Shojo Beat

Sweet Rein

2

Story & Art by Sakura Tsukuba

Sweet Rein

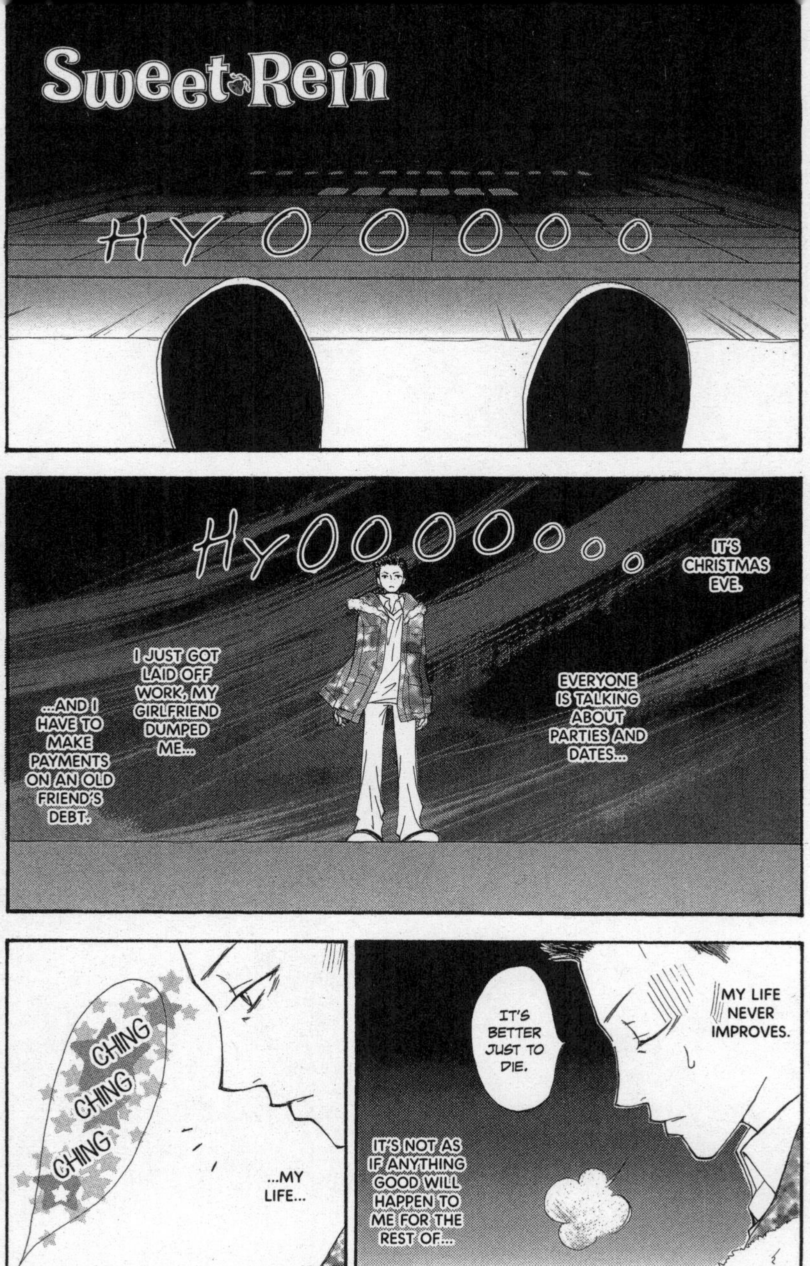
Sweet Rein
HYOOOOOO
HYOOOOOOO
IT'S CHRISTMAS EVE.
EVERYONE IS TALKING ABOUT PARTIES AND DATES...
I JUST GOT LAID OFF WORK, MY GIRLFRIEND DUMPED ME...
...AND I HAVE TO MAKE PAYMENTS ON AN OLD FRIEND'S DEBT.
MY LIFE NEVER IMPROVES.
IT'S BETTER JUST TO DIE.
IT'S NOT AS IF ANYTHING GOOD WILL HAPPEN TO ME FOR THE REST OF...
CHING CHING CHING
...MY LIFE...

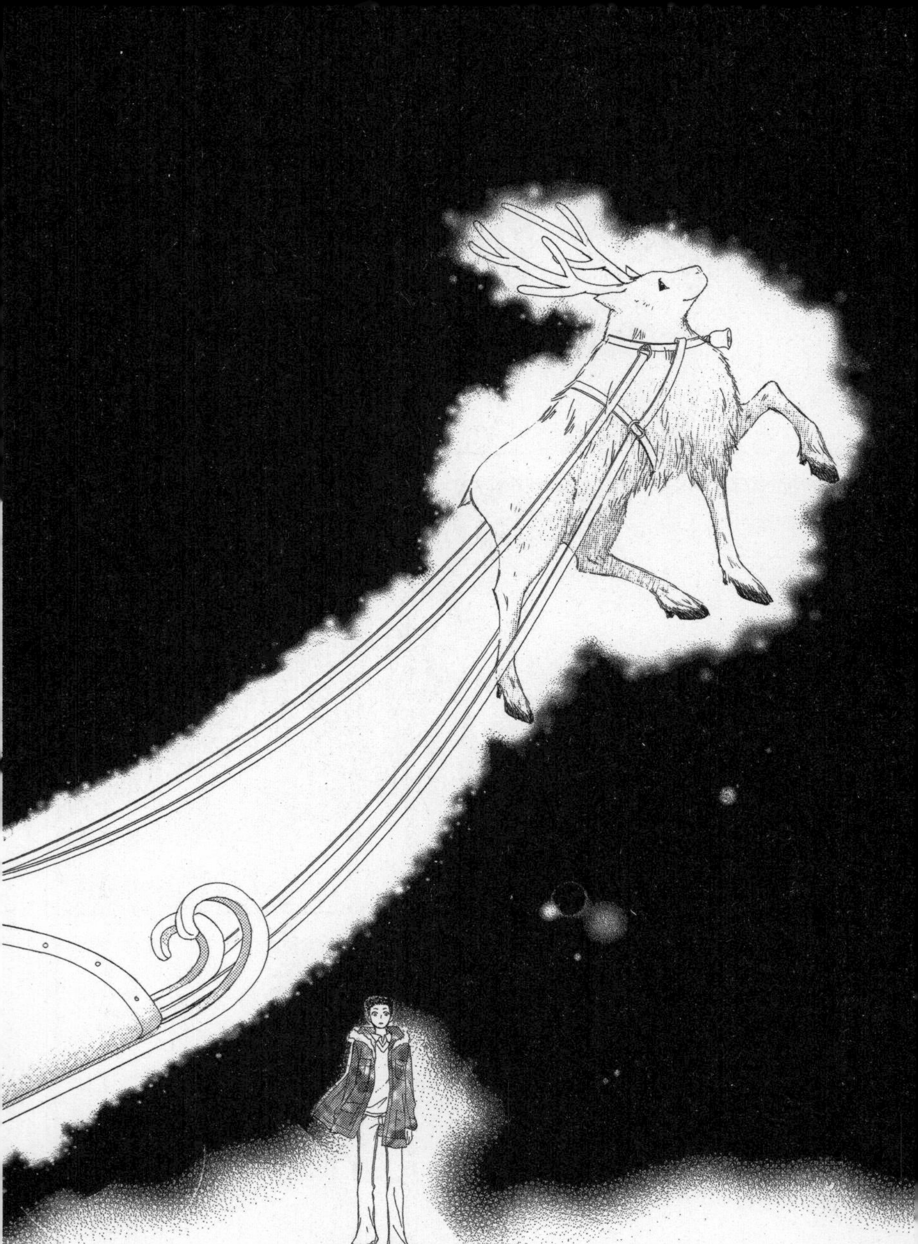

CHAPTER 4

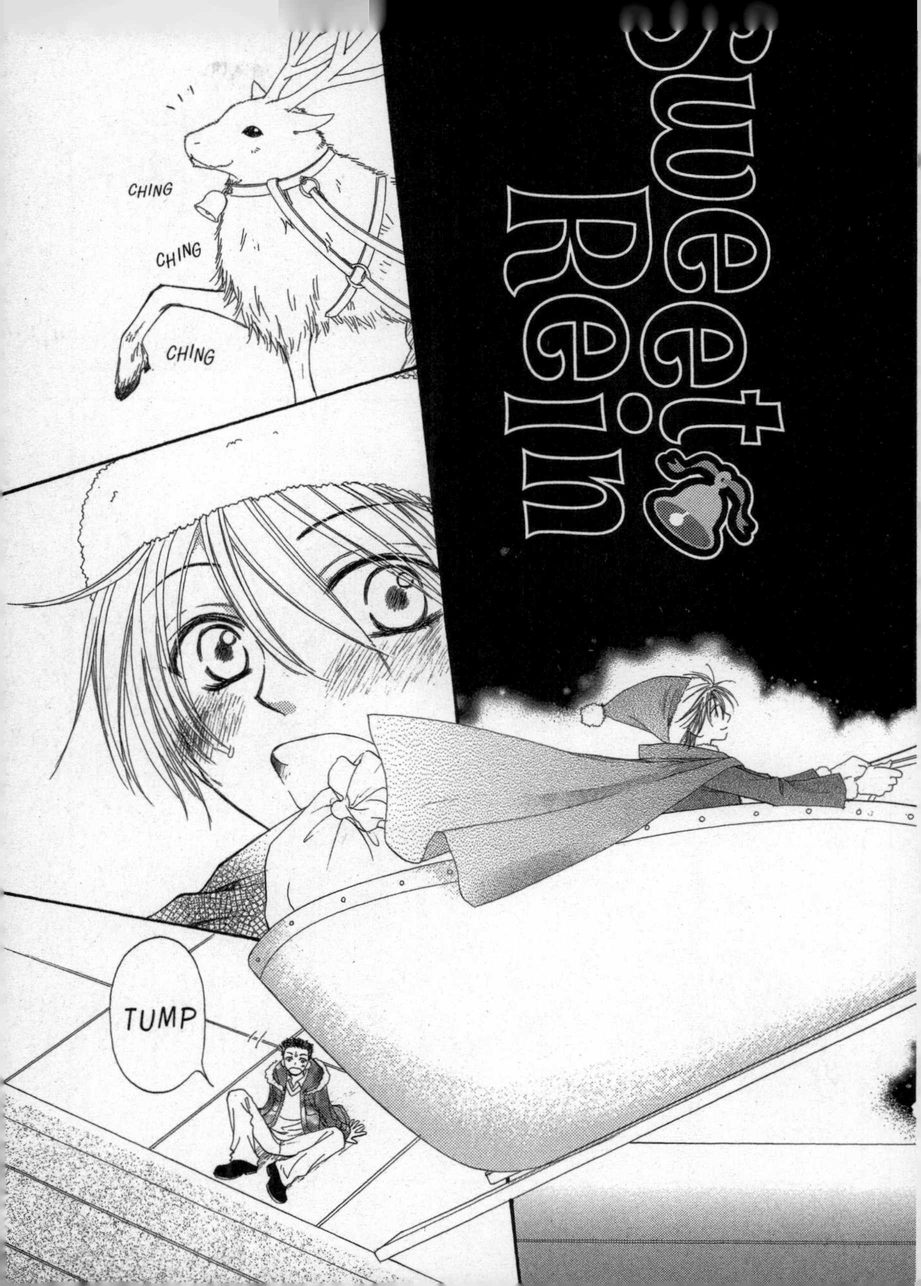
Sweet Rein
CHING
CHING
CHING
TUMP

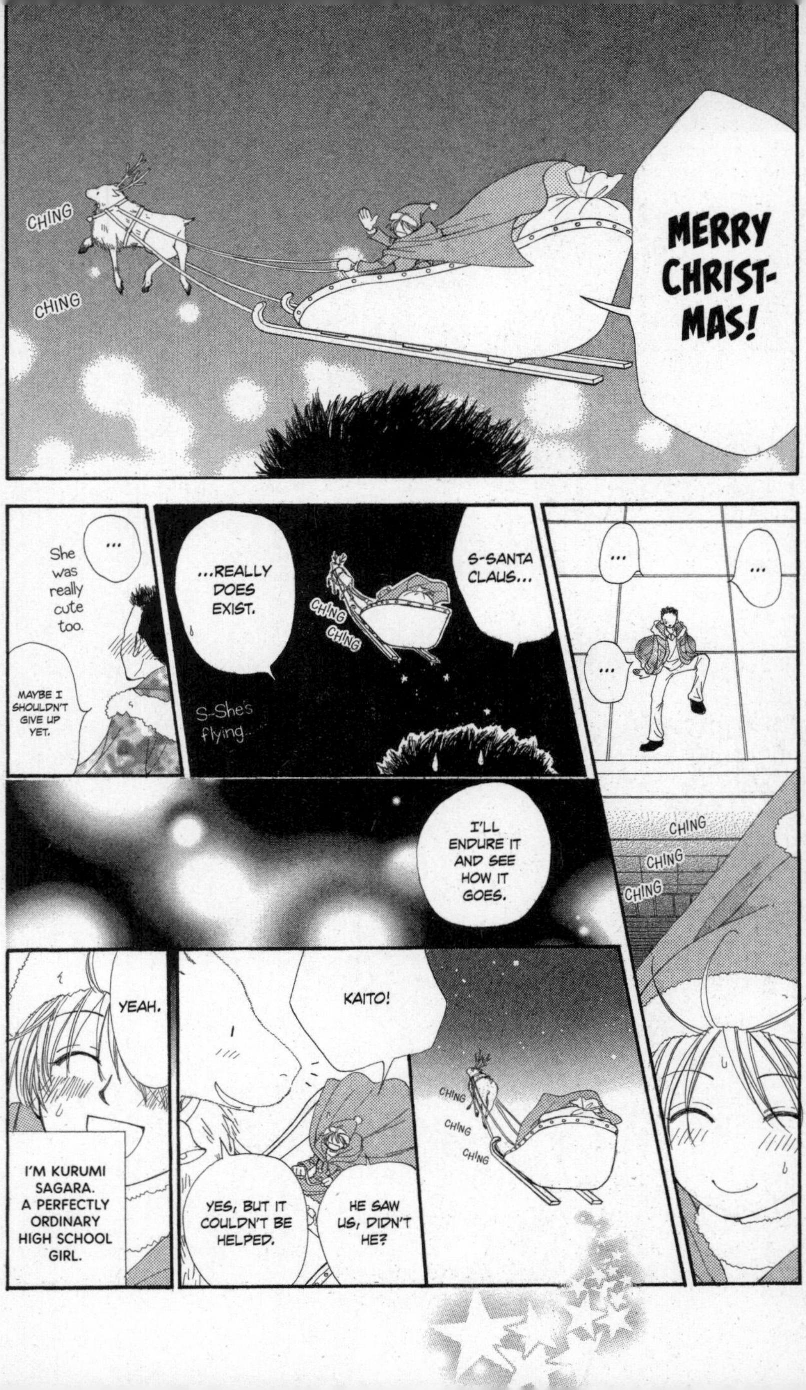
MERRY CHRISTMAS!
CHING
CHING
...
...
...
S-SANTA CLAUS...
...REALLY DOES EXIST.
CHING
CHING
S-She's flying...
...
She was really cute too.
MAYBE I SHOULDN'T GIVE UP YET.
CHING
CHING
CHING
I'LL ENDURE IT AND SEE HOW IT GOES.
CHING
CHING
CHING
KAITO!
HE SAW US, DIDN'T HE?
YES, BUT IT COULDN'T BE HELPED.
YEAH.
I'M KURUMI SAGARA. A PERFECTLY ORDINARY HIGH SCHOOL GIRL.

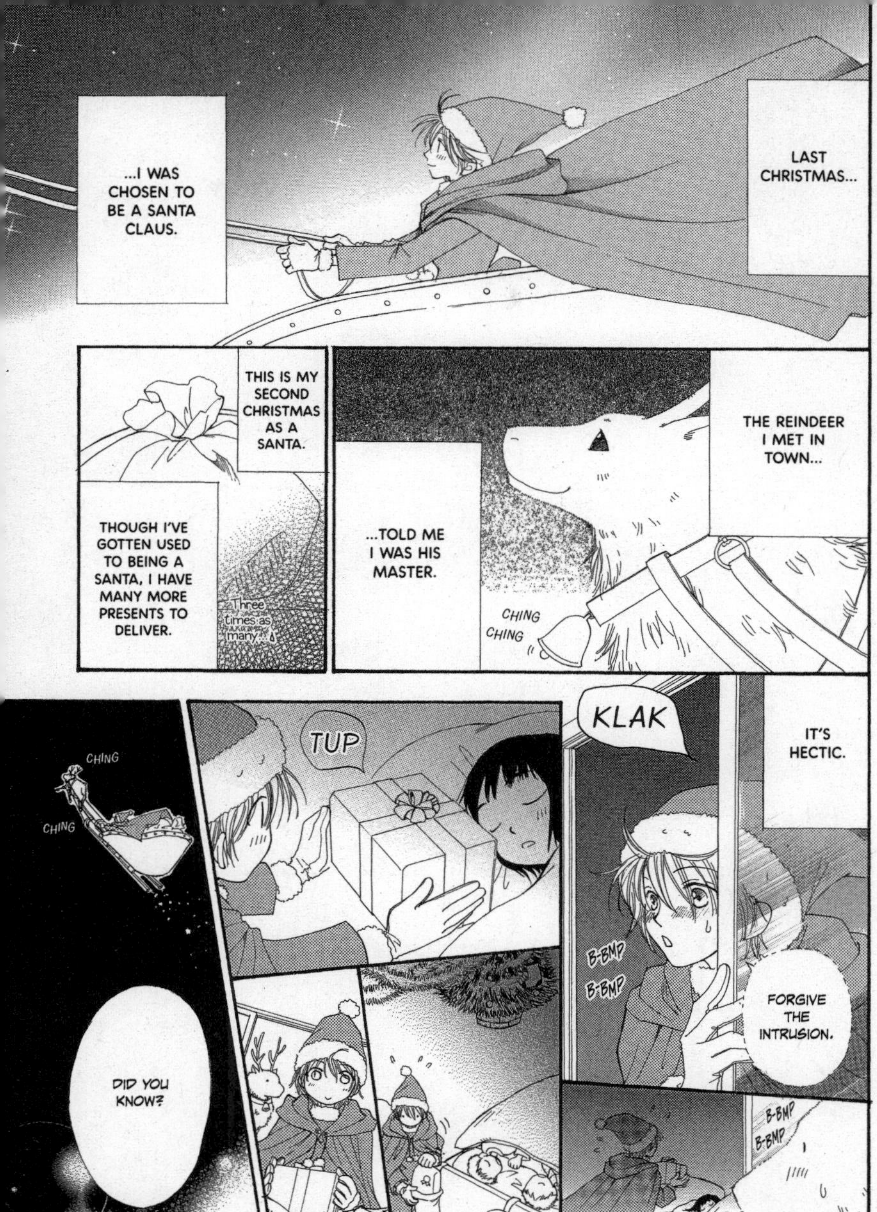
LAST CHRISTMAS...
...I WAS CHOSEN TO BE A SANTA CLAUS.
THE REINDEER I MET IN TOWN...
...TOLD ME I WAS HIS MASTER.
CHING CHING
THIS IS MY SECOND CHRISTMAS AS A SANTA.
THOUGH I'VE GOTTEN USED TO BEING A SANTA, I HAVE MANY MORE PRESENTS TO DELIVER.
Three times as many...
IT'S HECTIC.
KLAK
B-BMP B-BMP
FORGIVE THE INTRUSION.
B-BMP B-BMP
TUP
CHING
CHING
DID YOU KNOW?

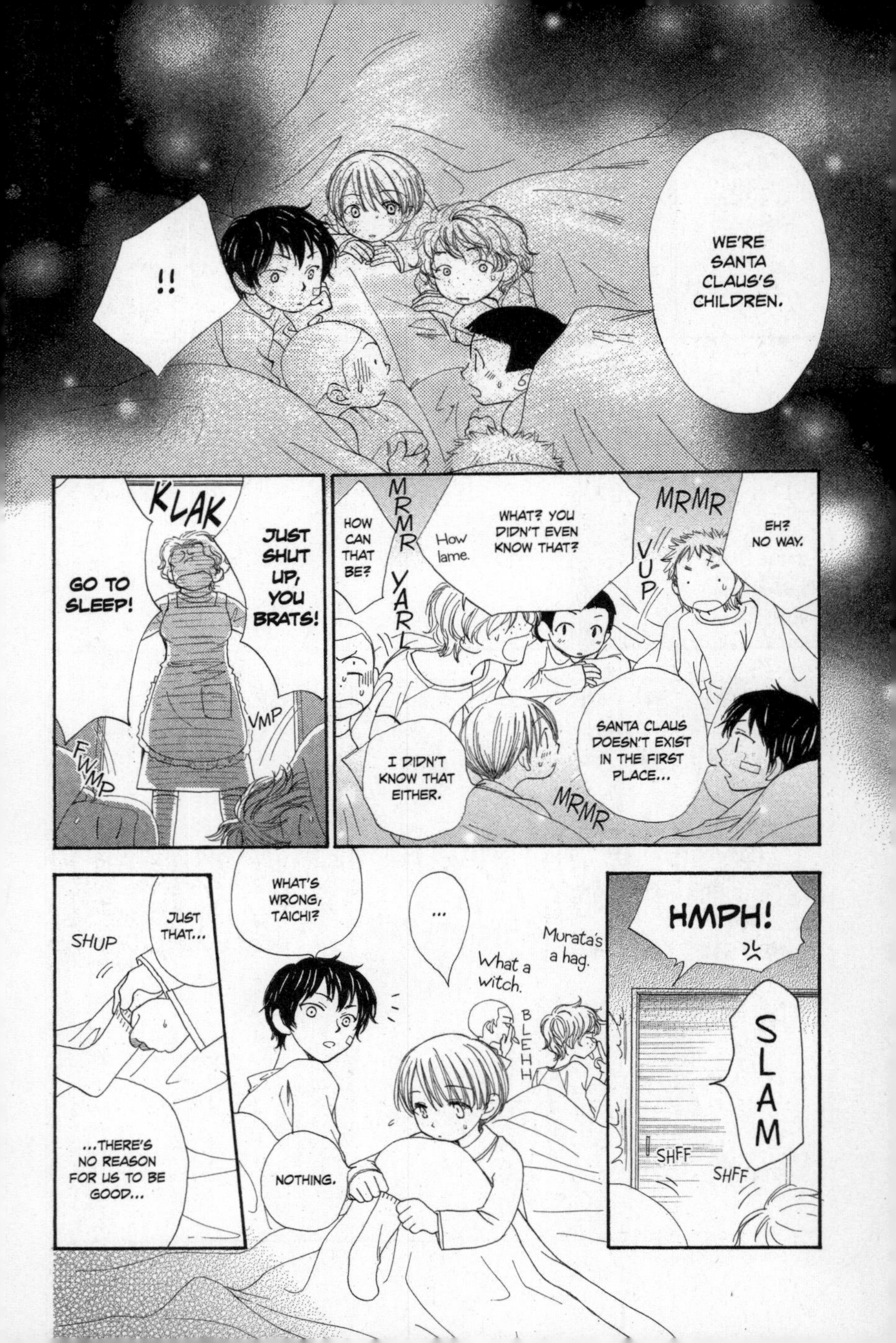
WE'RE SANTA CLAUS'S CHILDREN.
!!
EH? NO WAY.
MRMR
VUP
WHAT? YOU DIDN'T EVEN KNOW THAT?
How lame.
HOW CAN THAT BE?
MRMR YARL
SANTA CLAUS DOESN'T EXIST IN THE FIRST PLACE...
I DIDN'T KNOW THAT EITHER.
MRMR
KLAK
JUST SHUT UP, YOU BRATS!
GO TO SLEEP!
VMP
FWMP
HMPH!
SLAM
SHFF
SHFF
Murata's a hag.
What a witch.
BLEHH
...
WHAT'S WRONG, TAICHI?
JUST THAT...
SHUP
...THERE'S NO REASON FOR US TO BE GOOD...
NOTHING.

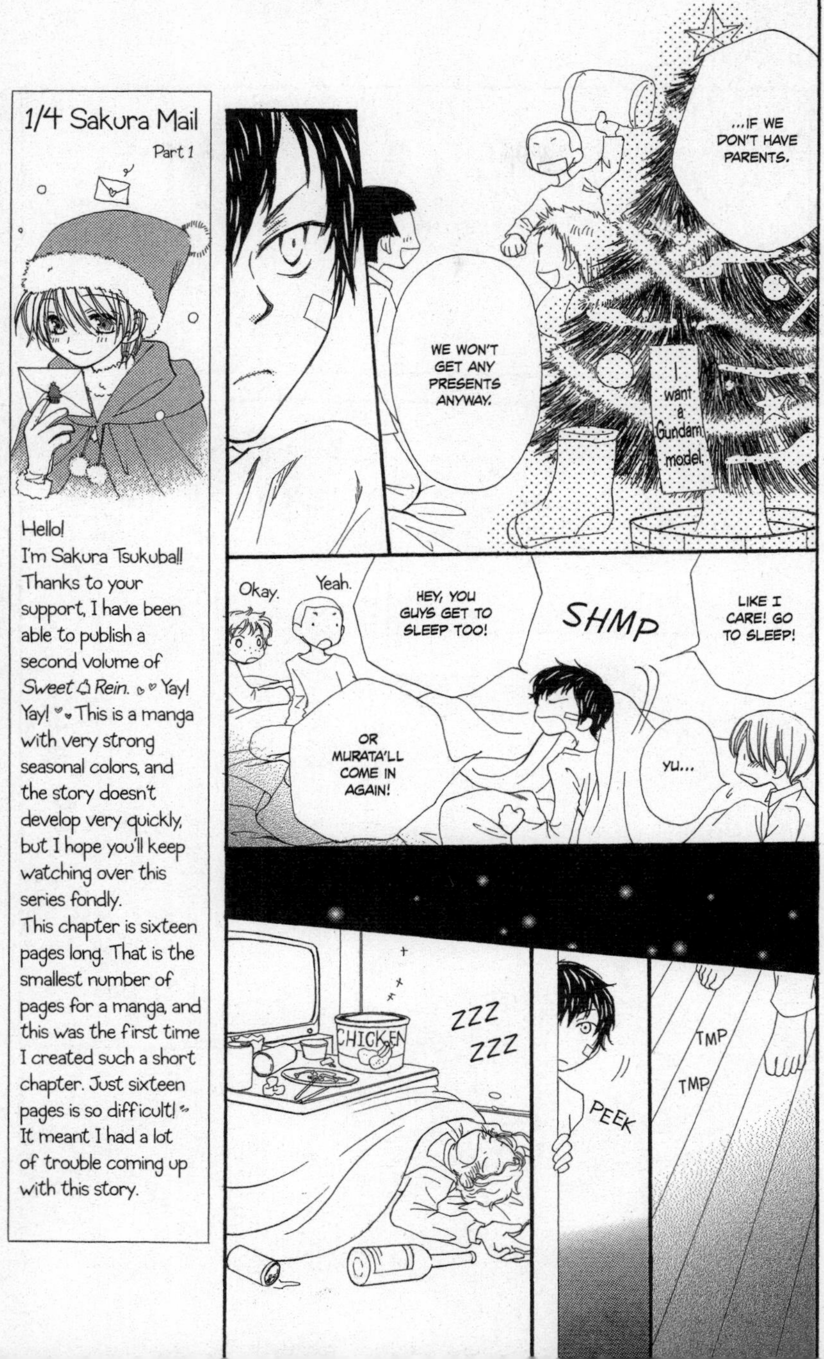
...IF WE DON'T HAVE PARENTS.
I want a Gundam model.
WE WON'T GET ANY PRESENTS ANYWAY.
LIKE I CARE! GO TO SLEEP!
SHMP
YU...
HEY, YOU GUYS GET TO SLEEP TOO!
OR MURATA'LL COME IN AGAIN!
Yeah.
Okay.
TMP
TMP
PEEK
ZZZ
ZZZ
CHICKEN

1/4 Sakura Mail

Part 1

Hello!
I'm Sakura Tsukuba!! Thanks to your support, I have been able to publish a second volume of *Sweet Rein*. Yay! Yay! This is a manga with very strong seasonal colors, and the story doesn't develop very quickly, but I hope you'll keep watching over this series fondly.
This chapter is sixteen pages long. That is the smallest number of pages for a manga, and this was the first time I created such a short chapter. Just sixteen pages is so difficult! It meant I had a lot of trouble coming up with this story.

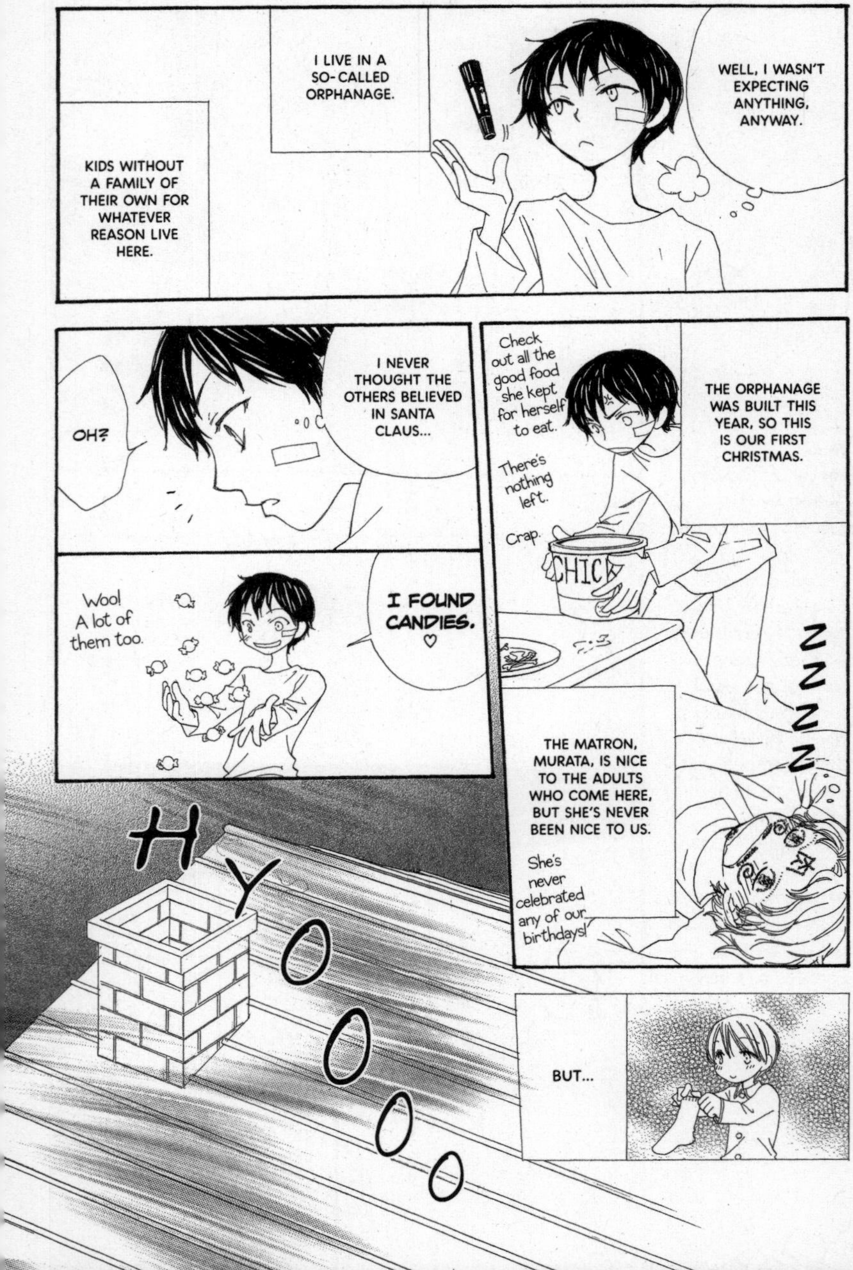
WELL, I WASN'T EXPECTING ANYTHING, ANYWAY.
I LIVE IN A SO-CALLED ORPHANAGE.
KIDS WITHOUT A FAMILY OF THEIR OWN FOR WHATEVER REASON LIVE HERE.
THE ORPHANAGE WAS BUILT THIS YEAR, SO THIS IS OUR FIRST CHRISTMAS.
Check out all the good food she kept for herself to eat.
There's nothing left.
Crap.
CHIC
ZZZZ
THE MATRON, MURATA, IS NICE TO THE ADULTS WHO COME HERE, BUT SHE'S NEVER BEEN NICE TO US.
She's never celebrated any of our birthdays!
I NEVER THOUGHT THE OTHERS BELIEVED IN SANTA CLAUS...
OH?
I FOUND CANDIES. ♡
Woo! A lot of them too.
BUT...
HYOOOO

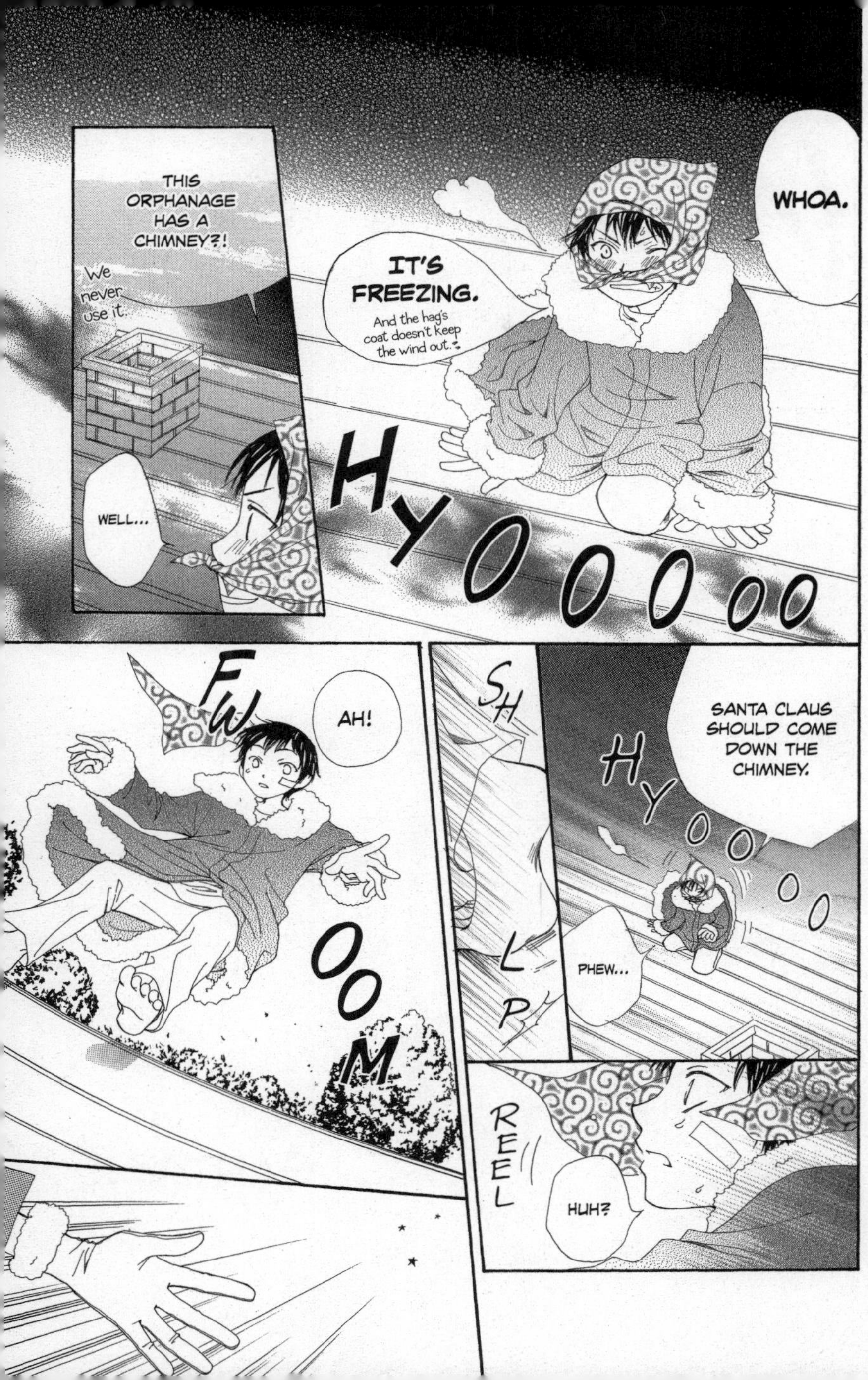
WHOA.
IT'S FREEZING.
And the hag's coat doesn't keep the wind out.
HYOOOOO
THIS ORPHANAGE HAS A CHIMNEY?!
We never use it.
WELL...
SANTA CLAUS SHOULD COME DOWN THE CHIMNEY.
HYOOOOO
SHLP
PHEW...
REEL
HUH?
FWOOOM
AH!

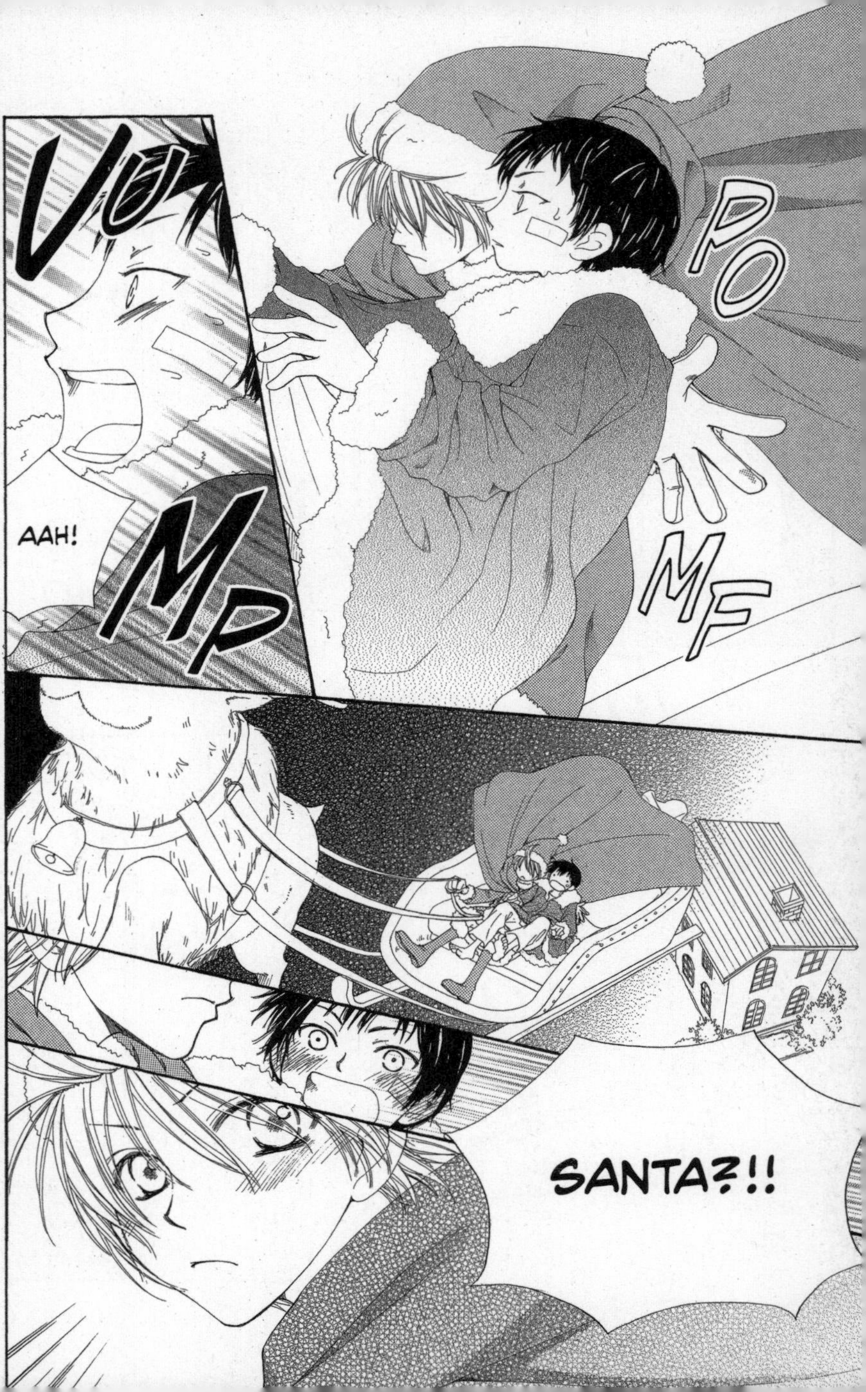
POMF
VUMP
AAH!
SANTA?!!

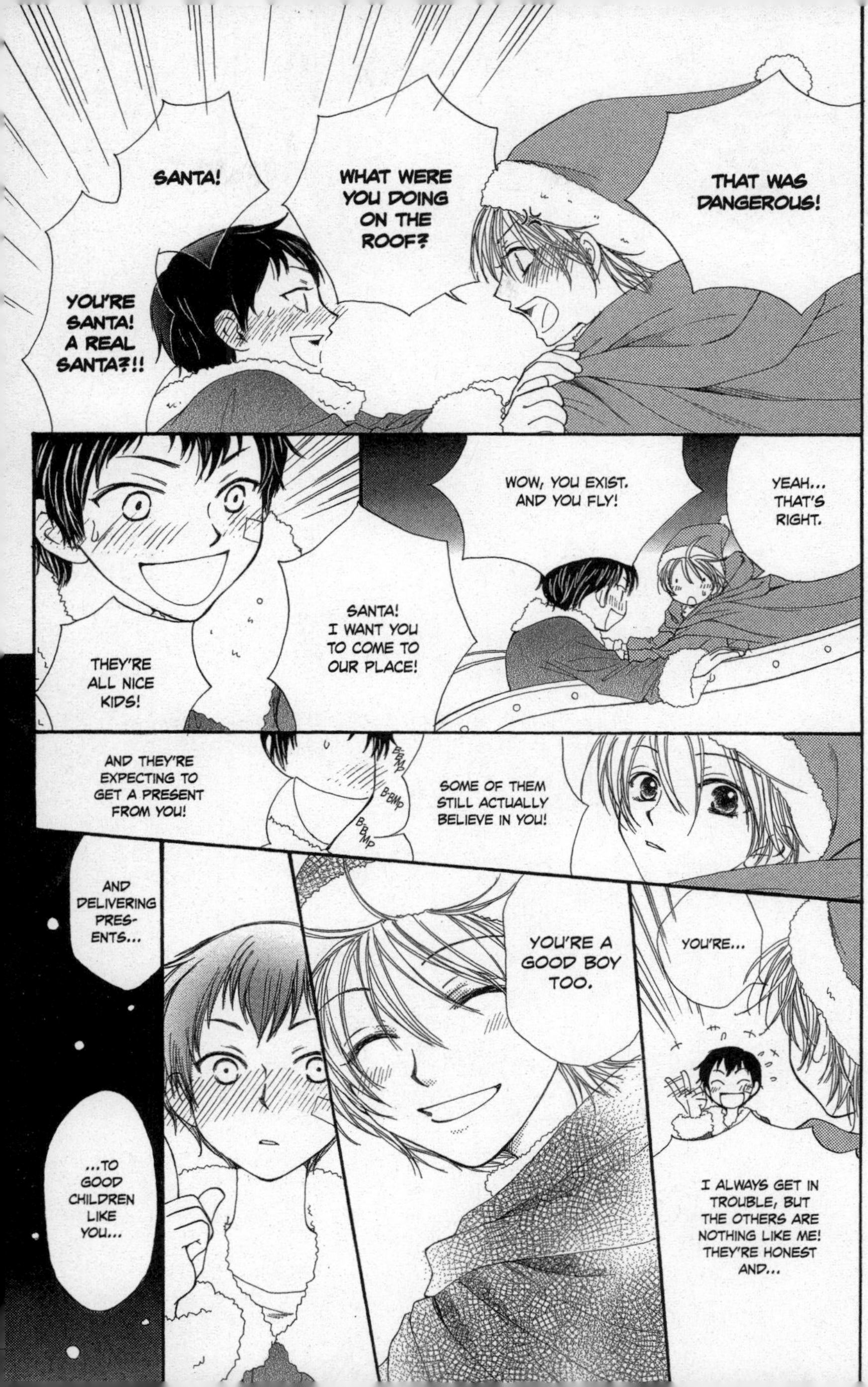
THAT WAS DANGEROUS!
WHAT WERE YOU DOING ON THE ROOF?
SANTA!
YOU'RE SANTA! A REAL SANTA?!!
YEAH... THAT'S RIGHT.
WOW, YOU EXIST. AND YOU FLY!
SANTA! I WANT YOU TO COME TO OUR PLACE!
THEY'RE ALL NICE KIDS!
SOME OF THEM STILL ACTUALLY BELIEVE IN YOU!
AND THEY'RE EXPECTING TO GET A PRESENT FROM YOU!
B-BMP
B-BMP
B-BMP
YOU'RE...
I ALWAYS GET IN TROUBLE, BUT THE OTHERS ARE NOTHING LIKE ME! THEY'RE HONEST AND...
YOU'RE A GOOD BOY TOO.
AND DELIVERING PRES-ENTS...
...TO GOOD CHILDREN LIKE YOU...

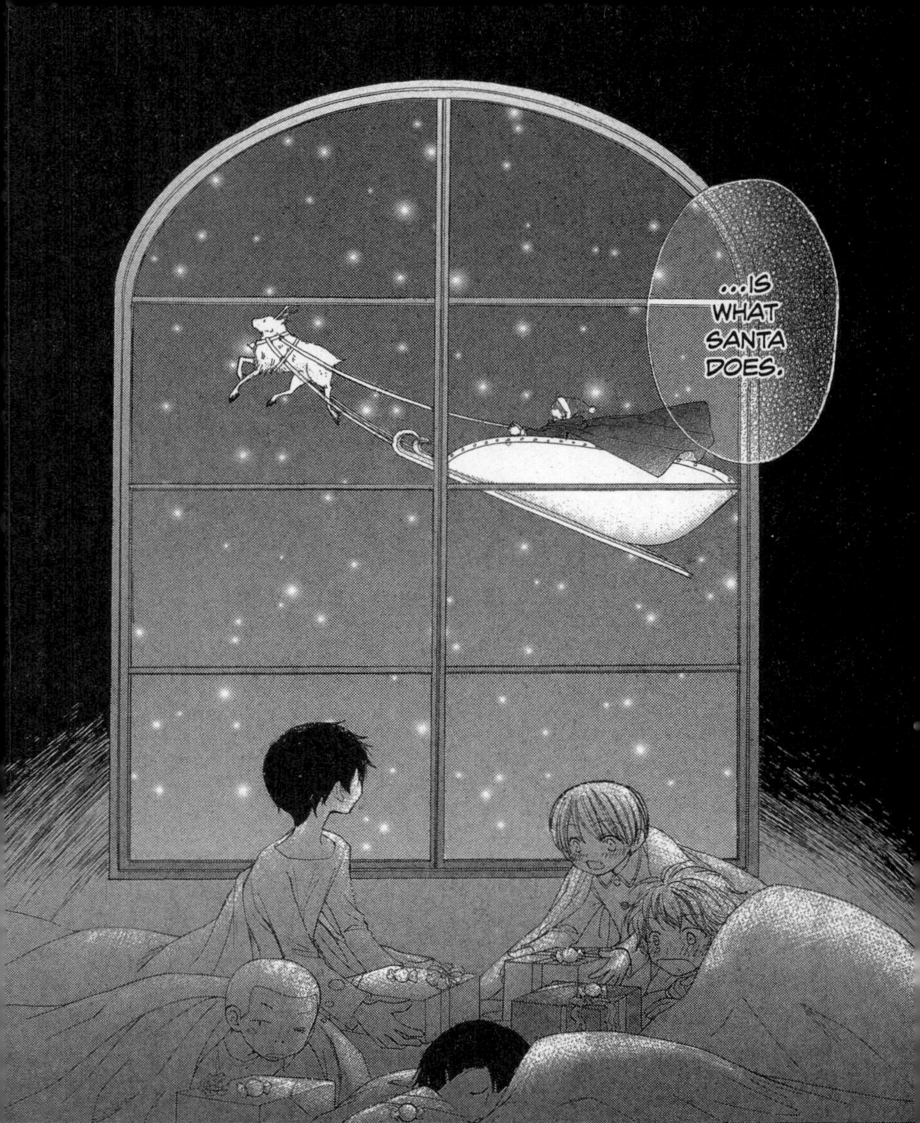
...IS WHAT SANTA DOES.
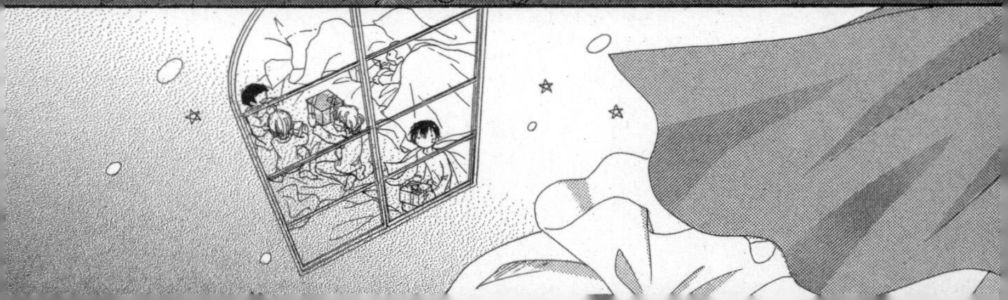

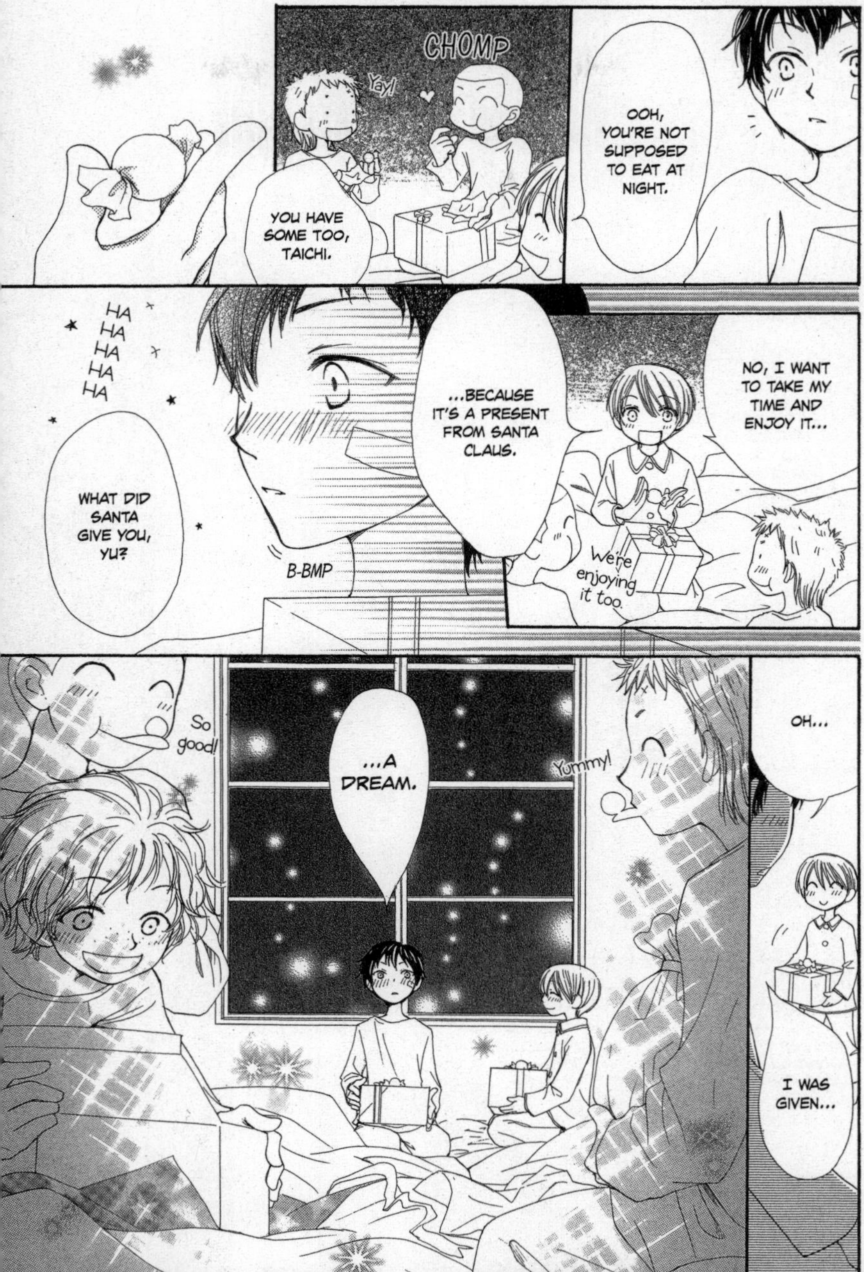
OOH, YOU'RE NOT SUPPOSED TO EAT AT NIGHT.
CHOMP
Yay!
YOU HAVE SOME TOO, TAICHI.
NO, I WANT TO TAKE MY TIME AND ENJOY IT...
...BECAUSE IT'S A PRESENT FROM SANTA CLAUS.
We're enjoying it too.
HA HA HA HA HA
B-BMP
WHAT DID SANTA GIVE YOU, YU?
OH...
I WAS GIVEN...
Yummy!
...A DREAM.
So good!

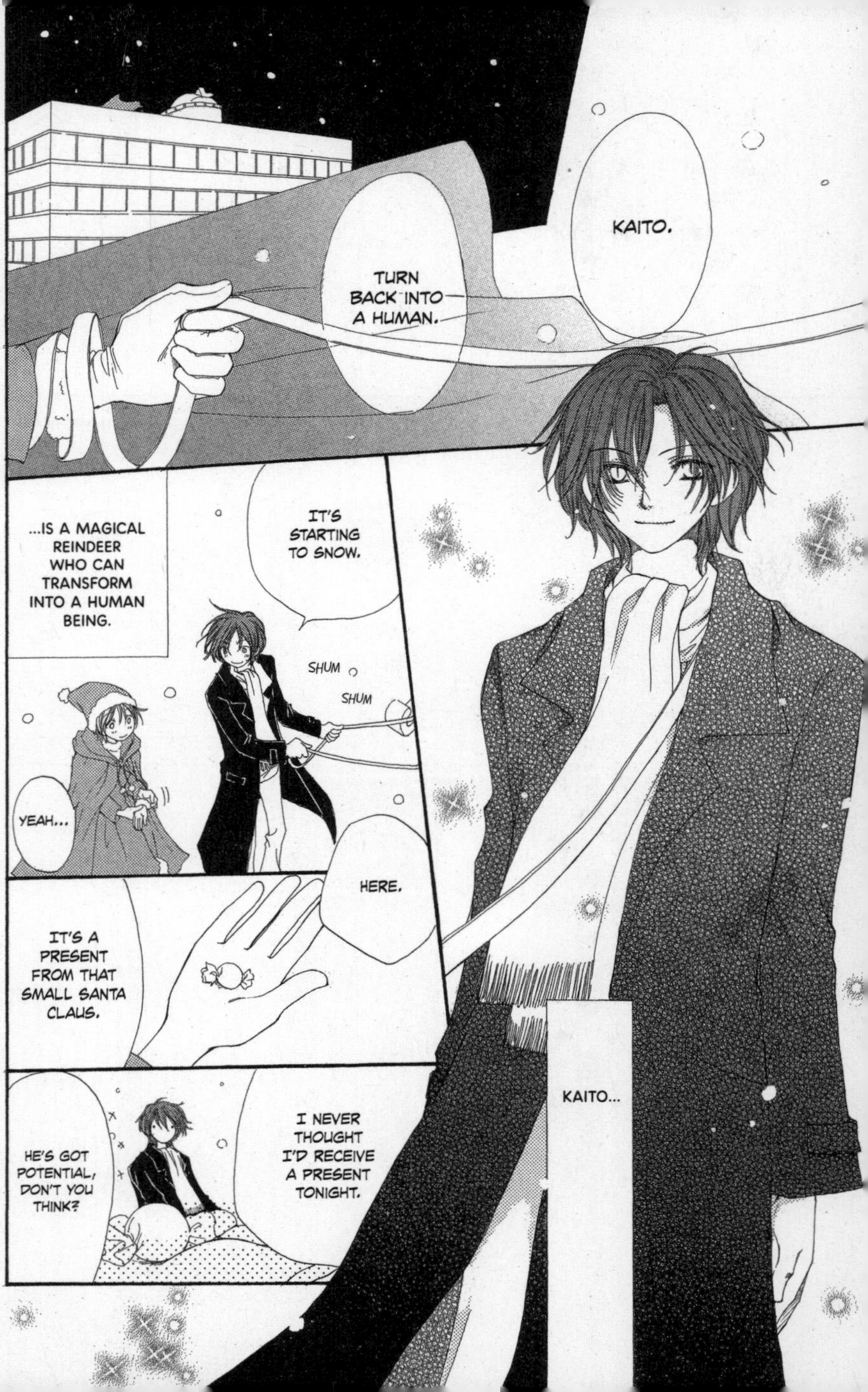
KAITO.
TURN BACK INTO A HUMAN.
KAITO...
IT'S STARTING TO SNOW.
...IS A MAGICAL REINDEER WHO CAN TRANSFORM INTO A HUMAN BEING.
SHUM
SHUM
YEAH...
HERE.
IT'S A PRESENT FROM THAT SMALL SANTA CLAUS.
I NEVER THOUGHT I'D RECEIVE A PRESENT TONIGHT.
HE'S GOT POTENTIAL, DON'T YOU THINK?

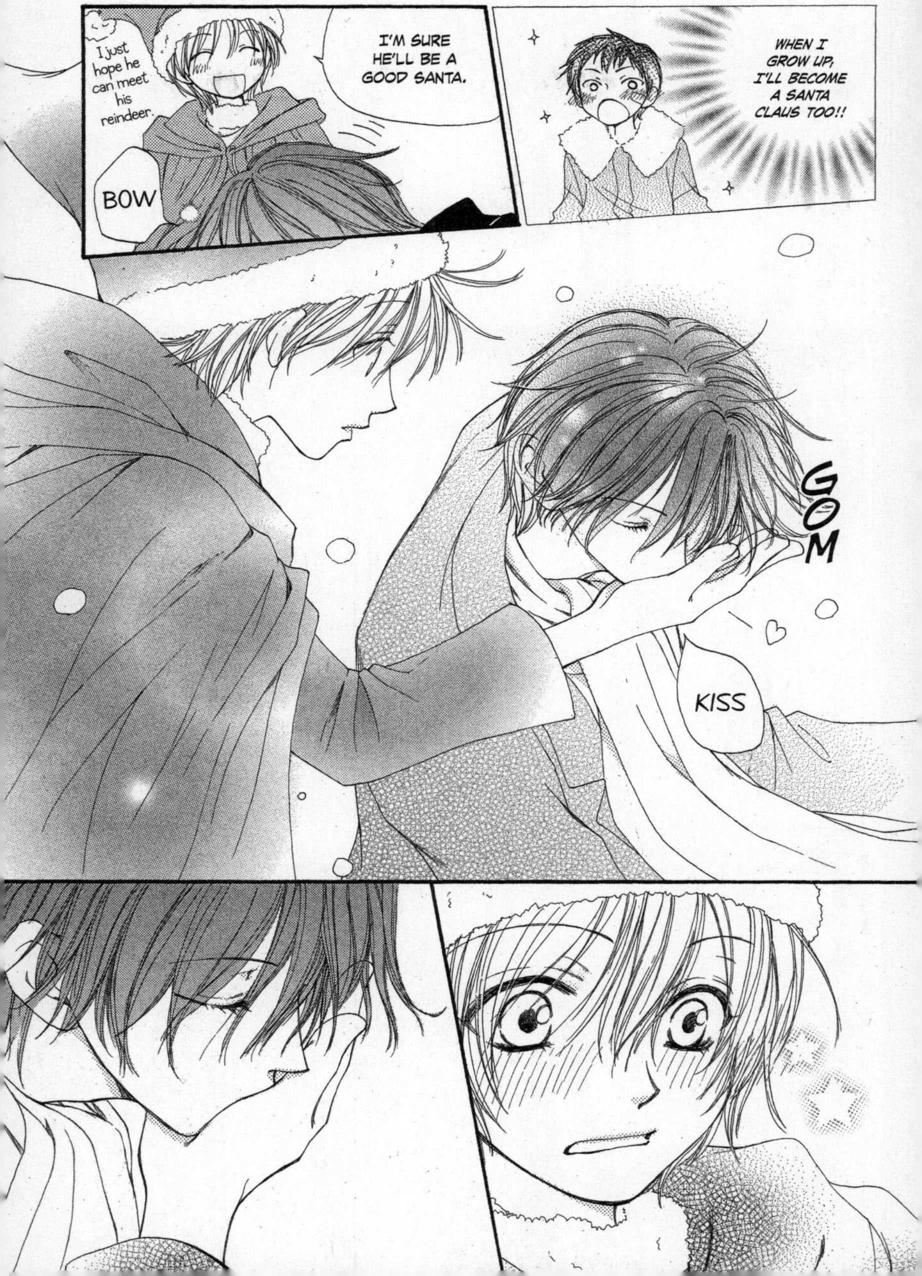
WHEN I GROW UP, I'LL BECOME A SANTA CLAUS TOO!!
I'M SURE HE'LL BE A GOOD SANTA.
I just hope he can meet his reindeer.
BOW
GOM
KISS

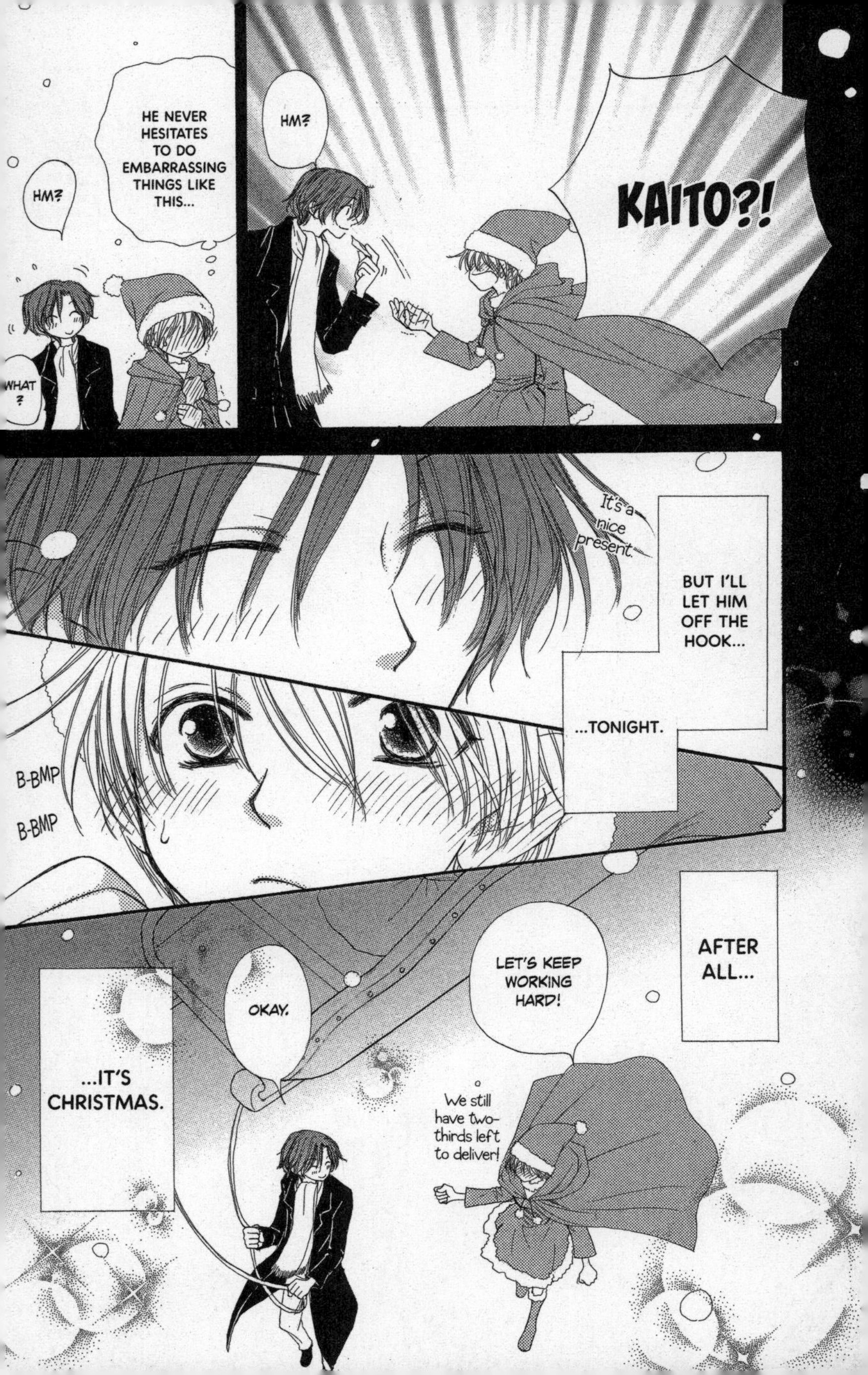
KAITO?!
HM?
HE NEVER HESITATES TO DO EMBARRASSING THINGS LIKE THIS...
HM?
WHAT?
It's a nice present.
BUT I'LL LET HIM OFF THE HOOK...
...TONIGHT.
B-BMP
B-BMP
AFTER ALL...
LET'S KEEP WORKING HARD!
We still have two-thirds left to deliver!
OKAY.
...IT'S CHRISTMAS.

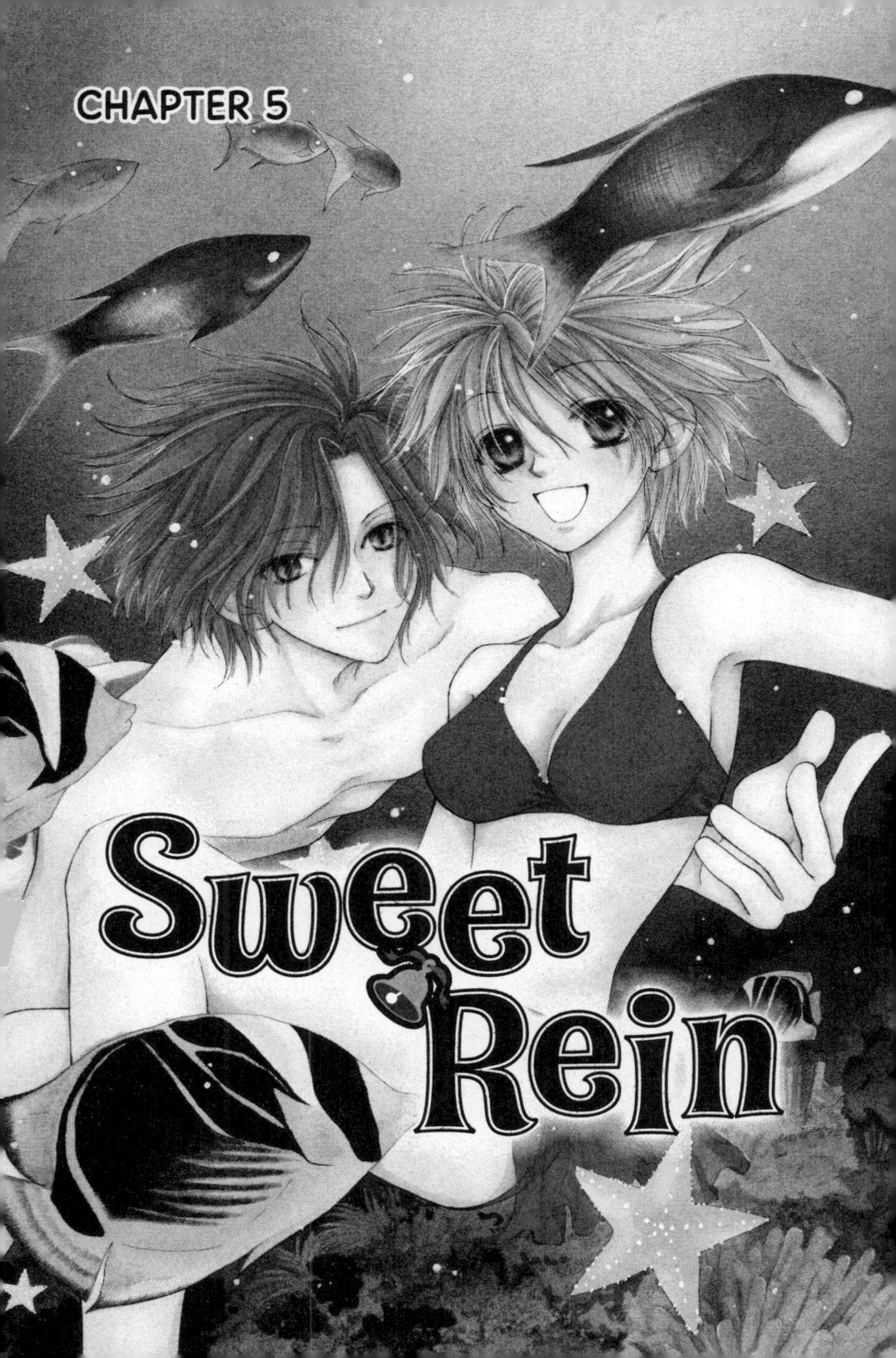
CHAPTER 5
Sweet Rein

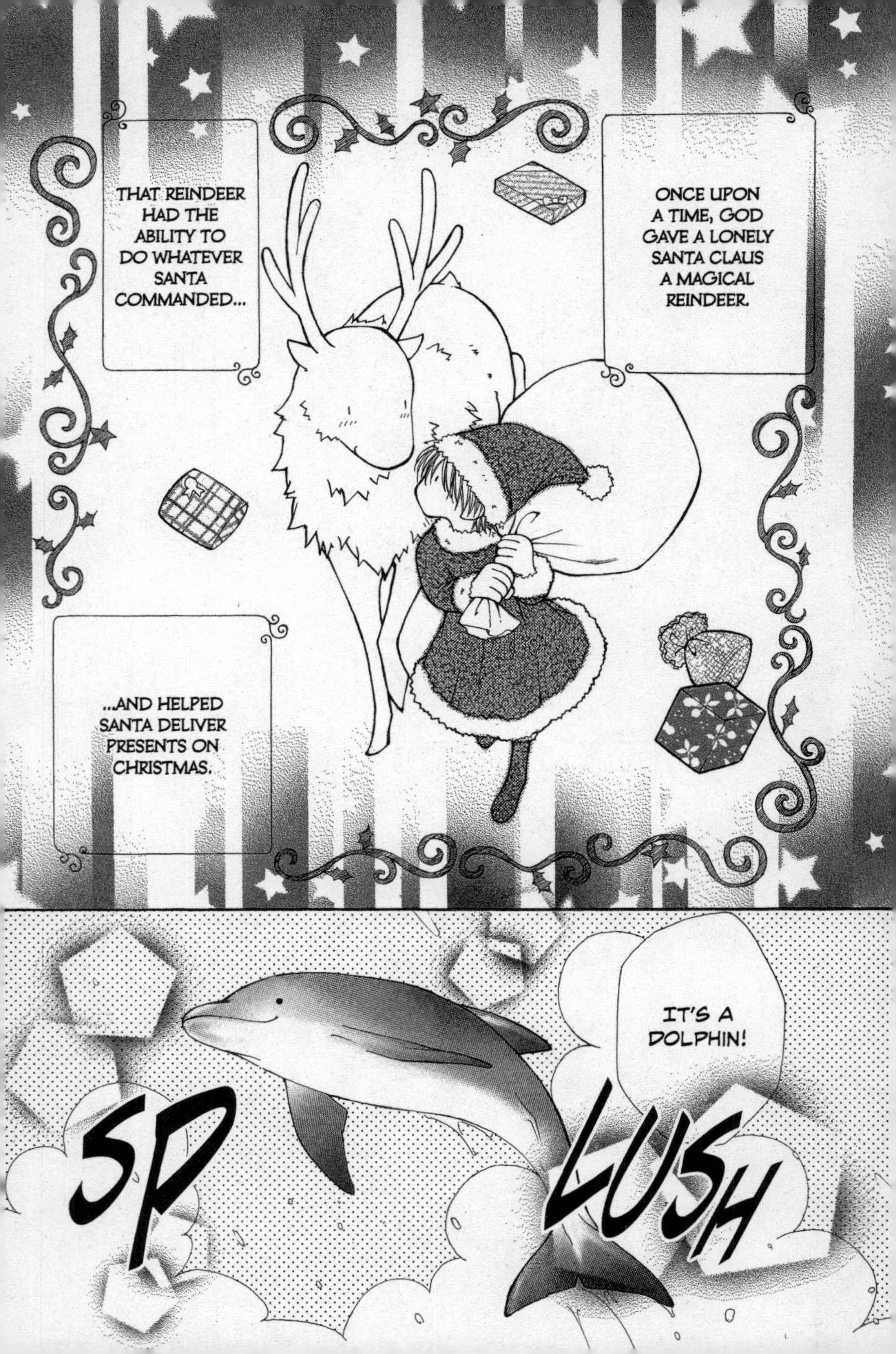
ONCE UPON A TIME, GOD GAVE A LONELY SANTA CLAUS A MAGICAL REINDEER.
THAT REINDEER HAD THE ABILITY TO DO WHATEVER SANTA COMMANDED...
...AND HELPED SANTA DELIVER PRESENTS ON CHRISTMAS.
IT'S A DOLPHIN!
SPLUSH

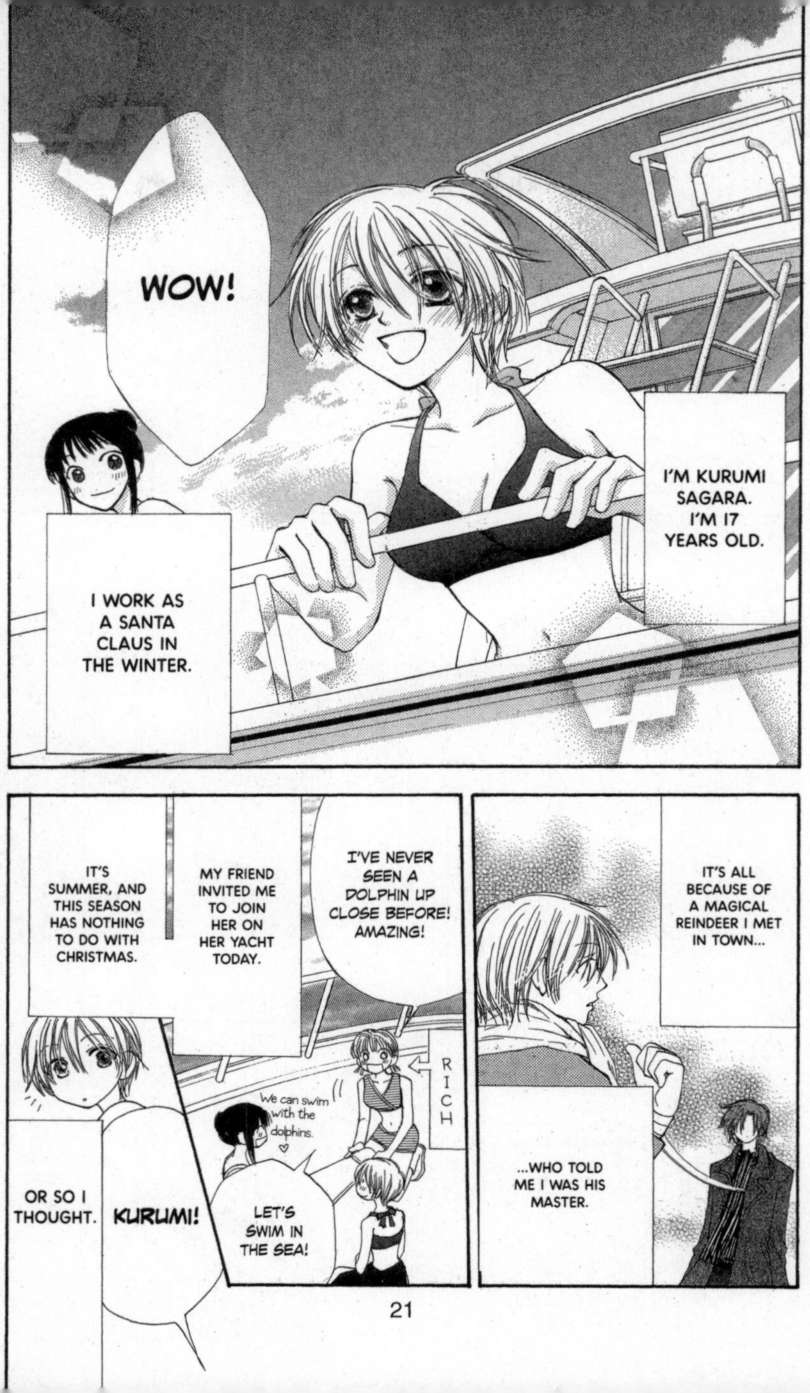

WOW!
I'M KURUMI SAGARA. I'M 17 YEARS OLD.
I WORK AS A SANTA CLAUS IN THE WINTER.
IT'S ALL BECAUSE OF A MAGICAL REINDEER I MET IN TOWN...
...WHO TOLD ME I WAS HIS MASTER.
I'VE NEVER SEEN A DOLPHIN UP CLOSE BEFORE! AMAZING!
MY FRIEND INVITED ME TO JOIN HER ON HER YACHT TODAY.
IT'S SUMMER, AND THIS SEASON HAS NOTHING TO DO WITH CHRISTMAS.
RICH
We can swim with the dolphins. ♥
LET'S SWIM IN THE SEA!
KURUMI!
OR SO I THOUGHT.

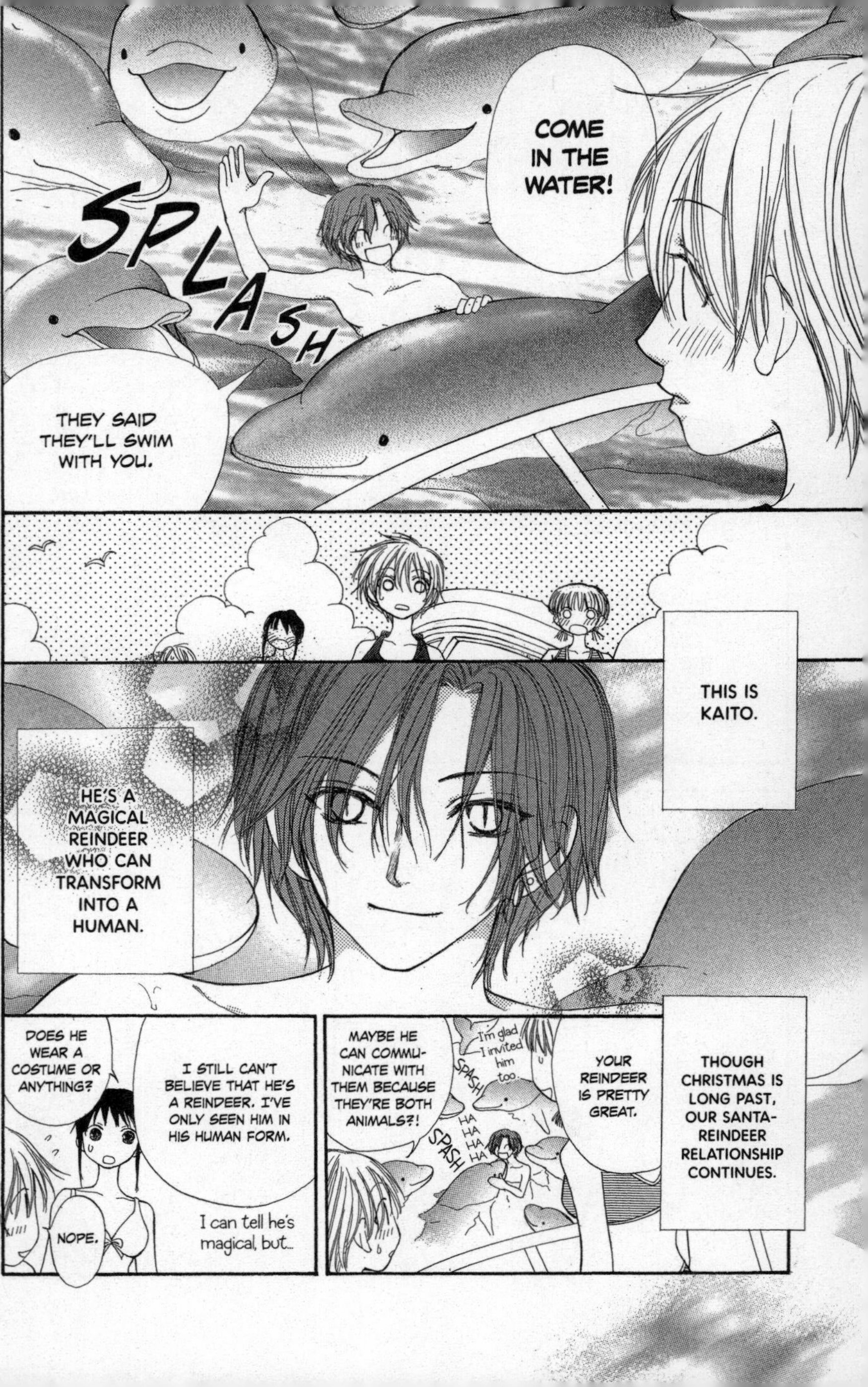
COME IN THE WATER!
SPLASH
THEY SAID THEY'LL SWIM WITH YOU.
THIS IS KAITO.
HE'S A MAGICAL REINDEER WHO CAN TRANSFORM INTO A HUMAN.
THOUGH CHRISTMAS IS LONG PAST, OUR SANTA-REINDEER RELATIONSHIP CONTINUES.
YOUR REINDEER IS PRETTY GREAT.
I'm glad I invited him too.
SPASH
MAYBE HE CAN COMMUNICATE WITH THEM BECAUSE THEY'RE BOTH ANIMALS?!
HA HA HA HA
SPASH
I STILL CAN'T BELIEVE THAT HE'S A REINDEER. I'VE ONLY SEEN HIM IN HIS HUMAN FORM.
DOES HE WEAR A COSTUME OR ANYTHING?
I can tell he's magical, but...
NOPE.

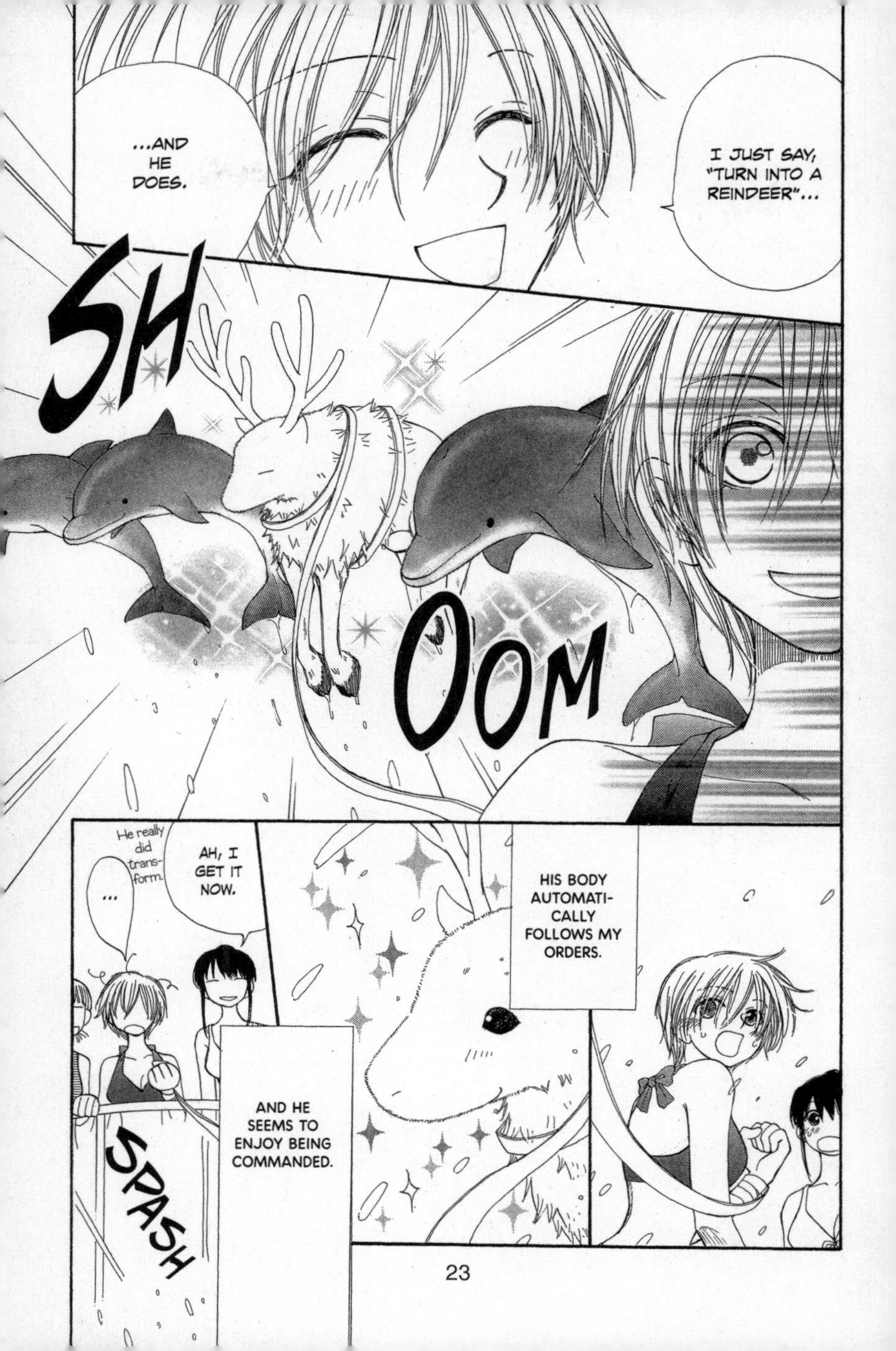
I JUST SAY, "TURN INTO A REINDEER"...
...AND HE DOES.
SHOOM
HIS BODY AUTOMATICALLY FOLLOWS MY ORDERS.
AND HE SEEMS TO ENJOY BEING COMMANDED.
AH, I GET IT NOW.
He really did transform.
...
SPASH

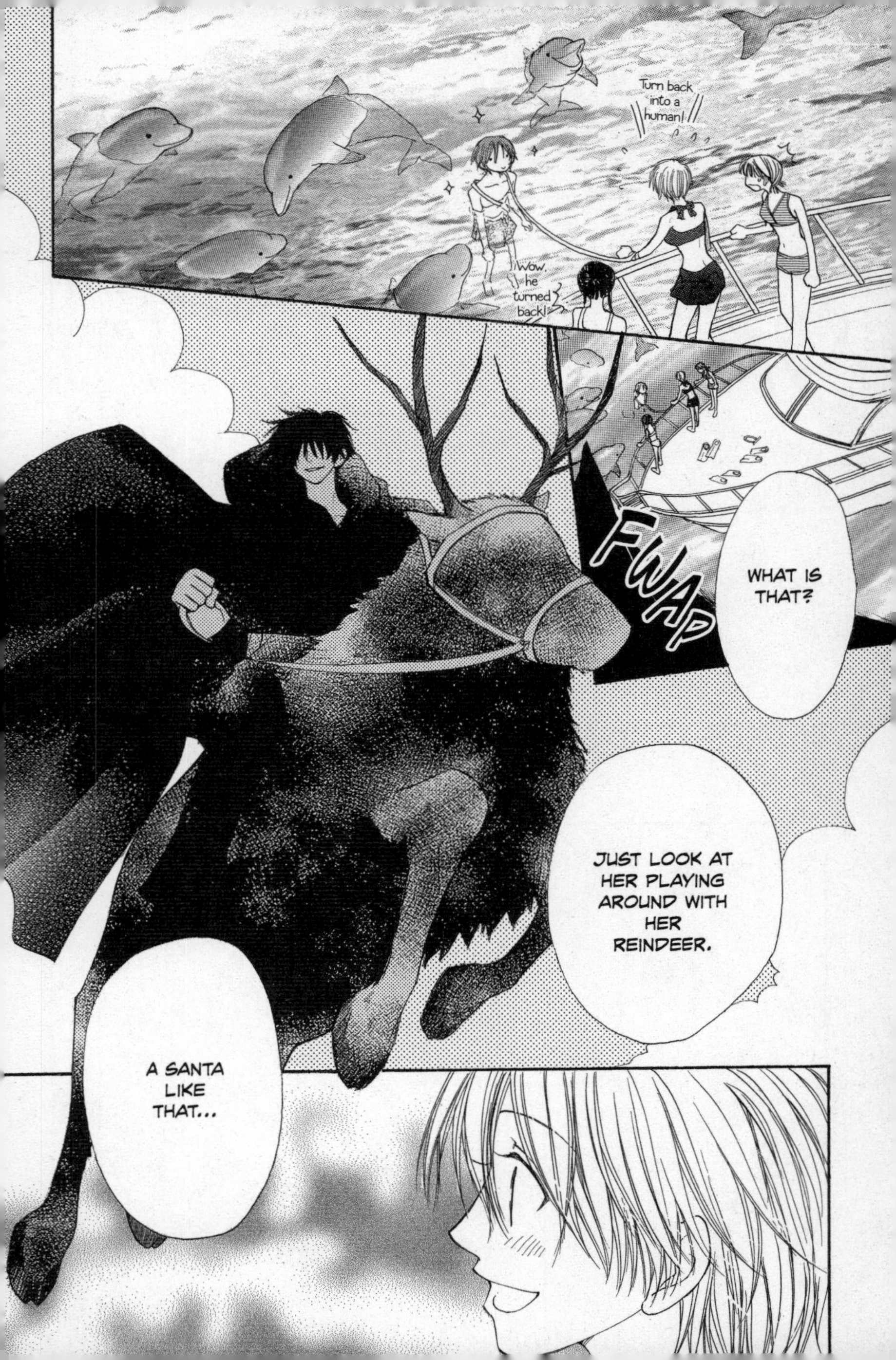
Turn back into a human!
Wow, he turned back!
FWAP
WHAT IS THAT?
JUST LOOK AT HER PLAYING AROUND WITH HER REINDEER.
A SANTA LIKE THAT...

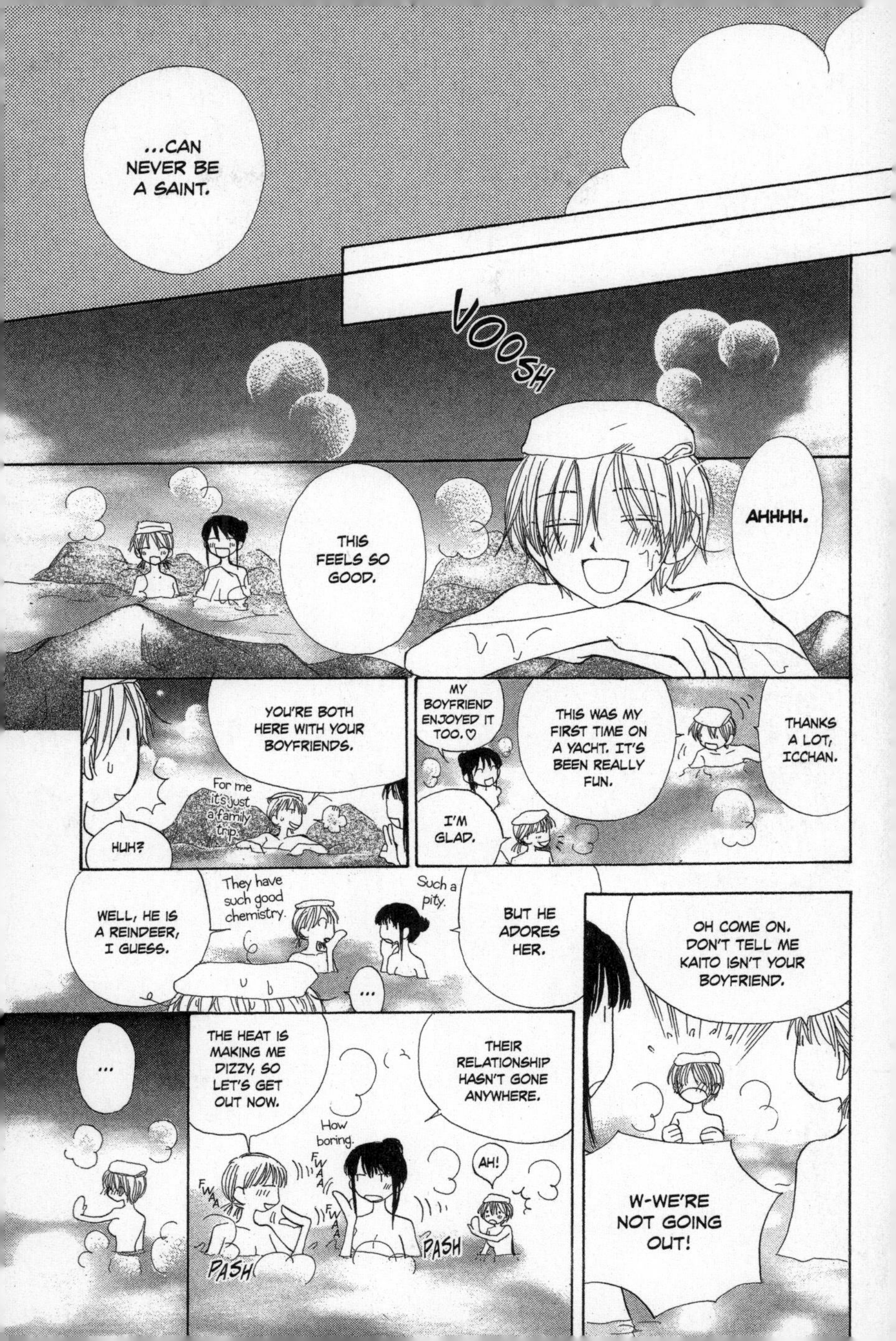
...CAN NEVER BE A SAINT.
VOOSH
AHHHH.
THIS FEELS SO GOOD.
THANKS A LOT, ICCHAN.
THIS WAS MY FIRST TIME ON A YACHT. IT'S BEEN REALLY FUN.
MY BOYFRIEND ENJOYED IT TOO.♡
I'M GLAD.
YOU'RE BOTH HERE WITH YOUR BOYFRIENDS.
For me it's just a family trip.
HUH?
OH COME ON. DON'T TELL ME KAITO ISN'T YOUR BOYFRIEND.
W-WE'RE NOT GOING OUT!
BUT HE ADORES HER.
Such a pity.
They have such good chemistry.
WELL, HE IS A REINDEER, I GUESS.
...
THEIR RELATIONSHIP HASN'T GONE ANYWHERE.
AH!
PASH
How boring.
FWAA
FWAA
THE HEAT IS MAKING ME DIZZY, SO LET'S GET OUT NOW.
FWAA
PASH
...

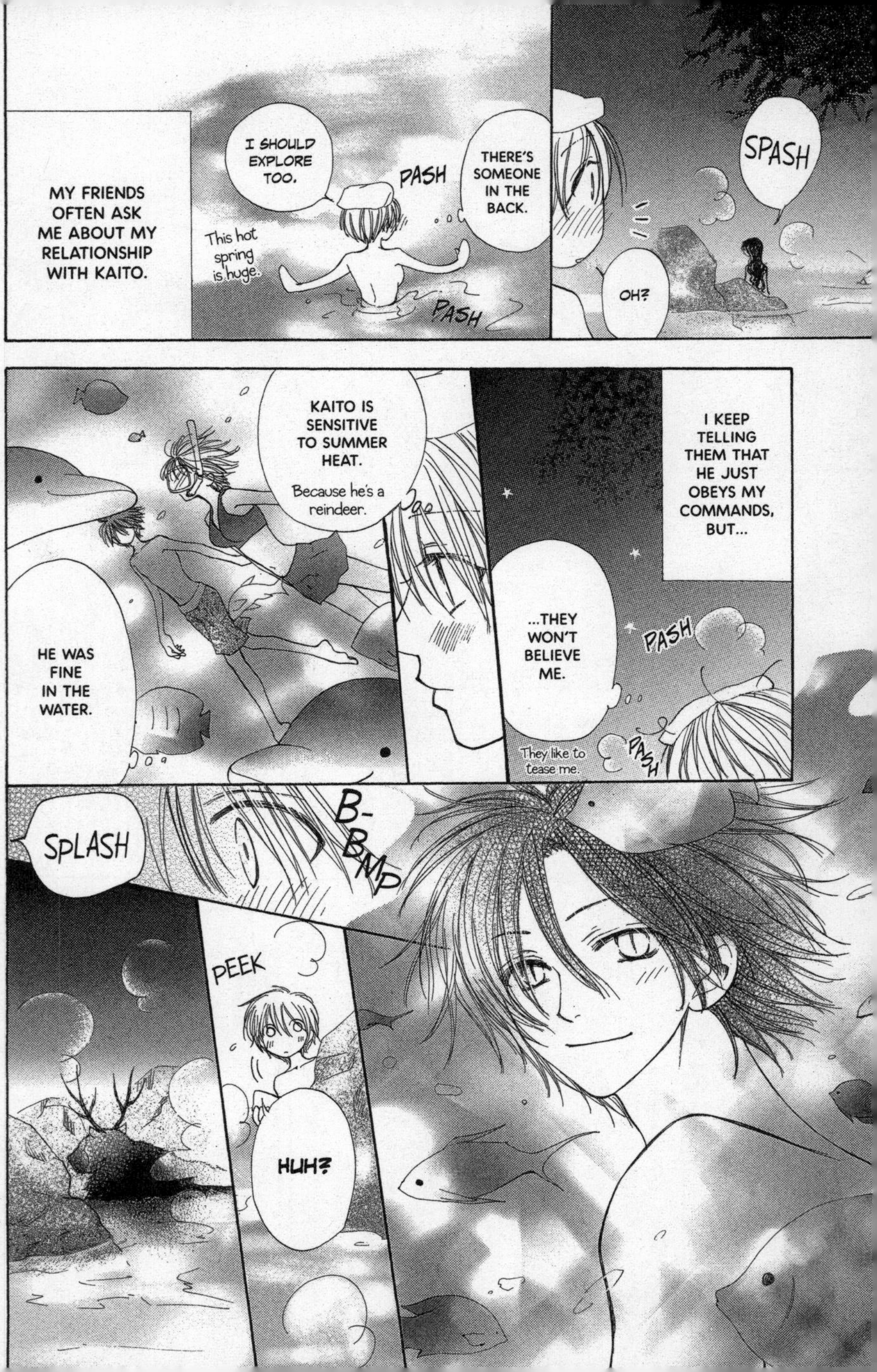
SPASH
OH?
THERE'S SOMEONE IN THE BACK.
PASH
I SHOULD EXPLORE TOO.
This hot spring is huge.
PASH
MY FRIENDS OFTEN ASK ME ABOUT MY RELATIONSHIP WITH KAITO.
I KEEP TELLING THEM THAT HE JUST OBEYS MY COMMANDS, BUT...
...THEY WON'T BELIEVE ME.
They like to tease me.
PASH
PASH
KAITO IS SENSITIVE TO SUMMER HEAT.
Because he's a reindeer.
HE WAS FINE IN THE WATER.
B-BMP
SPLASH
PEEK
HUH?

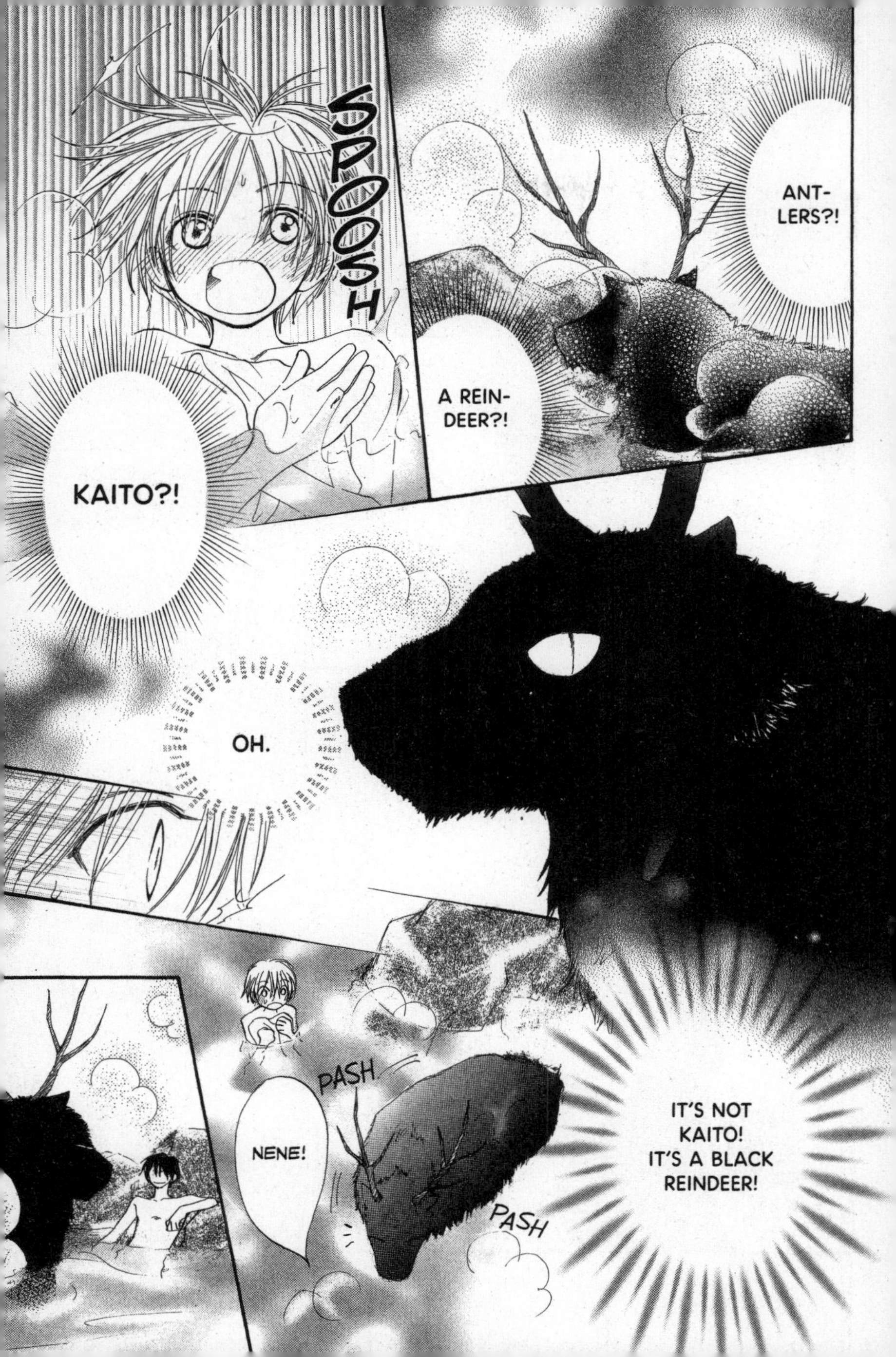
ANT-LERS?!
A REIN-DEER?!
SPOOSH
KAITO?!
OH.
IT'S NOT KAITO! IT'S A BLACK REINDEER!
PASH
PASH
NENE!

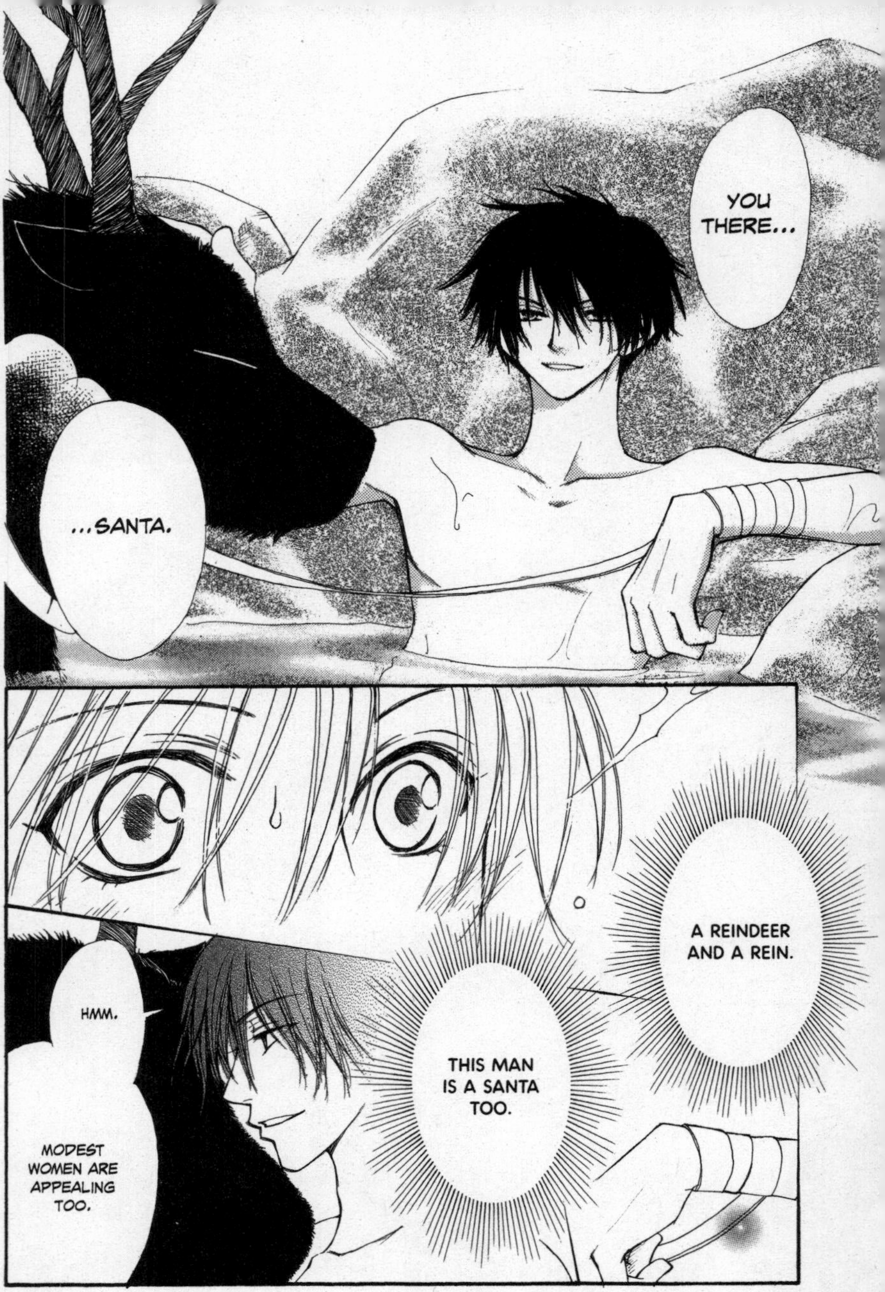
YOU THERE...
...SANTA.
A REINDEER AND A REIN.
THIS MAN IS A SANTA TOO.
HMM.
MODEST WOMEN ARE APPEALING TOO.

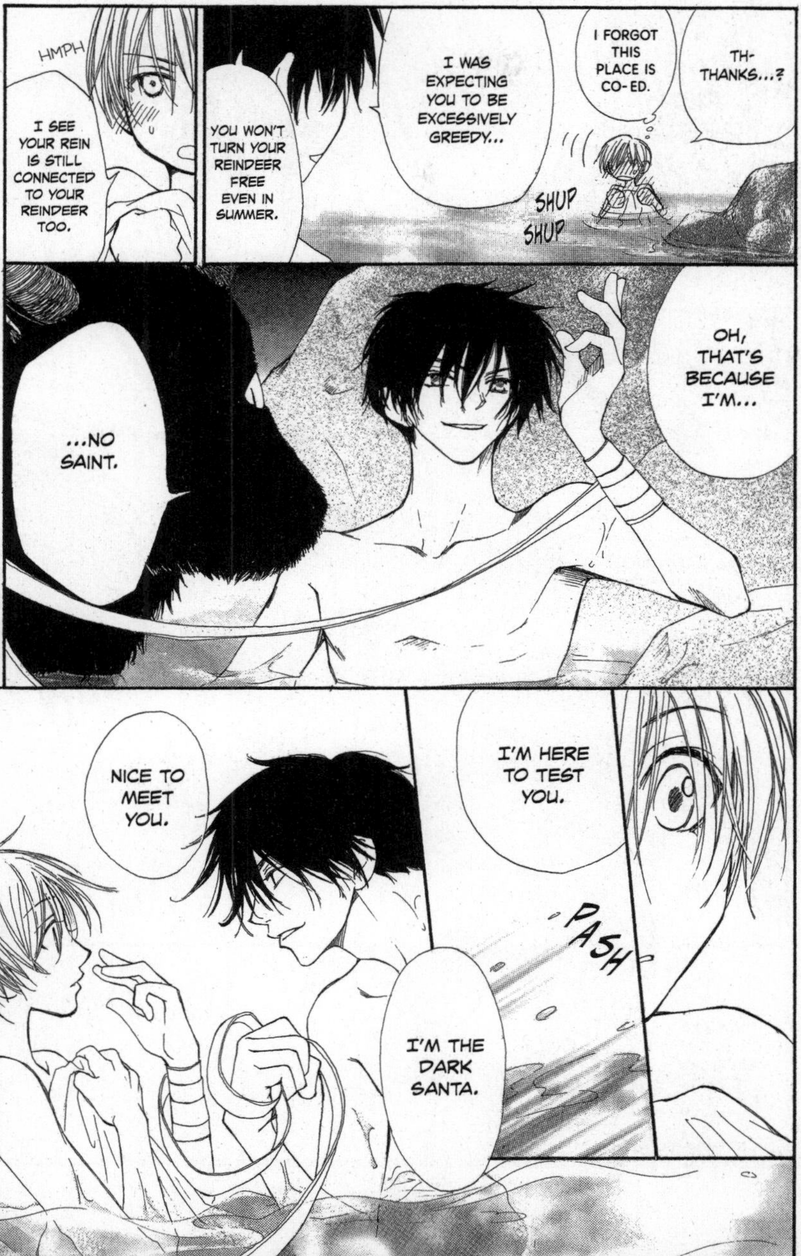
TH- THANKS...?
I FORGOT THIS PLACE IS CO-ED.
I WAS EXPECTING YOU TO BE EXCESSIVELY GREEDY...
SHUP SHUP
YOU WON'T TURN YOUR REINDEER FREE EVEN IN SUMMER.
HMPH
I SEE YOUR REIN IS STILL CONNECTED TO YOUR REINDEER TOO.
OH, THAT'S BECAUSE I'M...
...NO SAINT.
I'M HERE TO TEST YOU.
PASH
NICE TO MEET YOU.
I'M THE DARK SANTA.

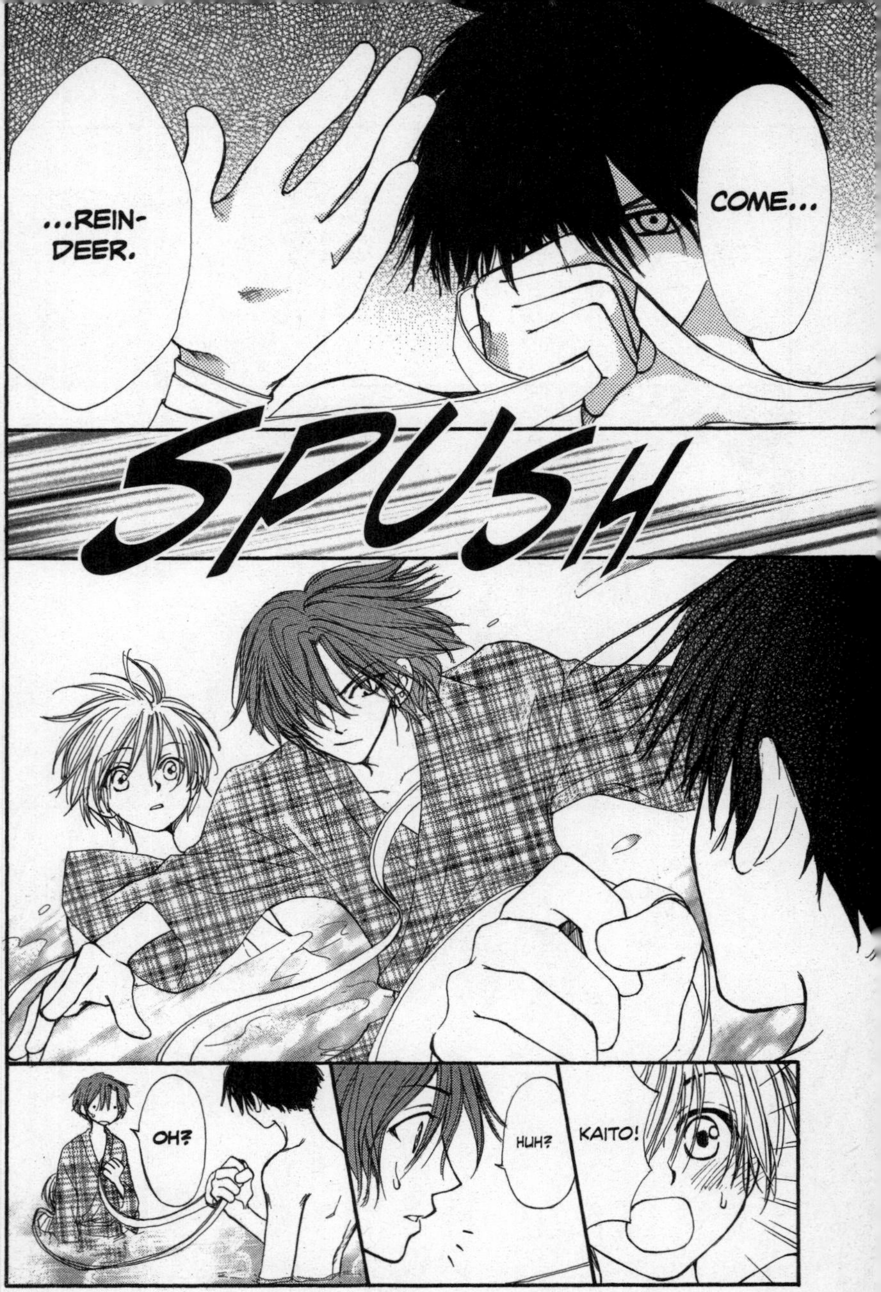
COME...
...REIN-
DEER.
SPUSH
KAITO!
HUH?
OH?

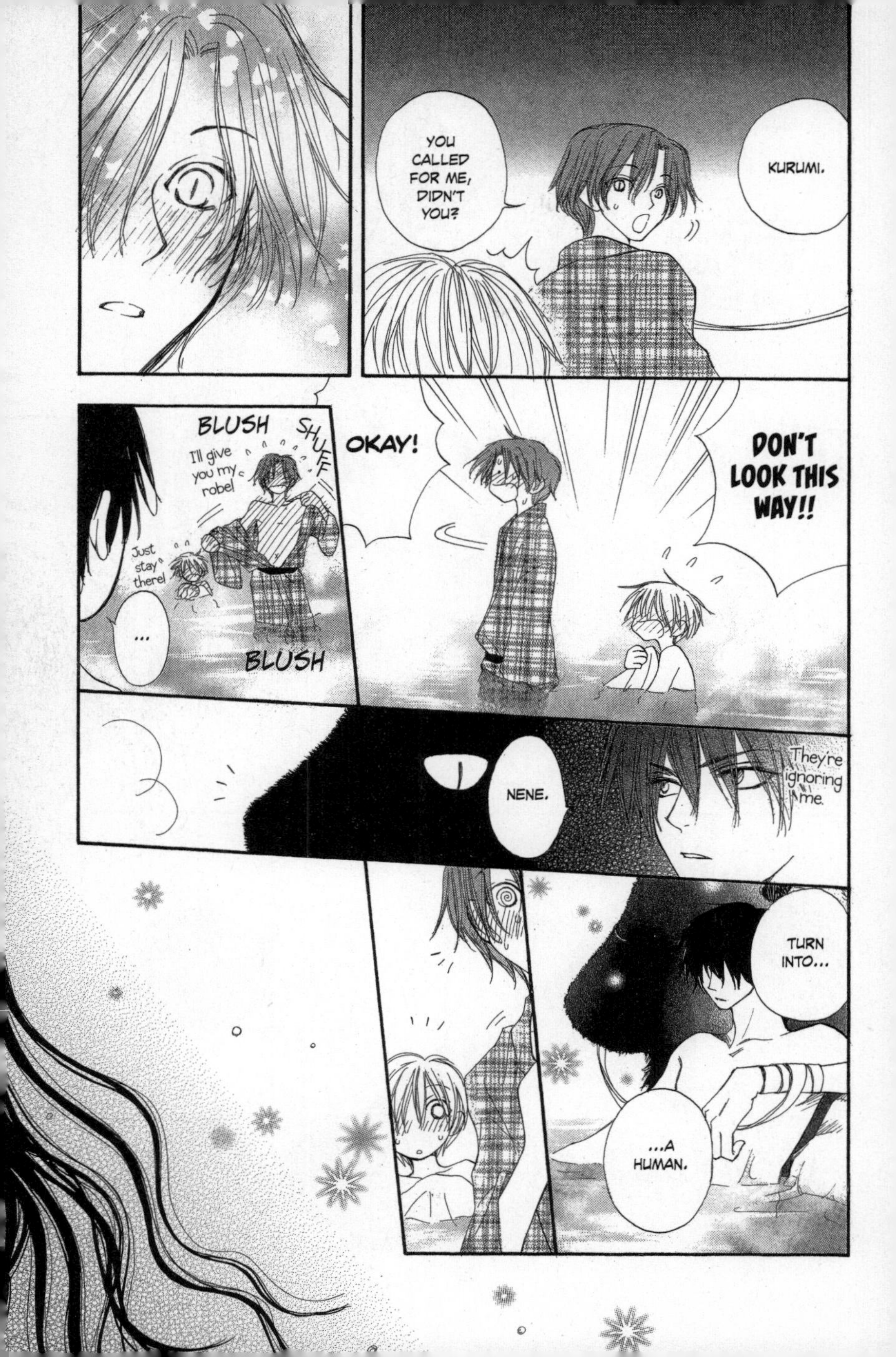
KURUMI.
YOU CALLED FOR ME, DIDN'T YOU?
DON'T LOOK THIS WAY!!
OKAY!
BLUSH
SHUFF
I'll give you my robe!
Just stay there!
...
BLUSH
They're ignoring me.
NENE.
TURN INTO...
...A HUMAN.

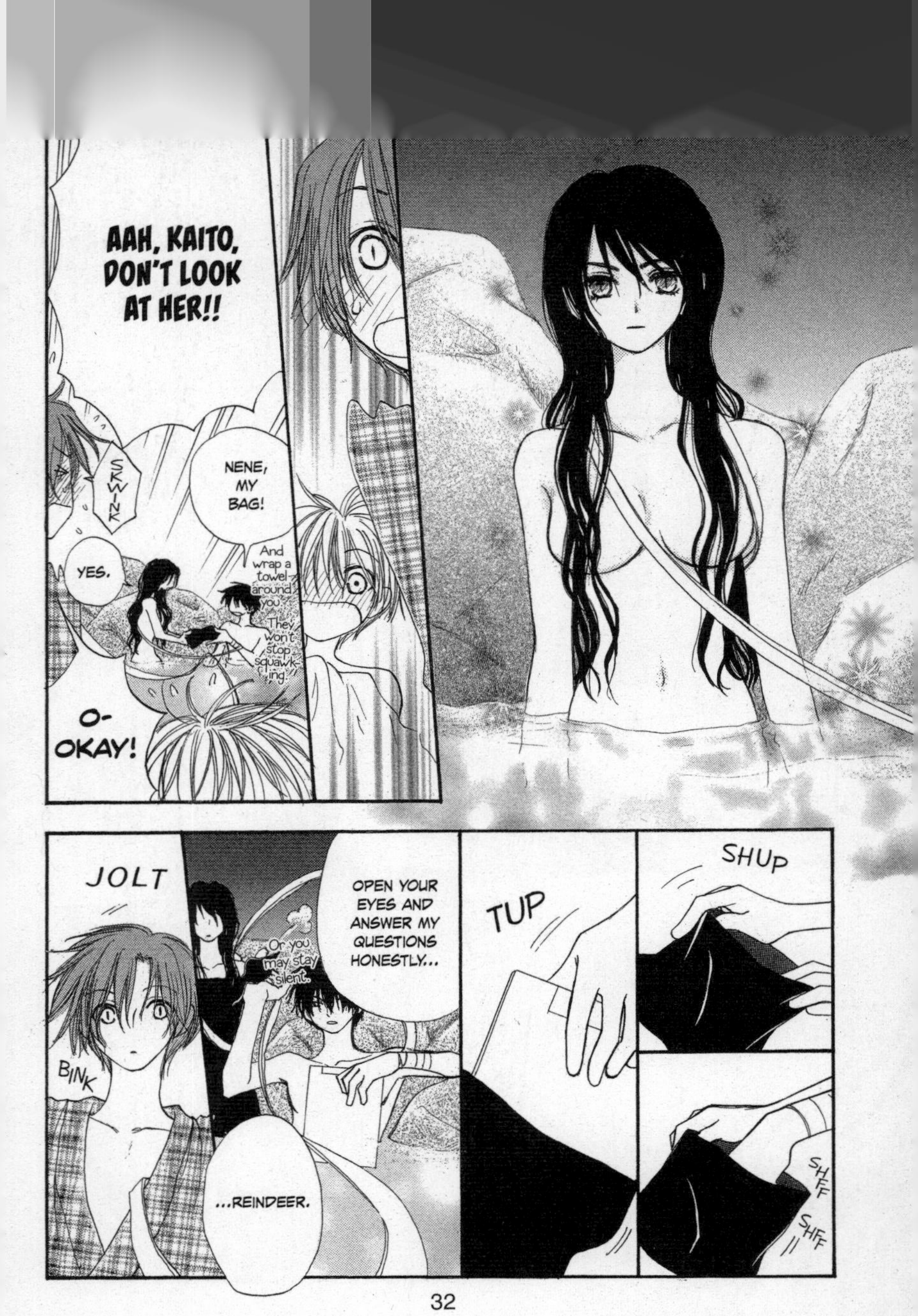
AAH, KAITO, DON'T LOOK AT HER!!
NENE, MY BAG!
And wrap a towel around you. They won't stop squawking.
SKWINK
YES.
O-OKAY!
SHUP
SHFF
SHFF
TUP
OPEN YOUR EYES AND ANSWER MY QUESTIONS HONESTLY...
Or you may stay silent.
JOLT
BINK
...REINDEER.

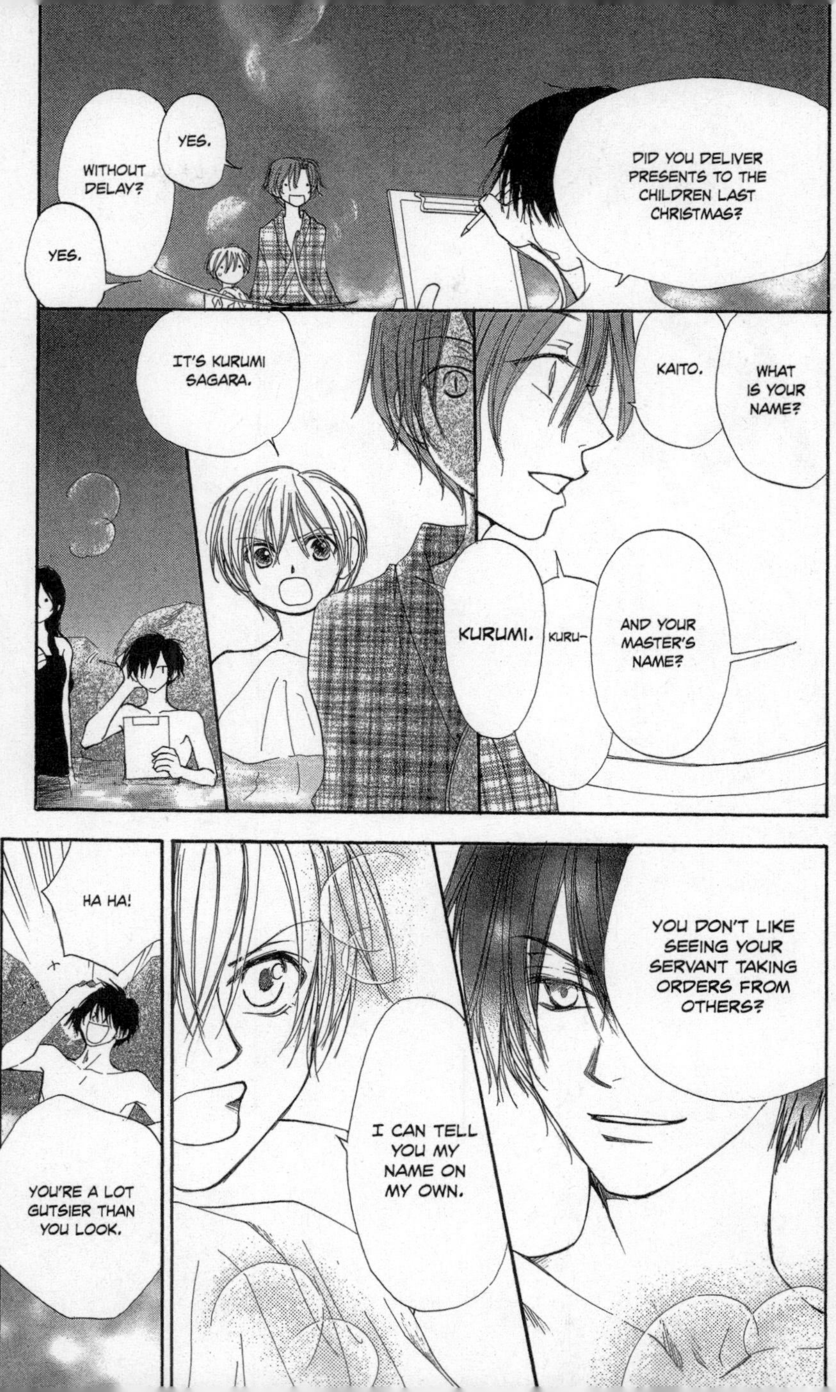
DID YOU DELIVER PRESENTS TO THE CHILDREN LAST CHRISTMAS?
YES.
WITHOUT DELAY?
YES.
WHAT IS YOUR NAME?
KAITO.
AND YOUR MASTER'S NAME?
KURU-
KURUMI.
IT'S KURUMI SAGARA.
YOU DON'T LIKE SEEING YOUR SERVANT TAKING ORDERS FROM OTHERS?
I CAN TELL YOU MY NAME ON MY OWN.
HA HA!
YOU'RE A LOT GUTSIER THAN YOU LOOK.

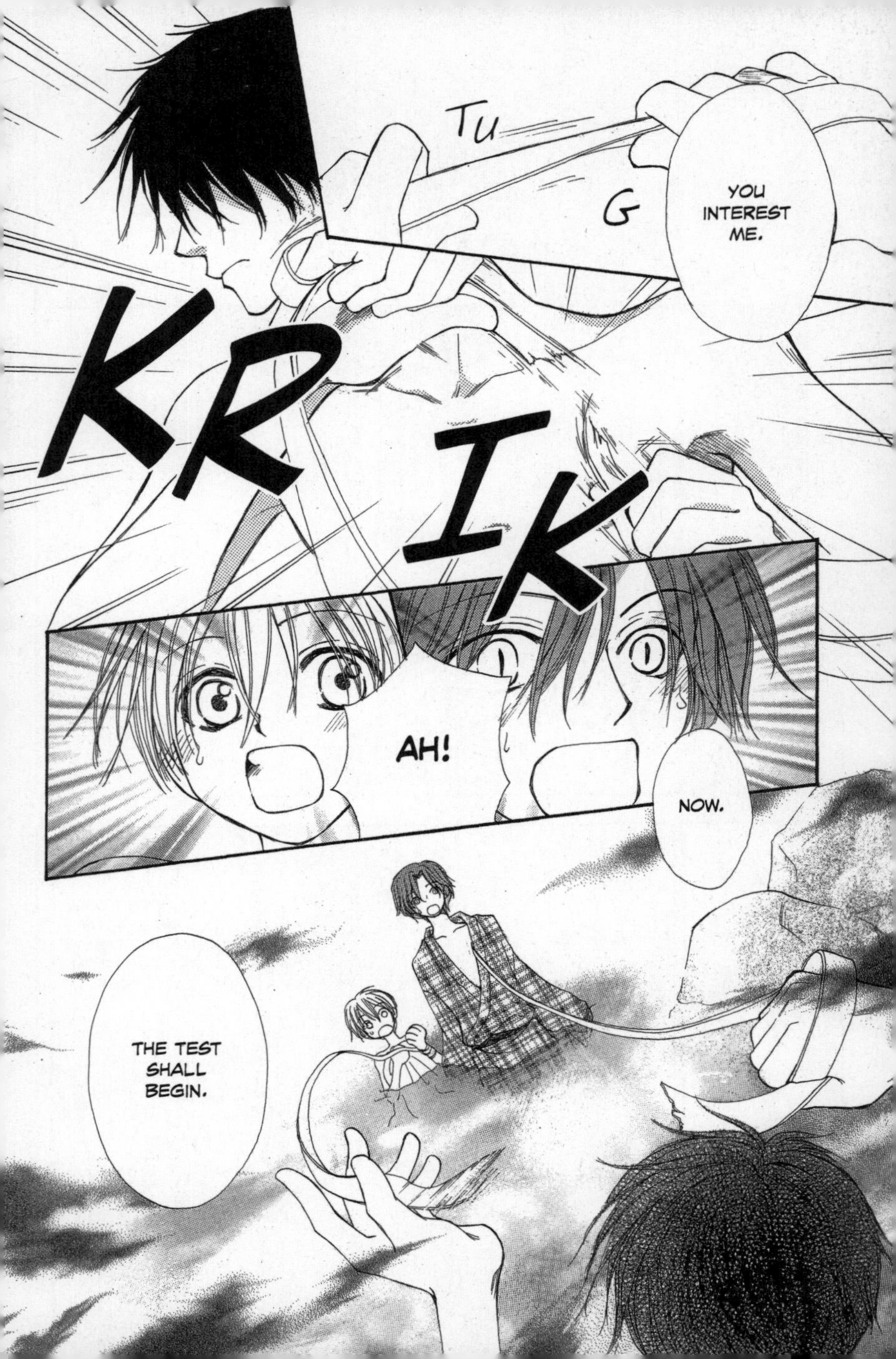
YOU INTEREST ME.
TU G
KRIK
NOW.
AH!
THE TEST SHALL BEGIN.

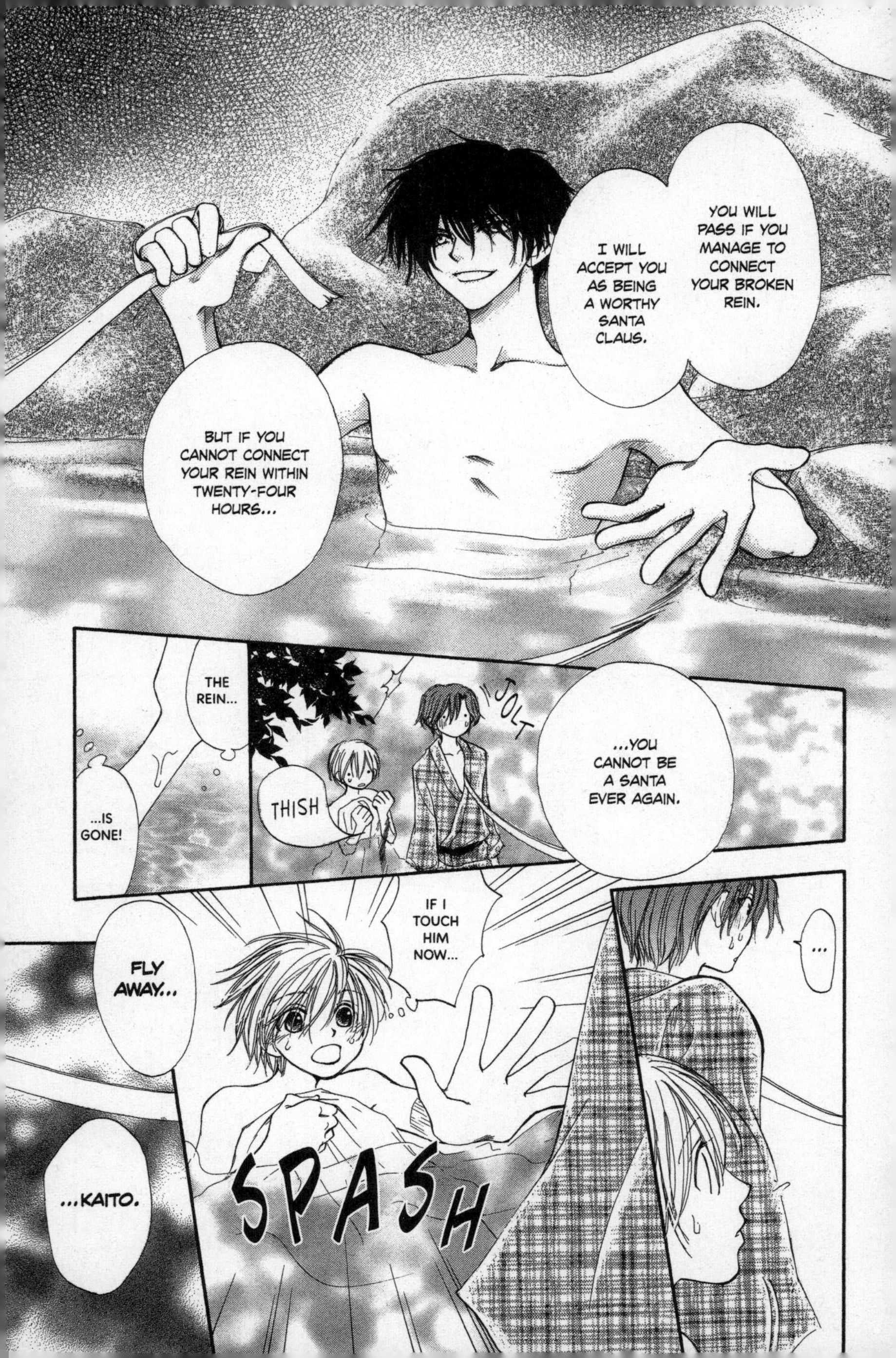
YOU WILL PASS IF YOU MANAGE TO CONNECT YOUR BROKEN REIN.
I WILL ACCEPT YOU AS BEING A WORTHY SANTA CLAUS.
BUT IF YOU CANNOT CONNECT YOUR REIN WITHIN TWENTY-FOUR HOURS...
...YOU CANNOT BE A SANTA EVER AGAIN.
JOLT
THISH
THE REIN...
...IS GONE!
...
IF I TOUCH HIM NOW...
FLY AWAY...
SPASH
...KAITO.

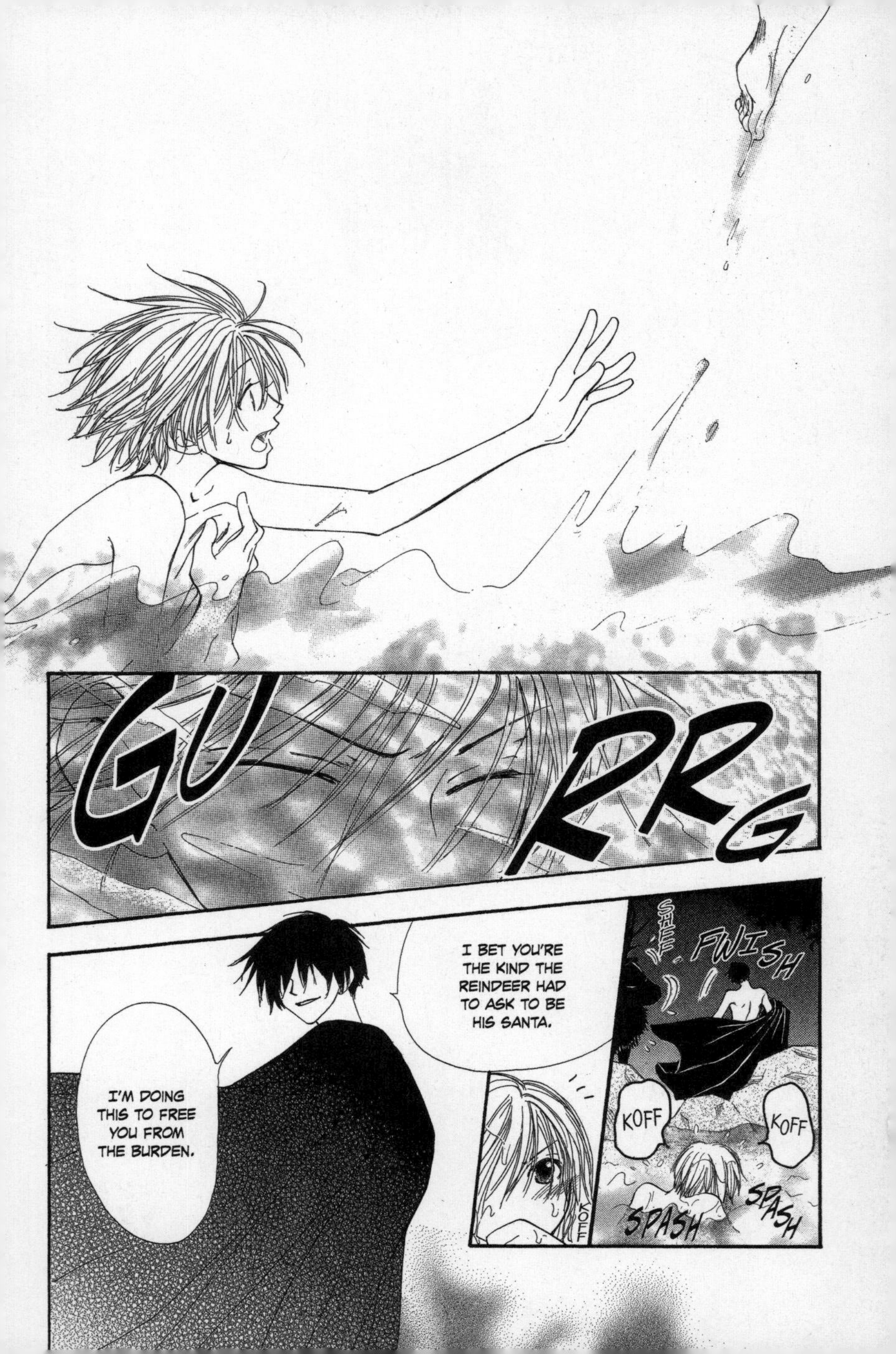
GU
KRRG
SHEF
FWISH
KOFF
KOFF
SPASH
SPASH
KOFF
I BET YOU'RE THE KIND THE REINDEER HAD TO ASK TO BE HIS SANTA.
I'M DOING THIS TO FREE YOU FROM THE BURDEN.

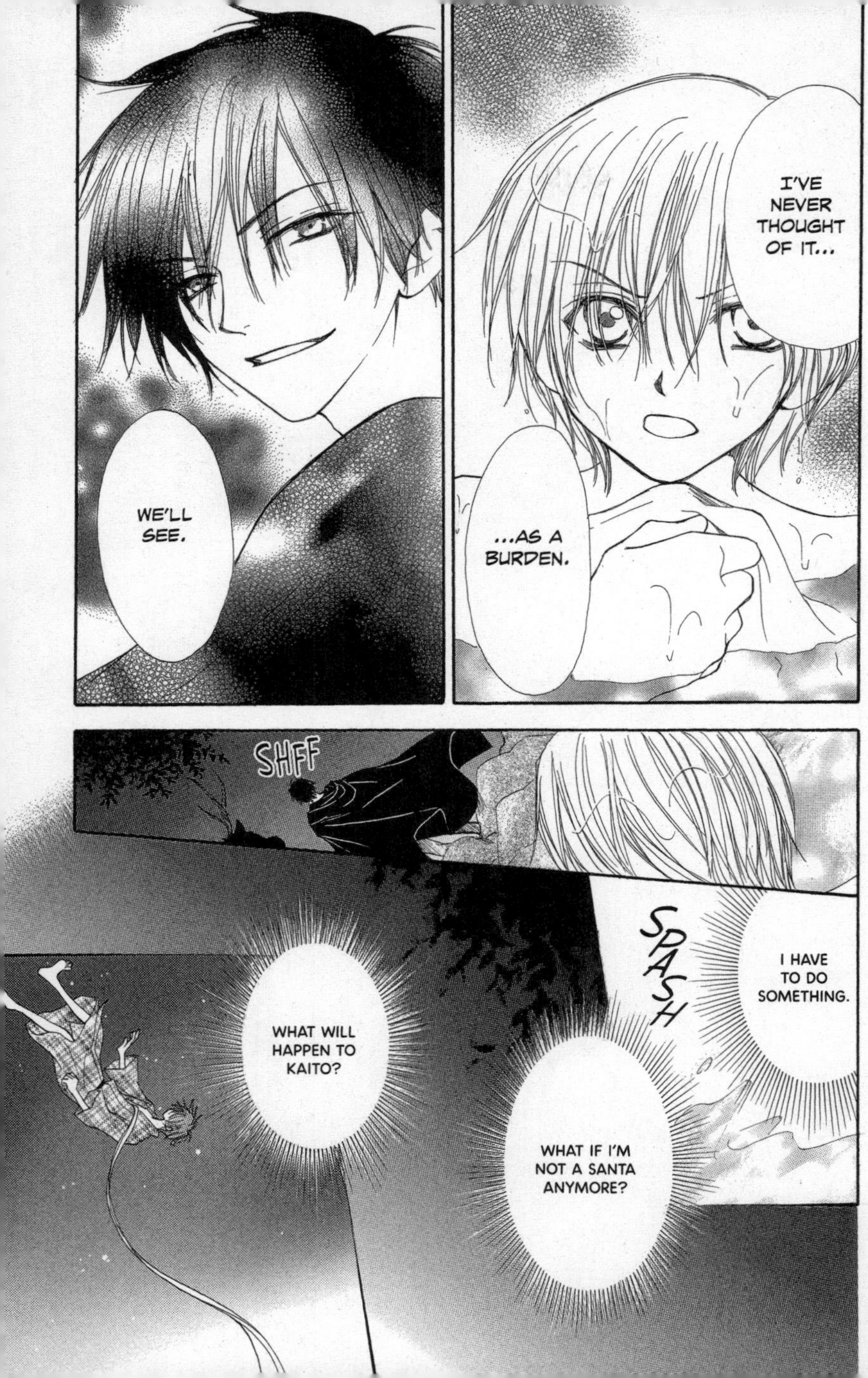
I'VE NEVER THOUGHT OF IT...
...AS A BURDEN.
WE'LL SEE.
SHFF
SPASH
I HAVE TO DO SOMETHING.
WHAT IF I'M NOT A SANTA ANYMORE?
WHAT WILL HAPPEN TO KAITO?

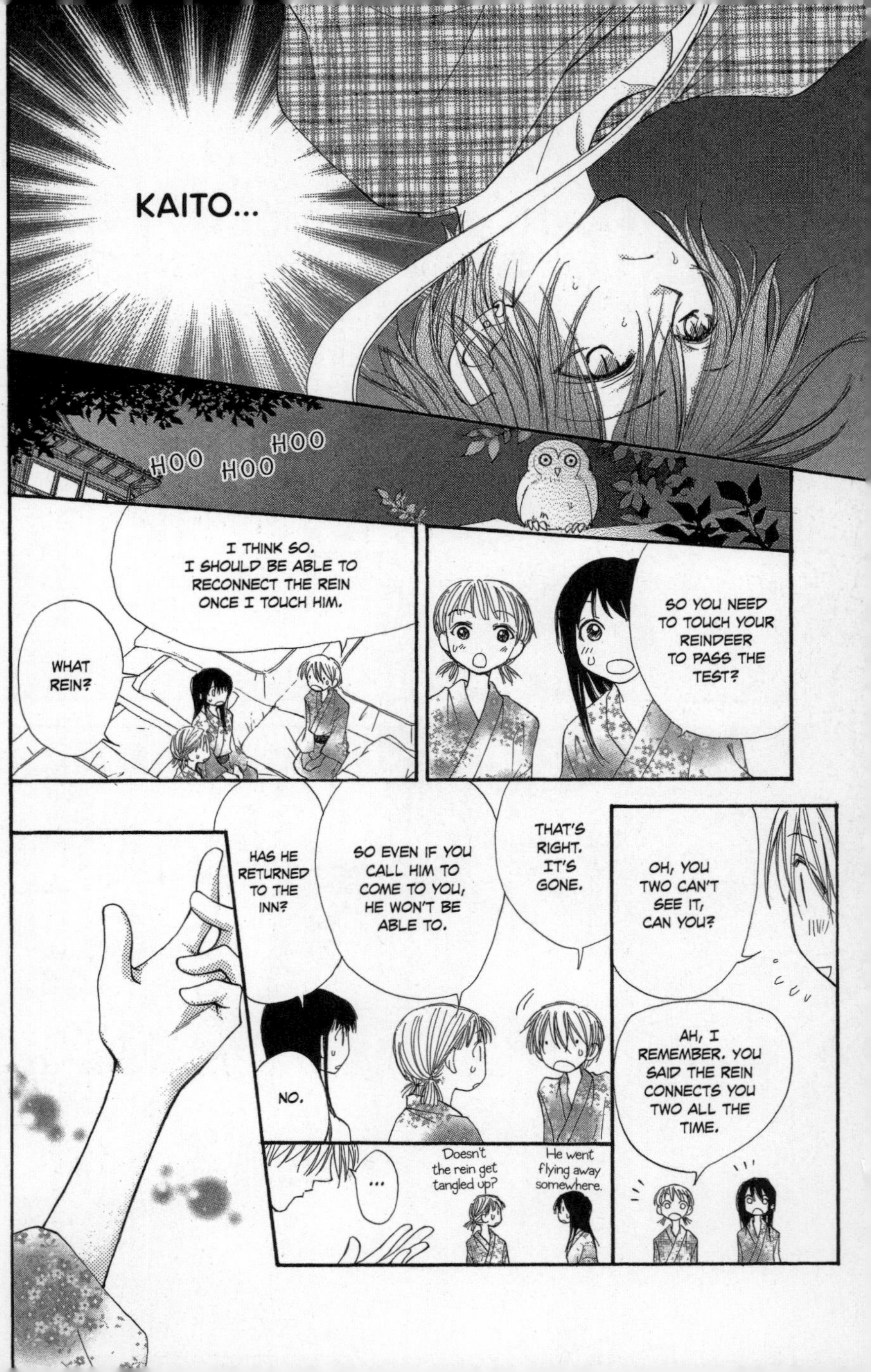

KAITO...
HOO HOO HOO
SO YOU NEED TO TOUCH YOUR REINDEER TO PASS THE TEST?
I THINK SO. I SHOULD BE ABLE TO RECONNECT THE REIN ONCE I TOUCH HIM.
WHAT REIN?
OH, YOU TWO CAN'T SEE IT, CAN YOU?
AH, I REMEMBER. YOU SAID THE REIN CONNECTS YOU TWO ALL THE TIME.
THAT'S RIGHT. IT'S GONE.
SO EVEN IF YOU CALL HIM TO COME TO YOU, HE WON'T BE ABLE TO.
HAS HE RETURNED TO THE INN?
NO.
He went flying away somewhere.
Doesn't the rein get tangled up?
...

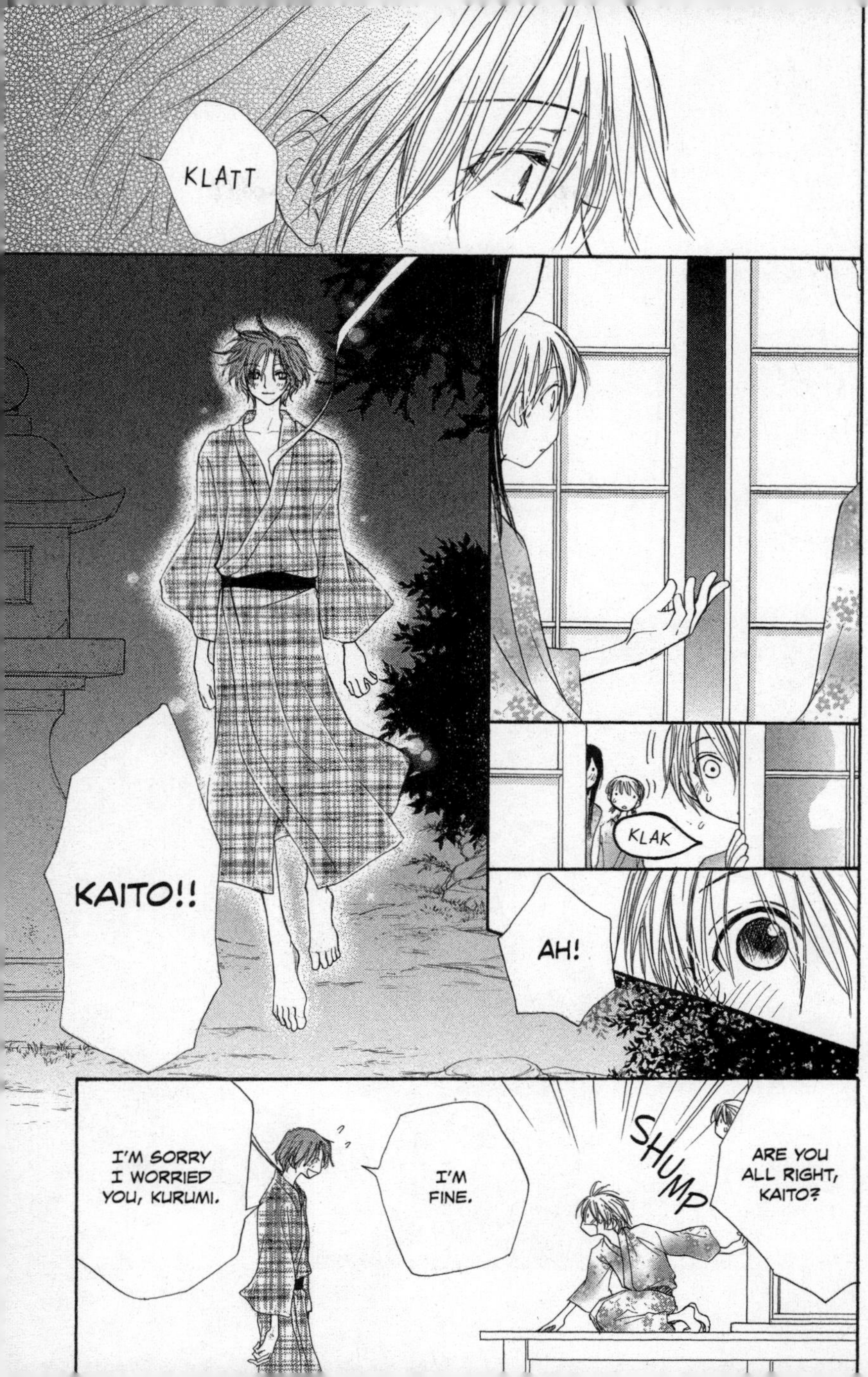
KLATT
KLAK
AH!
KAITO!!
ARE YOU ALL RIGHT, KAITO?
SHUMP
I'M FINE.
I'M SORRY I WORRIED YOU, KURUMI.

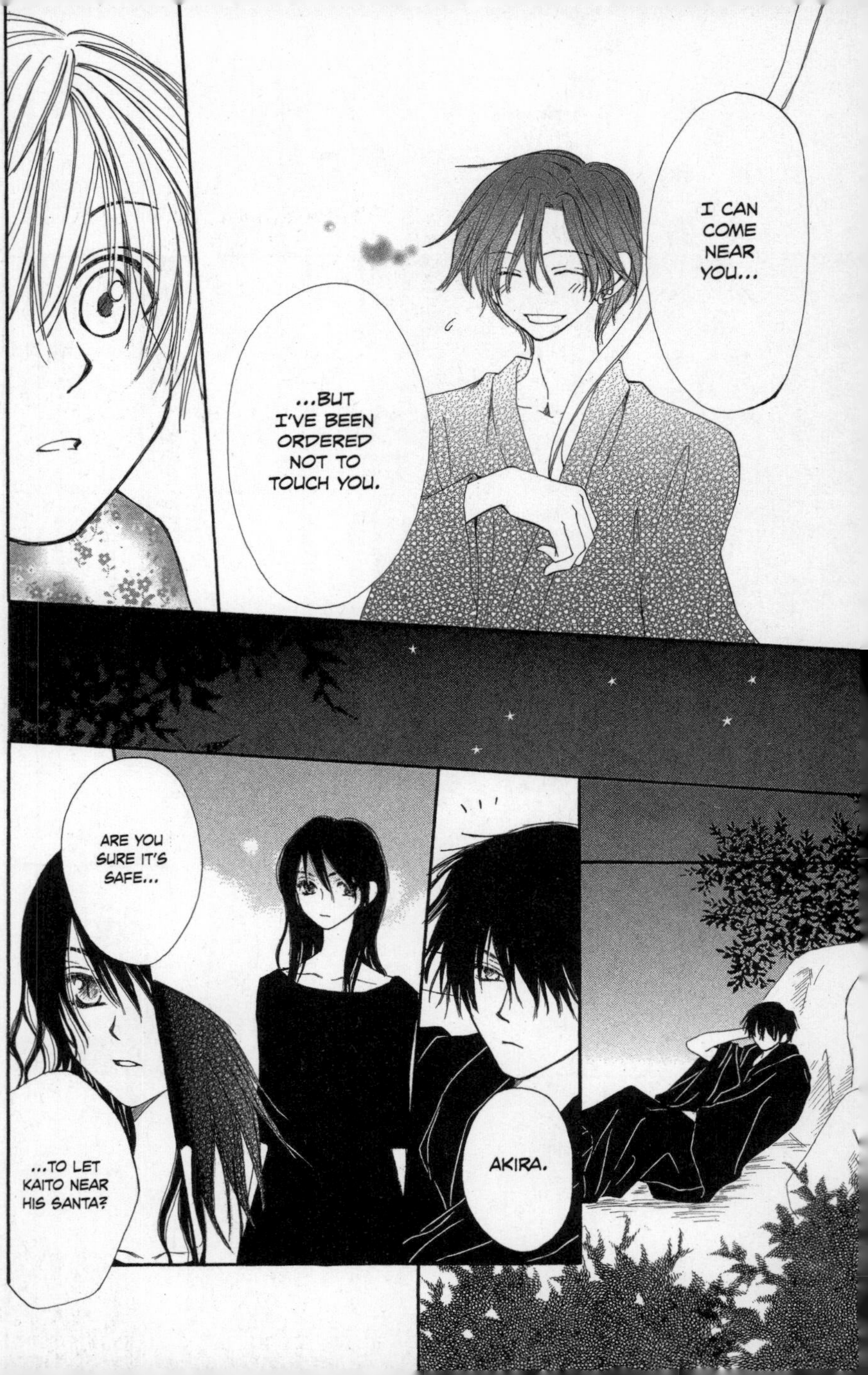
I CAN COME NEAR YOU...
...BUT I'VE BEEN ORDERED NOT TO TOUCH YOU.
AKIRA.
ARE YOU SURE IT'S SAFE...
...TO LET KAITO NEAR HIS SANTA?

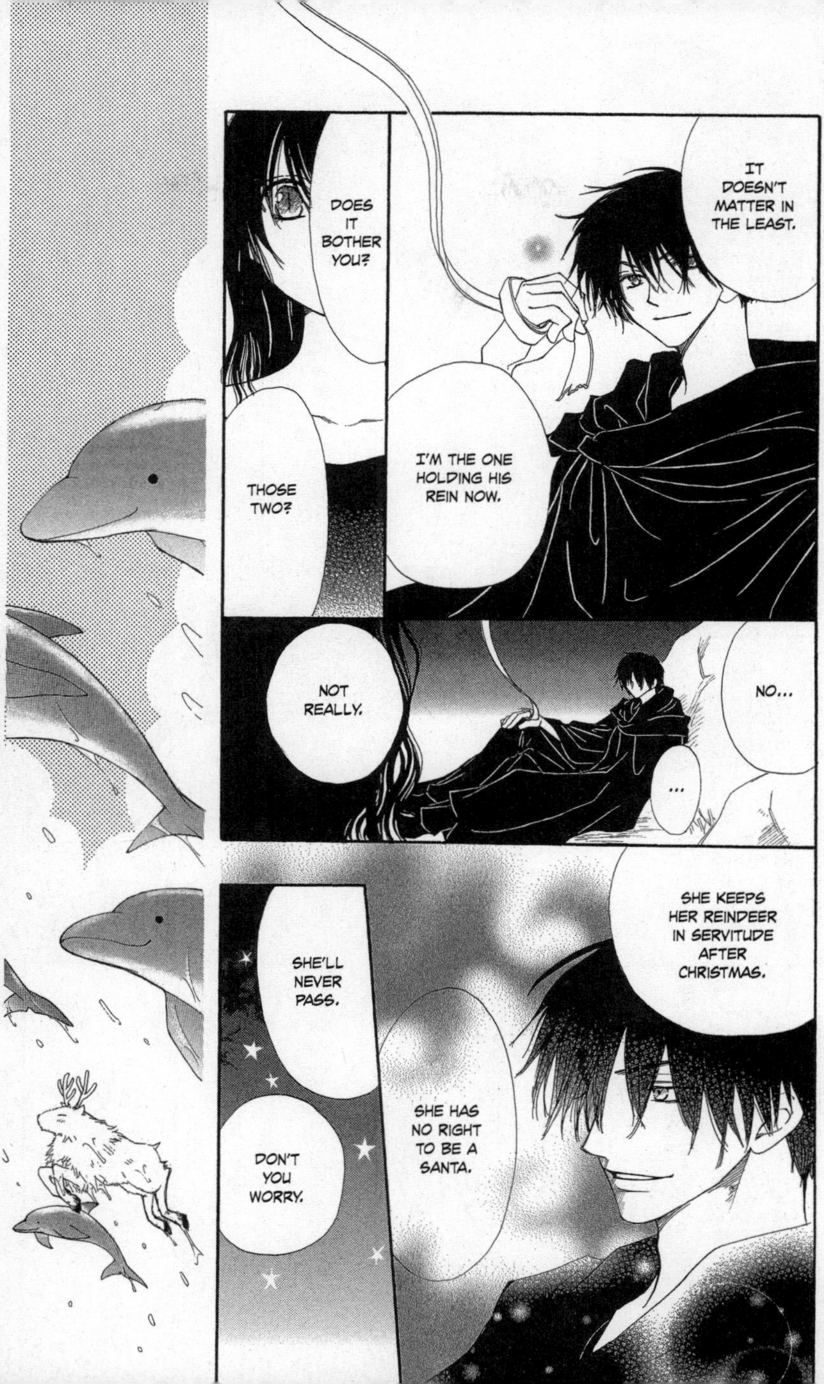
IT DOESN'T MATTER IN THE LEAST.
I'M THE ONE HOLDING HIS REIN NOW.
DOES IT BOTHER YOU?
THOSE TWO?
NO...
...
NOT REALLY.
SHE KEEPS HER REINDEER IN SERVITUDE AFTER CHRISTMAS.
SHE HAS NO RIGHT TO BE A SANTA.
SHE'LL NEVER PASS.
DON'T YOU WORRY.

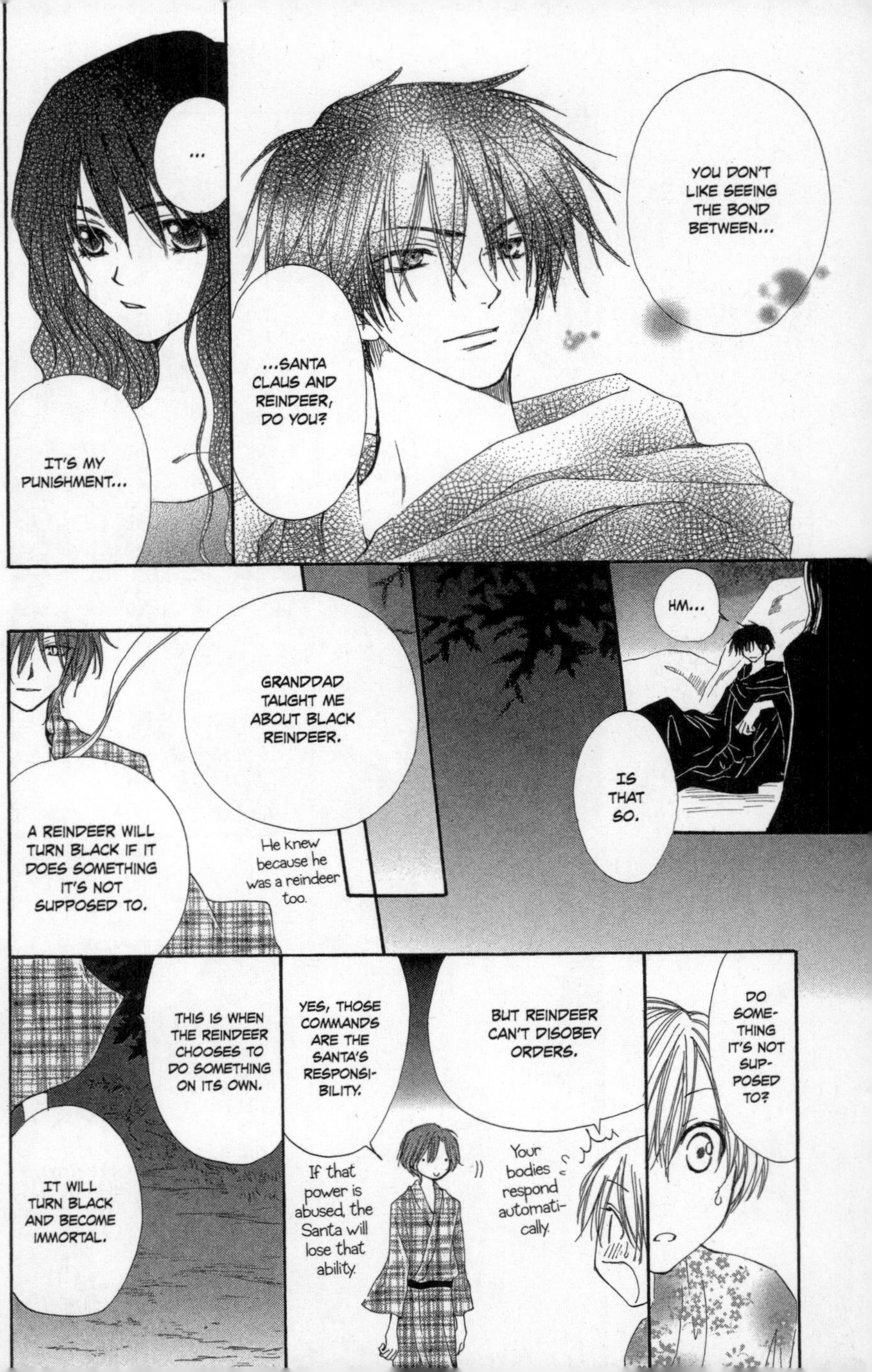
YOU DON'T LIKE SEEING THE BOND BETWEEN...
...SANTA CLAUS AND REINDEER, DO YOU?
...
IT'S MY PUNISHMENT...
HM...
IS THAT SO.
GRANDDAD TAUGHT ME ABOUT BLACK REINDEER.
He knew because he was a reindeer too.
A REINDEER WILL TURN BLACK IF IT DOES SOMETHING IT'S NOT SUPPOSED TO.
DO SOME-THING IT'S NOT SUP-POSED TO?
BUT REINDEER CAN'T DISOBEY ORDERS.
Your bodies respond automati-cally.
YES, THOSE COMMANDS ARE THE SANTA'S RESPONSI-BILITY.
If that power is abused, the Santa will lose that ability.
THIS IS WHEN THE REINDEER CHOOSES TO DO SOMETHING ON ITS OWN.
IT WILL TURN BLACK AND BECOME IMMORTAL.

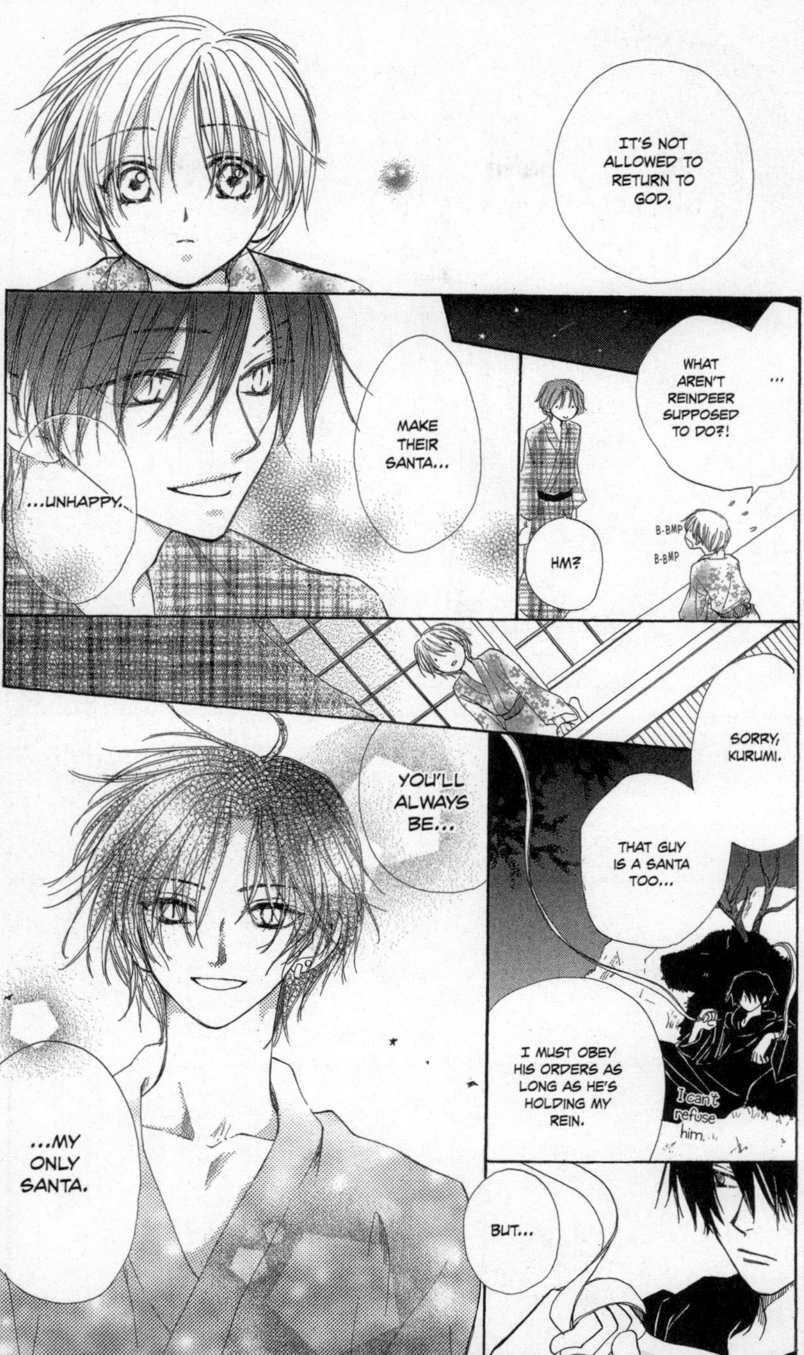

IT'S NOT ALLOWED TO RETURN TO GOD.
...
WHAT AREN'T REINDEER SUPPOSED TO DO?!
B-BMP
B-BMP
HM?
MAKE THEIR SANTA...
...UNHAPPY.
SORRY, KURUMI.
THAT GUY IS A SANTA TOO...
I MUST OBEY HIS ORDERS AS LONG AS HE'S HOLDING MY REIN.
I can't refuse him.
BUT...
YOU'LL ALWAYS BE...
...MY ONLY SANTA.

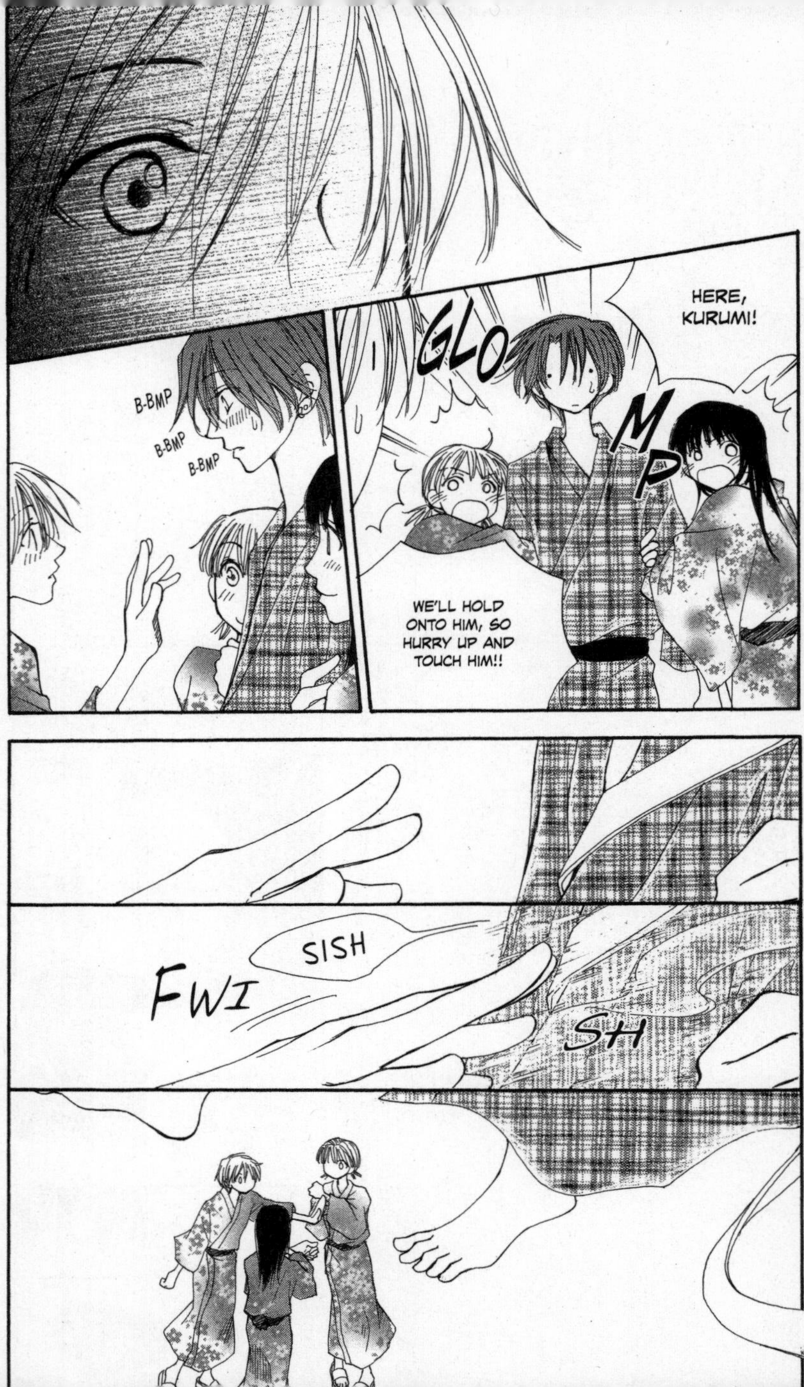
HERE, KURUMI!
GLOMP
WE'LL HOLD ONTO HIM, SO HURRY UP AND TOUCH HIM!!
B-BMP
B-BMP
B-BMP
SISH
SH
FWI

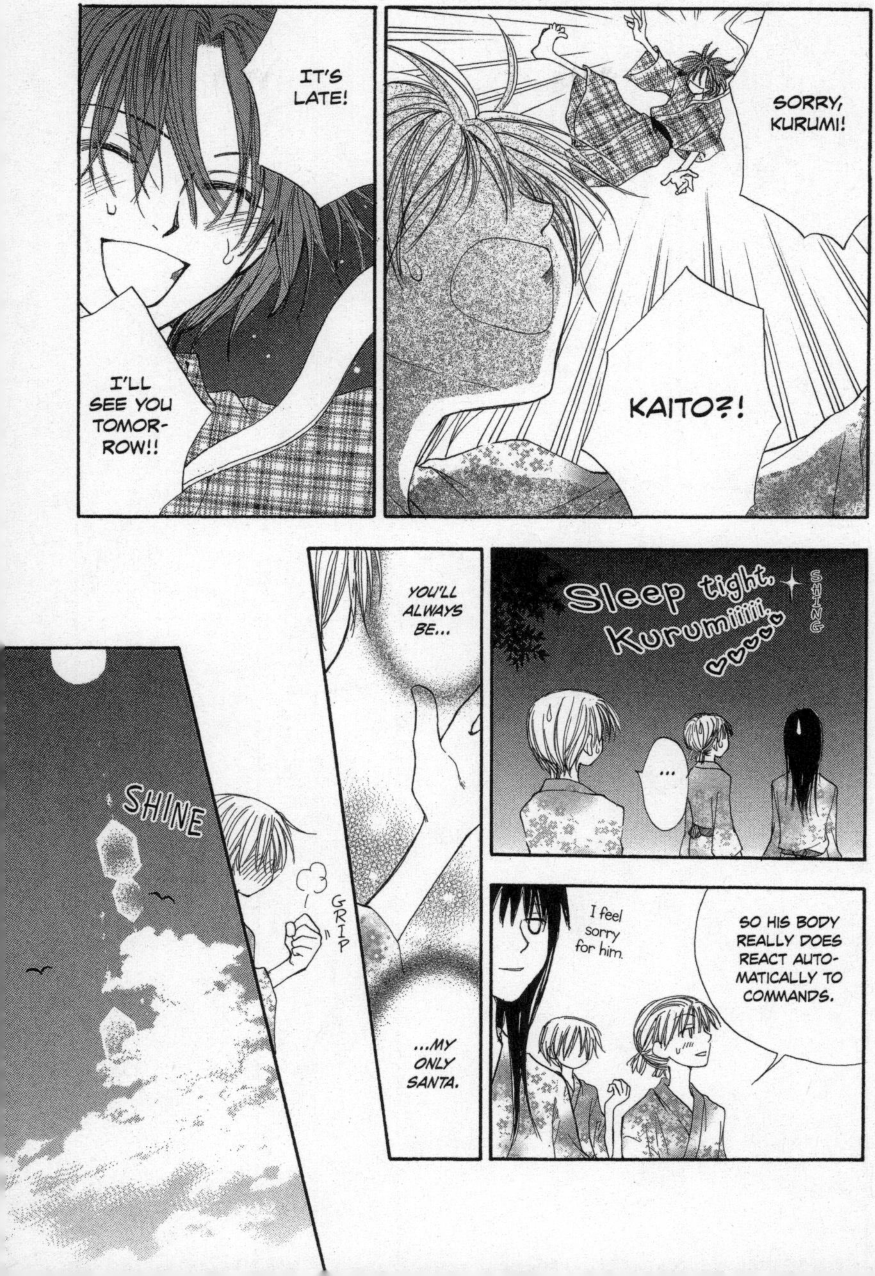
SORRY, KURUMI!
KAITO?!
IT'S LATE!
I'LL SEE YOU TOMOR-ROW!!
Sleep tight, Kurumiiiii.
SHING
...
SO HIS BODY REALLY DOES REACT AUTO-MATICALLY TO COMMANDS.
I feel sorry for him.
YOU'LL ALWAYS BE...
...MY ONLY SANTA.
SHINE
GRIP

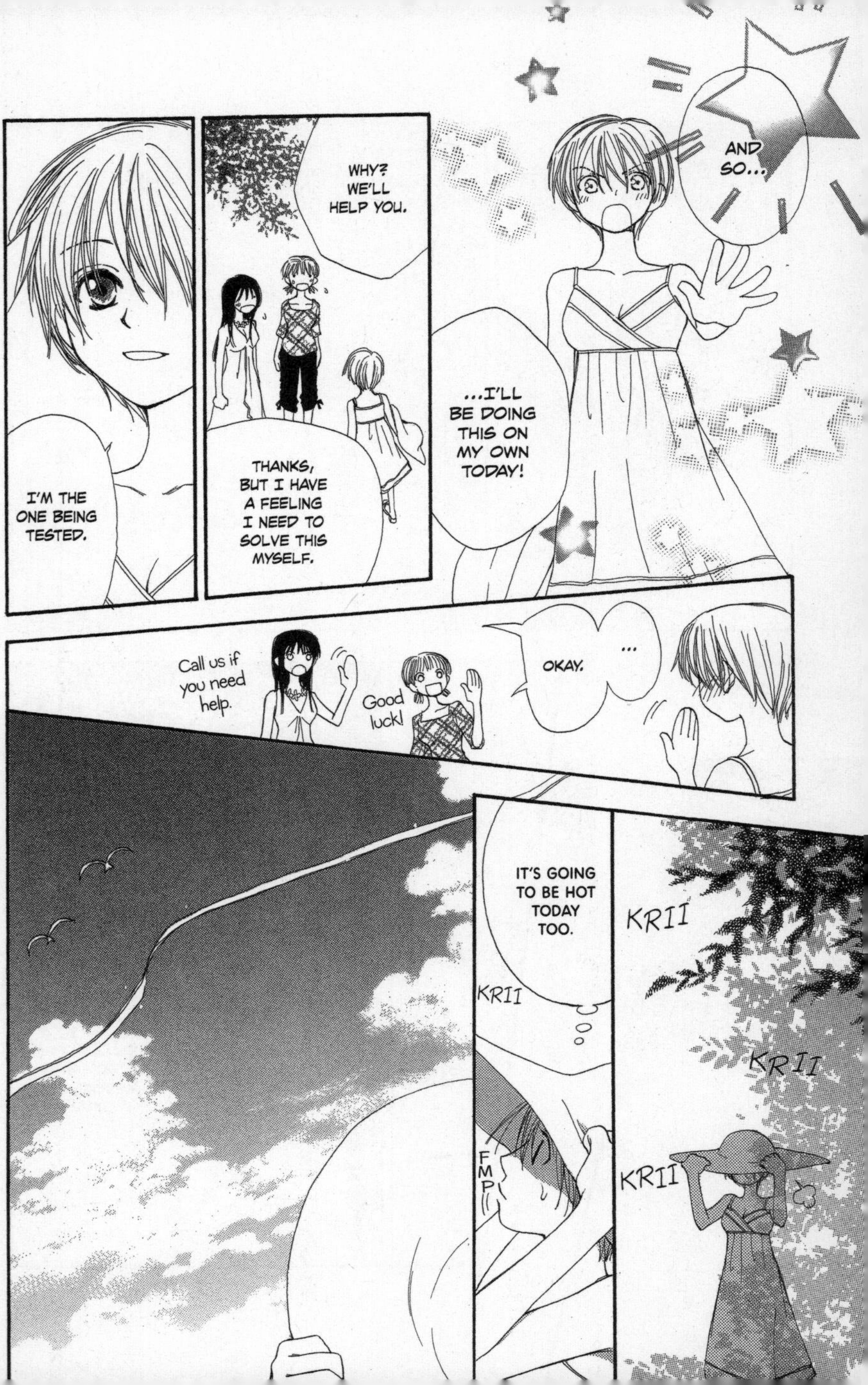
AND SO...
...I'LL BE DOING THIS ON MY OWN TODAY!
WHY? WE'LL HELP YOU.
THANKS, BUT I HAVE A FEELING I NEED TO SOLVE THIS MYSELF.
I'M THE ONE BEING TESTED.
...
OKAY.
Good luck!
Call us if you need help.
KRII
KRII
KRII
IT'S GOING TO BE HOT TODAY TOO.
KRII
FMP

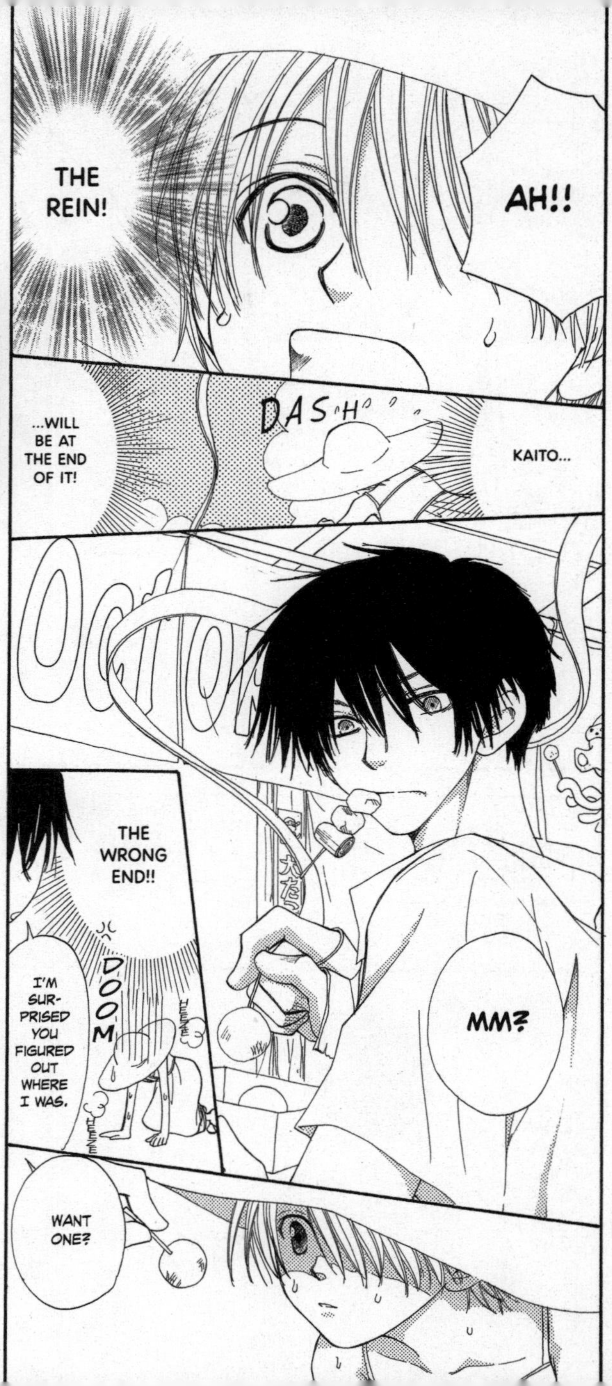
AH!!
THE REIN!
KAITO...
DASH
...WILL BE AT THE END OF IT!
MM?
THE WRONG END!!
DOOM
I'M SUR-PRISED YOU FIGURED OUT WHERE I WAS.
WANT ONE?

1/4 Sakura Mail

Part 2

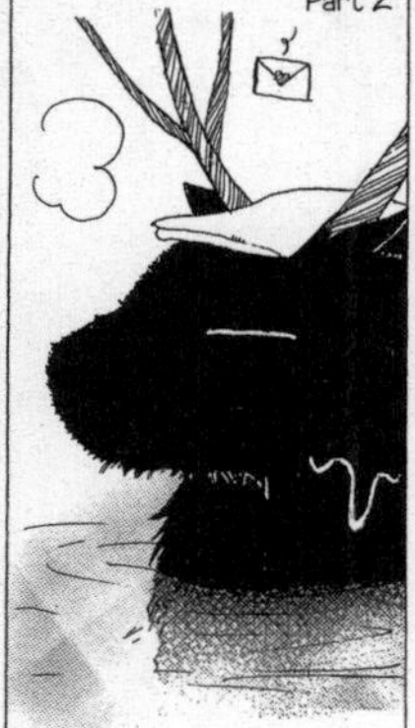

Now for the test. The reindeer can basically do anything the Santa orders, even if it's dangerous. So I decided to create a supervising entity. The black reindeer looks like one of those metal statues that children can climb on in department stores. I wanted to draw a female reindeer, so I had a lot of fun drawing Nene. She is naked in the hot spring scene, but the Dark Santa...

(continues)

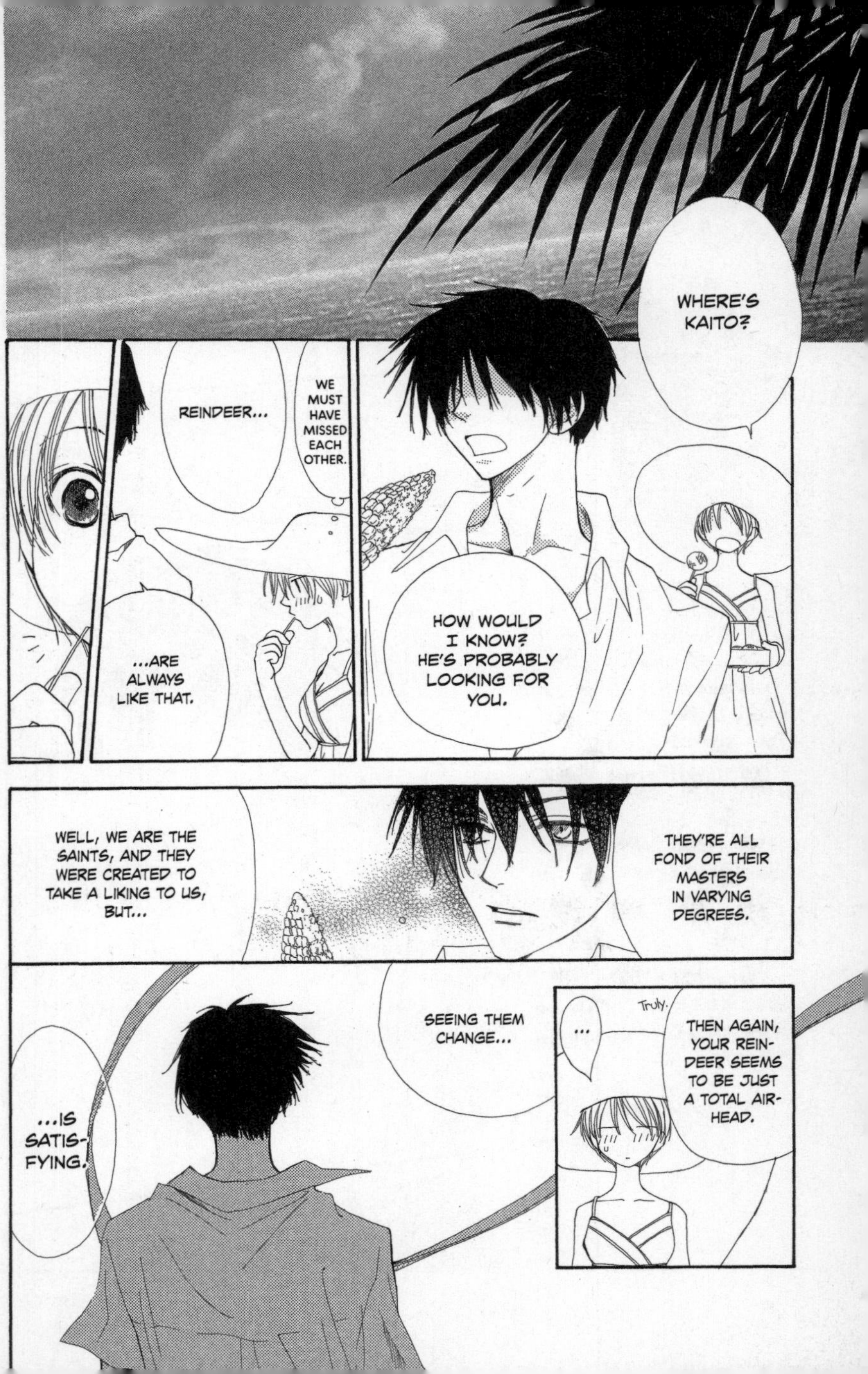
WHERE'S KAITO?
HOW WOULD I KNOW? HE'S PROBABLY LOOKING FOR YOU.
WE MUST HAVE MISSED EACH OTHER.
REINDEER...
...ARE ALWAYS LIKE THAT.
THEY'RE ALL FOND OF THEIR MASTERS IN VARYING DEGREES.
WELL, WE ARE THE SAINTS, AND THEY WERE CREATED TO TAKE A LIKING TO US, BUT...
Truly.
THEN AGAIN, YOUR REIN-DEER SEEMS TO BE JUST A TOTAL AIR-HEAD.
...
SEEING THEM CHANGE...
...IS SATIS-FYING.

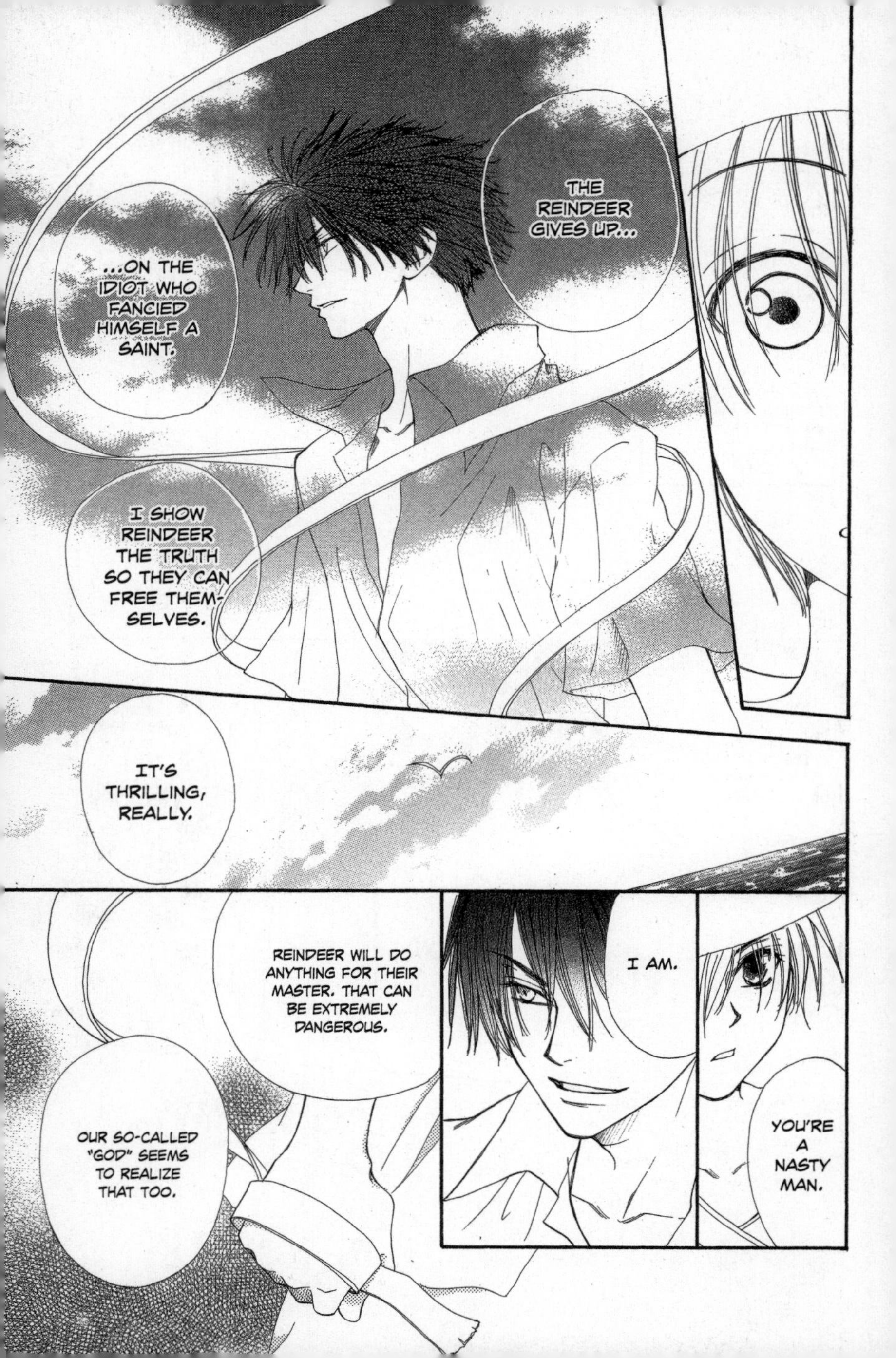
THE REINDEER GIVES UP...
...ON THE IDIOT WHO FANCIED HIMSELF A SAINT.
I SHOW REINDEER THE TRUTH SO THEY CAN FREE THEM-SELVES.
IT'S THRILLING, REALLY.
YOU'RE A NASTY MAN.
I AM.
REINDEER WILL DO ANYTHING FOR THEIR MASTER. THAT CAN BE EXTREMELY DANGEROUS.
OUR SO-CALLED "GOD" SEEMS TO REALIZE THAT TOO.

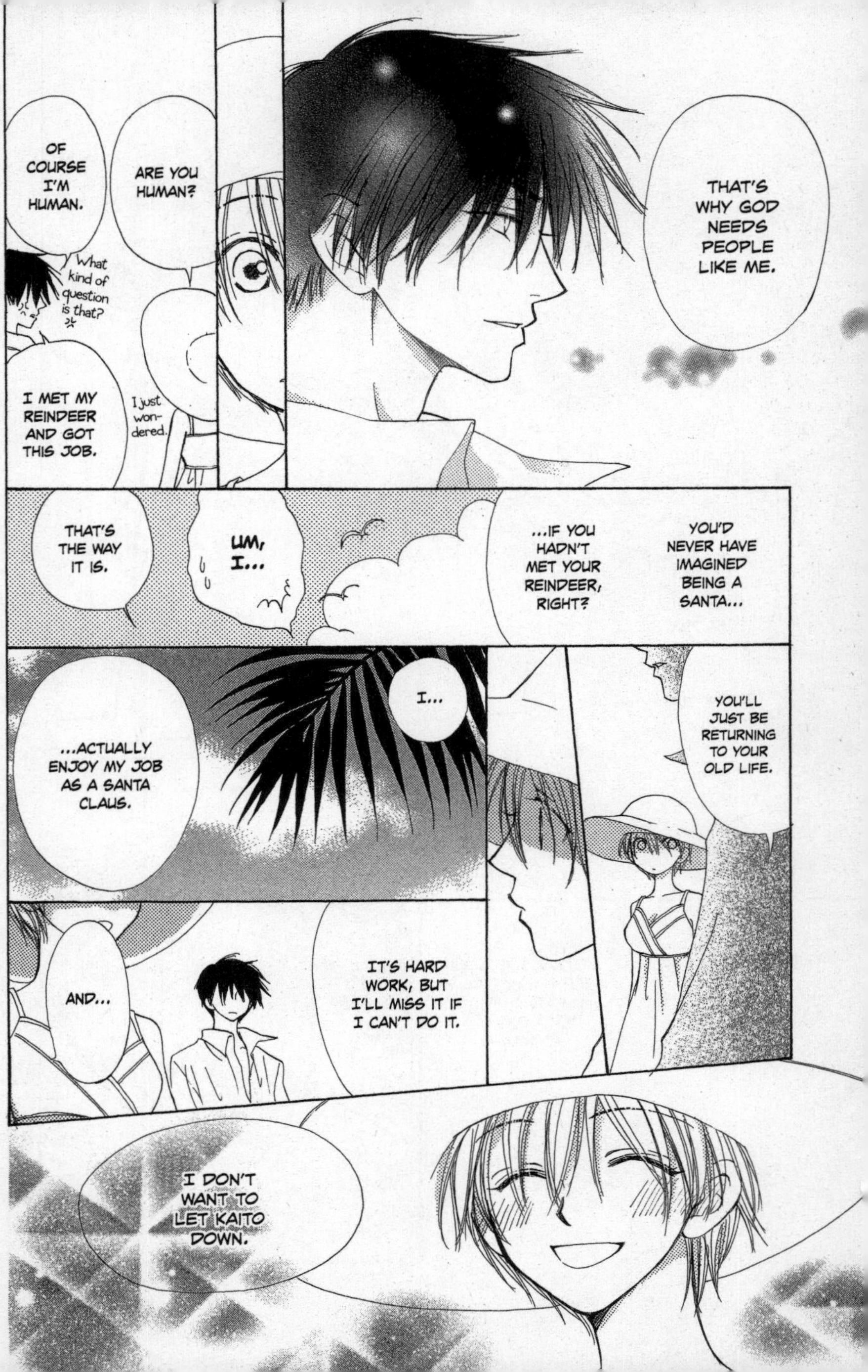
THAT'S WHY GOD NEEDS PEOPLE LIKE ME.
ARE YOU HUMAN?
I just wondered.
OF COURSE I'M HUMAN.
What kind of question is that?
I MET MY REINDEER AND GOT THIS JOB.
YOU'D NEVER HAVE IMAGINED BEING A SANTA...
...IF YOU HADN'T MET YOUR REINDEER, RIGHT?
UM, I...
THAT'S THE WAY IT IS.
YOU'LL JUST BE RETURNING TO YOUR OLD LIFE.
I...
...ACTUALLY ENJOY MY JOB AS A SANTA CLAUS.
IT'S HARD WORK, BUT I'LL MISS IT IF I CAN'T DO IT.
AND...
I DON'T WANT TO LET KAITO DOWN.

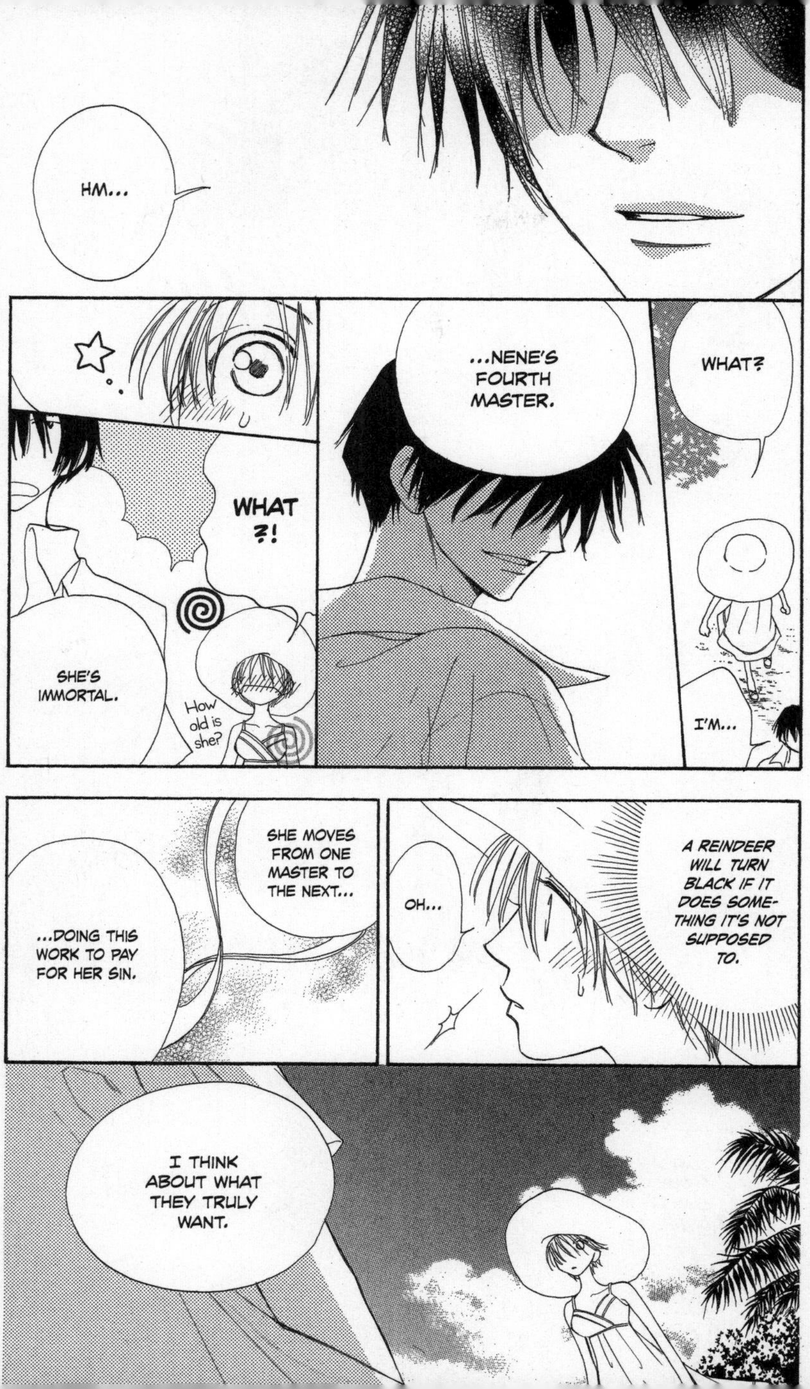
HM...
WHAT?
I'M...
...NENE'S FOURTH MASTER.
WHAT?!
SHE'S IMMORTAL.
How old is she?
A REINDEER WILL TURN BLACK IF IT DOES SOMETHING IT'S NOT SUPPOSED TO.
OH...
SHE MOVES FROM ONE MASTER TO THE NEXT...
...DOING THIS WORK TO PAY FOR HER SIN.
I THINK ABOUT WHAT THEY TRULY WANT.

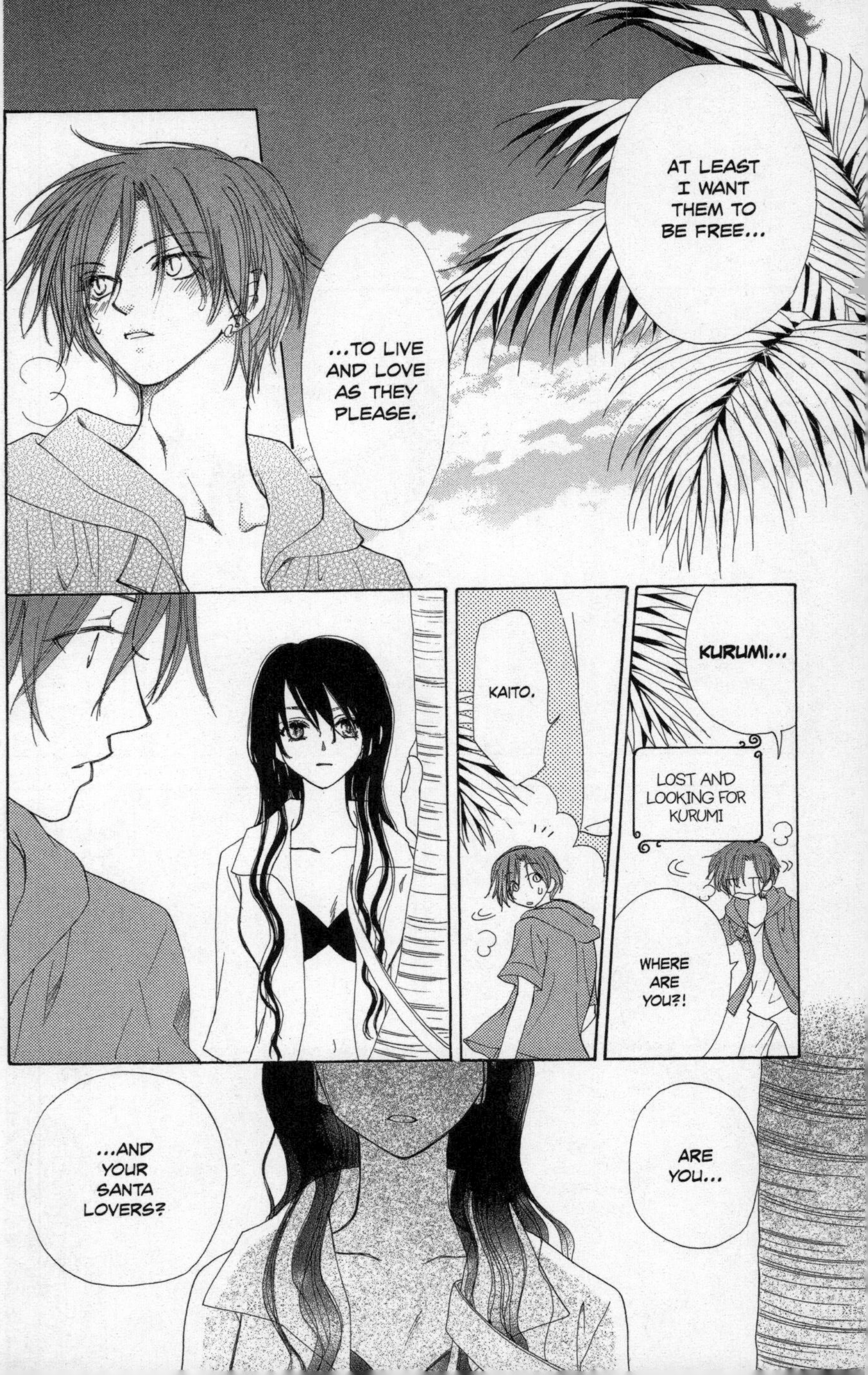
AT LEAST I WANT THEM TO BE FREE...
...TO LIVE AND LOVE AS THEY PLEASE.
KURUMI...
LOST AND LOOKING FOR KURUMI
WHERE ARE YOU?!
KAITO.
ARE YOU...
...AND YOUR SANTA LOVERS?

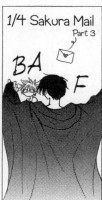

1/4 Sakura Mail

Part 3

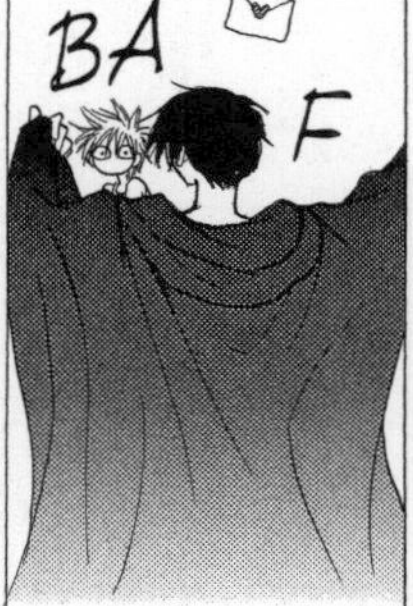
BA
F

...was nude too. I didn't take much notice of it until I actually drew it, but it looked like he was wearing a cape over his naked body, didn't it? I have an idea about what he looks like underneath that cape, but I'll keep that a secret. Thus, he has been branded as a pervert by my assistants. He's a bossy pervert too.

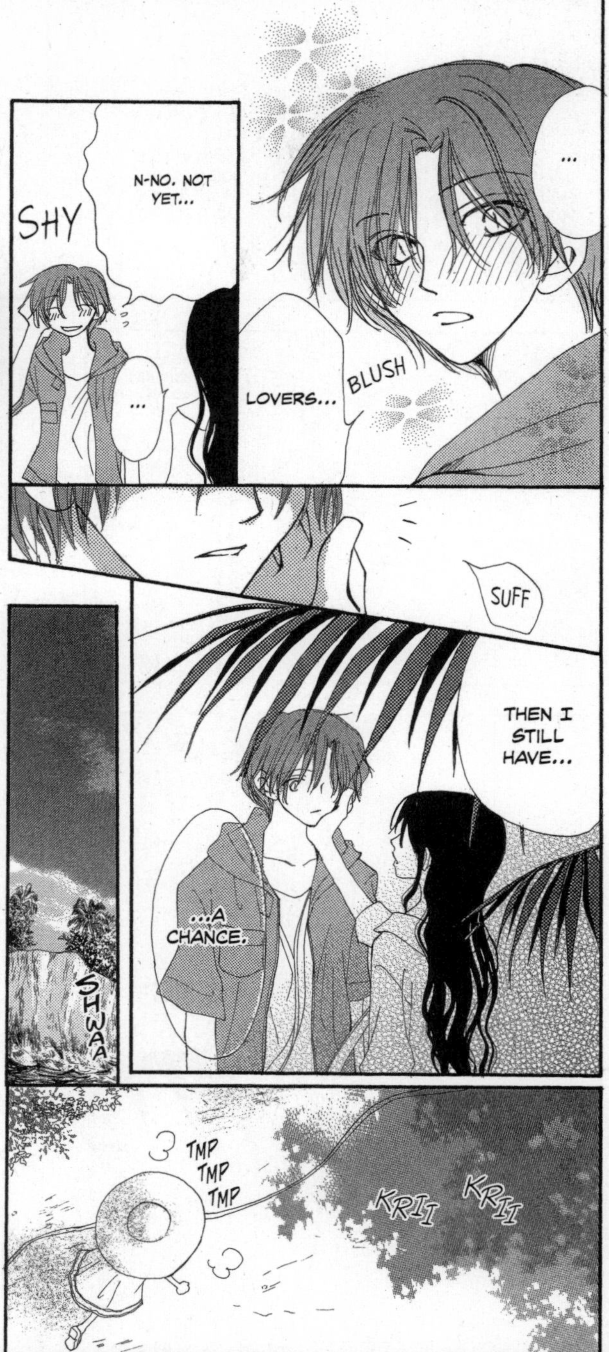
...
LOVERS...
BLUSH
N-NO. NOT YET...
SHY
...
SUFF
THEN I STILL HAVE...
...A CHANCE.
SHWAA
TMP
TMP
TMP
KRII
KRII

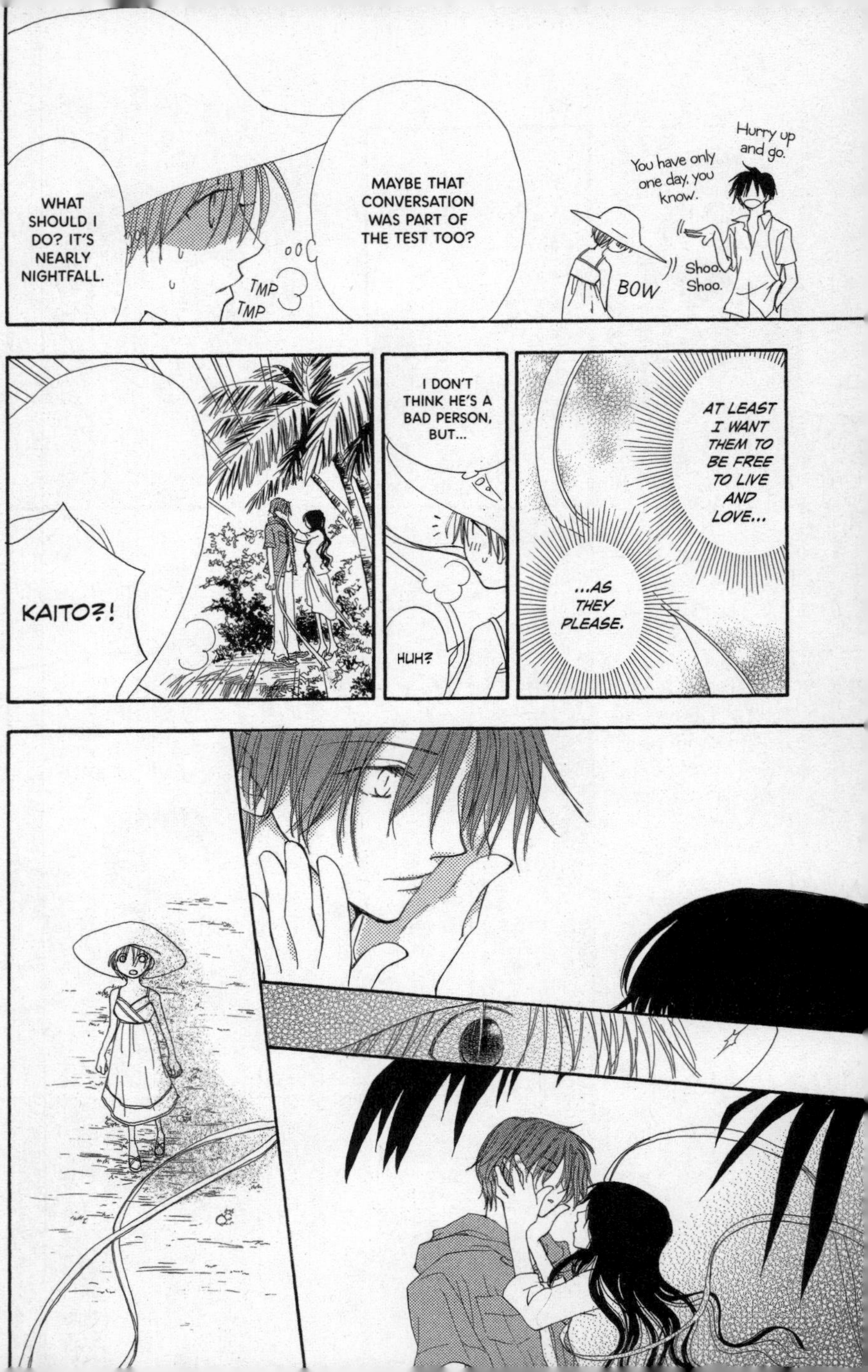

Hurry up and go.
You have only one day, you know.
BOW
Shoo. Shoo.
MAYBE THAT CONVERSATION WAS PART OF THE TEST TOO?
TMP TMP
WHAT SHOULD I DO? IT'S NEARLY NIGHTFALL.
AT LEAST I WANT THEM TO BE FREE TO LIVE AND LOVE...
...AS THEY PLEASE.
I DON'T THINK HE'S A BAD PERSON, BUT...
HUH?
KAITO?!

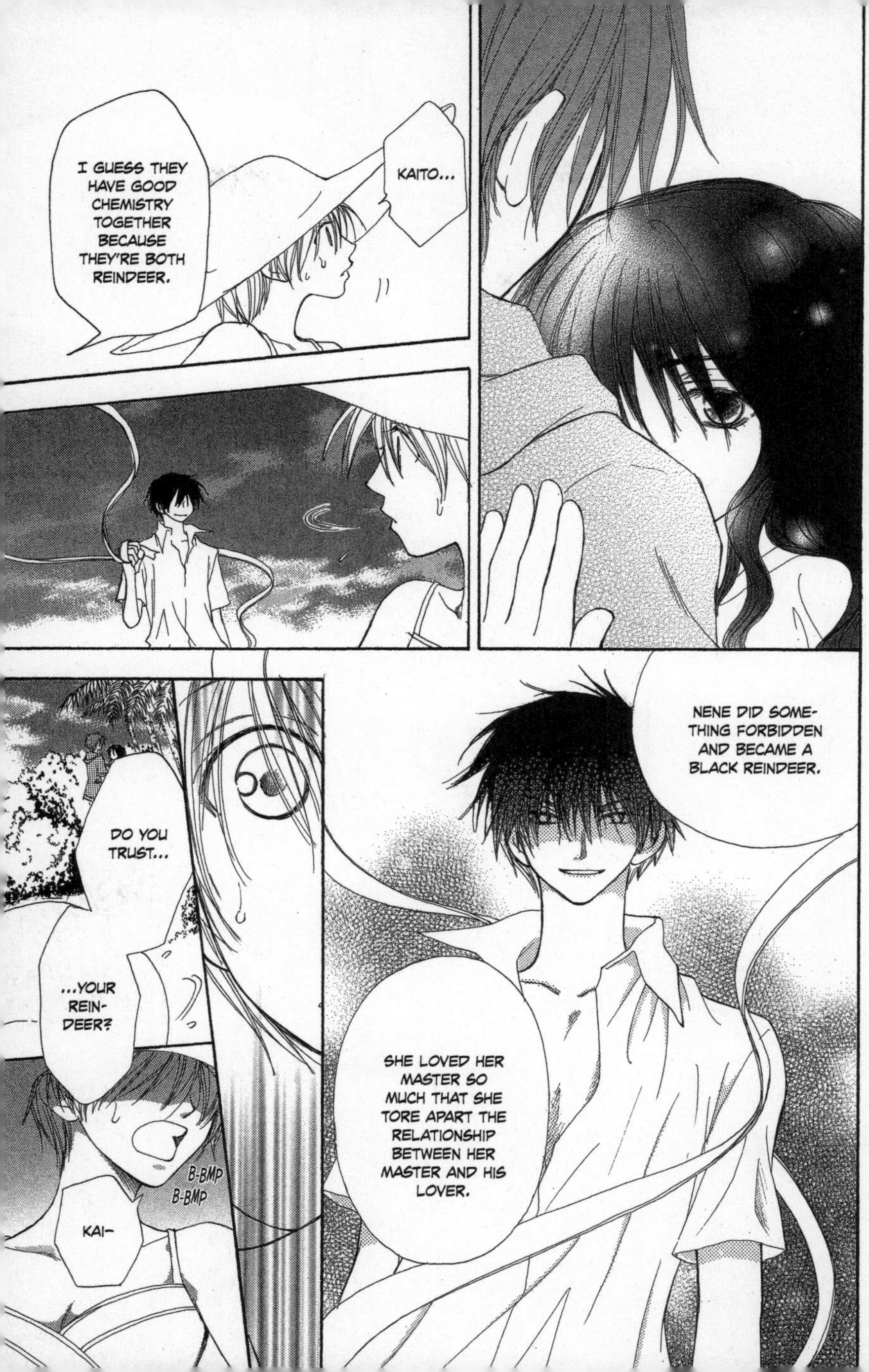

KAITO...
I GUESS THEY HAVE GOOD CHEMISTRY TOGETHER BECAUSE THEY'RE BOTH REINDEER.
NENE DID SOME-THING FORBIDDEN AND BECAME A BLACK REINDEER.
SHE LOVED HER MASTER SO MUCH THAT SHE TORE APART THE RELATIONSHIP BETWEEN HER MASTER AND HIS LOVER.
DO YOU TRUST...
...YOUR REIN-DEER?
B-BMP
B-BMP
KAI-

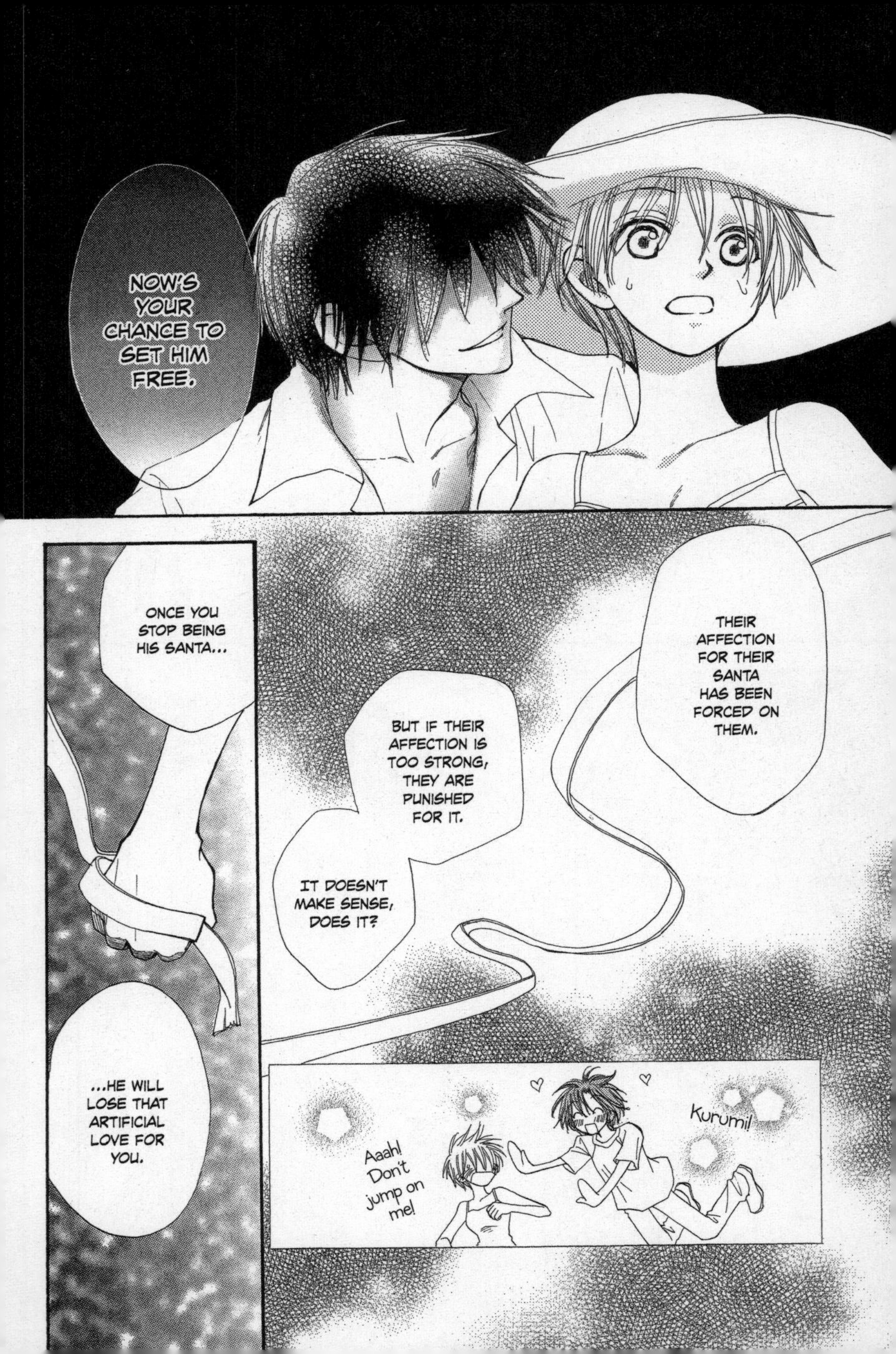
NOW'S YOUR CHANCE TO SET HIM FREE.
THEIR AFFECTION FOR THEIR SANTA HAS BEEN FORCED ON THEM.
BUT IF THEIR AFFECTION IS TOO STRONG, THEY ARE PUNISHED FOR IT.
IT DOESN'T MAKE SENSE, DOES IT?
Kurumi!
Aaah! Don't jump on me!
ONCE YOU STOP BEING HIS SANTA...
...HE WILL LOSE THAT ARTIFICIAL LOVE FOR YOU.

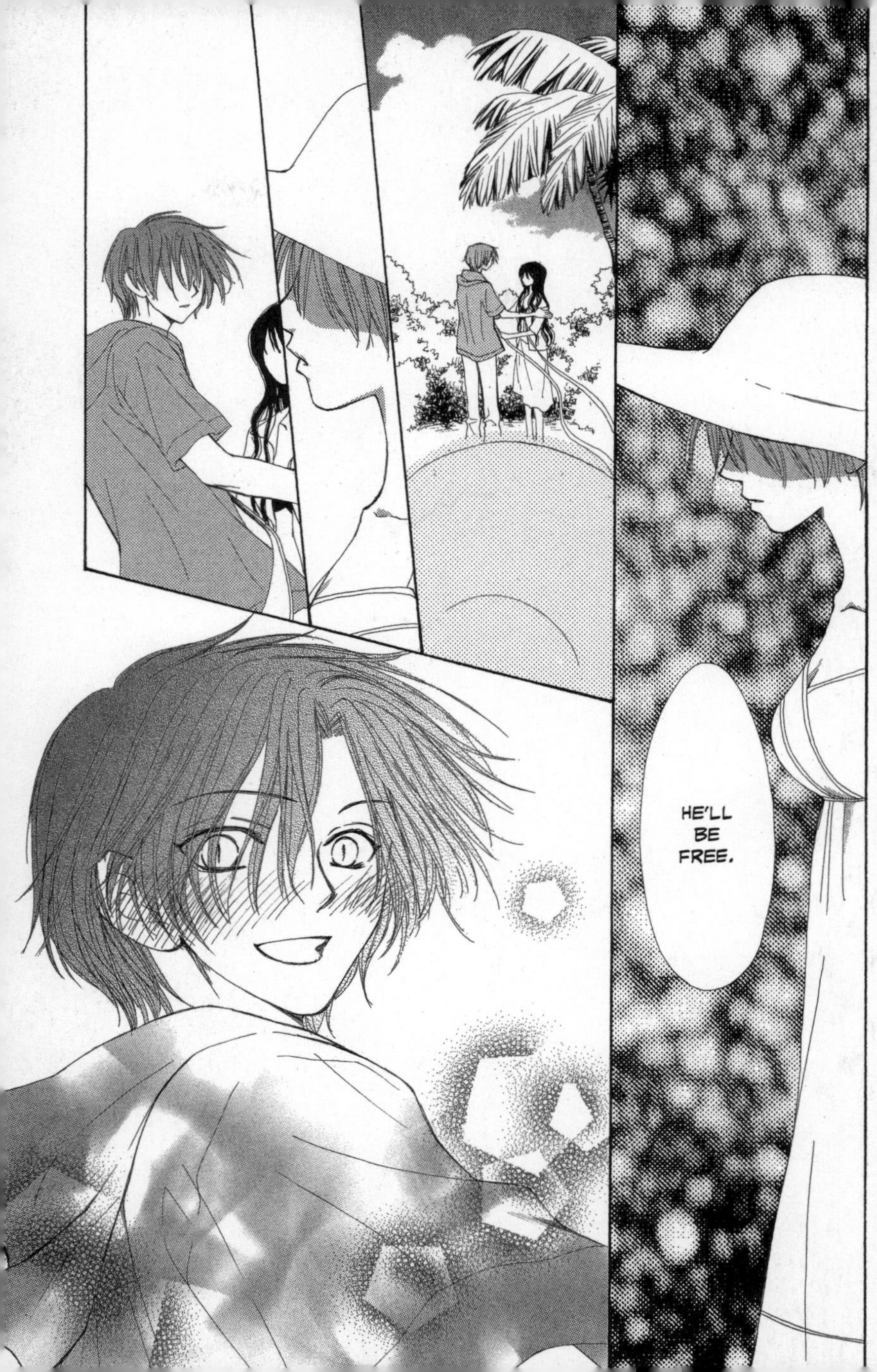
HE'LL BE FREE.

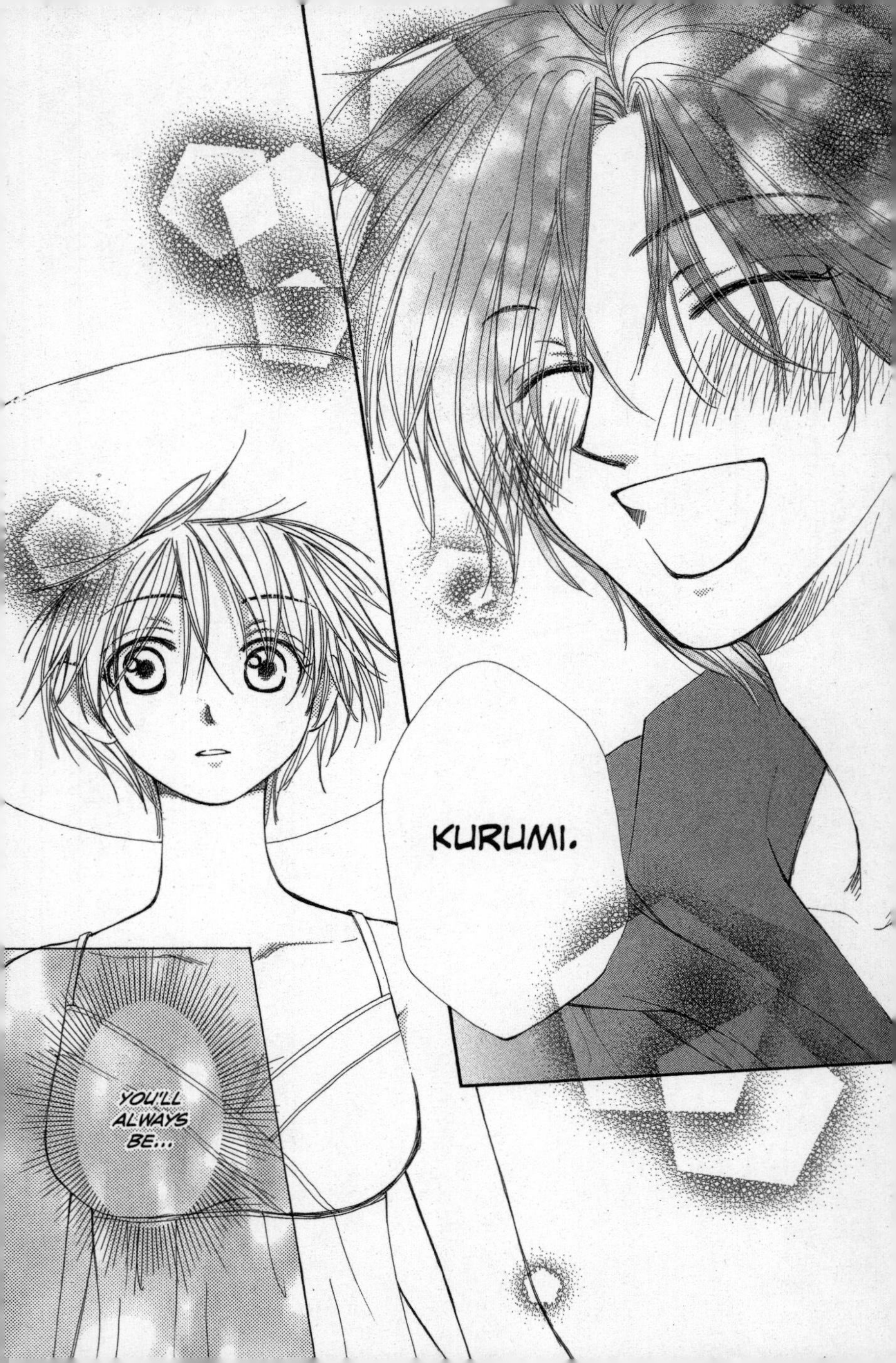
KURUMI.
YOU'LL ALWAYS BE...

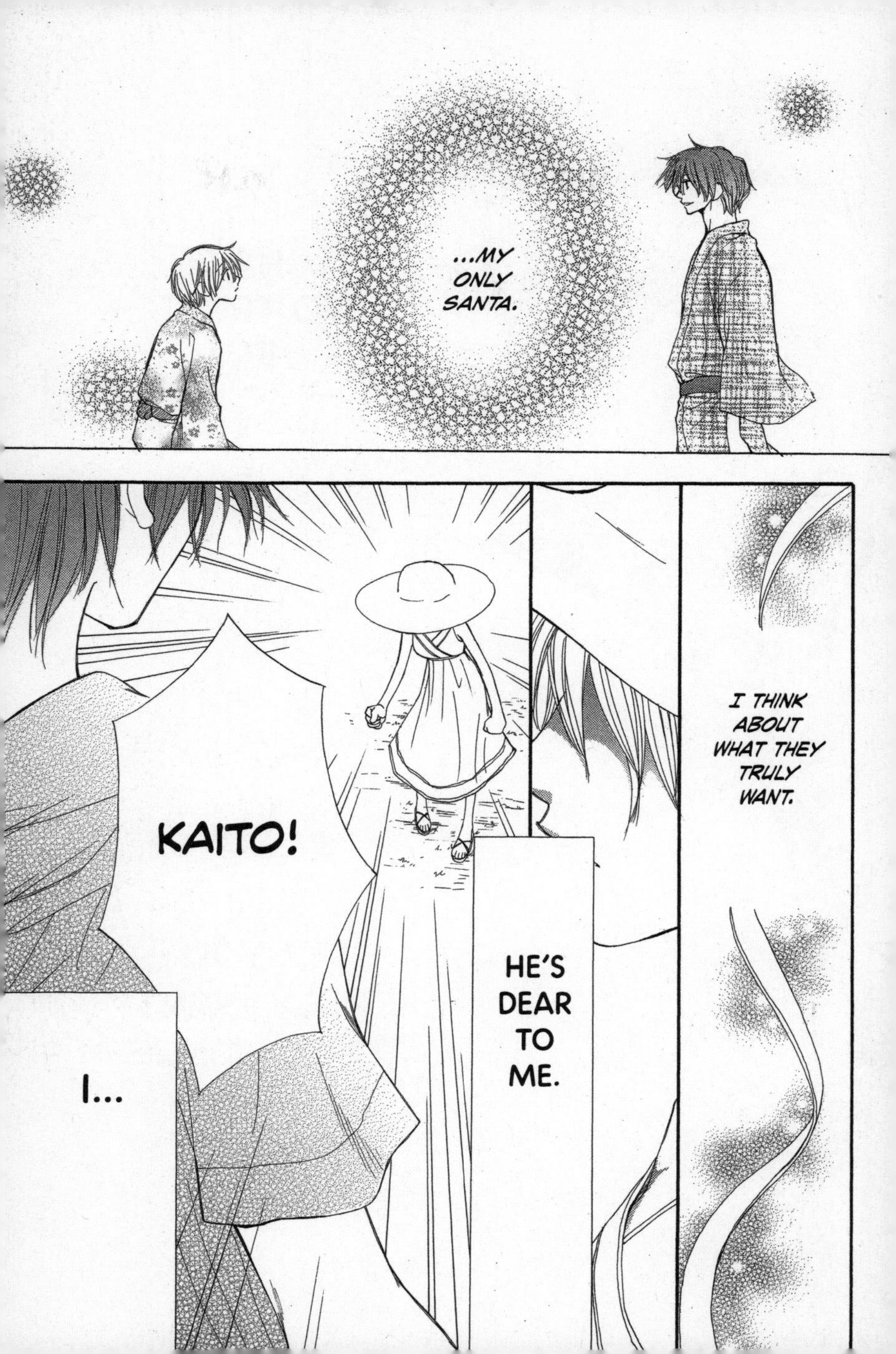
...MY ONLY SANTA.
I THINK ABOUT WHAT THEY TRULY WANT.
HE'S DEAR TO ME.
KAITO!
I...

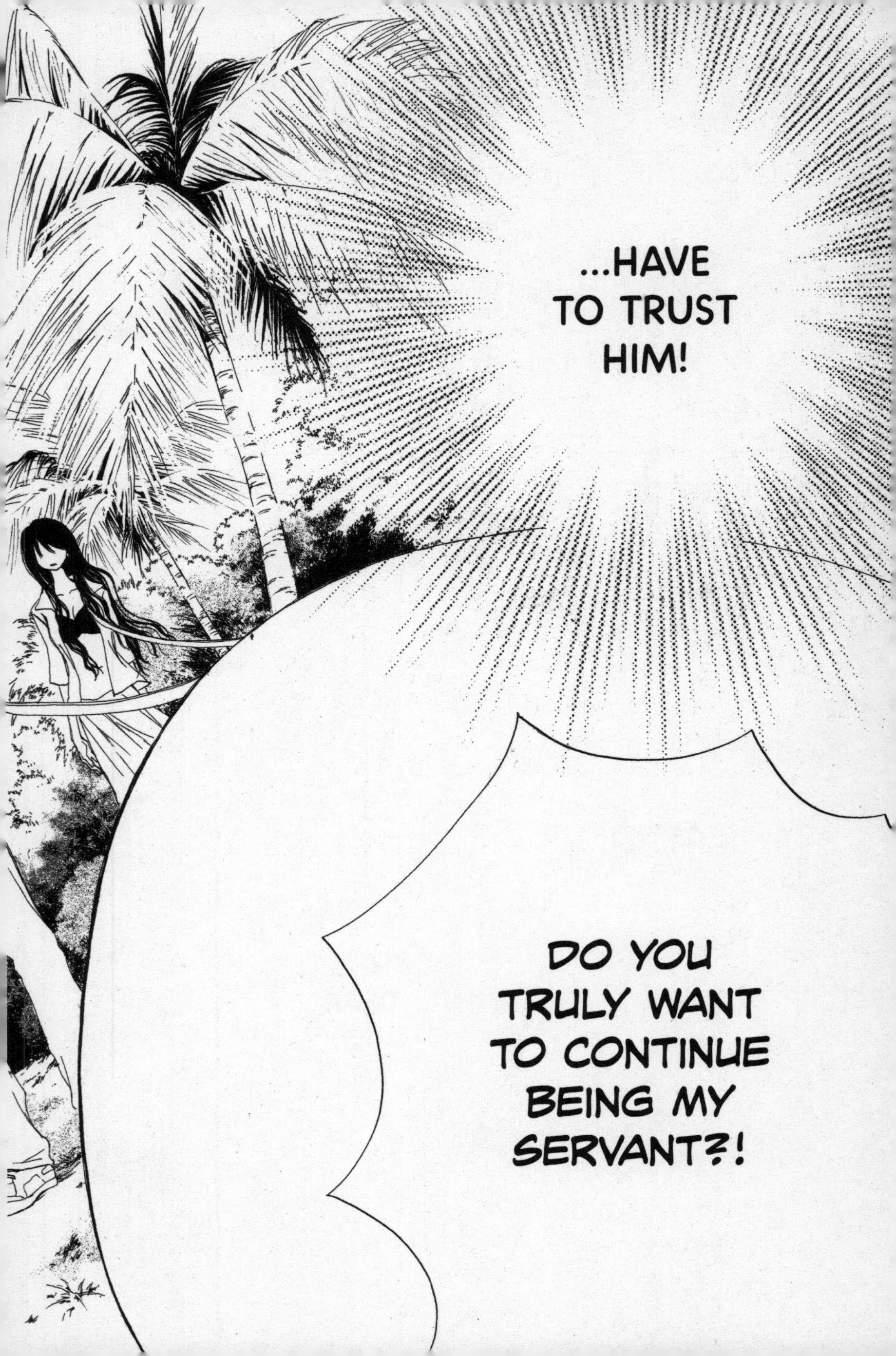
...HAVE TO TRUST HIM!
DO YOU TRULY WANT TO CONTINUE BEING MY SERVANT?!

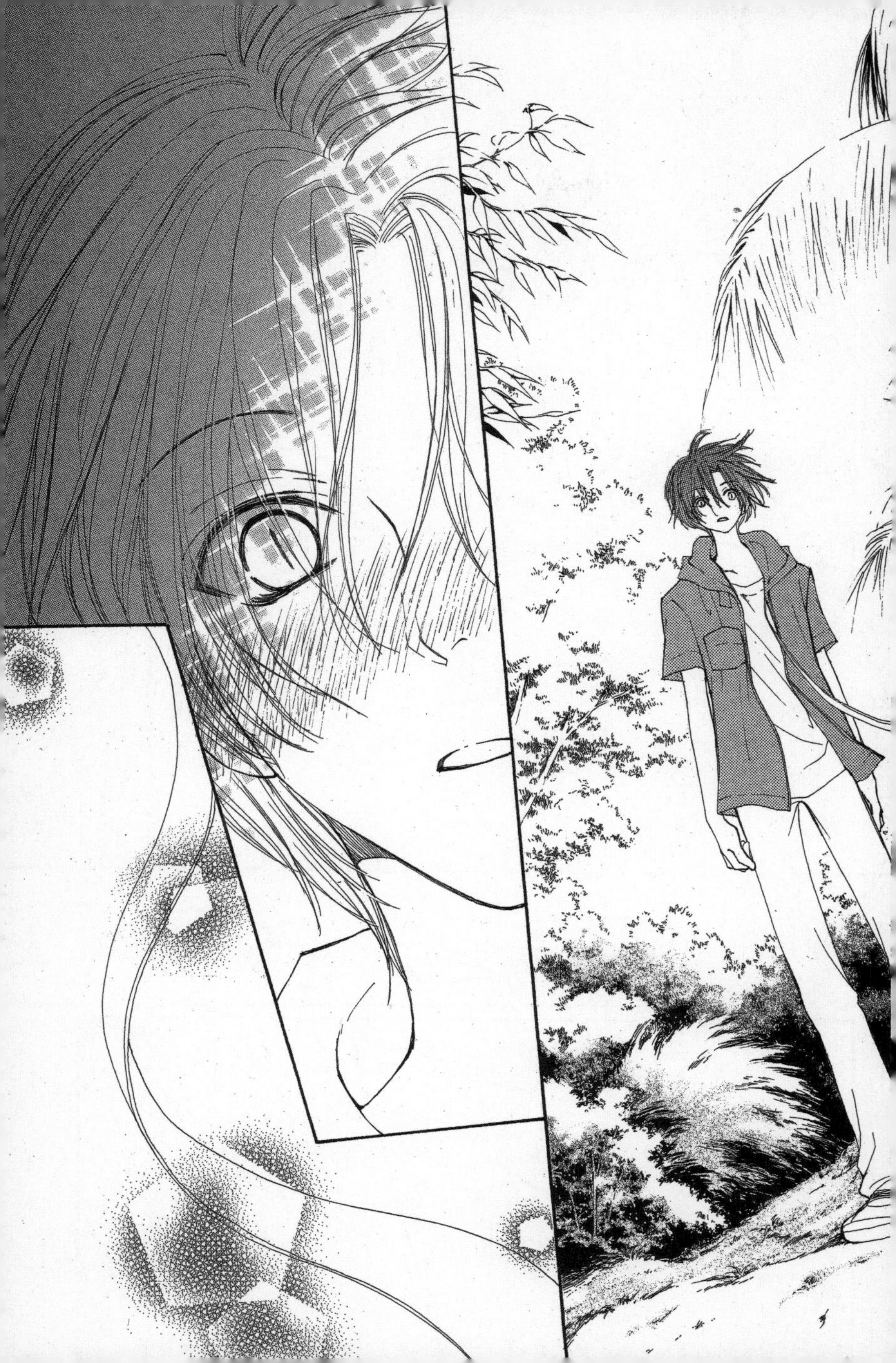

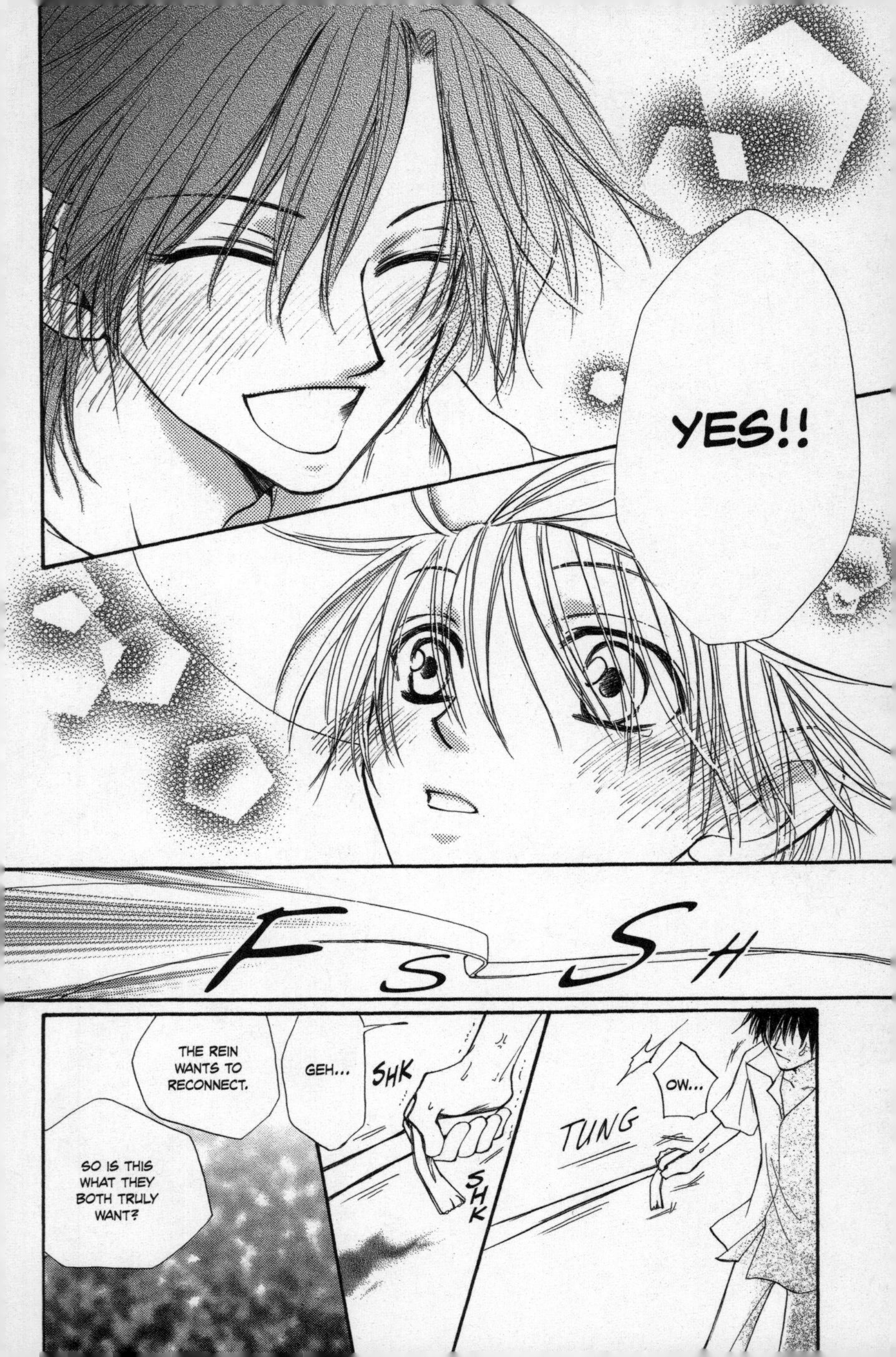
YES!!
FSSH
OW...
TUNG
SHK
GEH...
THE REIN WANTS TO RECONNECT.
SHK
SO IS THIS WHAT THEY BOTH TRULY WANT?

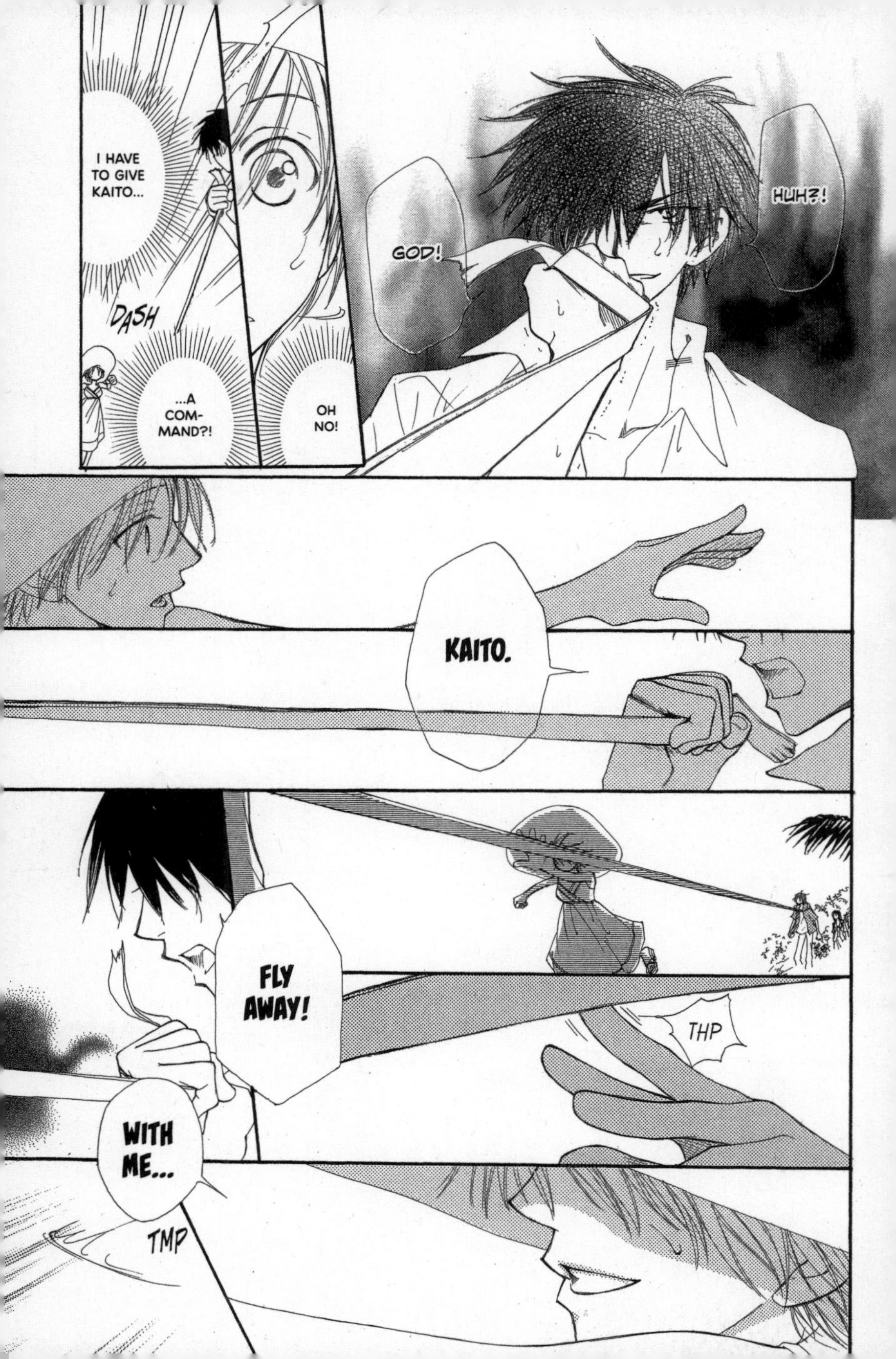
HUH?!
GOD!
OH NO!
I HAVE TO GIVE KAITO...
DASH
...A COMMAND?!
KAITO.
THP
FLY AWAY!
WITH ME...
TMP

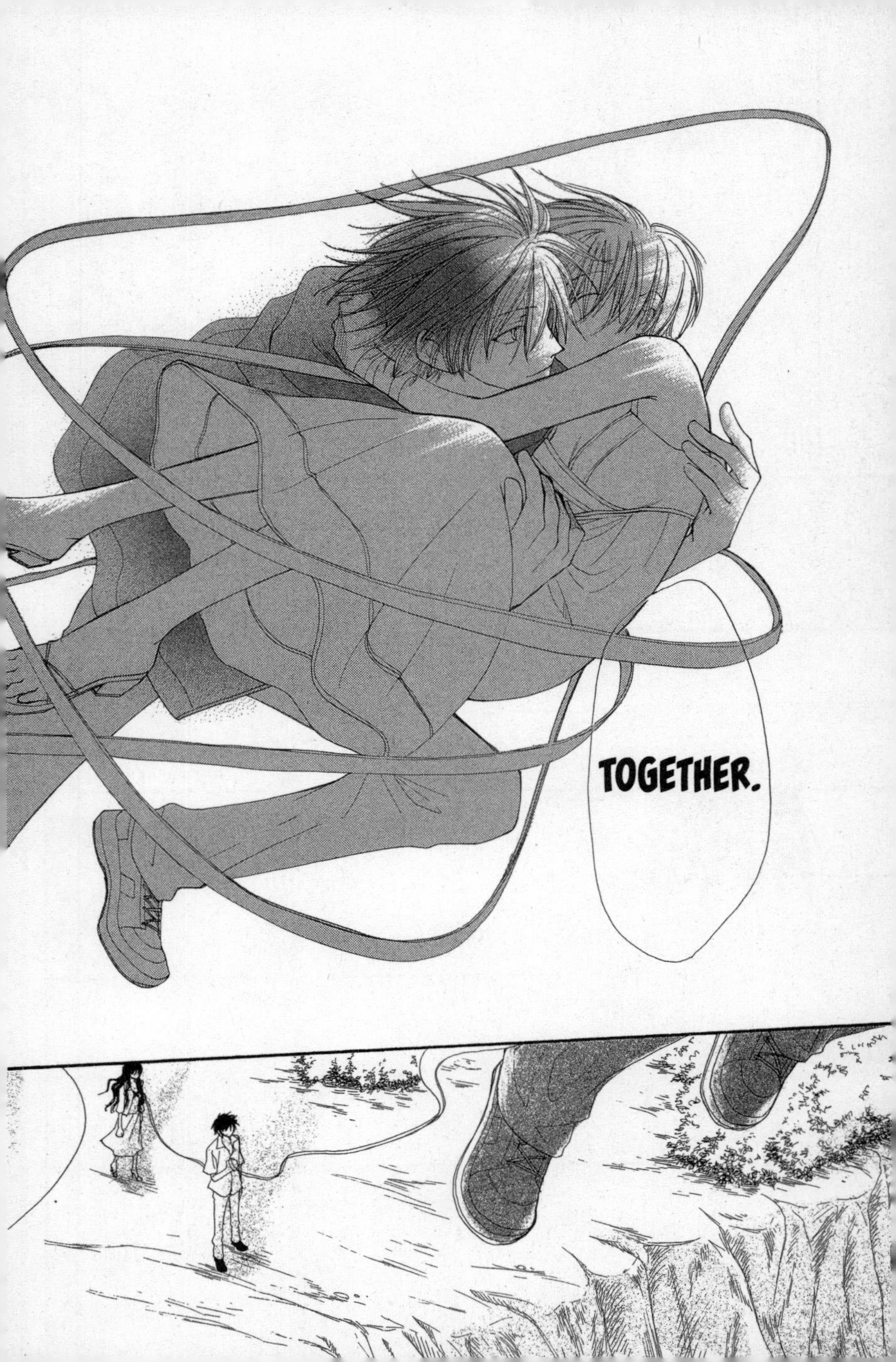
TOGETHER.

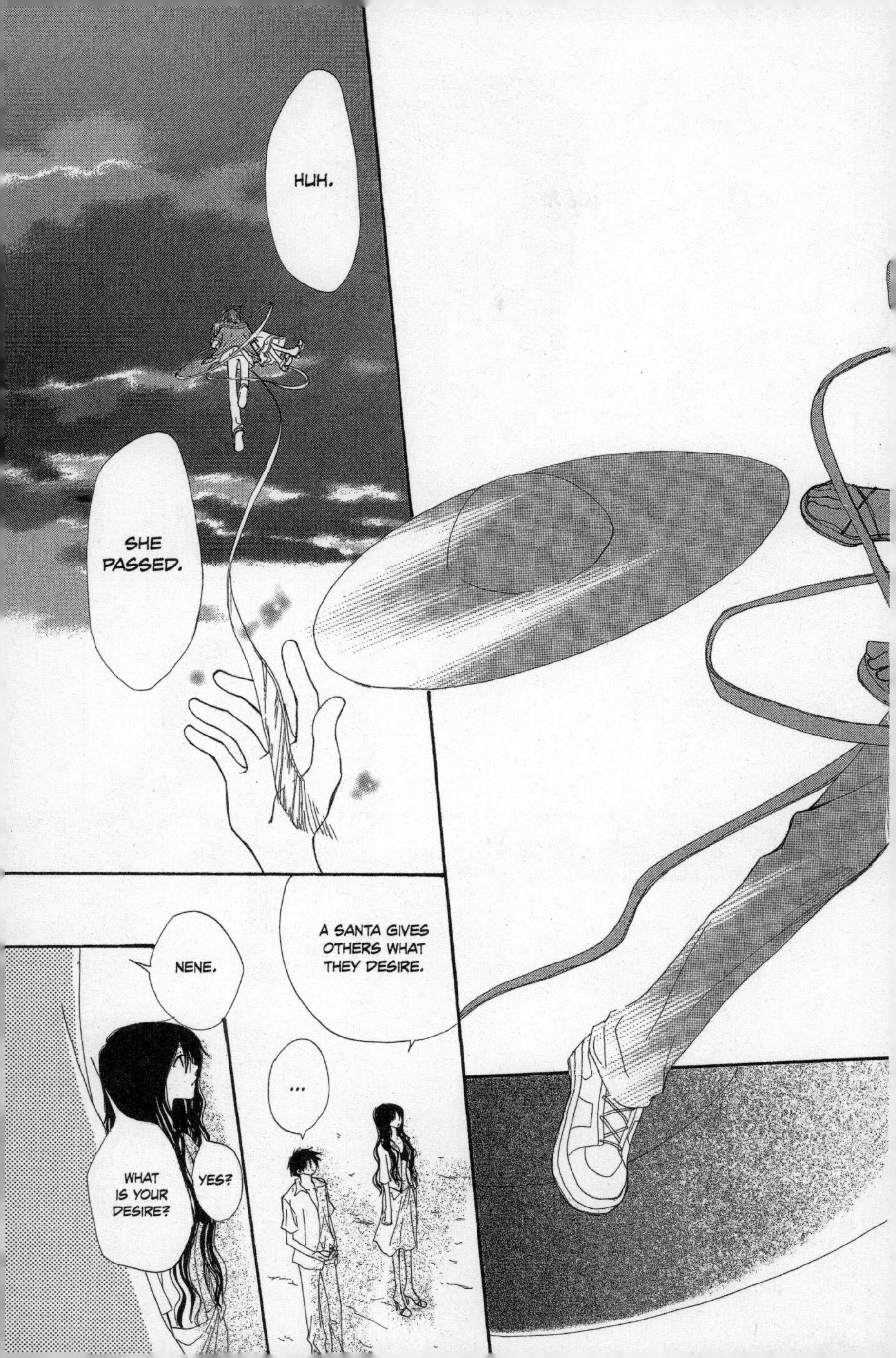
HUH.
SHE PASSED.
A SANTA GIVES OTHERS WHAT THEY DESIRE.
...
NENE.
YES?
WHAT IS YOUR DESIRE?

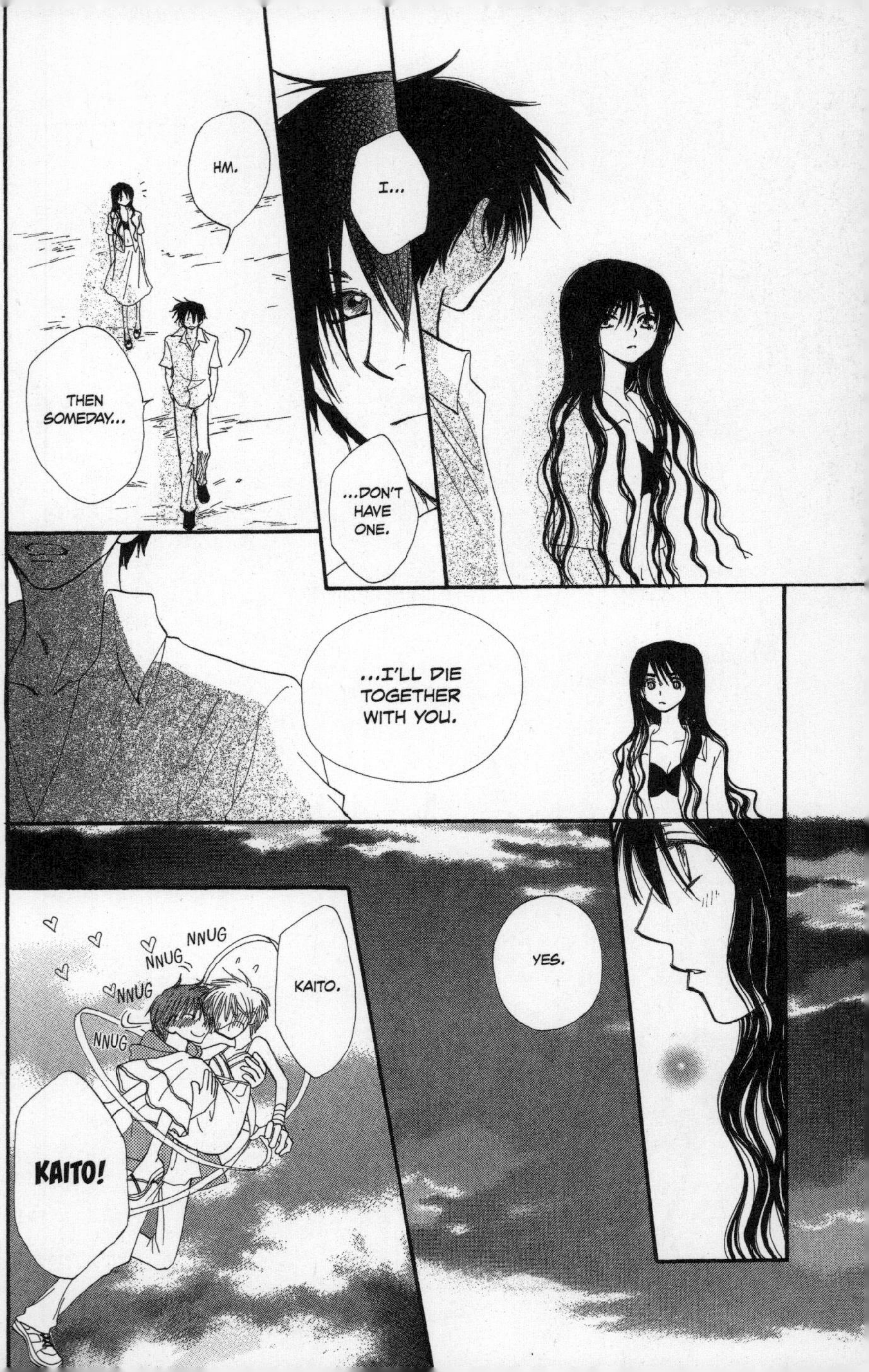
I...
...DON'T HAVE ONE.
HM.
THEN SOMEDAY...
...I'LL DIE TOGETHER WITH YOU.
YES.
KAITO.
NNUG NNUG
NNUG
NNUG
KAITO!

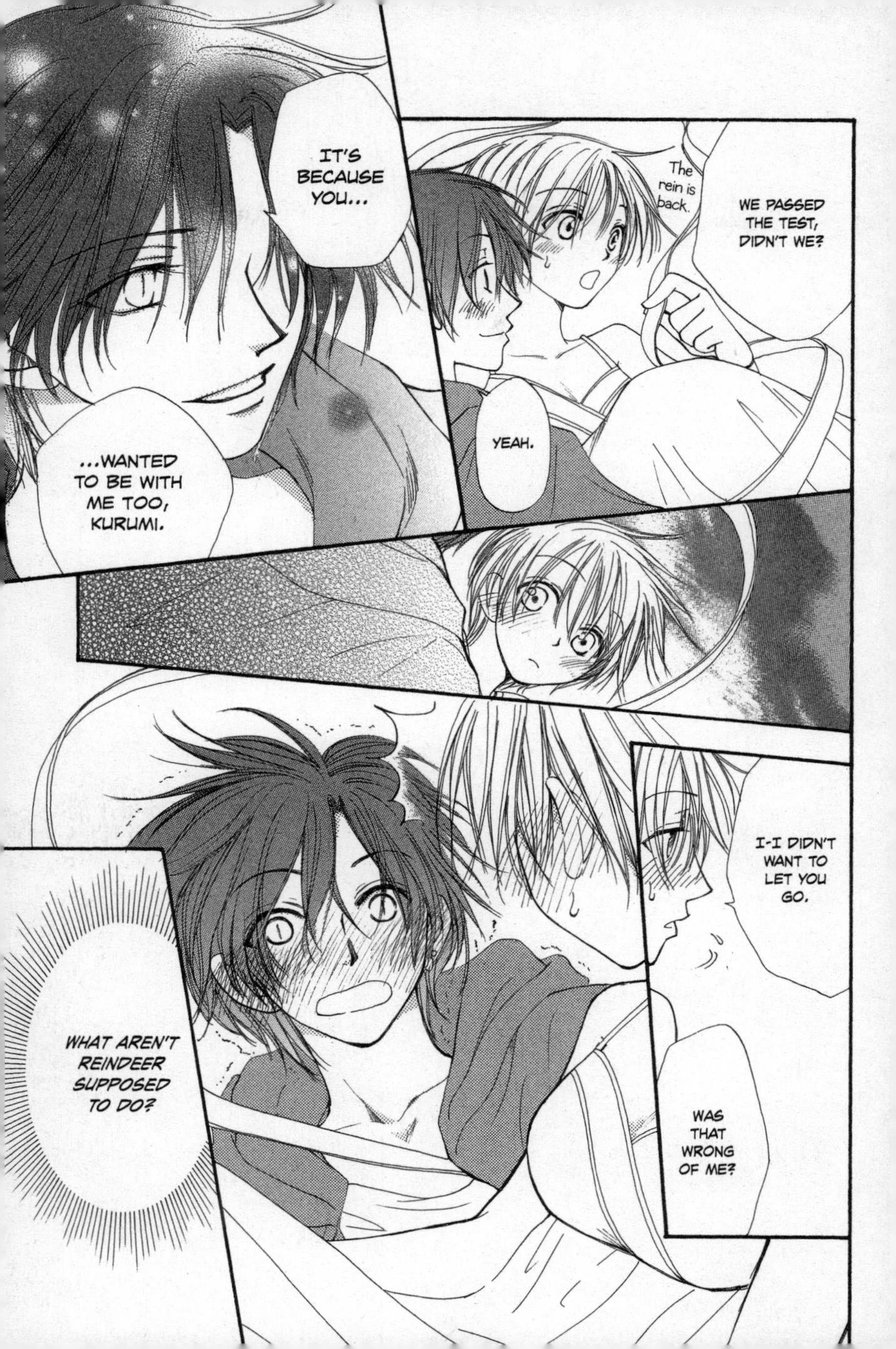

WE PASSED THE TEST, DIDN'T WE?
The rein is back.
YEAH.
IT'S BECAUSE YOU...
...WANTED TO BE WITH ME TOO, KURUMI.
I-I DIDN'T WANT TO LET YOU GO.
WAS THAT WRONG OF ME?
WHAT AREN'T REINDEER SUPPOSED TO DO?

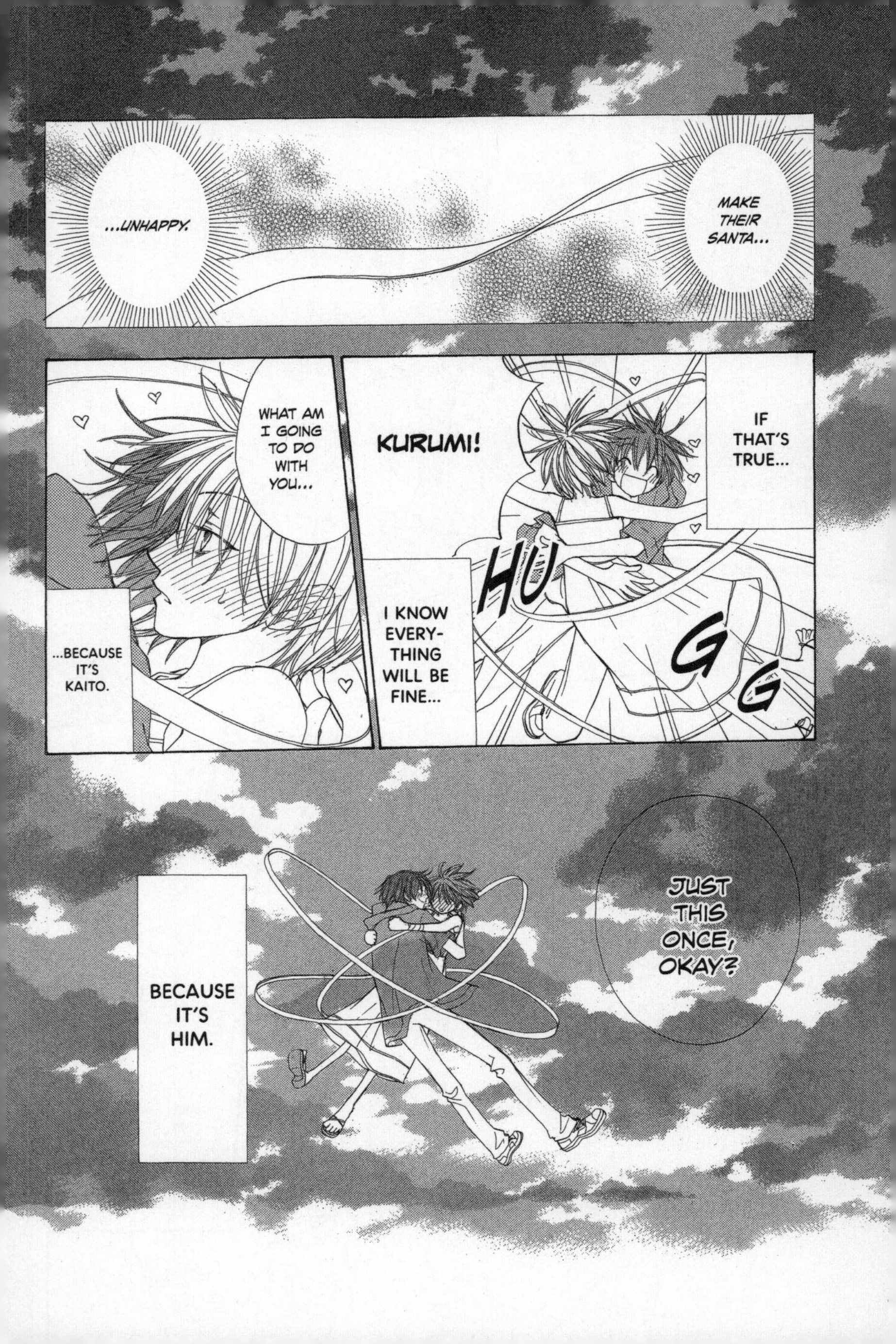
MAKE THEIR SANTA...
...UNHAPPY.
IF THAT'S TRUE...
KURUMI!
HUGG
I KNOW EVERY-THING WILL BE FINE...
WHAT AM I GOING TO DO WITH YOU...
...BECAUSE IT'S KAITO.
JUST THIS ONCE, OKAY?
BECAUSE IT'S HIM.

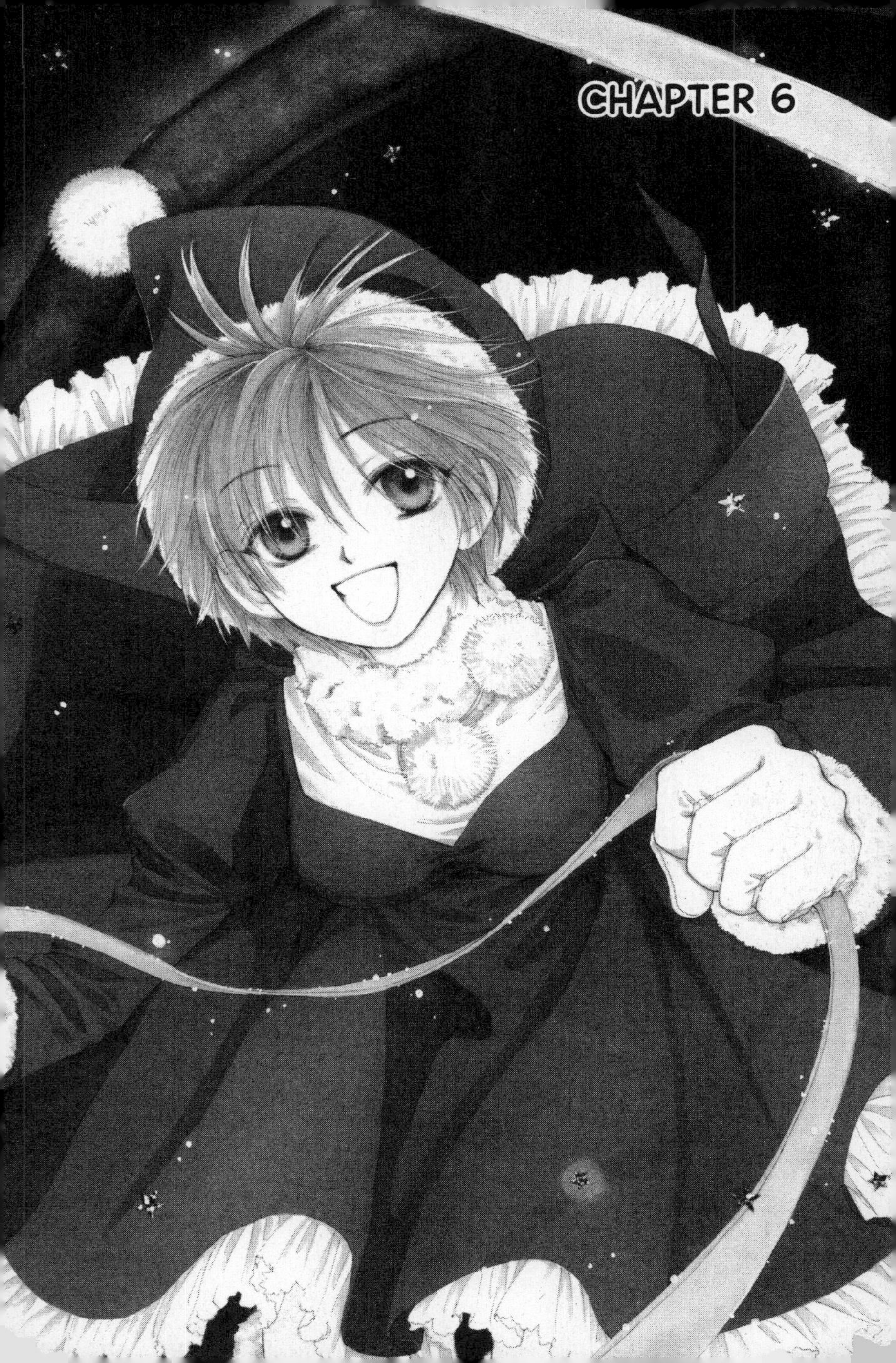
CHAPTER 6

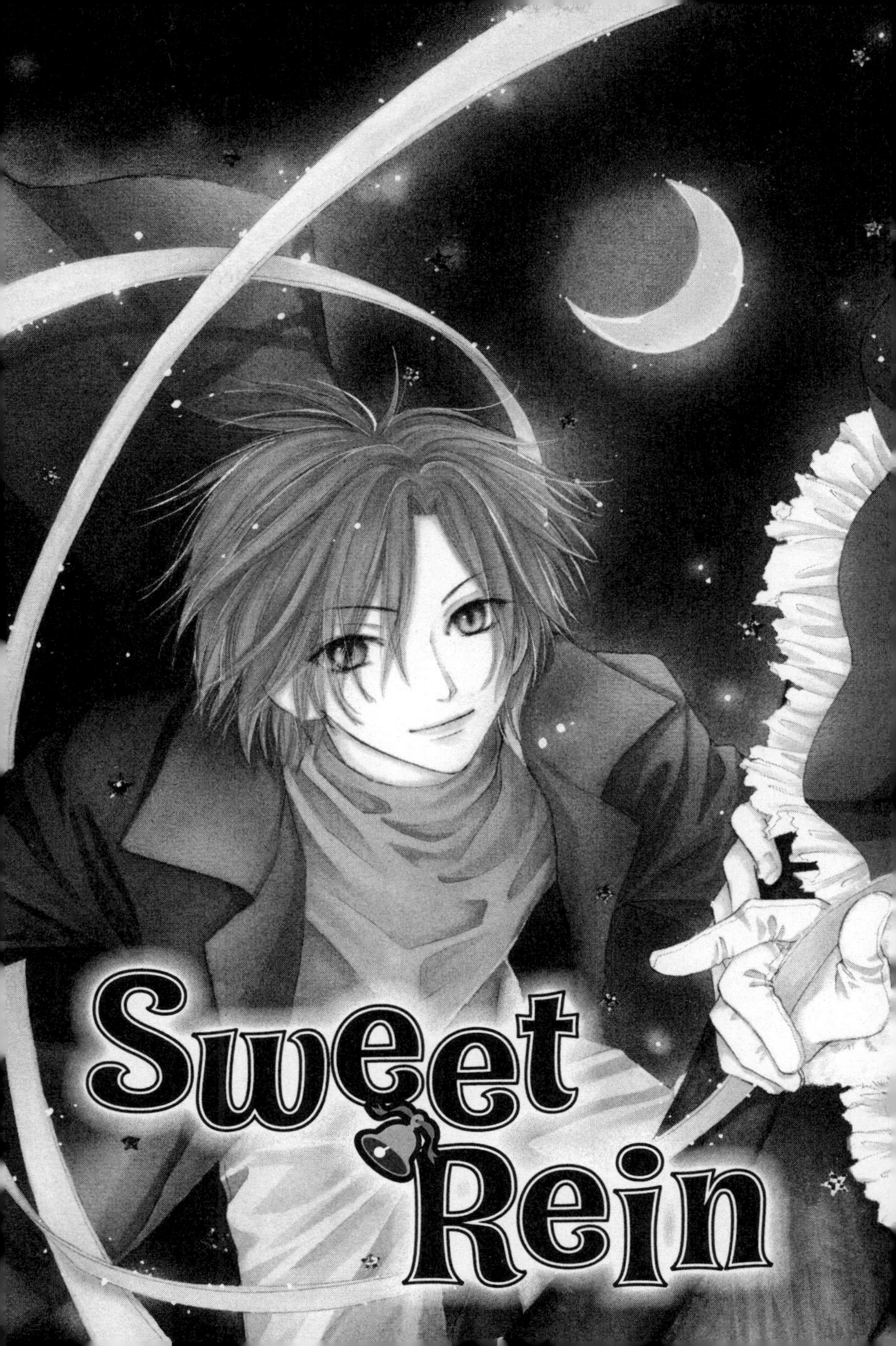
Sweet Rein

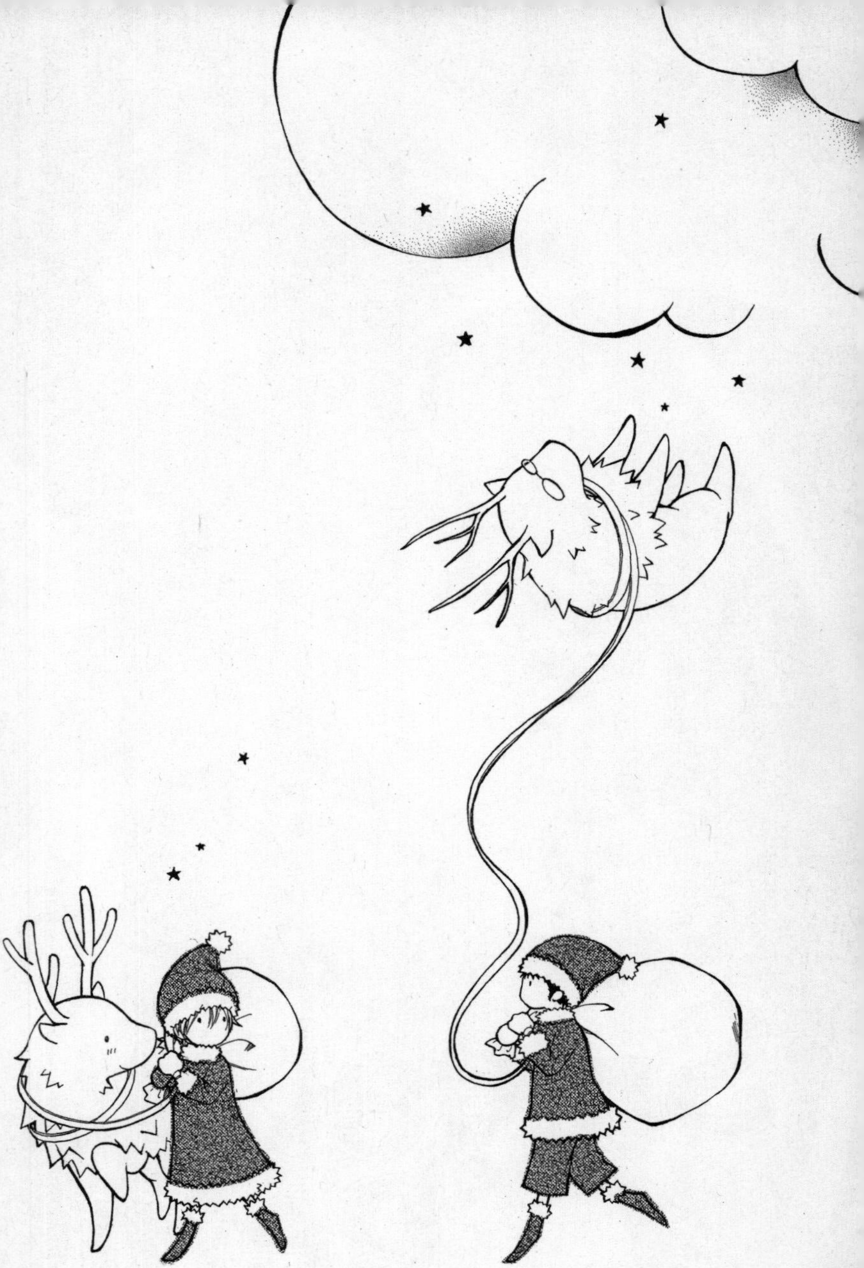

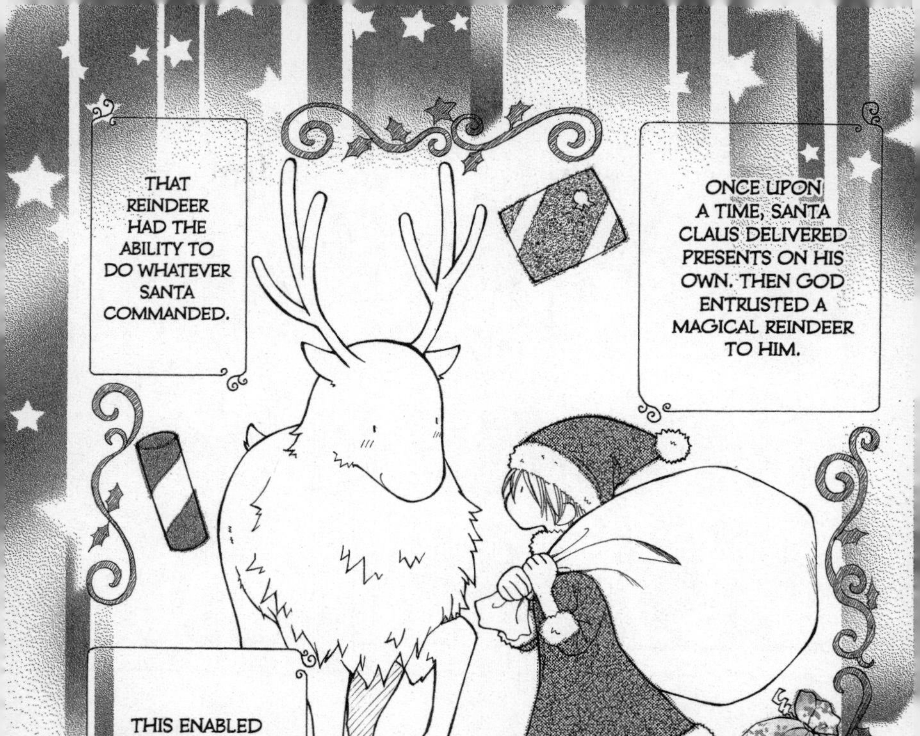
ONCE UPON A TIME, SANTA CLAUS DELIVERED PRESENTS ON HIS OWN. THEN GOD ENTRUSTED A MAGICAL REINDEER TO HIM.
THAT REINDEER HAD THE ABILITY TO DO WHATEVER SANTA COMMANDED.
THIS ENABLED SANTA CLAUS TO DELIVER PRESENTS TO GOOD CHILDREN EVERYWHERE.
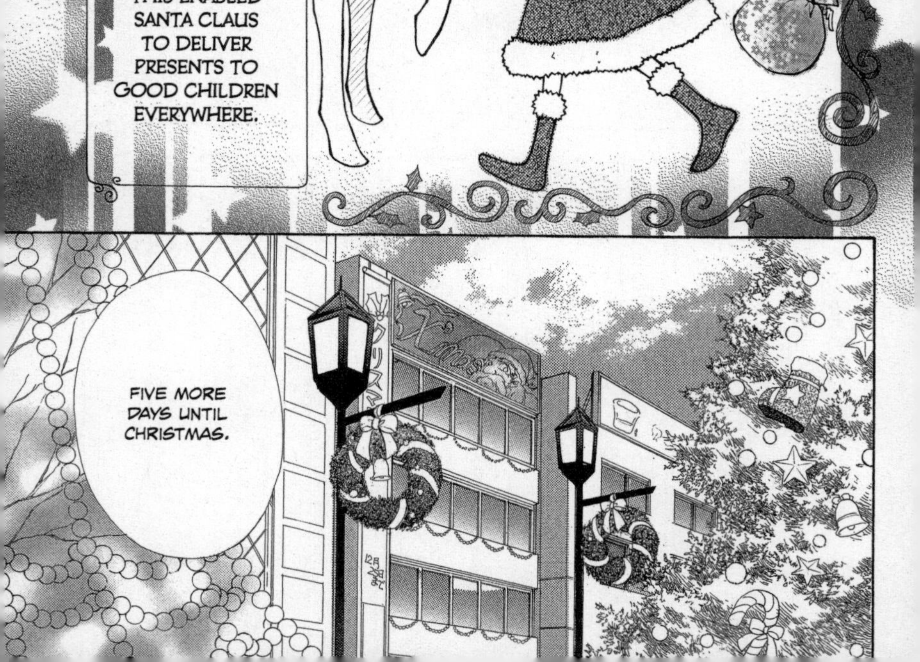
FIVE MORE DAYS UNTIL CHRISTMAS.

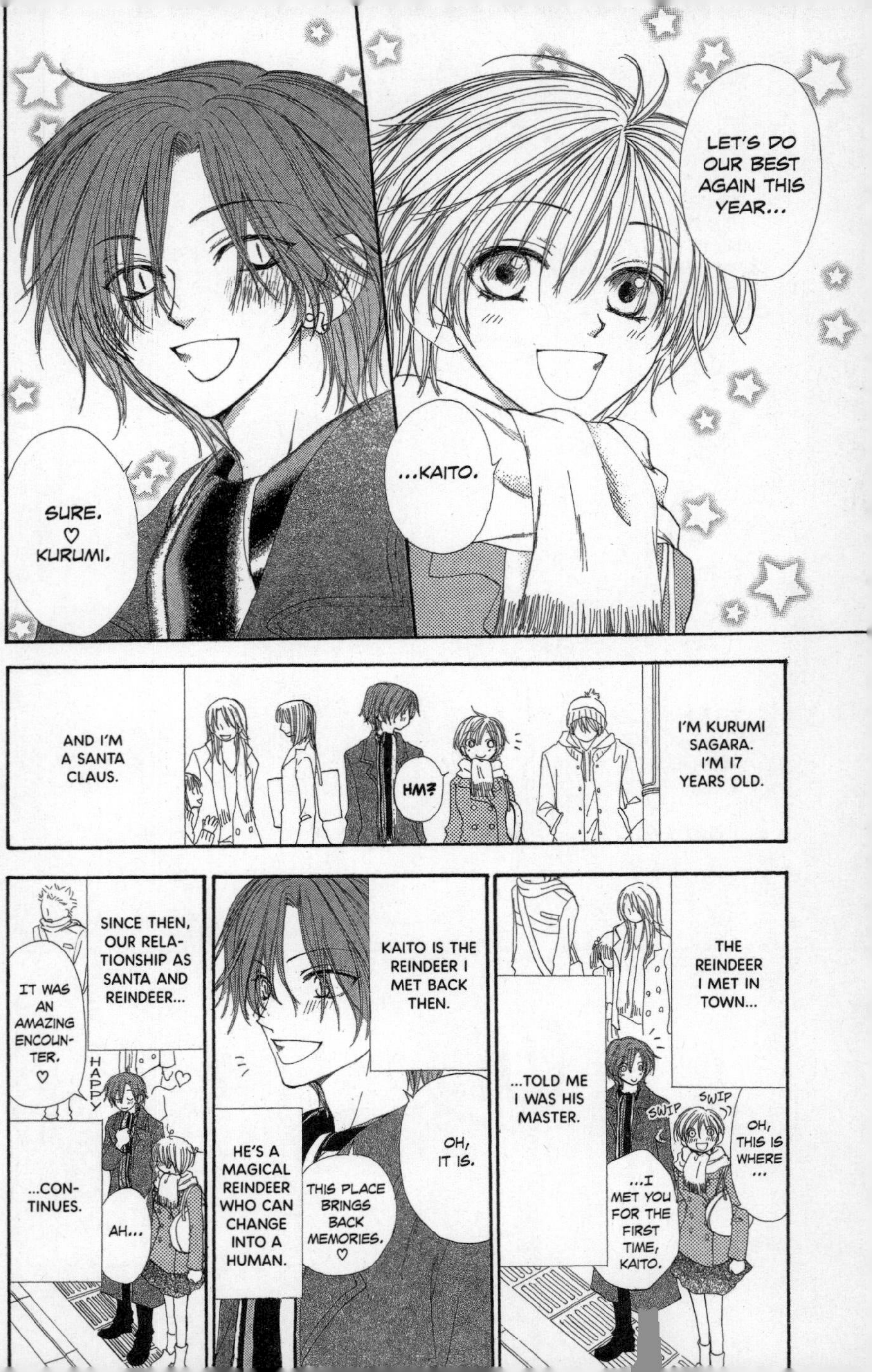
LET'S DO OUR BEST AGAIN THIS YEAR...
...KAITO.
SURE. ♡ KURUMI.
I'M KURUMI SAGARA. I'M 17 YEARS OLD.
HM?
AND I'M A SANTA CLAUS.
THE REINDEER I MET IN TOWN...
OH, THIS IS WHERE...
SWIP
SWIP
...I MET YOU FOR THE FIRST TIME, KAITO.
...TOLD ME I WAS HIS MASTER.
KAITO IS THE REINDEER I MET BACK THEN.
OH, IT IS.
THIS PLACE BRINGS BACK MEMORIES. ♡
HE'S A MAGICAL REINDEER WHO CAN CHANGE INTO A HUMAN.
SINCE THEN, OUR RELATIONSHIP AS SANTA AND REINDEER...
IT WAS AN AMAZING ENCOUNTER. ♡
HAPPY
AH...
...CONTINUES.

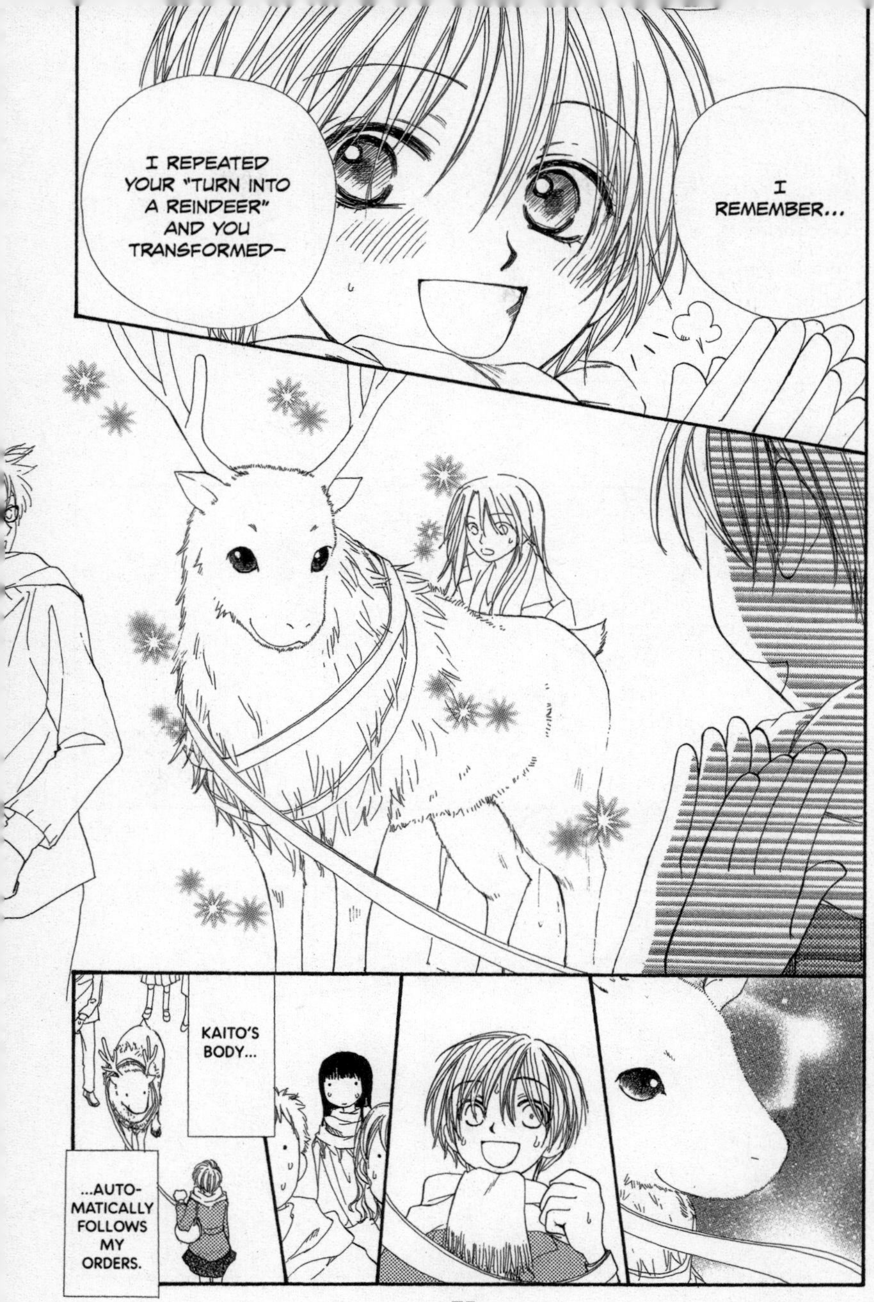
I REMEMBER...
I REPEATED YOUR "TURN INTO A REINDEER" AND YOU TRANSFORMED—
KAITO'S BODY...
...AUTO-MATICALLY FOLLOWS MY ORDERS.

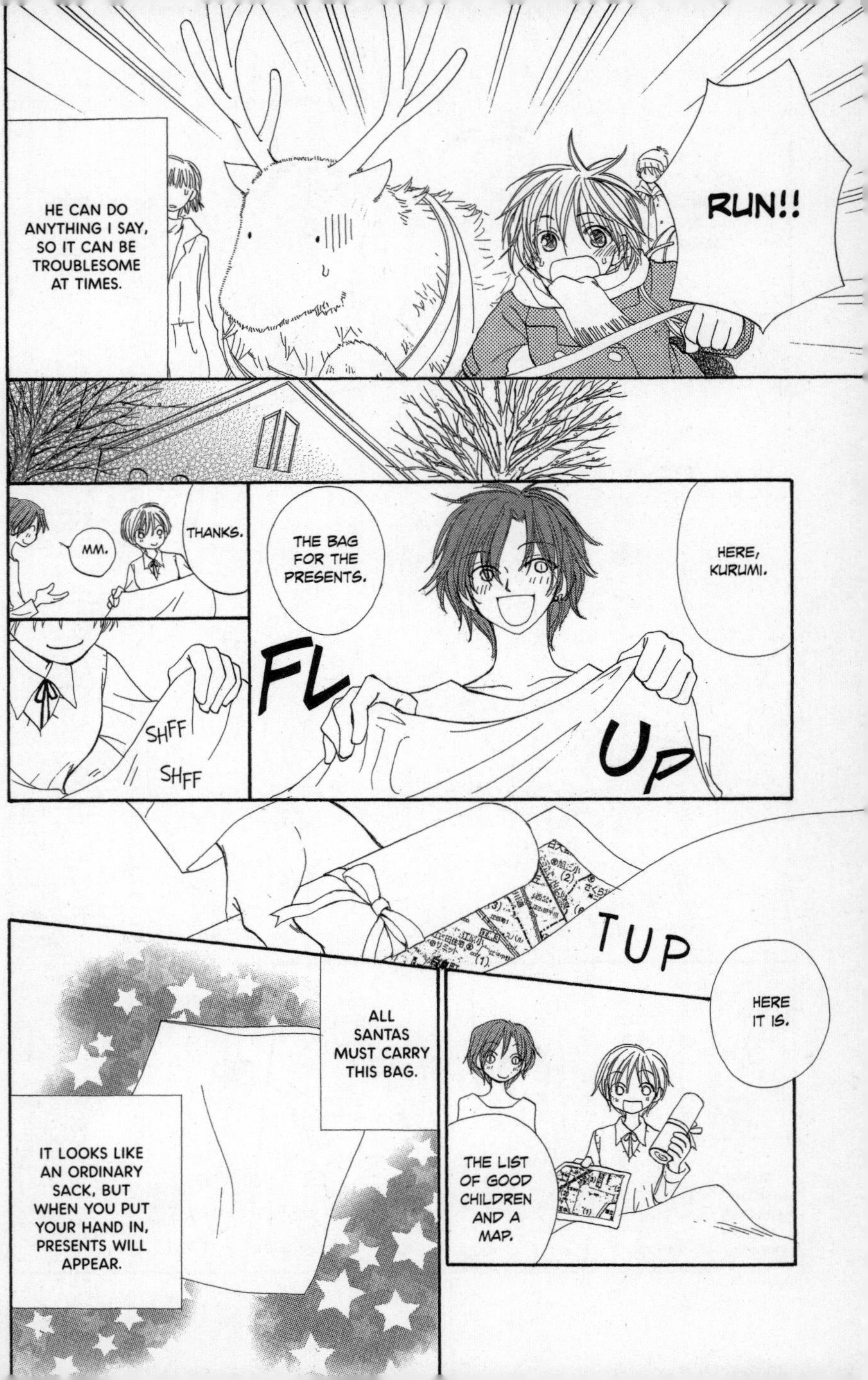
RUN!!
HE CAN DO ANYTHING I SAY, SO IT CAN BE TROUBLESOME AT TIMES.
HERE, KURUMI.
THE BAG FOR THE PRESENTS.
FL UP
THANKS.
MM.
SHFF
SHFF
TUP
HERE IT IS.
THE LIST OF GOOD CHILDREN AND A MAP.
ALL SANTAS MUST CARRY THIS BAG.
IT LOOKS LIKE AN ORDINARY SACK, BUT WHEN YOU PUT YOUR HAND IN, PRESENTS WILL APPEAR.

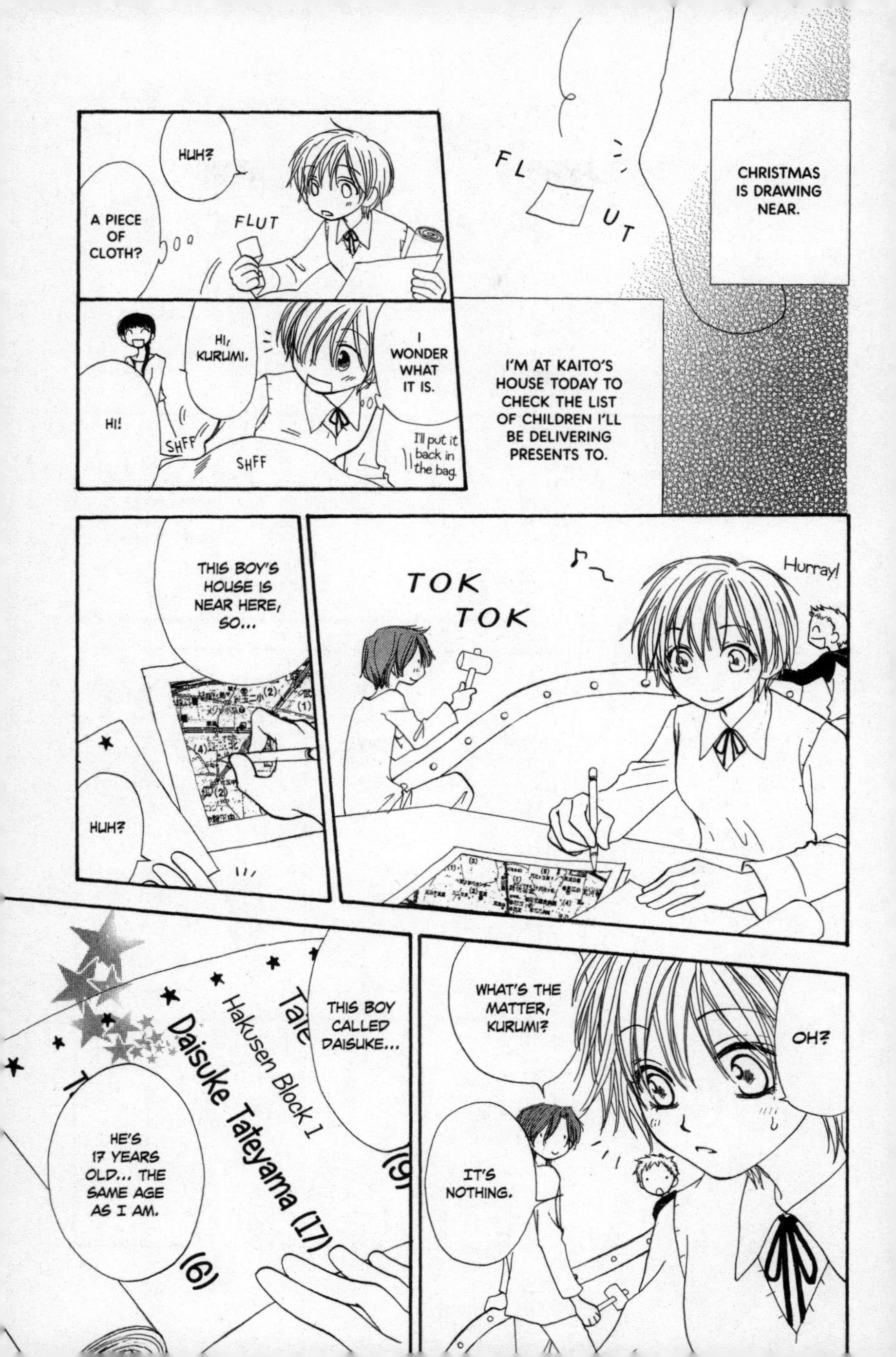
CHRISTMAS IS DRAWING NEAR.
FL UT
I'M AT KAITO'S HOUSE TODAY TO CHECK THE LIST OF CHILDREN I'LL BE DELIVERING PRESENTS TO.
HUH?
A PIECE OF CLOTH?
FLUT
I WONDER WHAT IT IS.
I'll put it back in the bag.
HI, KURUMI.
HI!
SHFF
SHFF
Hurray!
TOK TOK
THIS BOY'S HOUSE IS NEAR HERE, SO...
HUH?
OH?
WHAT'S THE MATTER, KURUMI?
IT'S NOTHING.
THIS BOY CALLED DAISUKE...
Tale
Hakusen Block 1
Daisuke Tateyama (17)
(9)
(6)
HE'S 17 YEARS OLD... THE SAME AGE AS I AM.

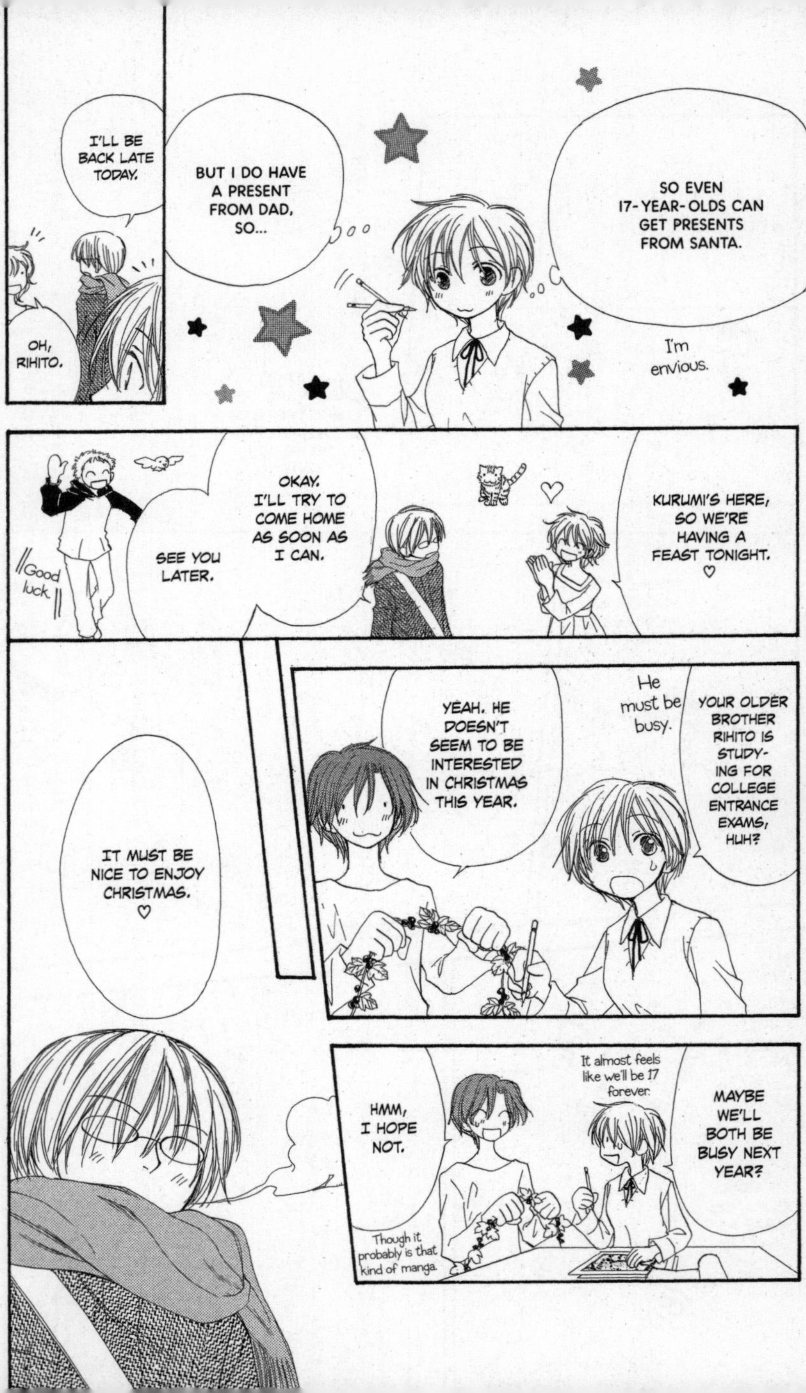
SO EVEN 17-YEAR-OLDS CAN GET PRESENTS FROM SANTA.
I'm envious.
BUT I DO HAVE A PRESENT FROM DAD, SO...
I'LL BE BACK LATE TODAY.
OH, RIHITO.
KURUMI'S HERE, SO WE'RE HAVING A FEAST TONIGHT. ♡
OKAY. I'LL TRY TO COME HOME AS SOON AS I CAN.
SEE YOU LATER.
Good luck.
YOUR OLDER BROTHER RIHITO IS STUDYING FOR COLLEGE ENTRANCE EXAMS, HUH?
He must be busy.
YEAH. HE DOESN'T SEEM TO BE INTERESTED IN CHRISTMAS THIS YEAR.
MAYBE WE'LL BOTH BE BUSY NEXT YEAR?
It almost feels like we'll be 17 forever.
HMM, I HOPE NOT.
Though it probably is that kind of manga.
IT MUST BE NICE TO ENJOY CHRISTMAS. ♡

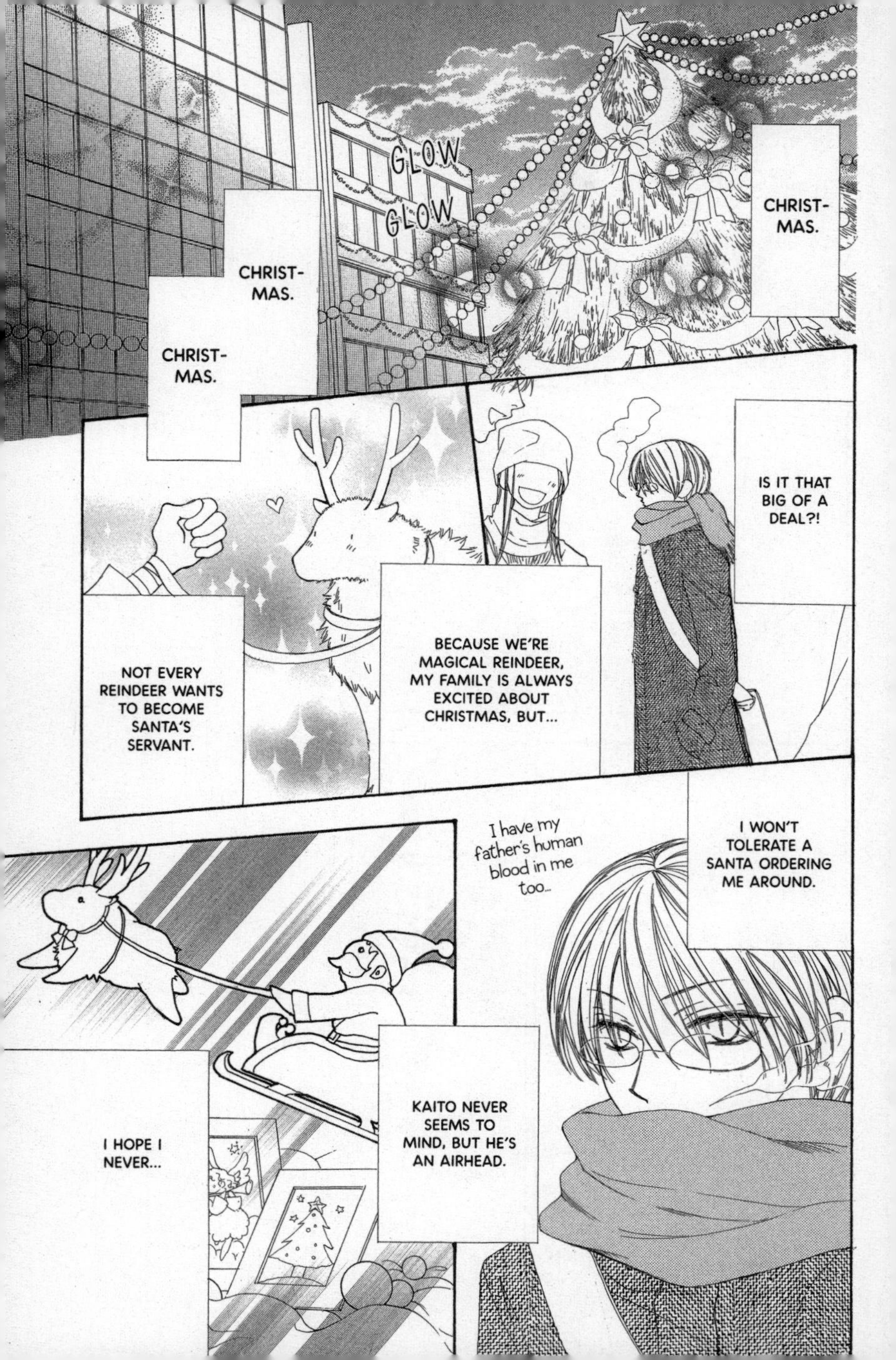

CHRIST-MAS.
GLOW GLOW
CHRIST-MAS.
CHRIST-MAS.
IS IT THAT BIG OF A DEAL?!
BECAUSE WE'RE MAGICAL REINDEER, MY FAMILY IS ALWAYS EXCITED ABOUT CHRISTMAS, BUT...
NOT EVERY REINDEER WANTS TO BECOME SANTA'S SERVANT.
I WON'T TOLERATE A SANTA ORDERING ME AROUND.
I have my father's human blood in me too...
KAITO NEVER SEEMS TO MIND, BUT HE'S AN AIRHEAD.
I HOPE I NEVER...

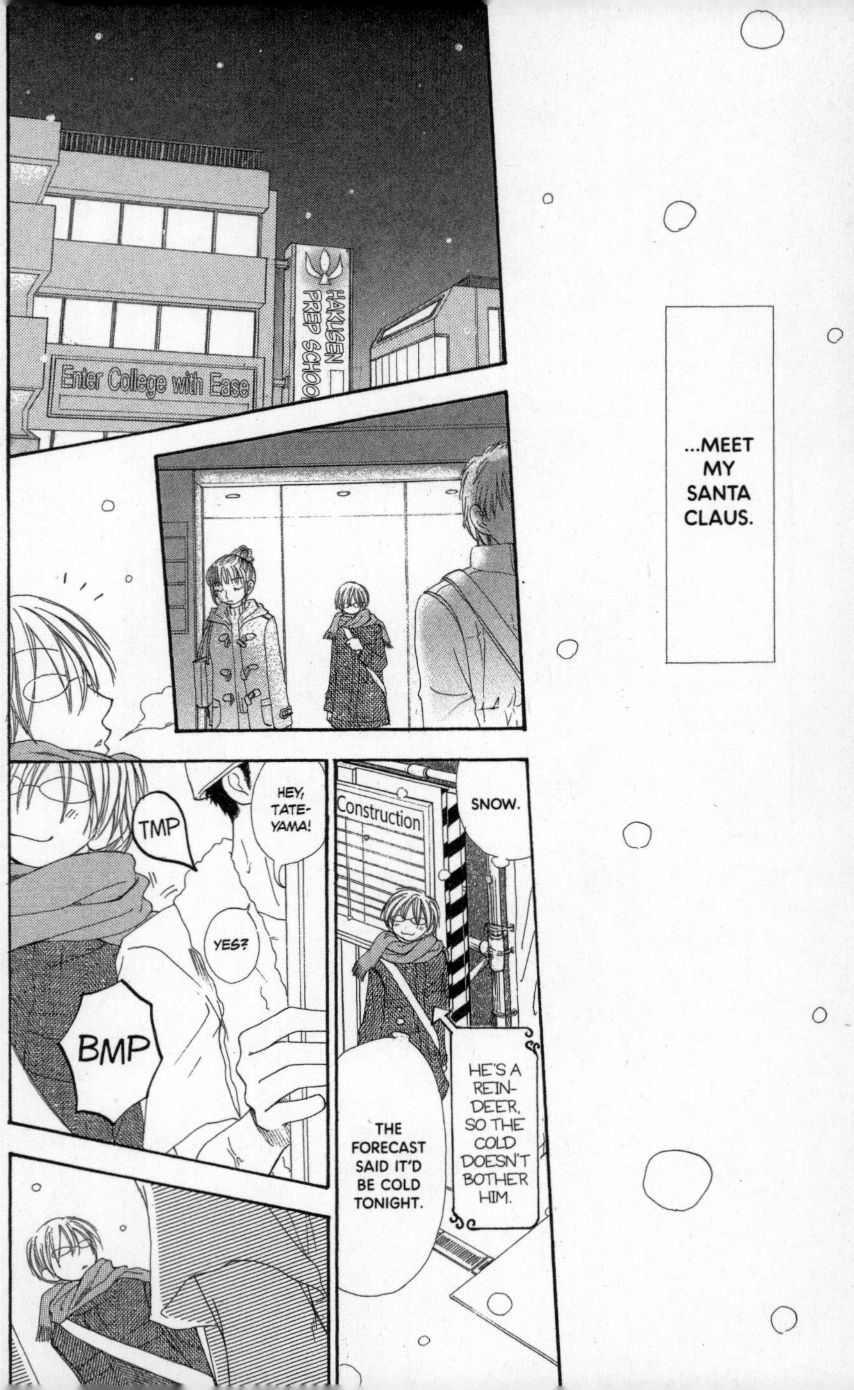
...MEET MY SANTA CLAUS.
HAKUSEN PREP SCHOOL
Enter College with Ease
SNOW.
Construction
HE'S A REIN-DEER, SO THE COLD DOESN'T BOTHER HIM.
HEY, TATE-YAMA!
TMP
YES?
BMP
THE FORECAST SAID IT'D BE COLD TONIGHT.

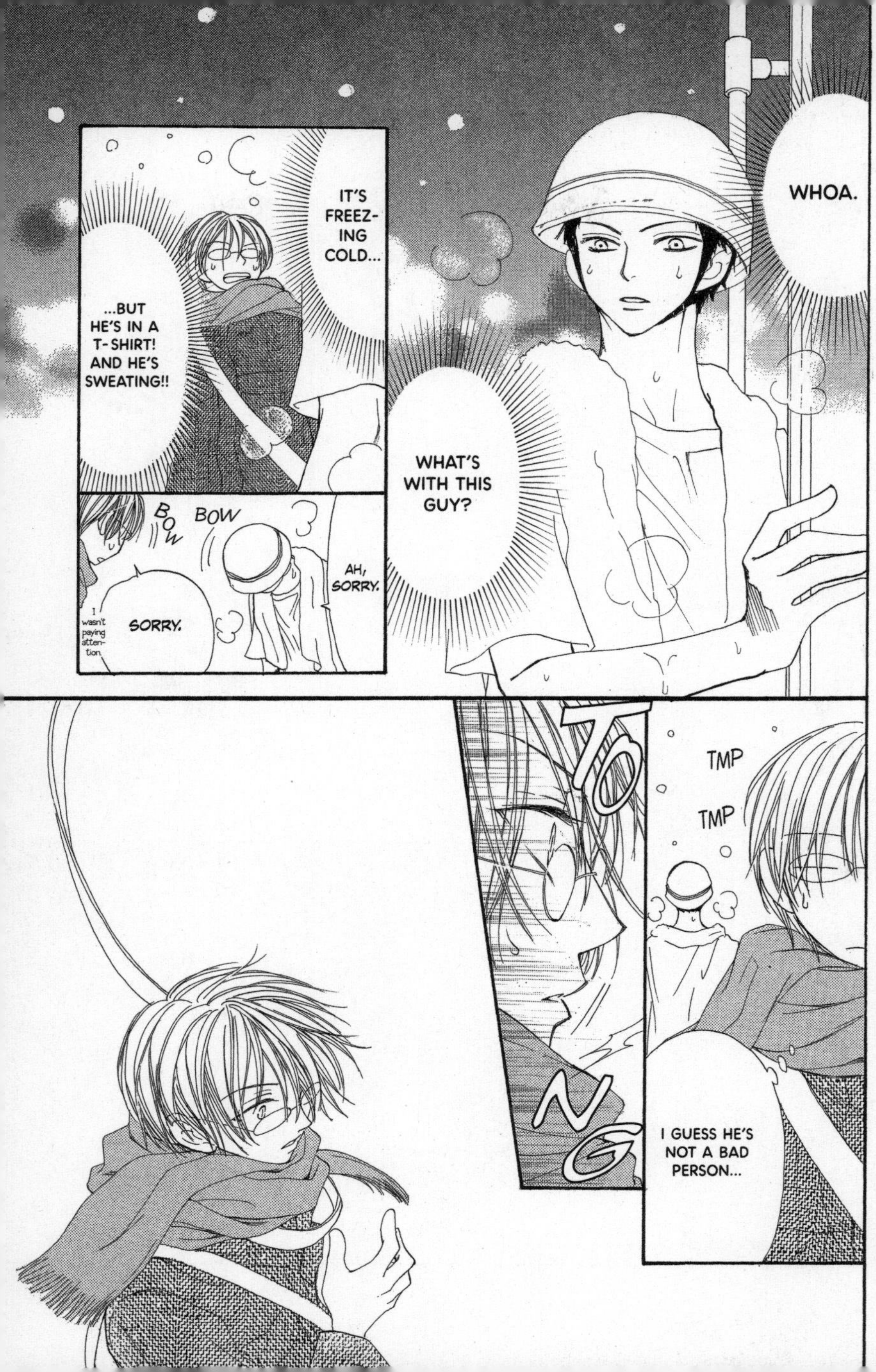
WHOA.
WHAT'S WITH THIS GUY?
IT'S FREEZ-ING COLD...
...BUT HE'S IN A T-SHIRT! AND HE'S SWEATING!!
AH, SORRY.
BOW BOW
SORRY.
I wasn't paying atten-tion.
TMP TMP
I GUESS HE'S NOT A BAD PERSON...
TONG

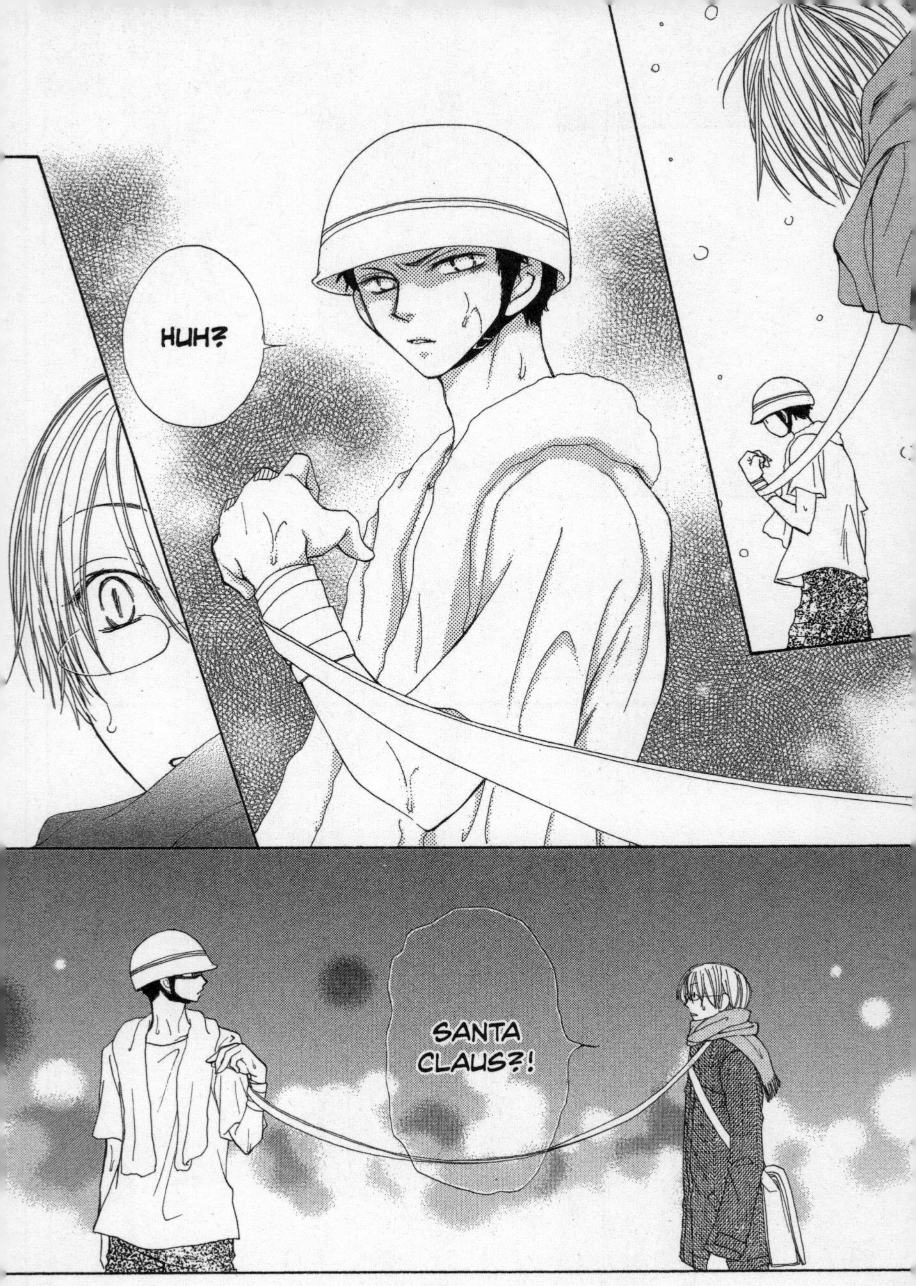
HUH?
SANTA CLAUS?!

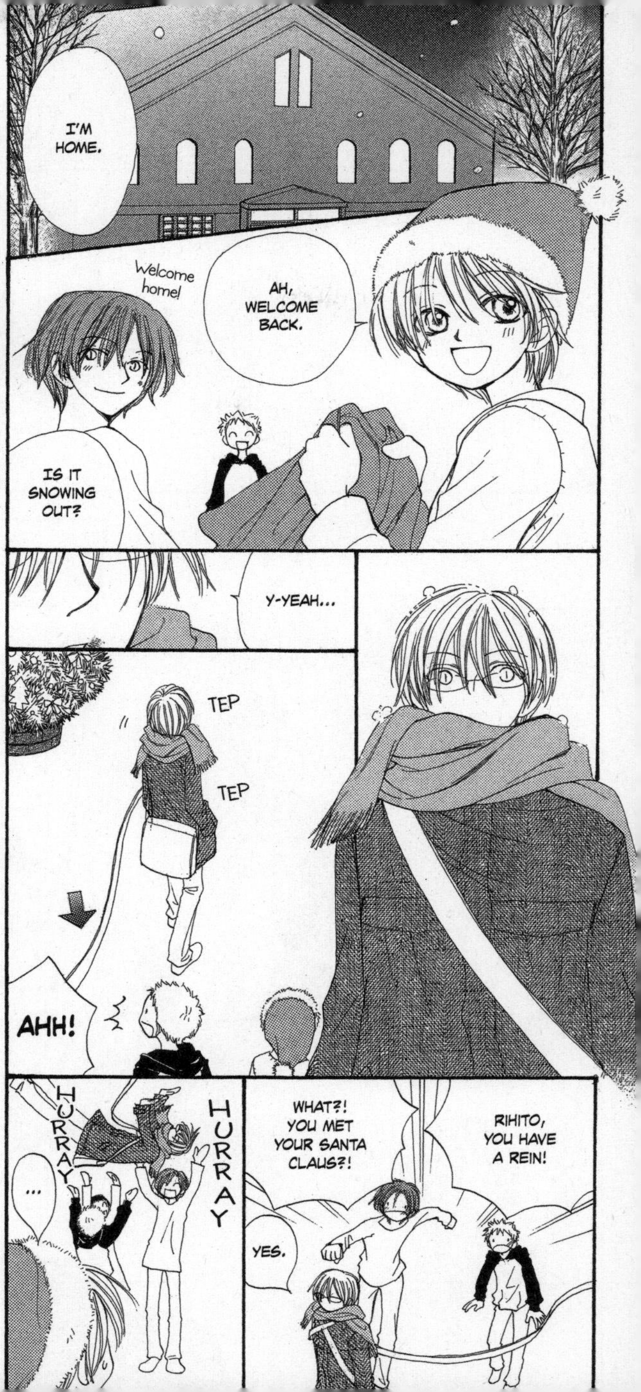
I'M HOME.
AH, WELCOME BACK.
Welcome home!
IS IT SNOWING OUT?
Y-YEAH...
TEP
TEP
AHH!
RIHITO, YOU HAVE A REIN!
WHAT?! YOU MET YOUR SANTA CLAUS?!
YES.
HURRAY
HURRAY
...

1/4 Sakura Mail

Part 4

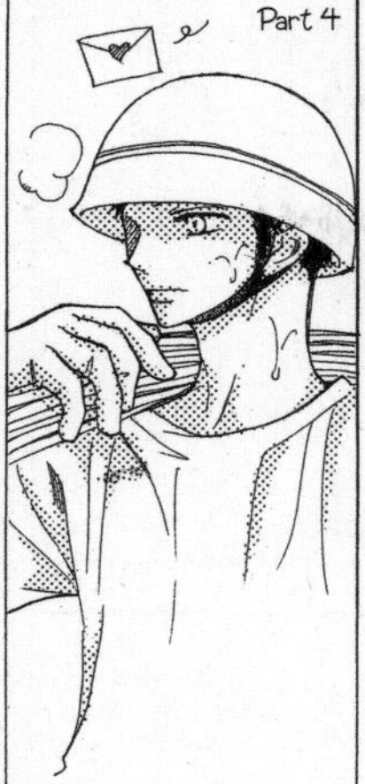

Rihito has been caught now too. Most magical reindeer never meet their Santa Claus, so I think quite a lot them feel the same way Rihito does. And, if you think about it, it would be difficult if they do meet their Santa. On the other hand, Kaito is always carefree. One reason is because of the way his family and grandfather brought him up, but Kaito has always had that disposition.

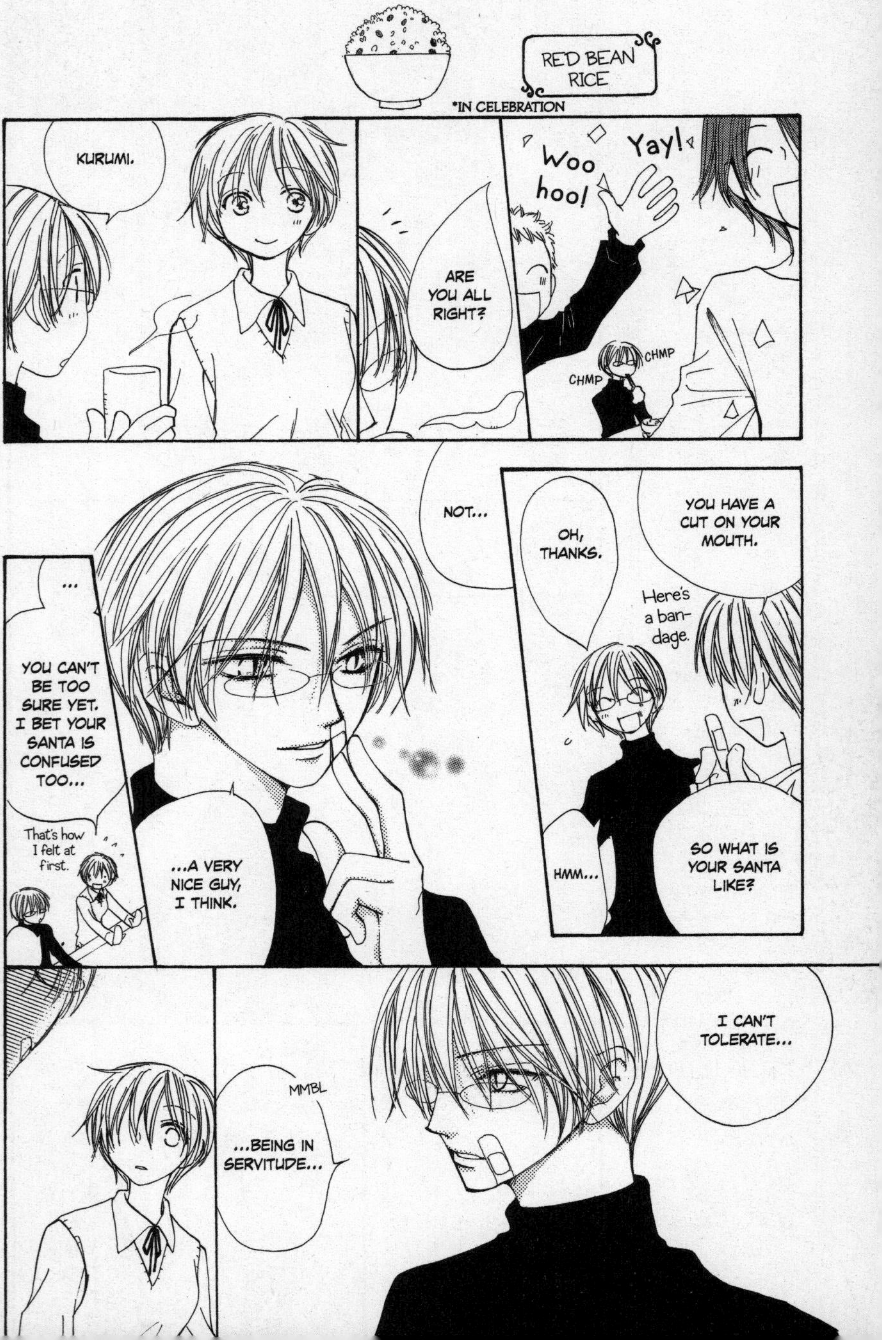
RED BEAN RICE
*IN CELEBRATION
Woo hoo!
Yay!
CHMP
CHMP
ARE YOU ALL RIGHT?
KURUMI.
YOU HAVE A CUT ON YOUR MOUTH.
Here's a ban-dage.
OH, THANKS.
SO WHAT IS YOUR SANTA LIKE?
HMM...
NOT...
...A VERY NICE GUY, I THINK.
...
YOU CAN'T BE TOO SURE YET. I BET YOUR SANTA IS CONFUSED TOO...
That's how I felt at first.
I CAN'T TOLERATE...
MMBL
...BEING IN SERVITUDE...

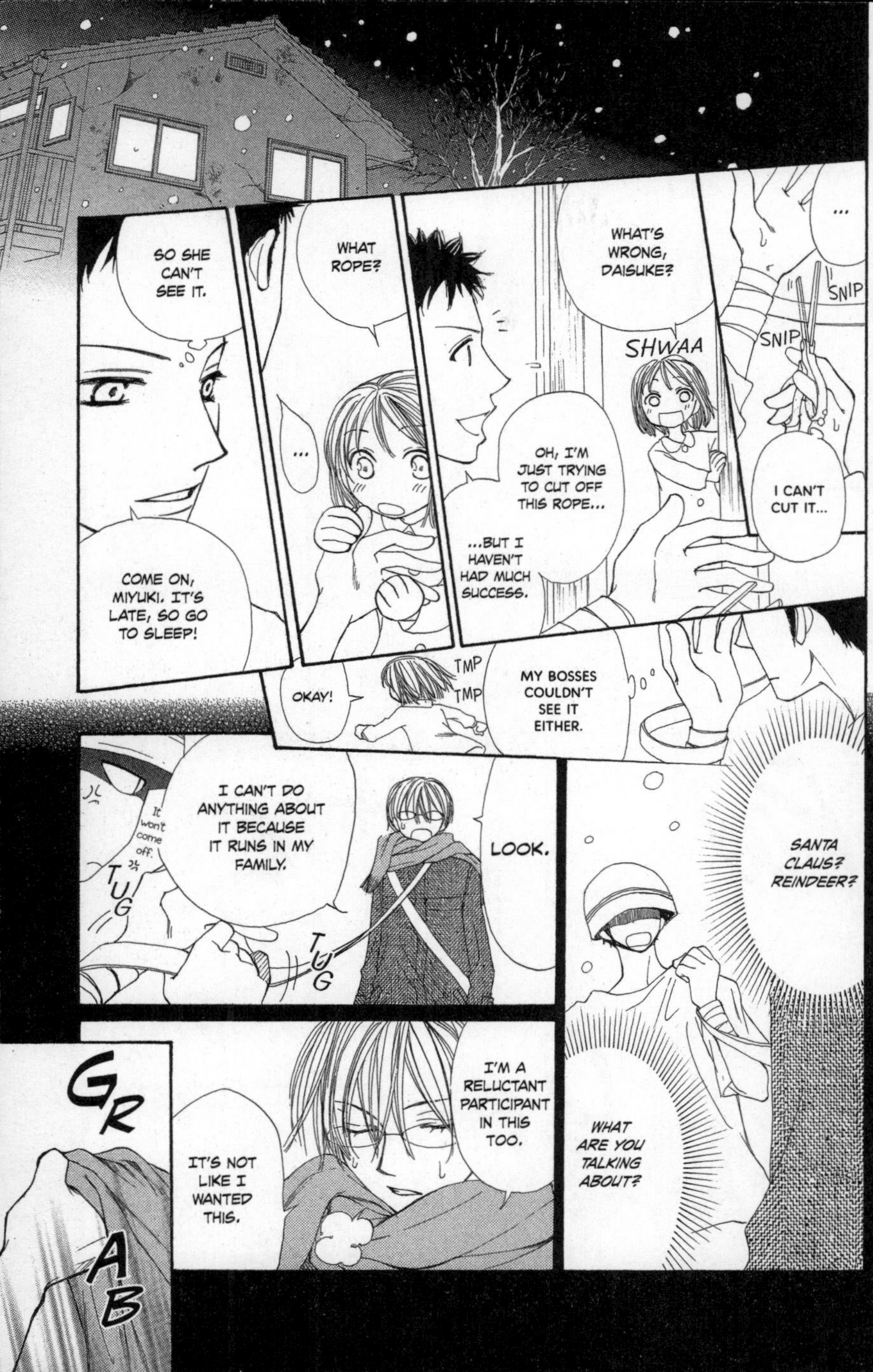
...
SNIP
SNIP
I CAN'T CUT IT...
WHAT'S WRONG, DAISUKE?
SHWAA
OH, I'M JUST TRYING TO CUT OFF THIS ROPE...
...BUT I HAVEN'T HAD MUCH SUCCESS.
WHAT ROPE?
...
SO SHE CAN'T SEE IT.
COME ON, MIYUKI. IT'S LATE, SO GO TO SLEEP!
MY BOSSES COULDN'T SEE IT EITHER.
TMP
TMP
OKAY!
SANTA CLAUS? REINDEER?
WHAT ARE YOU TALKING ABOUT?
LOOK.
I CAN'T DO ANYTHING ABOUT IT BECAUSE IT RUNS IN MY FAMILY.
It won't come off.
TUG
TUG
I'M A RELUCTANT PARTICIPANT IN THIS TOO.
IT'S NOT LIKE I WANTED THIS.
GRAB

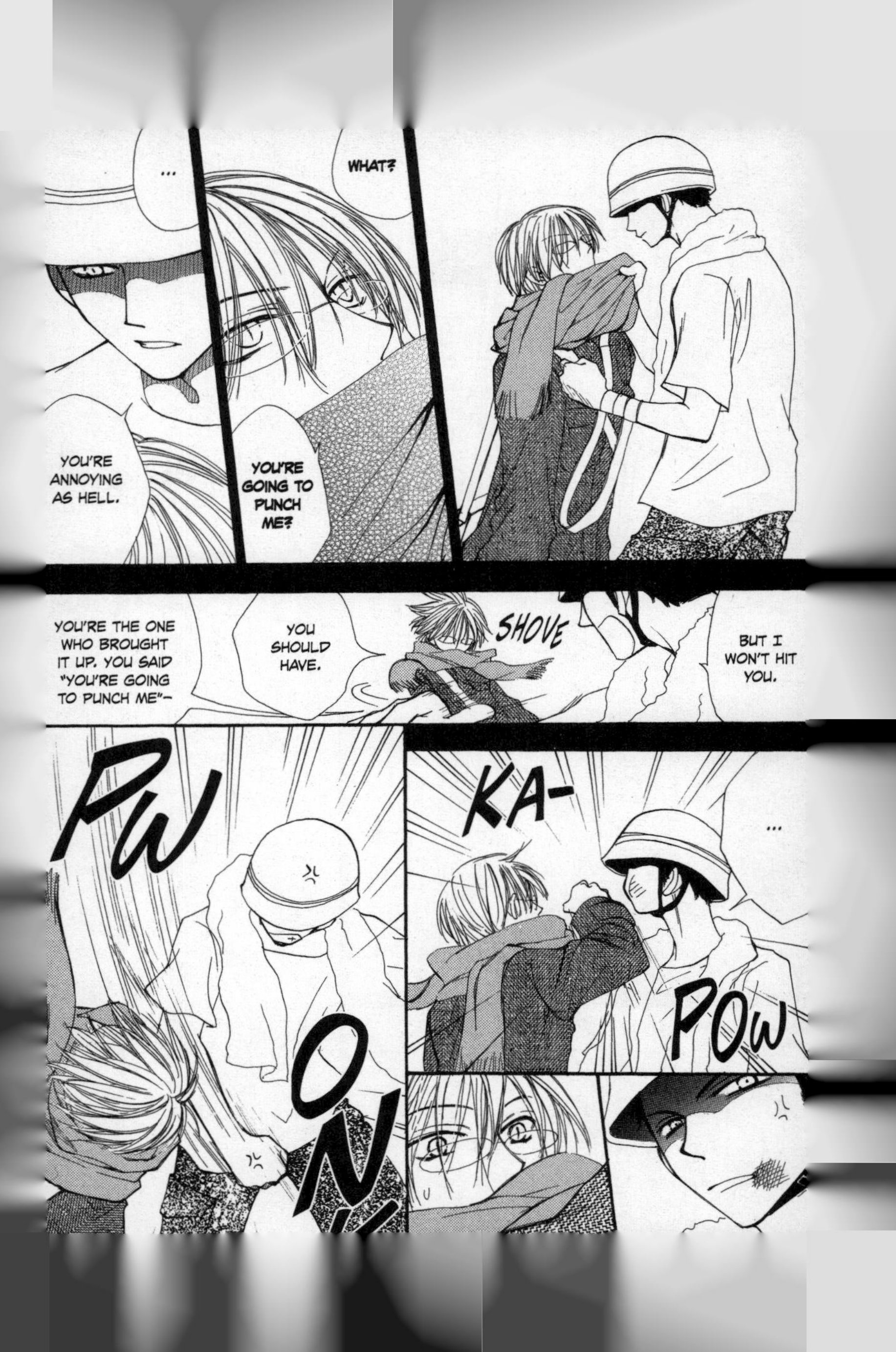
WHAT?
YOU'RE GOING TO PUNCH ME?
...
YOU'RE ANNOYING AS HELL.
BUT I WON'T HIT YOU.
SHOVE
YOU SHOULD HAVE.
YOU'RE THE ONE WHO BROUGHT IT UP. YOU SAID "YOU'RE GOING TO PUNCH ME"–
KA-
...
POW
PWON

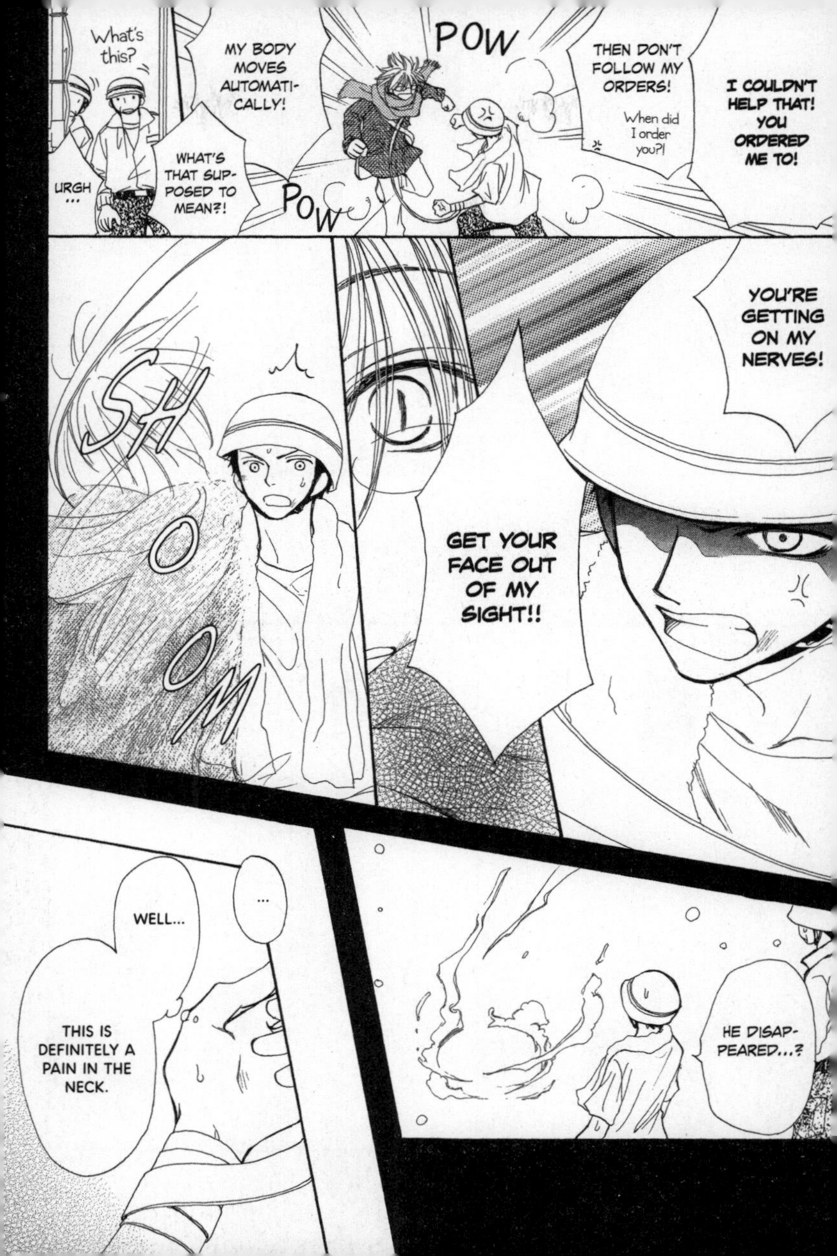
I COULDN'T HELP THAT! YOU ORDERED ME TO!
THEN DON'T FOLLOW MY ORDERS!
When did I order you?!
POW
POW
MY BODY MOVES AUTOMATI-CALLY!
WHAT'S THAT SUP-POSED TO MEAN?!
What's this?
URGH...
YOU'RE GETTING ON MY NERVES!
GET YOUR FACE OUT OF MY SIGHT!!
SHOOOM
HE DISAP-PEARED...?
...
WELL...
THIS IS DEFINITELY A PAIN IN THE NECK.

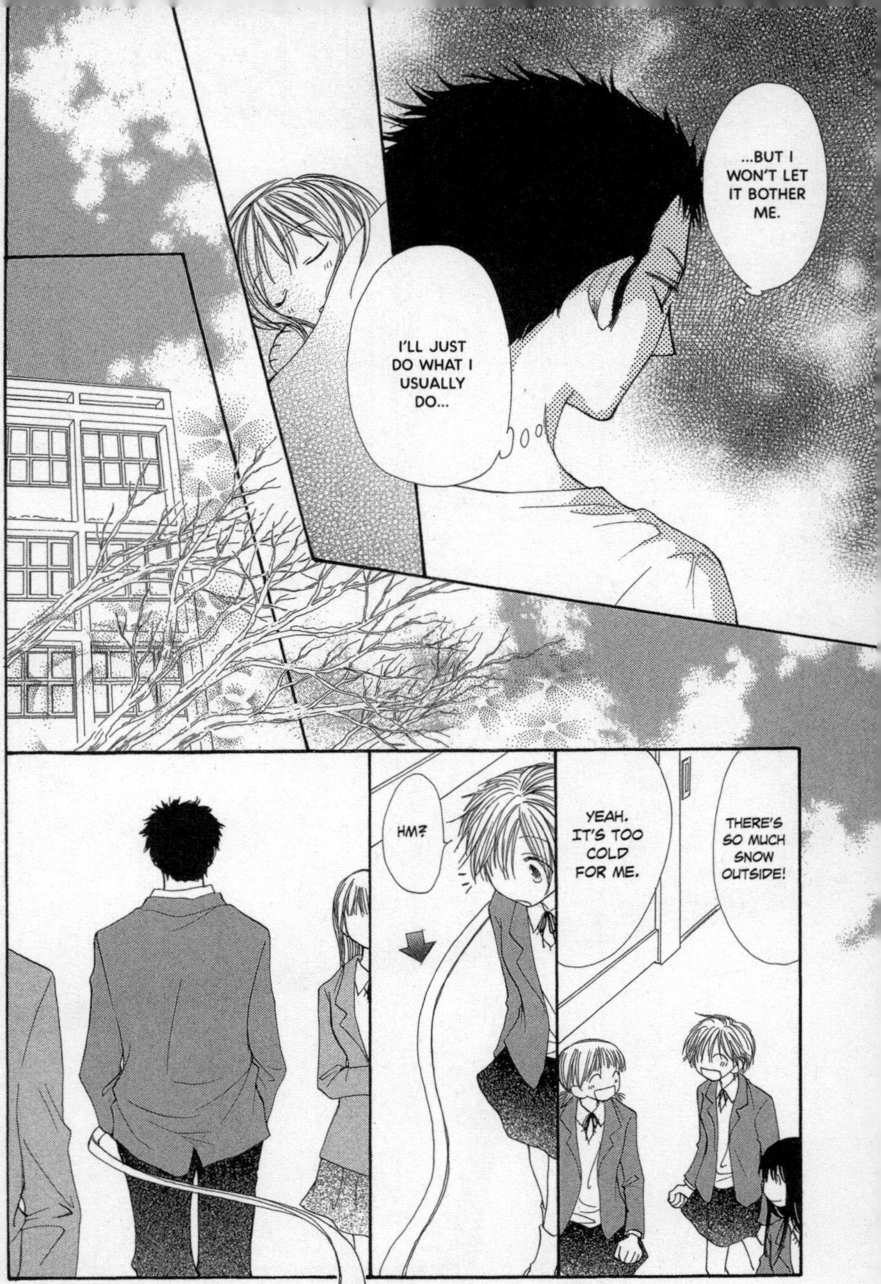
...BUT I WON'T LET IT BOTHER ME.
I'LL JUST DO WHAT I USUALLY DO...
THERE'S SO MUCH SNOW OUTSIDE!
YEAH. IT'S TOO COLD FOR ME.
HM?

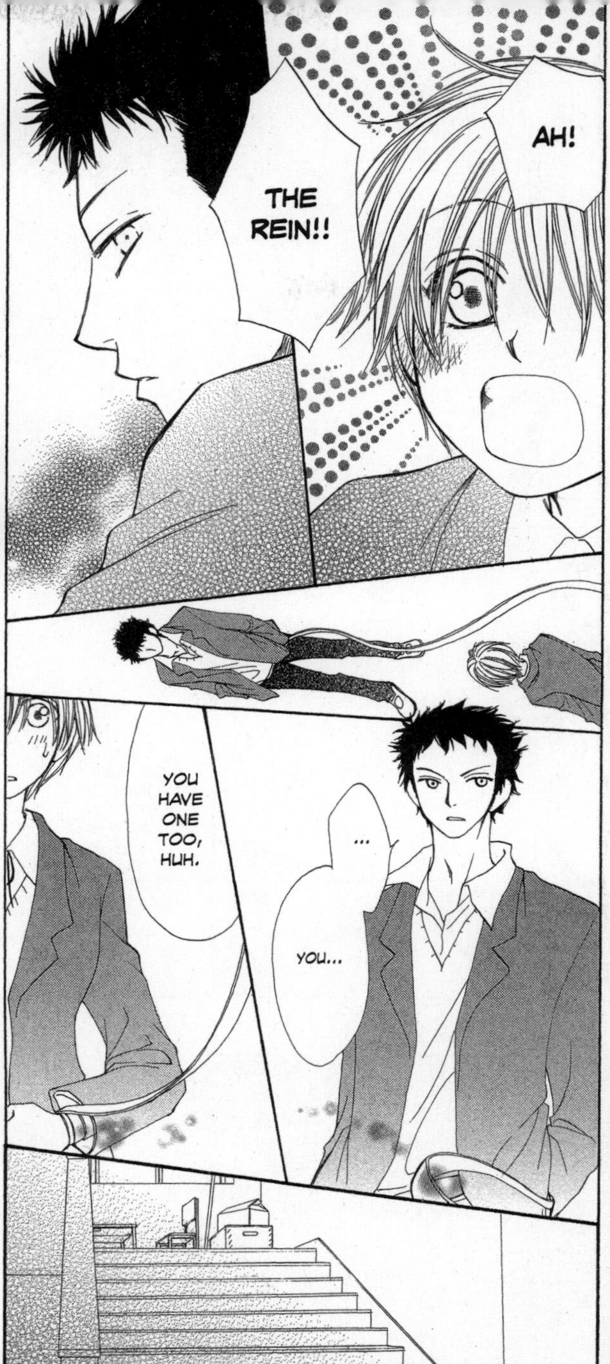
AH!
THE REIN!!
...
YOU...
YOU HAVE ONE TOO, HUH.

1/4 Sakura Mail

Part 5

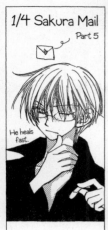

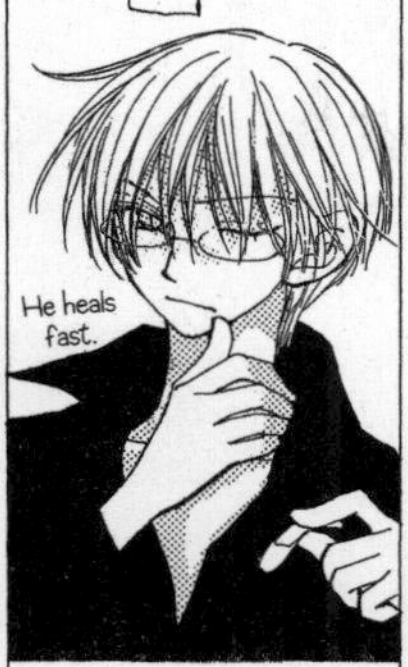
He heals fast.

The main stories are set during Christmas because this manga is about Santa Claus and reindeer. So seasonal! But of the three chapters in volume 1, two of them were set in summer. This time, two out of four chapters were set in winter, so I feel a little better. And, um... this chapter marks Kurumi's third Santa duty. But she's still 17!!

(continues)

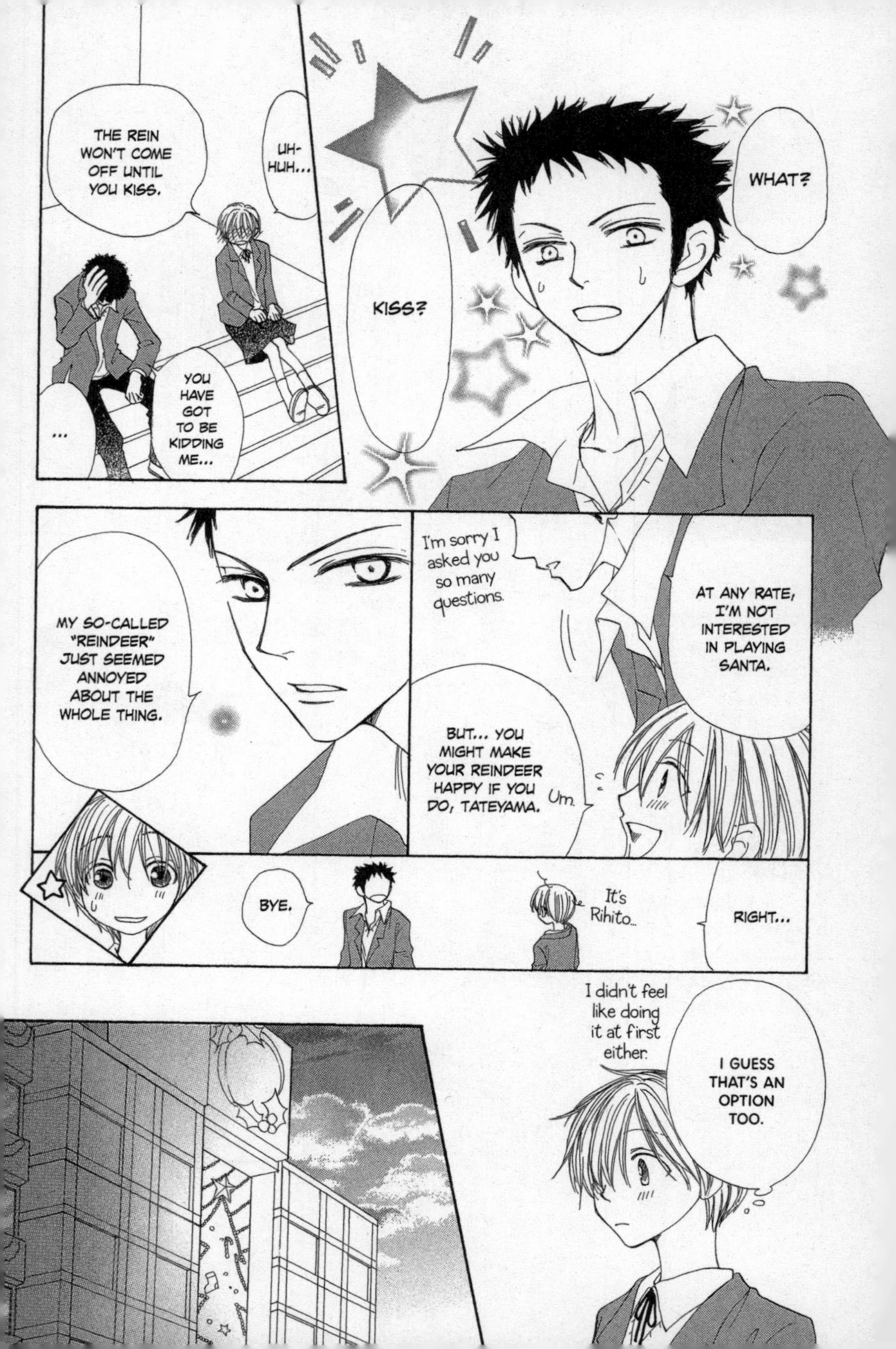
WHAT?
KISS?
THE REIN WON'T COME OFF UNTIL YOU KISS.
UH-HUH...
YOU HAVE GOT TO BE KIDDING ME...
...
AT ANY RATE, I'M NOT INTERESTED IN PLAYING SANTA.
I'm sorry I asked you so many questions.
Um.
BUT... YOU MIGHT MAKE YOUR REINDEER HAPPY IF YOU DO, TATEYAMA.
MY SO-CALLED "REINDEER" JUST SEEMED ANNOYED ABOUT THE WHOLE THING.
RIGHT...
It's Rihito...
BYE.
I GUESS THAT'S AN OPTION TOO.
I didn't feel like doing it at first either.

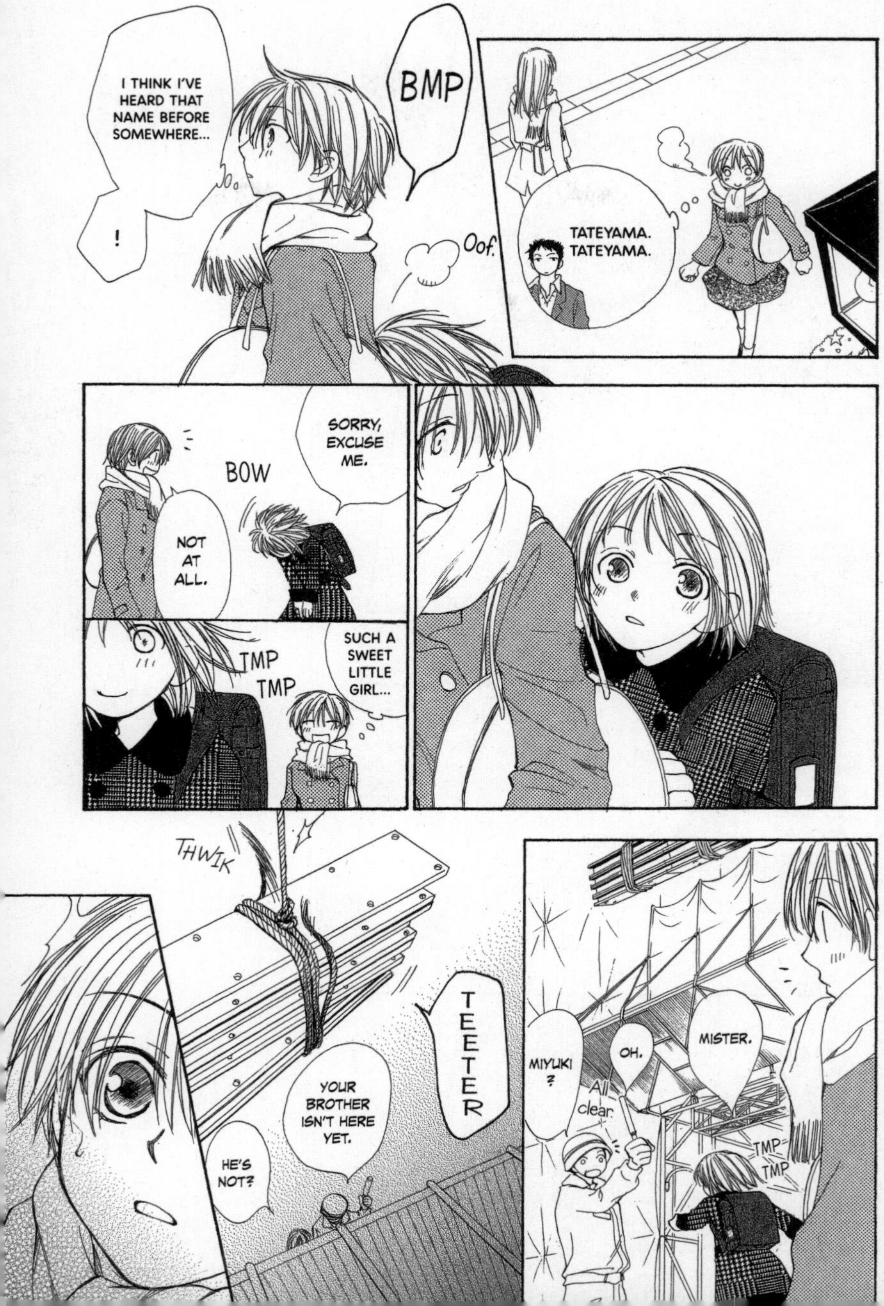

TATEYAMA. TATEYAMA.
BMP
Oof.
I THINK I'VE HEARD THAT NAME BEFORE SOMEWHERE...
!
SORRY, EXCUSE ME.
BOW
NOT AT ALL.
SUCH A SWEET LITTLE GIRL...
TMP TMP
MISTER.
OH.
MIYUKI?
All clear.
TMP TMP
THWIK
TEETER
YOUR BROTHER ISN'T HERE YET.
HE'S NOT?

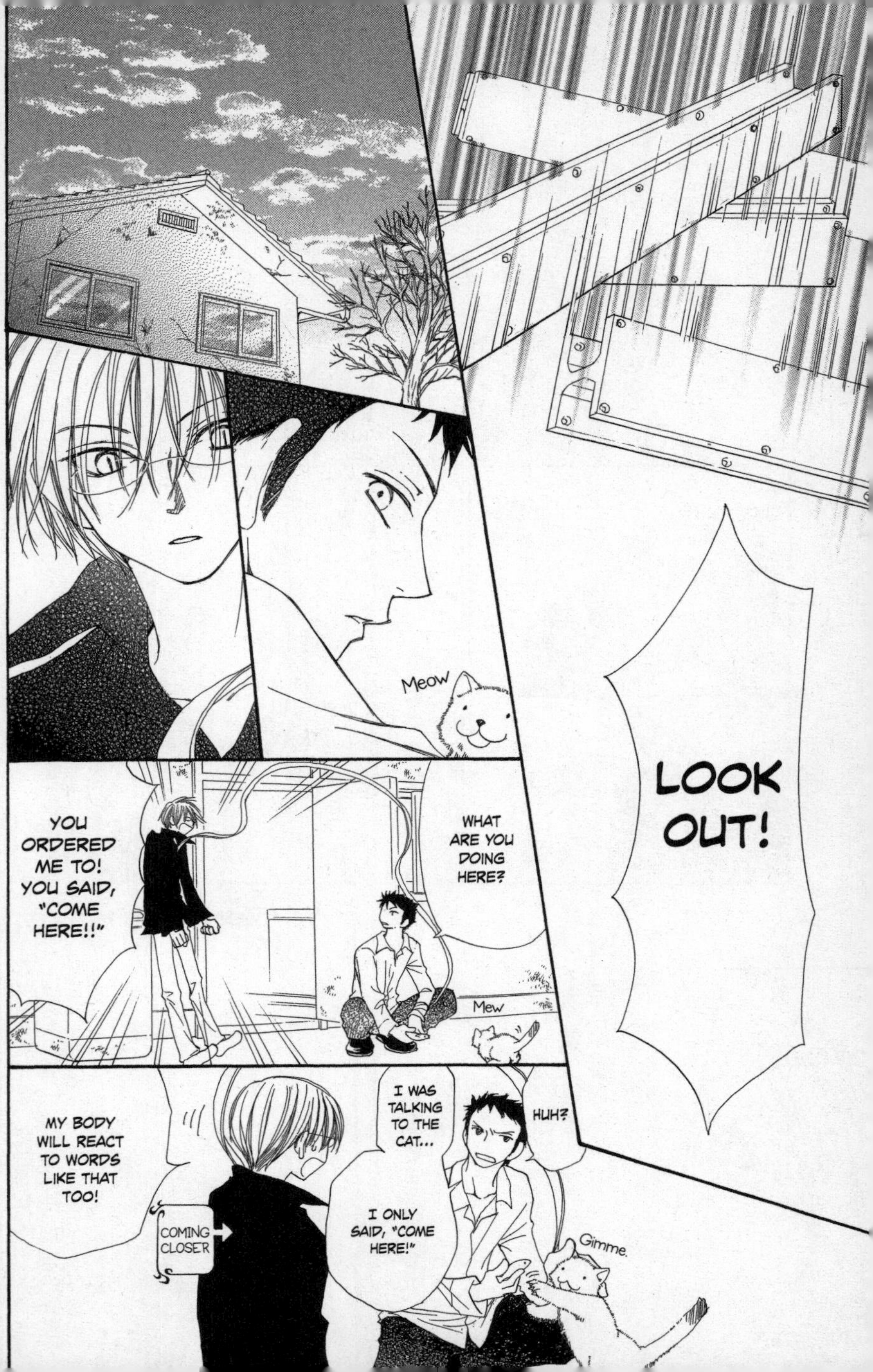

LOOK OUT!
Meow
WHAT ARE YOU DOING HERE?
YOU ORDERED ME TO! YOU SAID, "COME HERE!!"
Mew
HUH?
I WAS TALKING TO THE CAT...
I ONLY SAID, "COME HERE!"
MY BODY WILL REACT TO WORDS LIKE THAT TOO!
COMING CLOSER
Gimme.

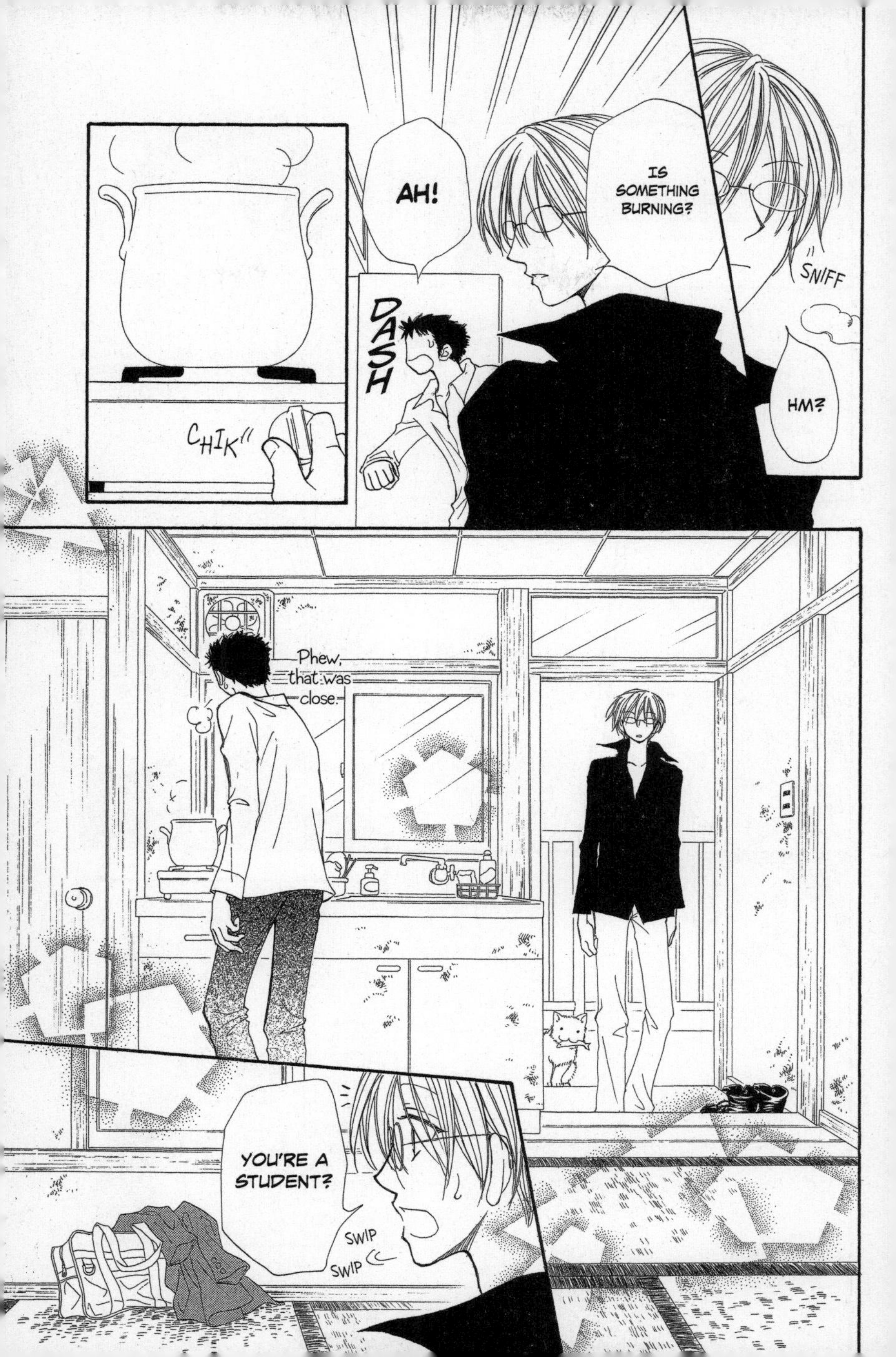
SNIFF
HM?
IS SOMETHING BURNING?
AH!
DASH
CHIK
Phew, that was close.
YOU'RE A STUDENT?
SWIP
SWIP

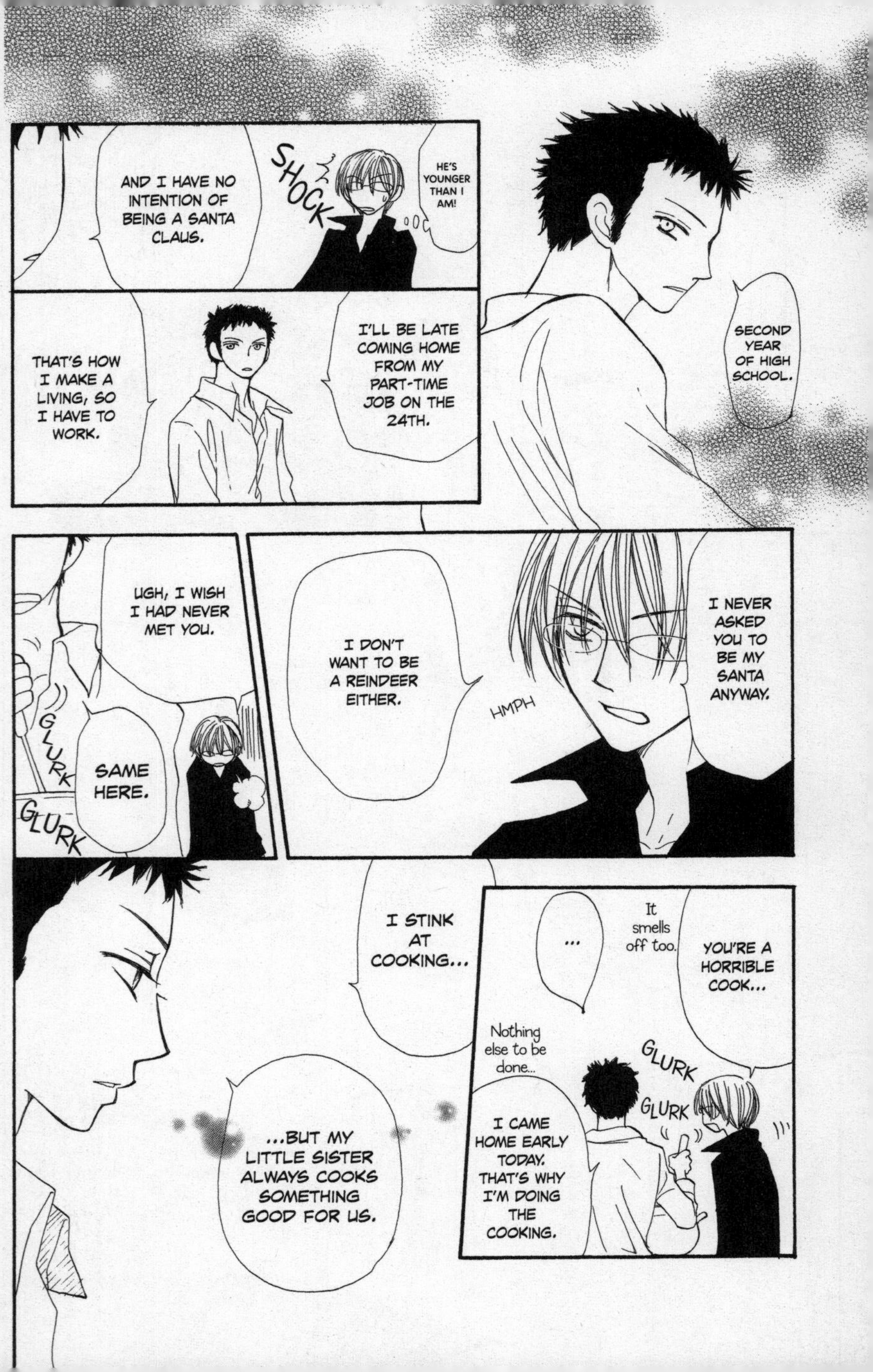
SECOND YEAR OF HIGH SCHOOL.
HE'S YOUNGER THAN I AM!
SHOCK
AND I HAVE NO INTENTION OF BEING A SANTA CLAUS.
I'LL BE LATE COMING HOME FROM MY PART-TIME JOB ON THE 24TH.
THAT'S HOW I MAKE A LIVING, SO I HAVE TO WORK.
I NEVER ASKED YOU TO BE MY SANTA ANYWAY.
HMPH
I DON'T WANT TO BE A REINDEER EITHER.
UGH, I WISH I HAD NEVER MET YOU.
SAME HERE.
GLURK
GLURK
YOU'RE A HORRIBLE COOK...
It smells off too.
...
GLURK
GLURK
Nothing else to be done...
I CAME HOME EARLY TODAY. THAT'S WHY I'M DOING THE COOKING.
I STINK AT COOKING...
...BUT MY LITTLE SISTER ALWAYS COOKS SOMETHING GOOD FOR US.

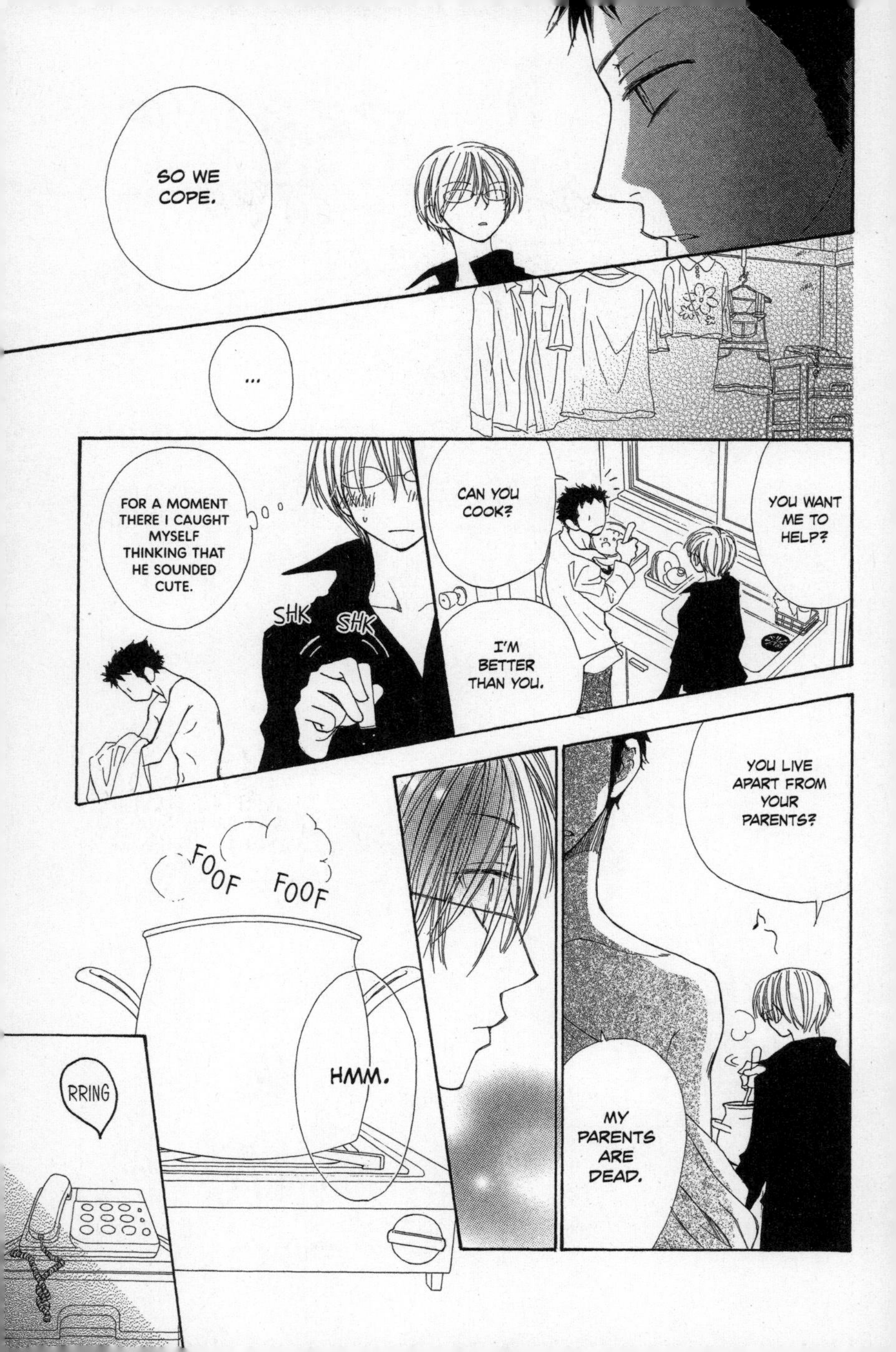
SO WE COPE.
...
YOU WANT ME TO HELP?
CAN YOU COOK?
I'M BETTER THAN YOU.
FOR A MOMENT THERE I CAUGHT MYSELF THINKING THAT HE SOUNDED CUTE.
SHK SHK
YOU LIVE APART FROM YOUR PARENTS?
MY PARENTS ARE DEAD.
HMM.
FOOF FOOF
RRING

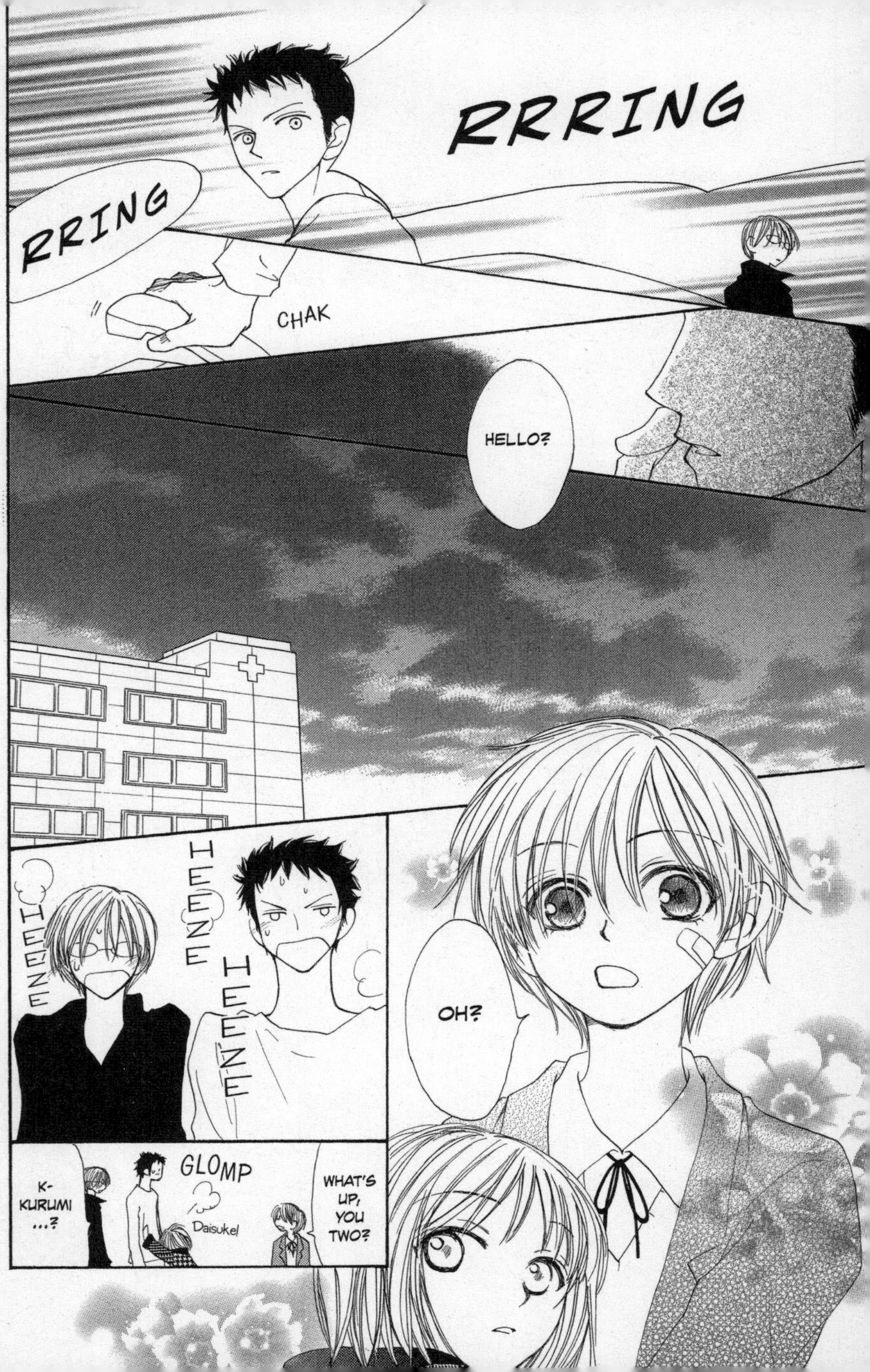

RRRING
RRING
CHAK
HELLO?
OH?
HEEZE HEEZE
HEEZE HEEZE
HEEZE HEEZE
WHAT'S UP, YOU TWO?
GLOMP
Daisuke!
K-KURUMI...?

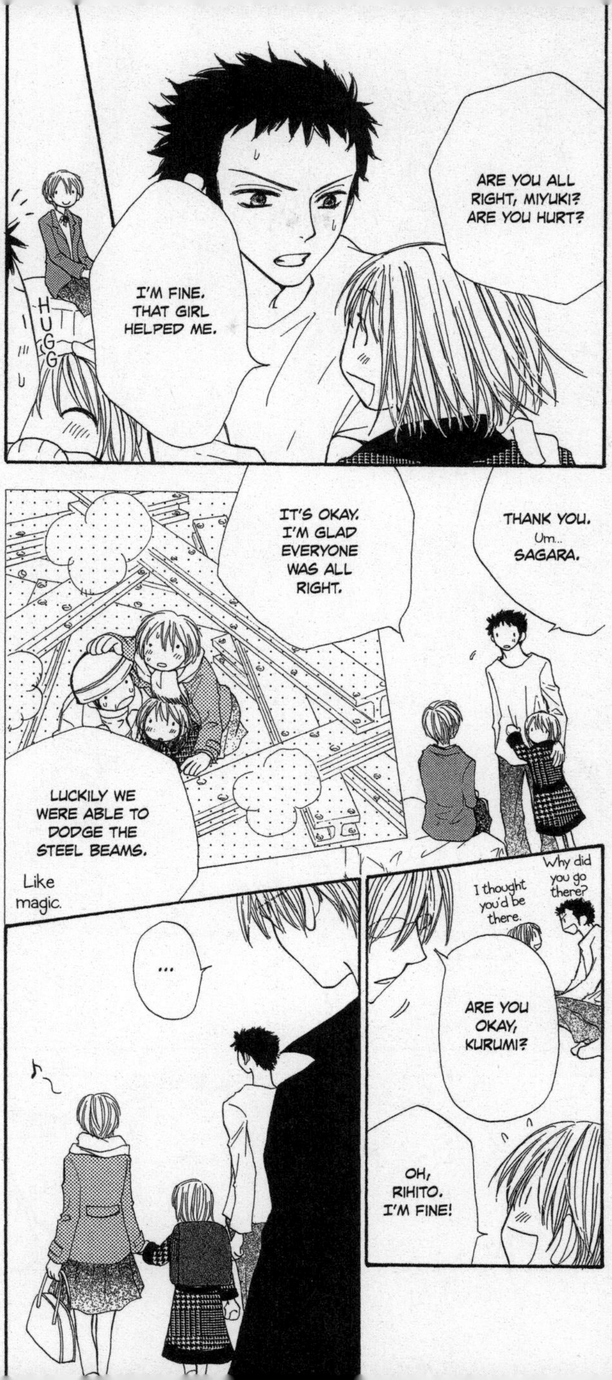
ARE YOU ALL RIGHT, MIYUKI? ARE YOU HURT?
I'M FINE. THAT GIRL HELPED ME.
HUGG
THANK YOU. Um... SAGARA.
IT'S OKAY. I'M GLAD EVERYONE WAS ALL RIGHT.
LUCKILY WE WERE ABLE TO DODGE THE STEEL BEAMS.
Like magic.
Why did you go there?
I thought you'd be there.
ARE YOU OKAY, KURUMI?
OH, RIHITO. I'M FINE!
...

1/4 Sakura Mail

Part 6

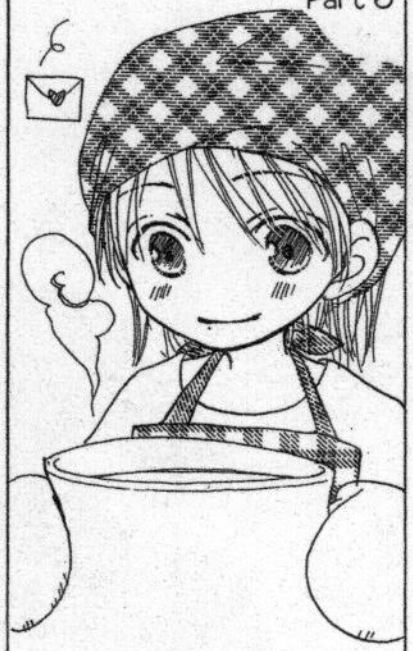

She will forever be 17! Time will pass, Kurumi will continue to gain experience, but she will not age. I think the important thing is to draw the story of how she changes as a person. And Kaito too!! He's foolish, but I think he's also enlightened in a way because he has such a straightforward way of thinking. But I want him to grow up more too! And because he's foolish...I enjoy drawing him.

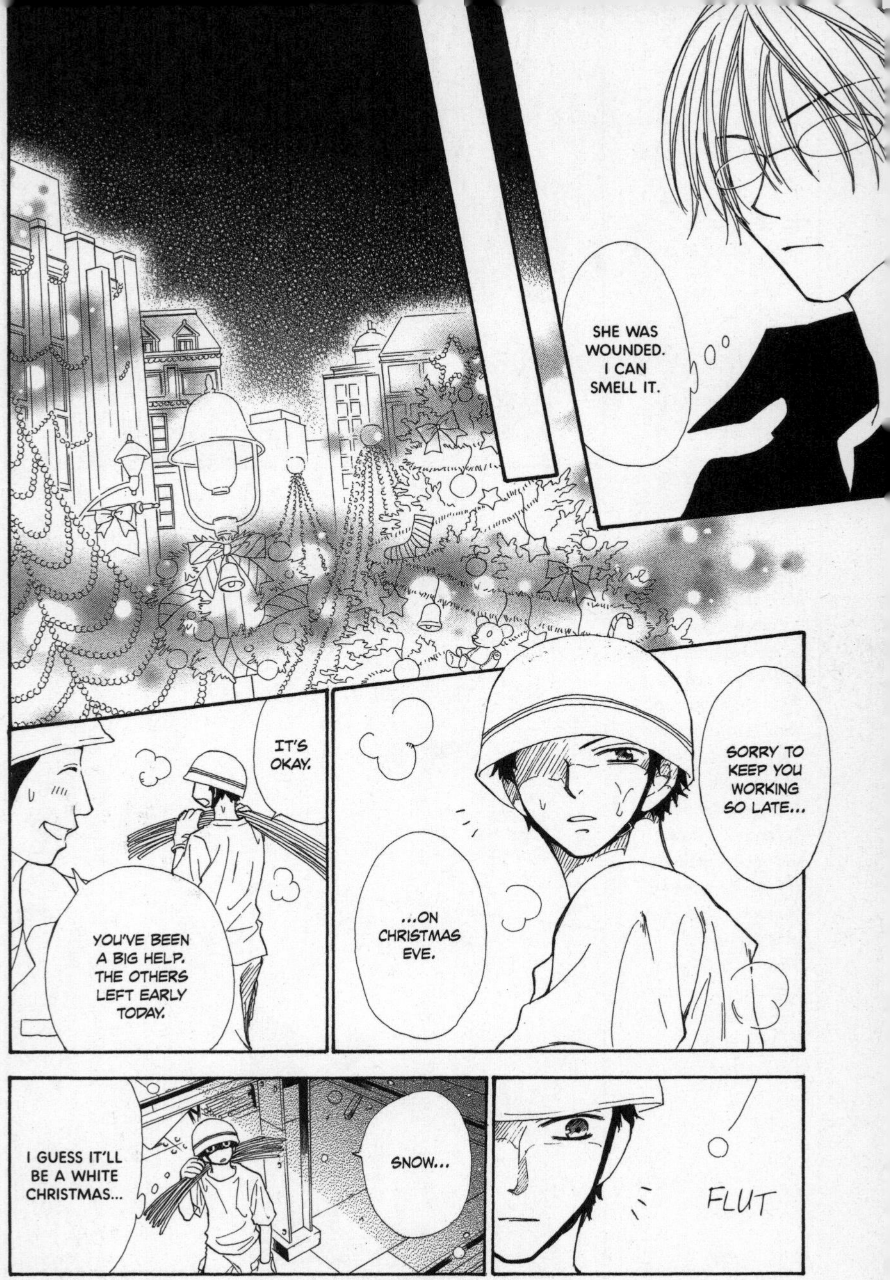
SHE WAS WOUNDED. I CAN SMELL IT.
SORRY TO KEEP YOU WORKING SO LATE...
...ON CHRISTMAS EVE.
IT'S OKAY.
YOU'VE BEEN A BIG HELP. THE OTHERS LEFT EARLY TODAY.
FLUT
SNOW...
I GUESS IT'LL BE A WHITE CHRISTMAS...

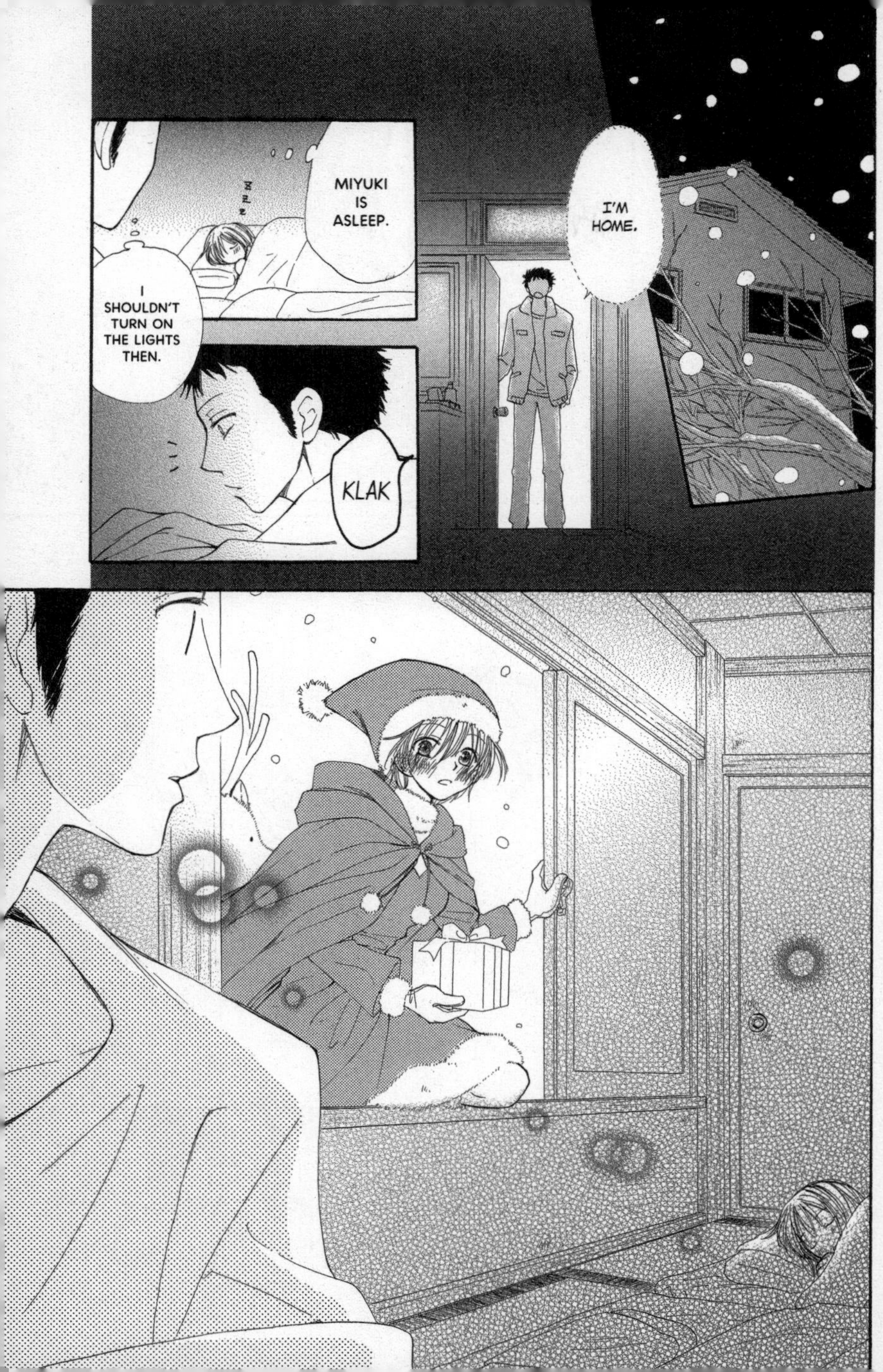
I'M HOME.
MIYUKI IS ASLEEP.
I SHOULDN'T TURN ON THE LIGHTS THEN.
KLAK

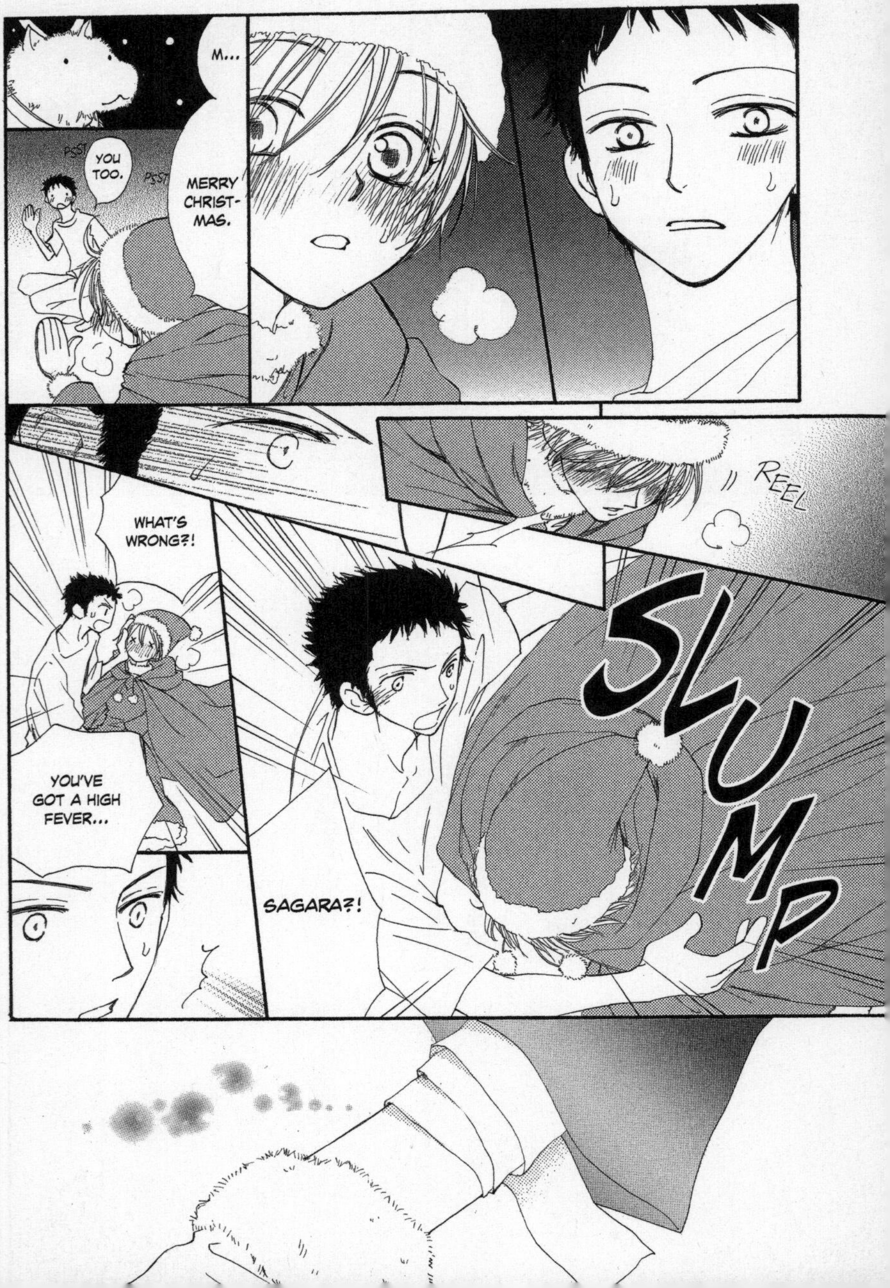
M...
MERRY CHRIST-MAS.
PSST
YOU TOO.
PSST
REEL
SLUMP
SAGARA?!
WHAT'S WRONG?!
YOU'VE GOT A HIGH FEVER...

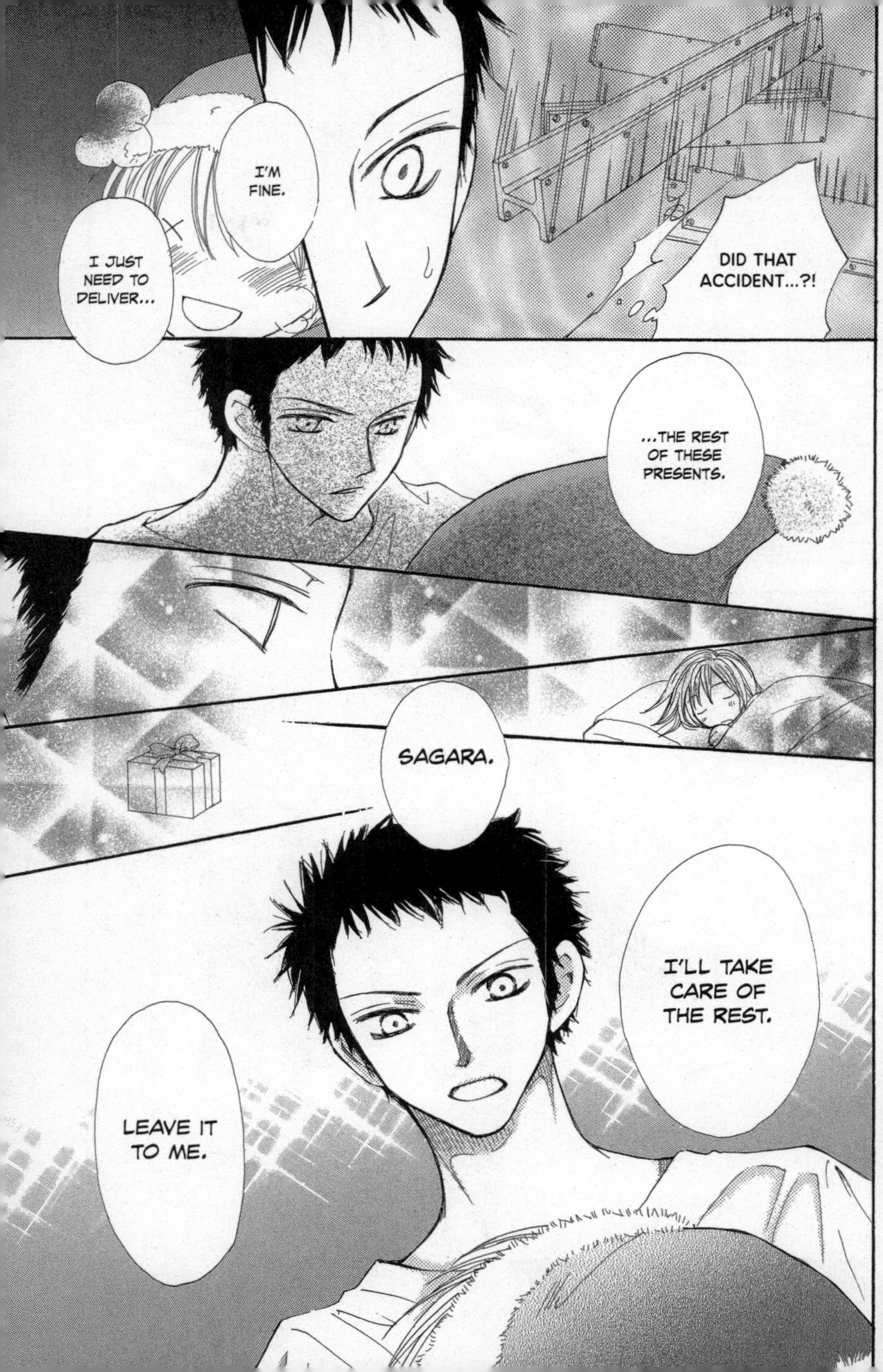
DID THAT ACCIDENT...?!
I'M FINE.
I JUST NEED TO DELIVER...
...THE REST OF THESE PRESENTS.
SAGARA.
I'LL TAKE CARE OF THE REST.
LEAVE IT TO ME.

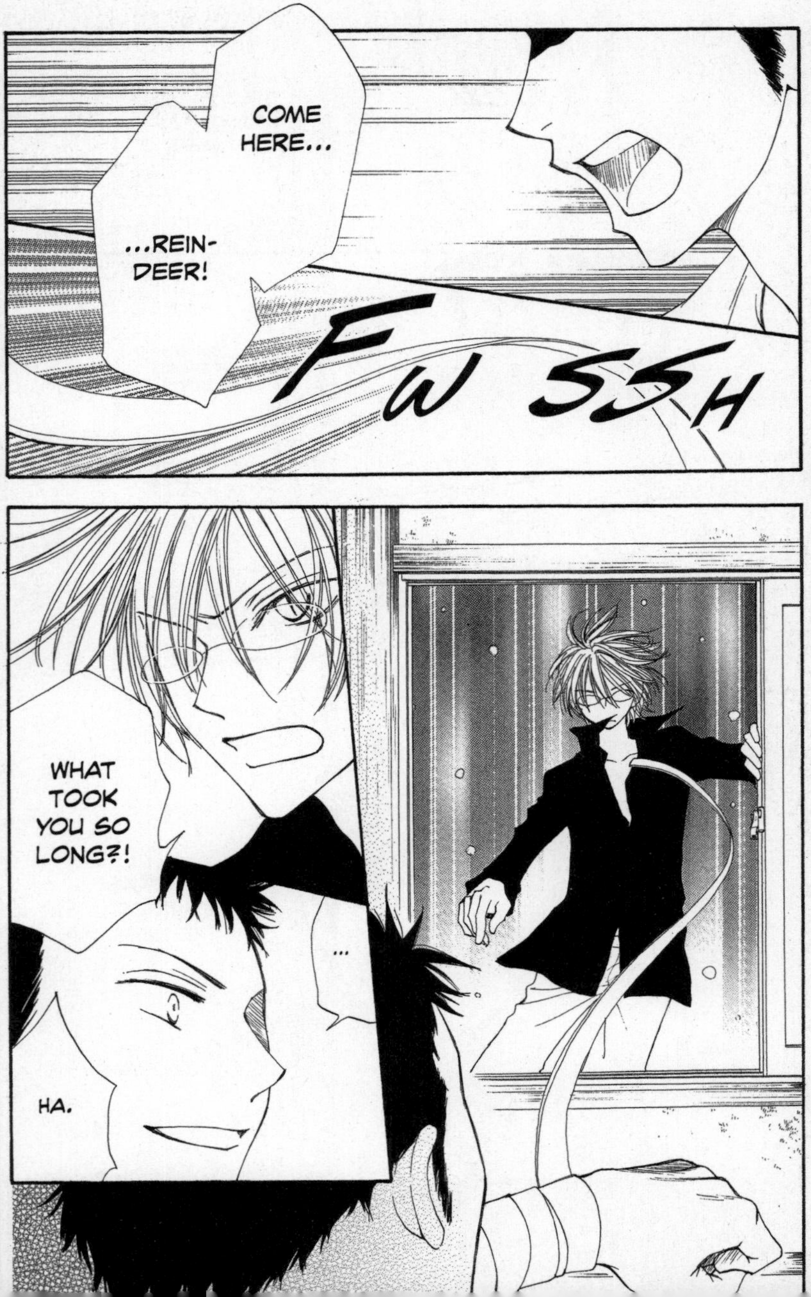
COME HERE...
...REIN-DEER!
FWSSH
WHAT TOOK YOU SO LONG?!
...
HA.

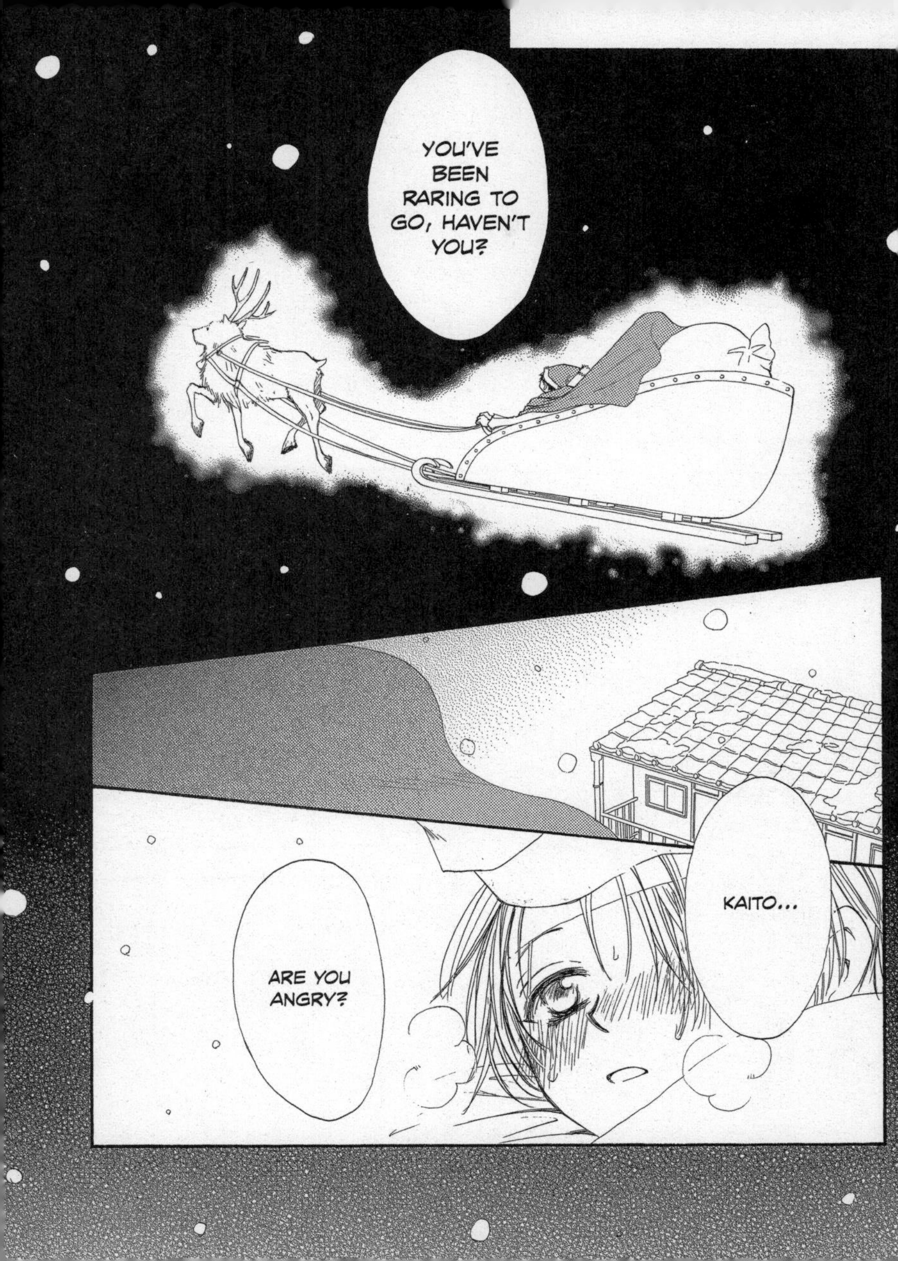
YOU'VE BEEN RARING TO GO, HAVEN'T YOU?
KAITO...
ARE YOU ANGRY?

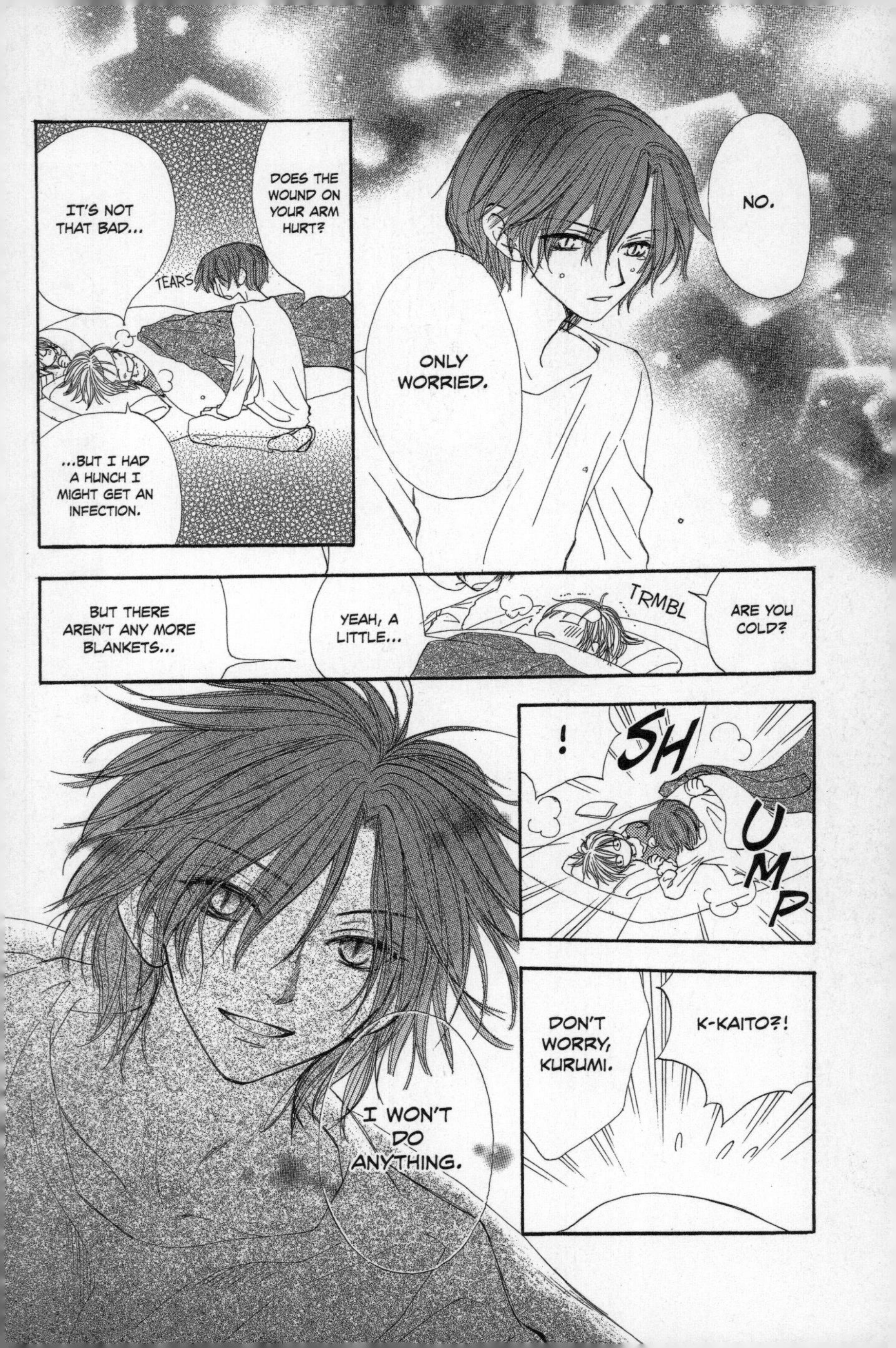
NO.
ONLY WORRIED.
DOES THE WOUND ON YOUR ARM HURT?
IT'S NOT THAT BAD...
TEARS
...BUT I HAD A HUNCH I MIGHT GET AN INFECTION.
ARE YOU COLD?
TRMBL
YEAH, A LITTLE...
BUT THERE AREN'T ANY MORE BLANKETS...
SHUMP
!
K-KAITO?!
DON'T WORRY, KURUMI.
I WON'T DO ANYTHING.

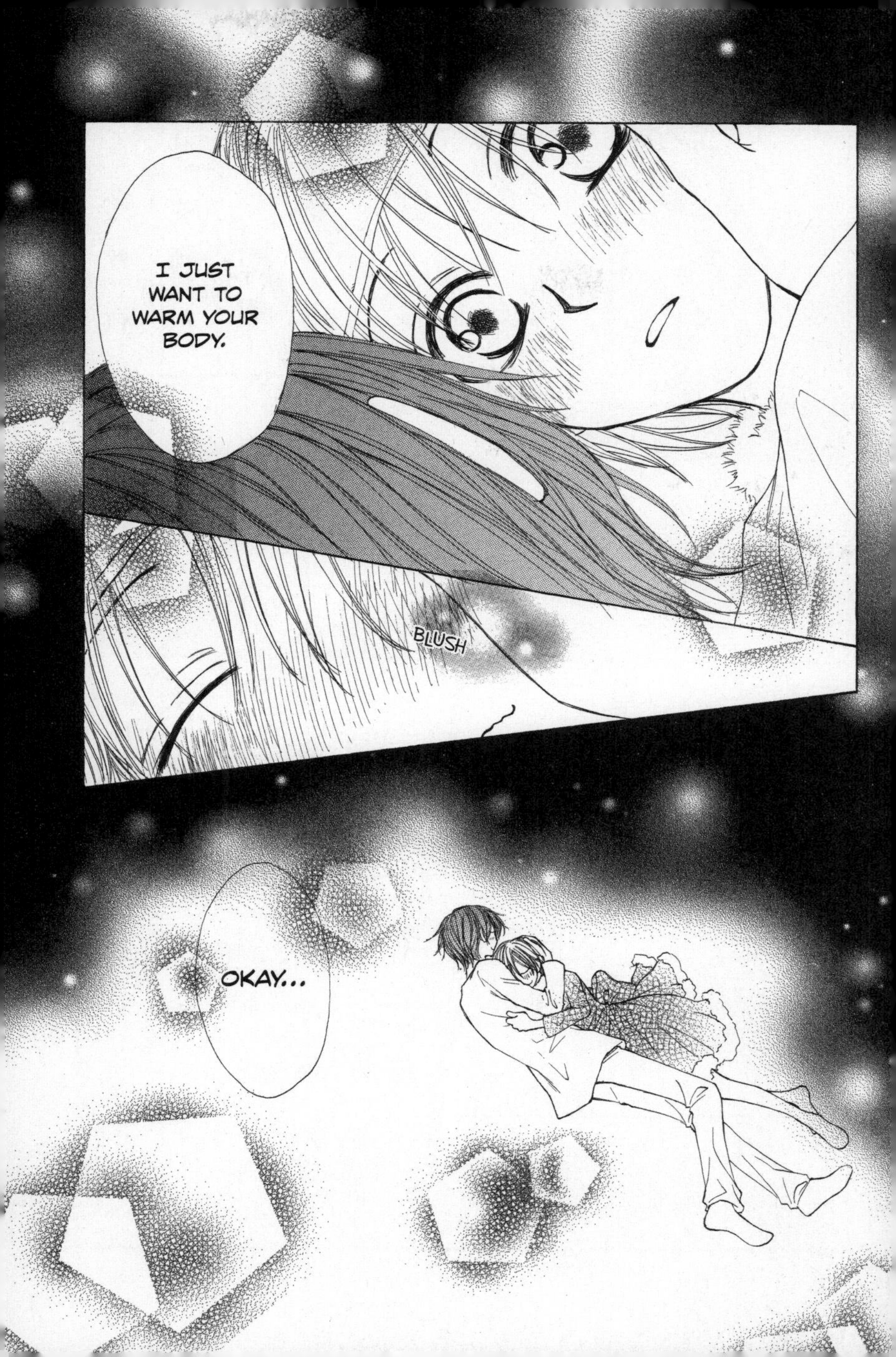
I JUST WANT TO WARM YOUR BODY.
BLUSH
OKAY...

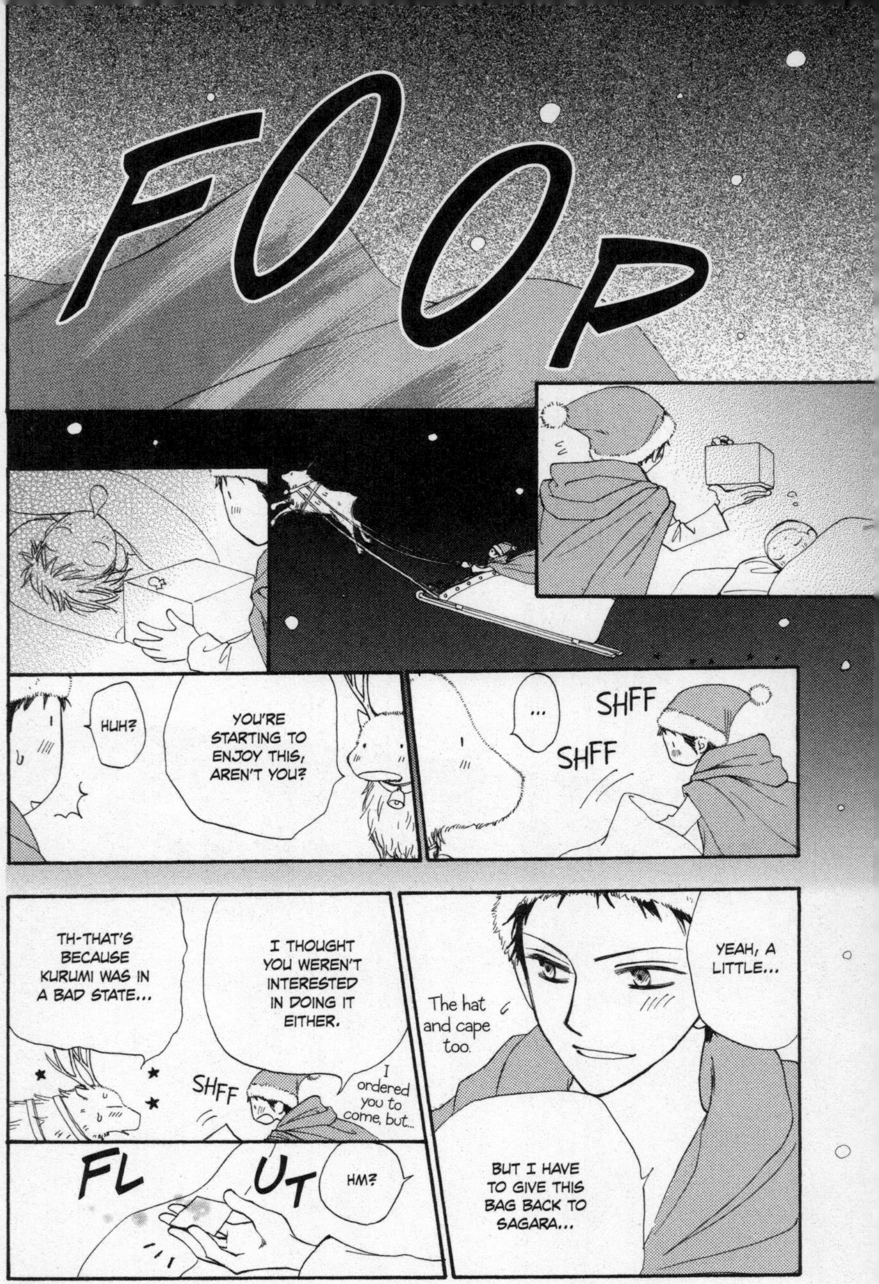
FOOP
...
SHFF
SHFF
YOU'RE STARTING TO ENJOY THIS, AREN'T YOU?
HUH?
YEAH, A LITTLE...
The hat and cape too.
BUT I HAVE TO GIVE THIS BAG BACK TO SAGARA...
I THOUGHT YOU WEREN'T INTERESTED IN DOING IT EITHER.
TH-THAT'S BECAUSE KURUMI WAS IN A BAD STATE...
I ordered you to come, but...
SHFF
HM?
FLUT

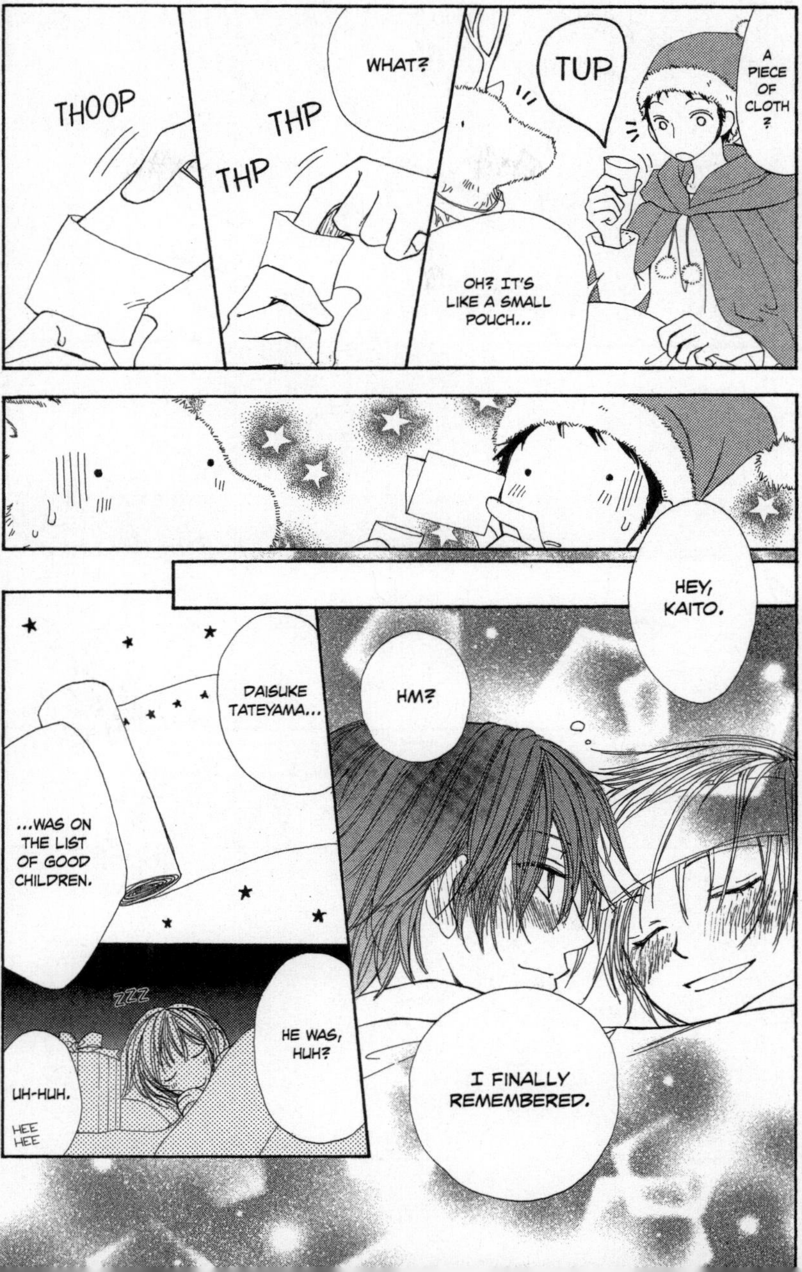
A PIECE OF CLOTH?
TUP
OH? IT'S LIKE A SMALL POUCH...
WHAT?
THP
THP
THOOP
HEY, KAITO.
HM?
I FINALLY REMEMBERED.
DAISUKE TATEYAMA...
...WAS ON THE LIST OF GOOD CHILDREN.
HE WAS, HUH?
ZZZ
UH-HUH.
HEE HEE

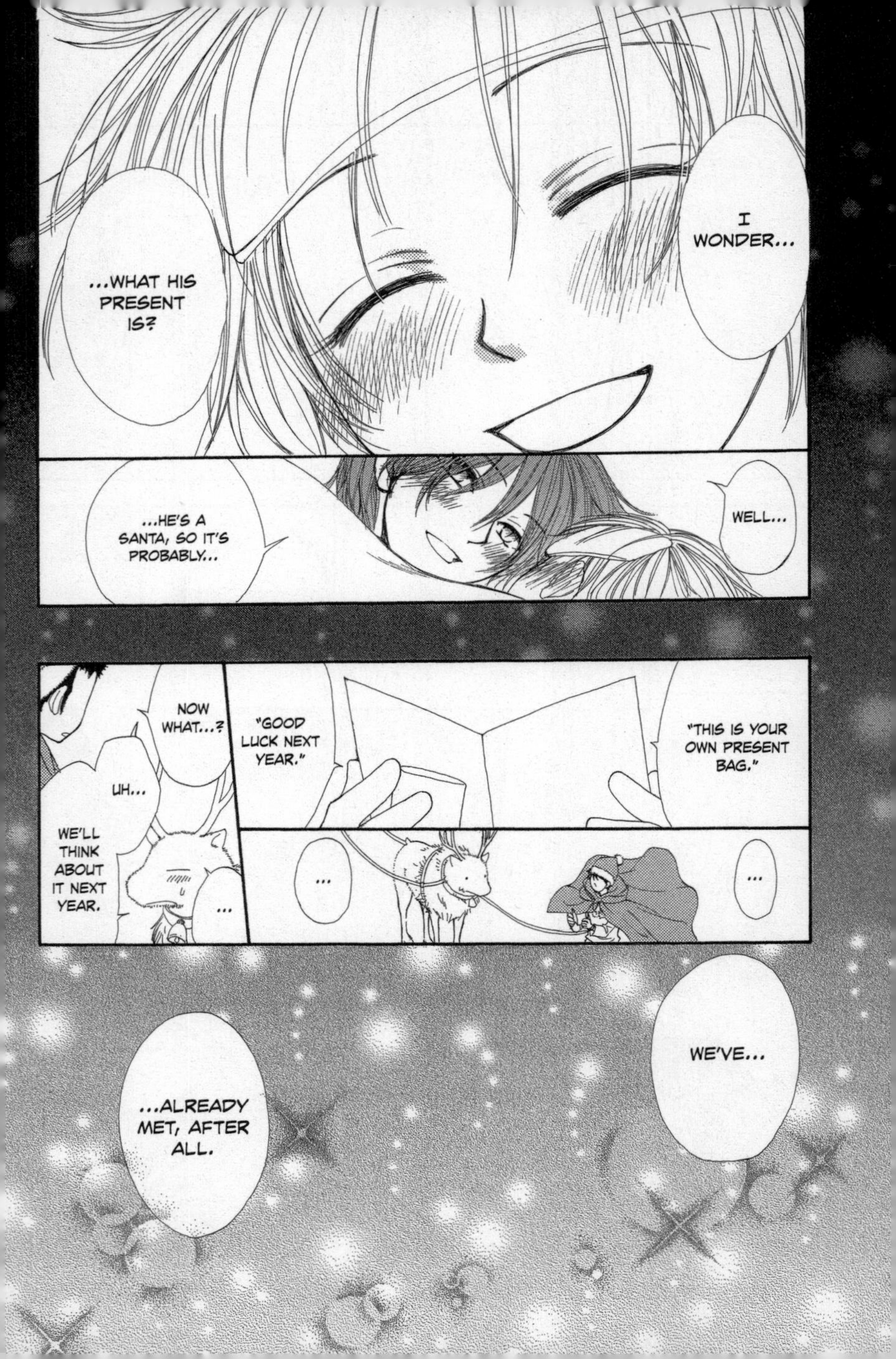
I WONDER...
...WHAT HIS PRESENT IS?
WELL...
...HE'S A SANTA, SO IT'S PROBABLY...
"THIS IS YOUR OWN PRESENT BAG."
"GOOD LUCK NEXT YEAR."
...
...
NOW WHAT...?
UH...
WE'LL THINK ABOUT IT NEXT YEAR.
...
WE'VE...
...ALREADY MET, AFTER ALL.

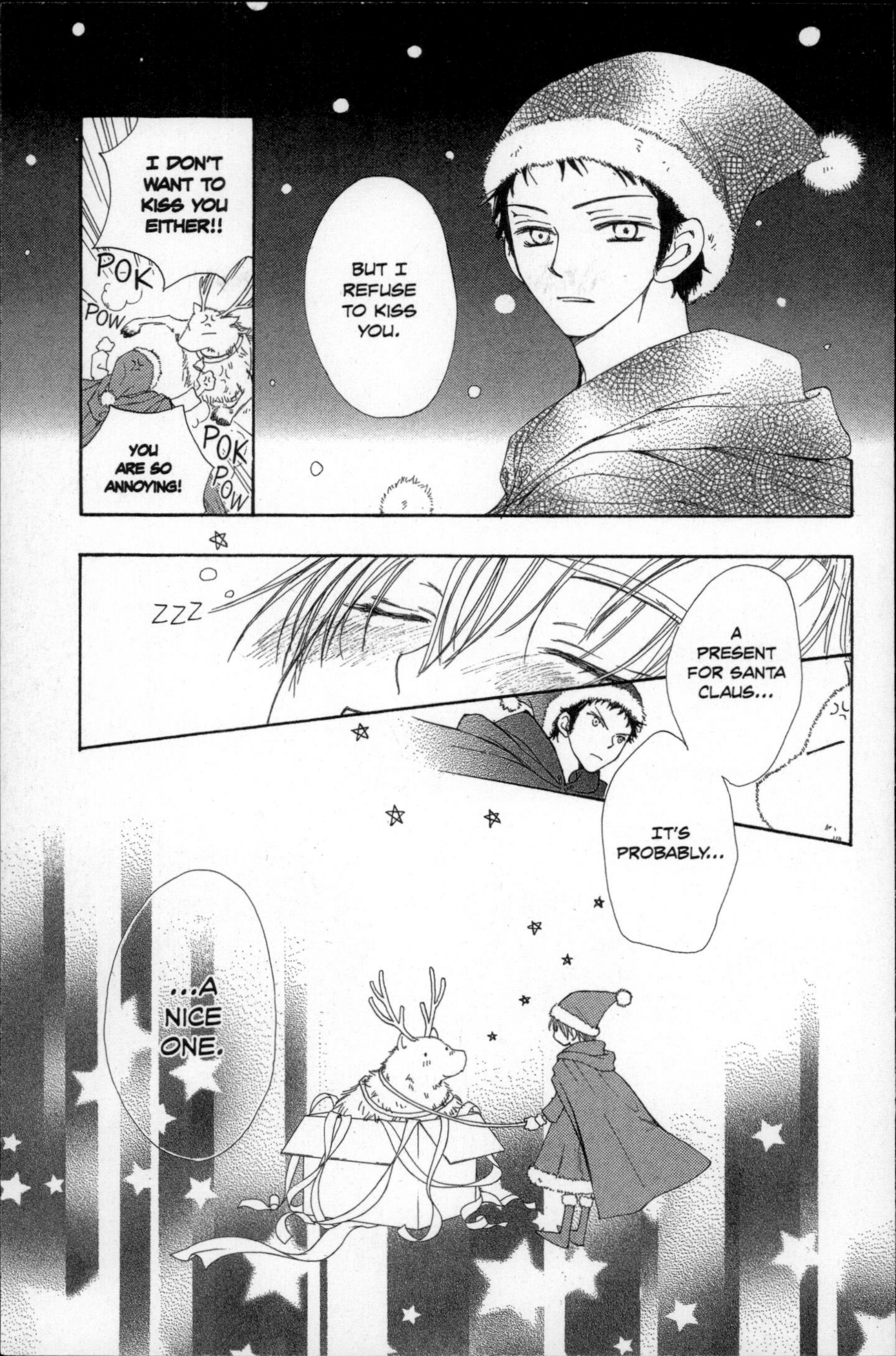
BUT I REFUSE TO KISS YOU.
I DON'T WANT TO KISS YOU EITHER!!
POK
POW
POK
POW
YOU ARE SO ANNOYING!
A PRESENT FOR SANTA CLAUS...
ZZZ
IT'S PROBABLY...
...A NICE ONE.

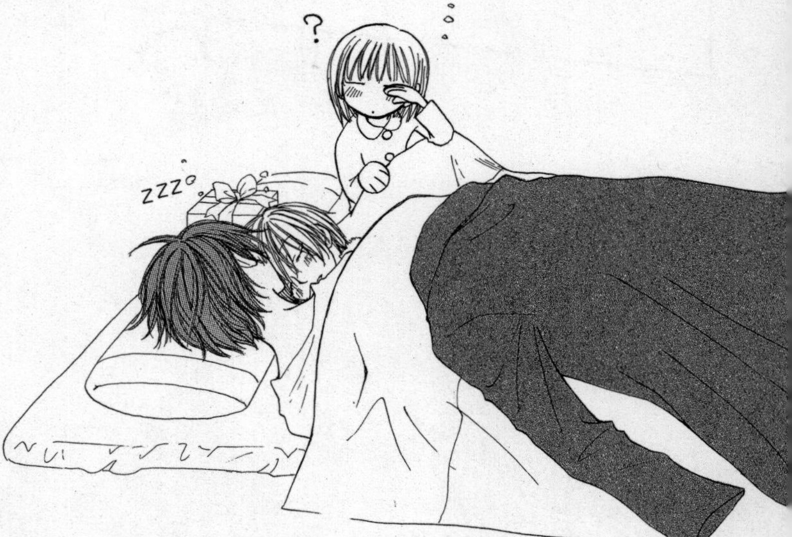
ZZZ

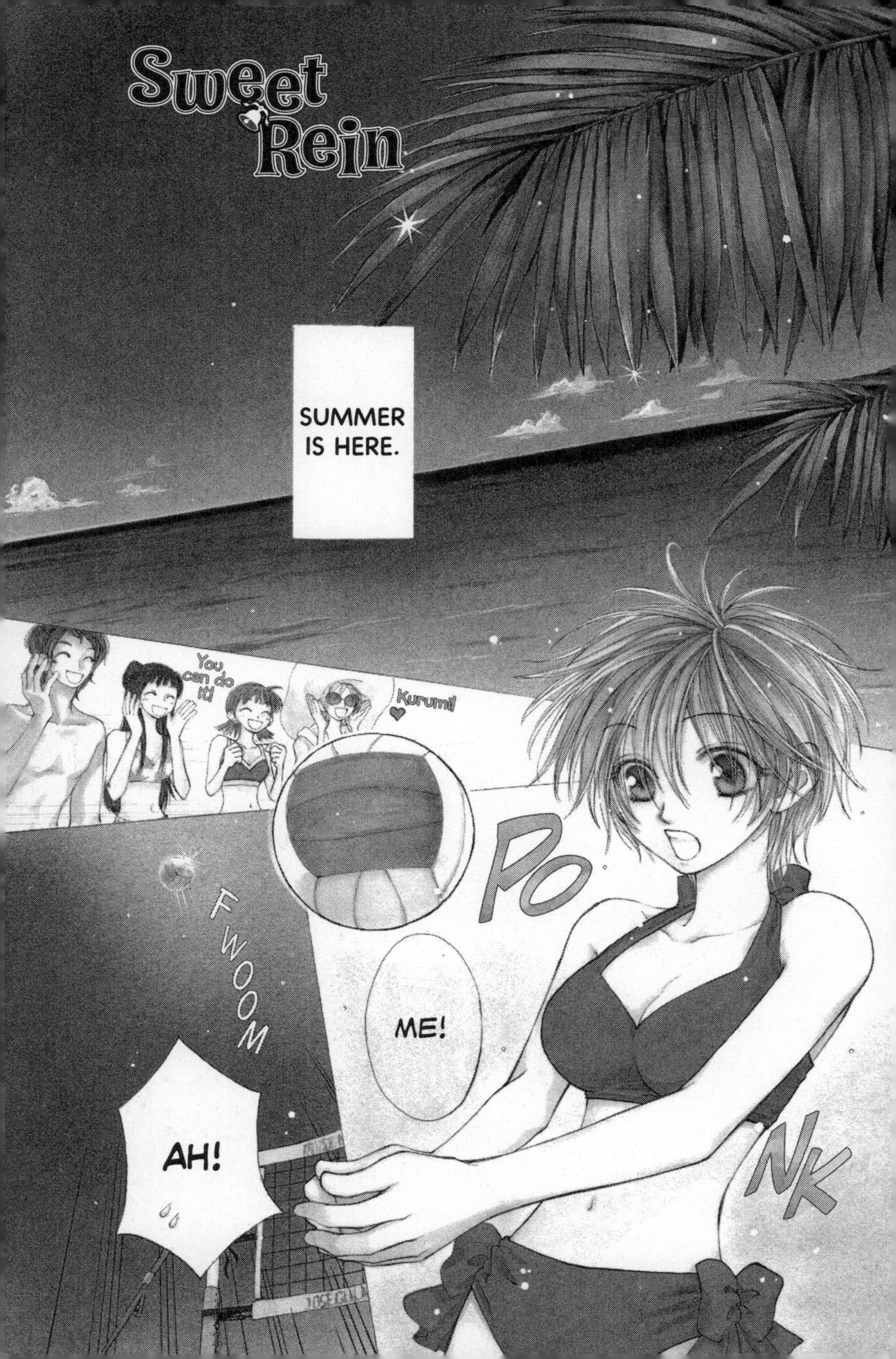
Sweet Rein
SUMMER IS HERE.
Kurumi! ♥
You can do it!
PO
NK
ME!
FWOOM
AH!

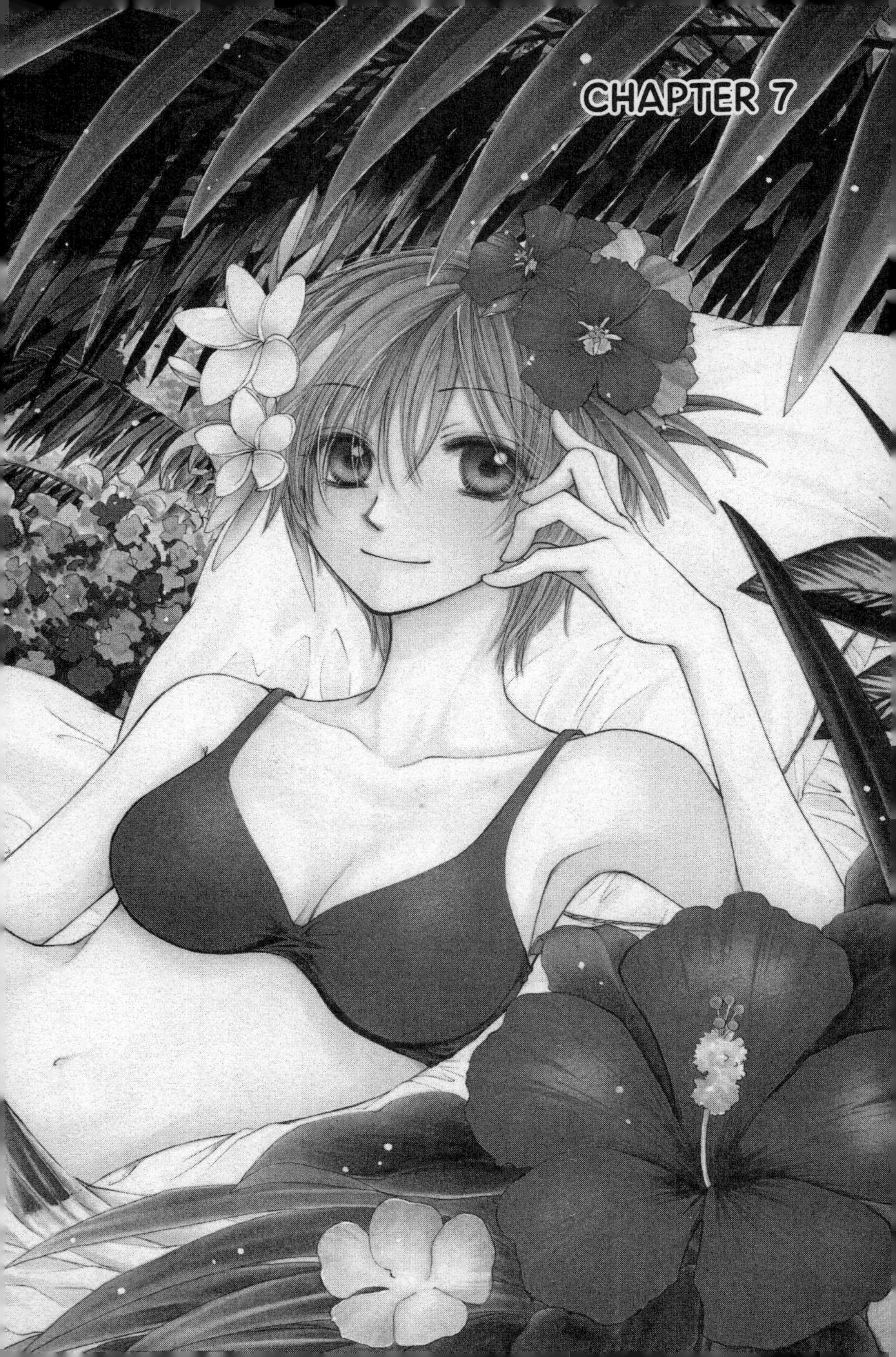
CHAPTER 7

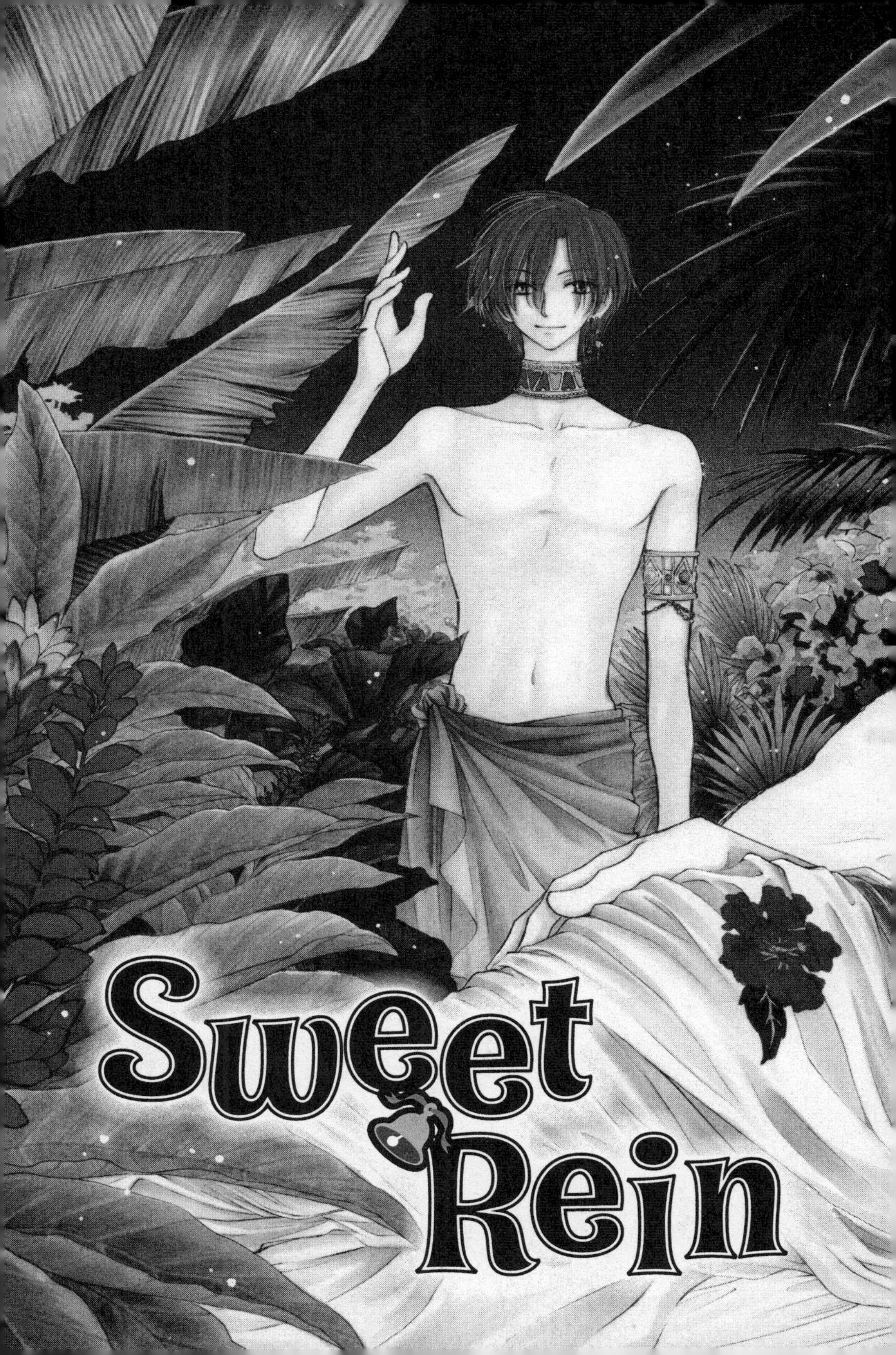
Sweet
Rein

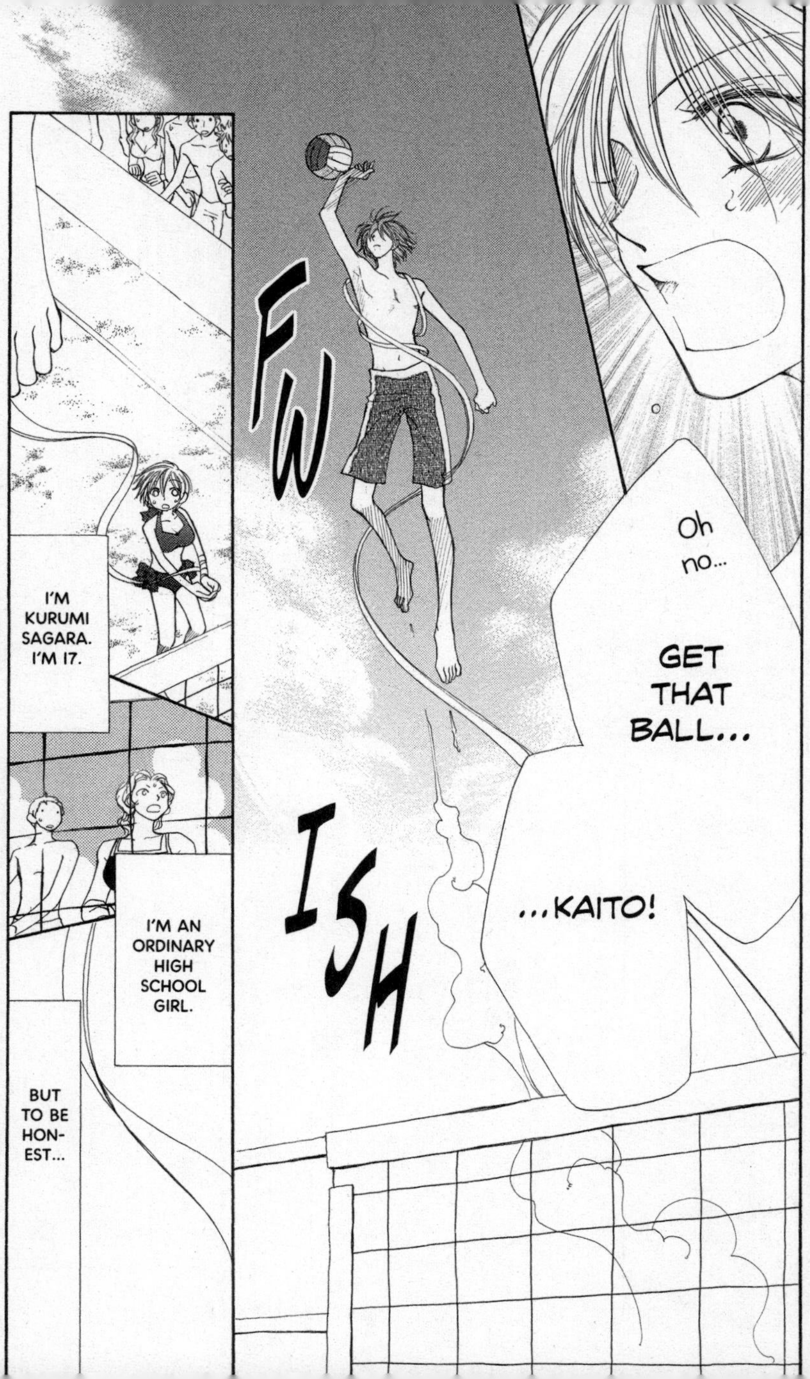
Oh no...
GET THAT BALL...
...KAITO!
FWISH
I'M KURUMI SAGARA. I'M 17.
I'M AN ORDINARY HIGH SCHOOL GIRL.
BUT TO BE HONEST...

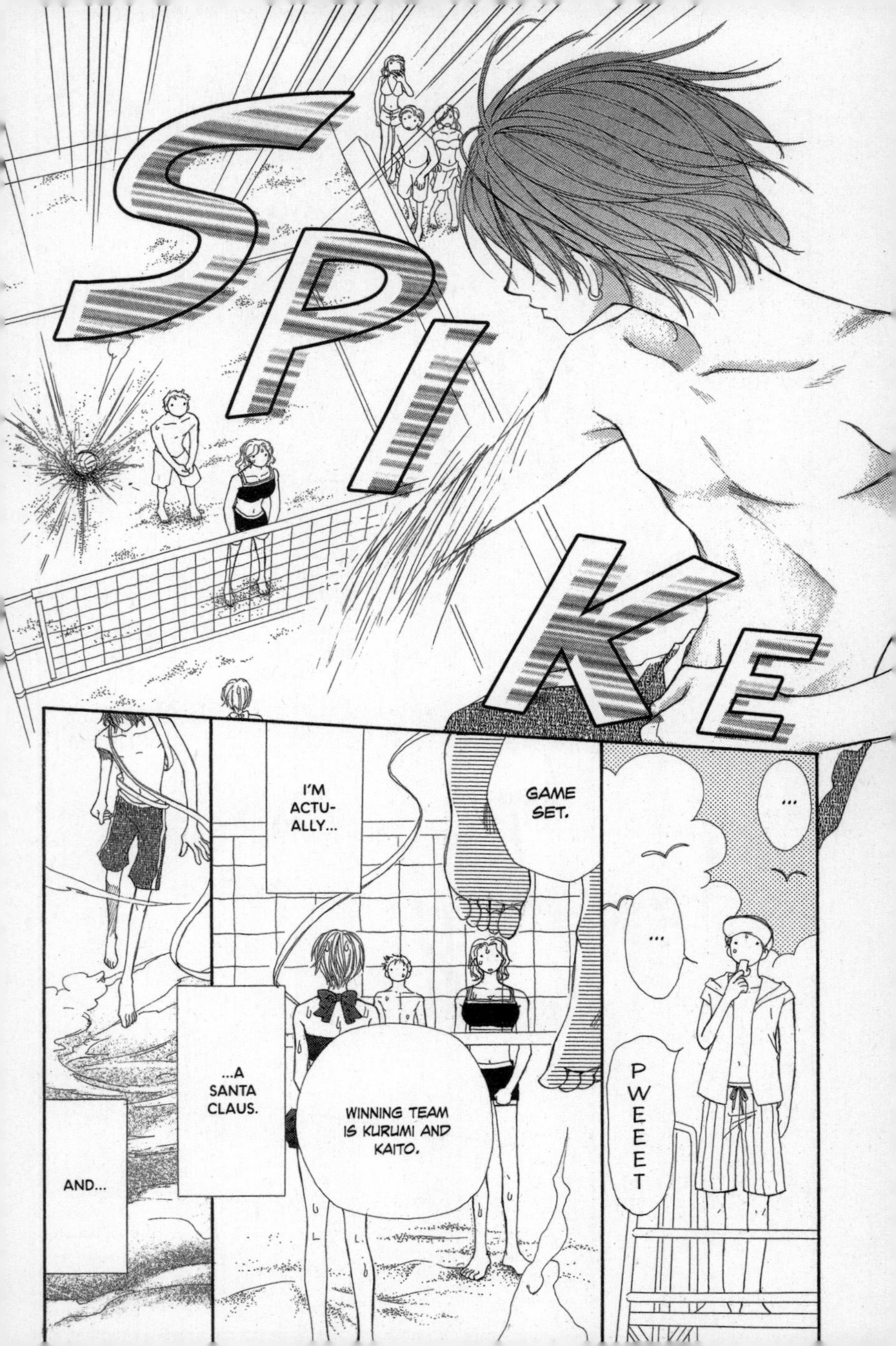
SPIKE
...
...
PWEEET
GAME SET.
I'M ACTUALLY...
WINNING TEAM IS KURUMI AND KAITO.
...A SANTA CLAUS.
AND...

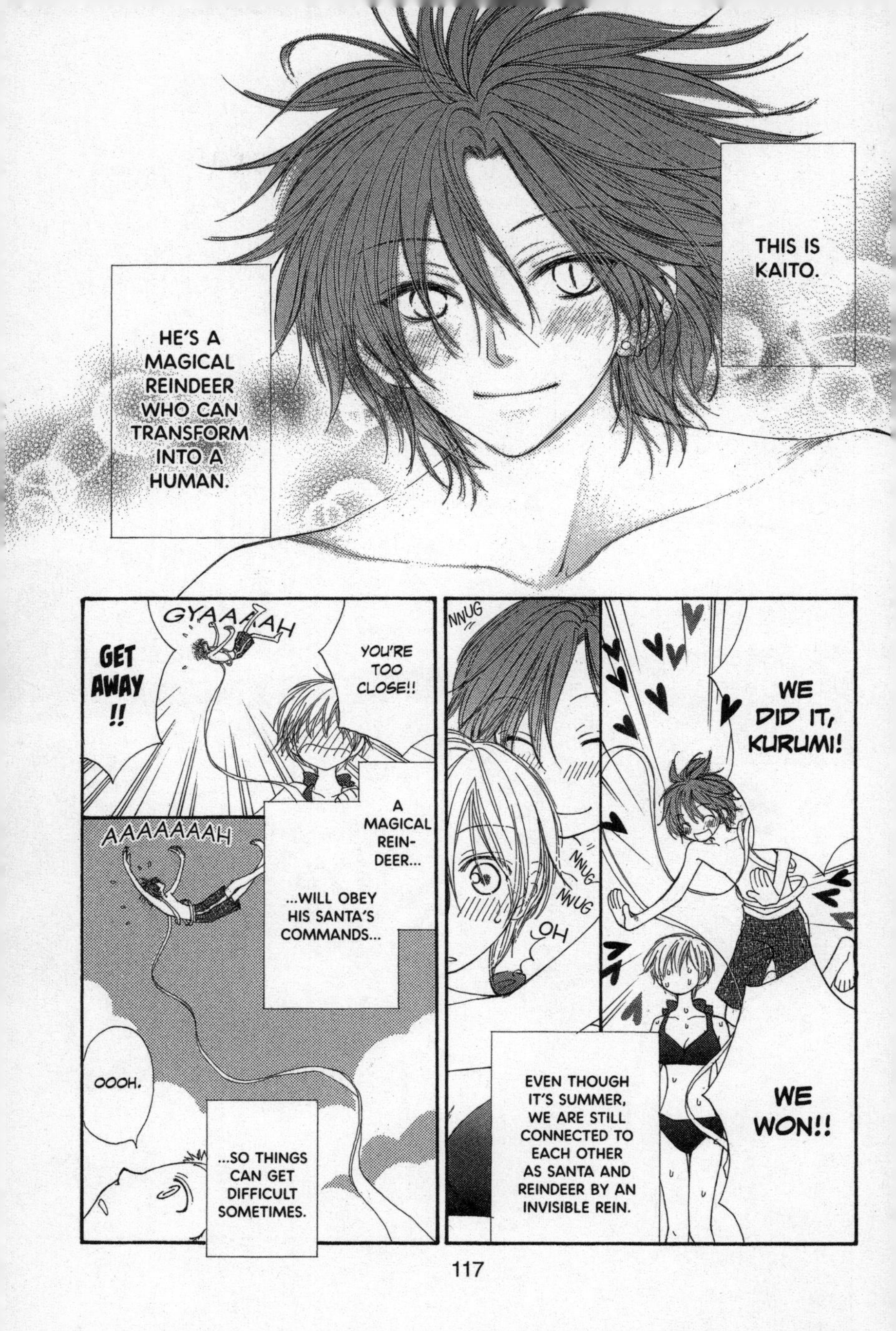
THIS IS KAITO.
HE'S A MAGICAL REINDEER WHO CAN TRANSFORM INTO A HUMAN.
WE DID IT, KURUMI!
NNUG
NNUG
NNUG
OH
WE WON!!
EVEN THOUGH IT'S SUMMER, WE ARE STILL CONNECTED TO EACH OTHER AS SANTA AND REINDEER BY AN INVISIBLE REIN.
GYAAAAAH
YOU'RE TOO CLOSE!!
GET AWAY!!
A MAGICAL REIN-DEER...
...WILL OBEY HIS SANTA'S COMMANDS...
AAAAAAAH
OOOH.
...SO THINGS CAN GET DIFFICULT SOMETIMES.

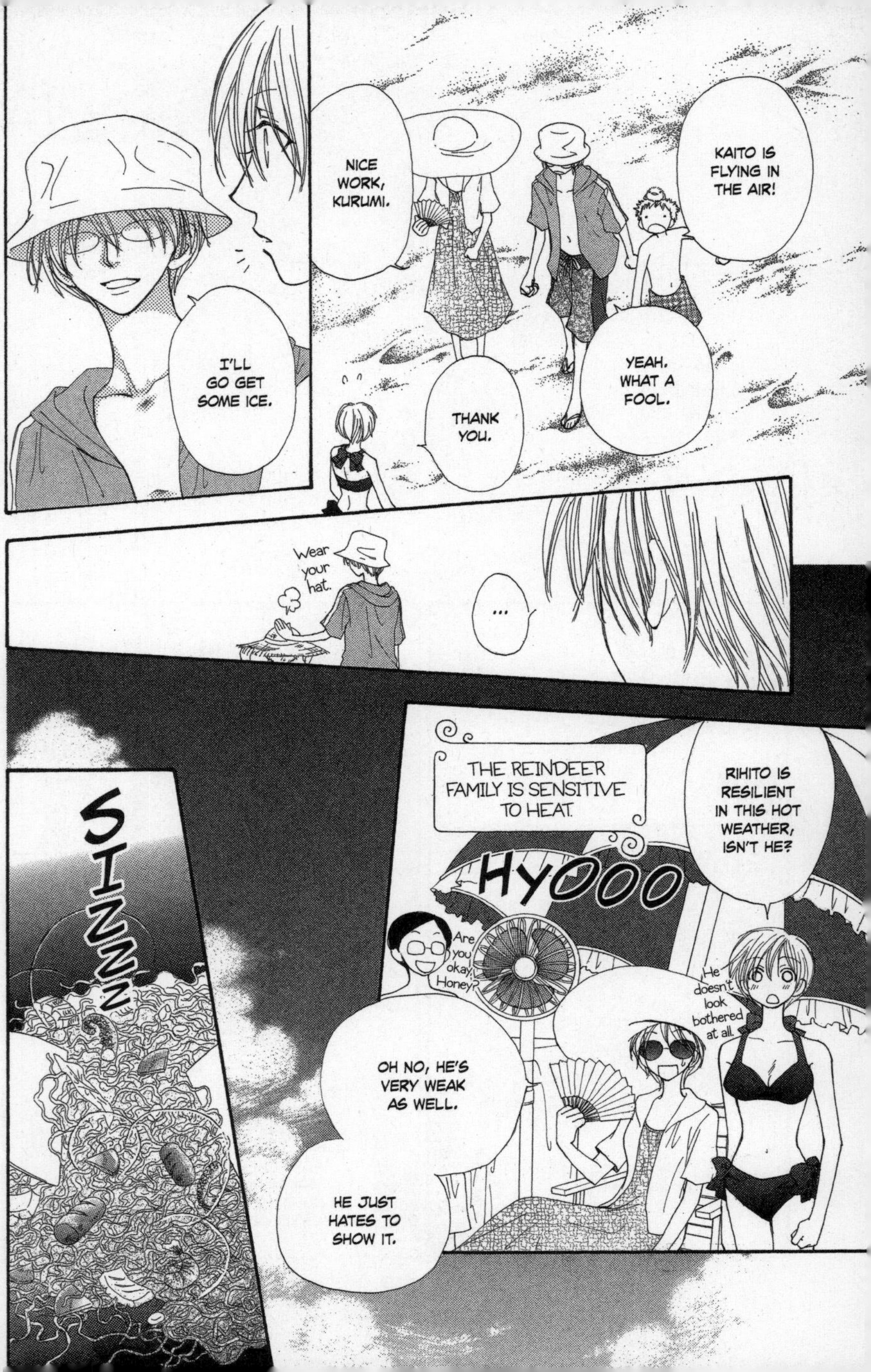
KAITO IS FLYING IN THE AIR!
NICE WORK, KURUMI.
YEAH. WHAT A FOOL.
THANK YOU.
I'LL GO GET SOME ICE.
...
Wear your hat.
THE REINDEER FAMILY IS SENSITIVE TO HEAT.
RIHITO IS RESILIENT IN THIS HOT WEATHER, ISN'T HE?
HYOOO
Are you okay, Honey?
He doesn't look bothered at all.
OH NO, HE'S VERY WEAK AS WELL.
HE JUST HATES TO SHOW IT.
SIZZZ

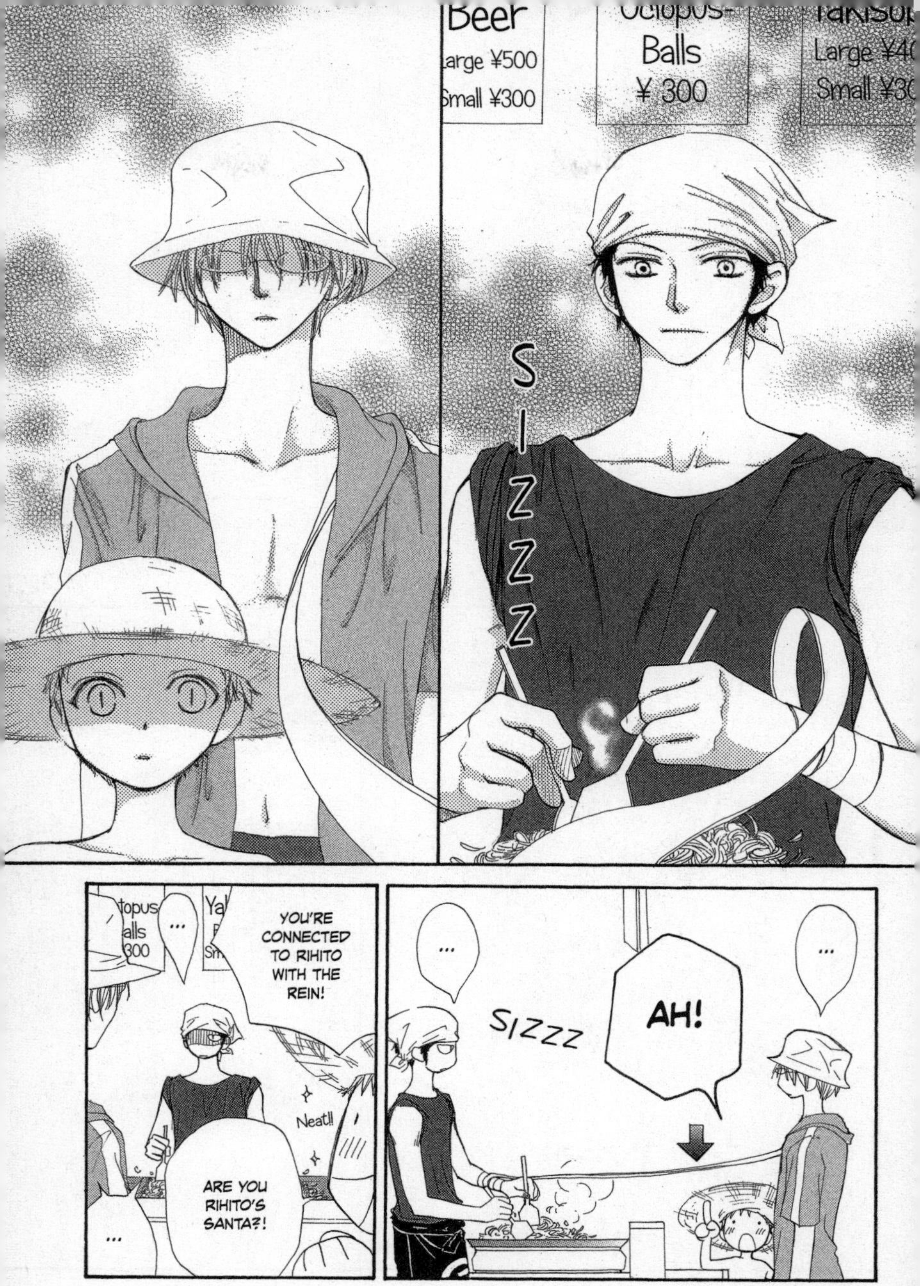
Balls
¥ 300
SIZZZ
Beer
Small ¥300
...
AH!
SIZZZ
...
YOU'RE CONNECTED TO RIHITO WITH THE REIN!
...
Neat!!
ARE YOU RIHITO'S SANTA?!
...

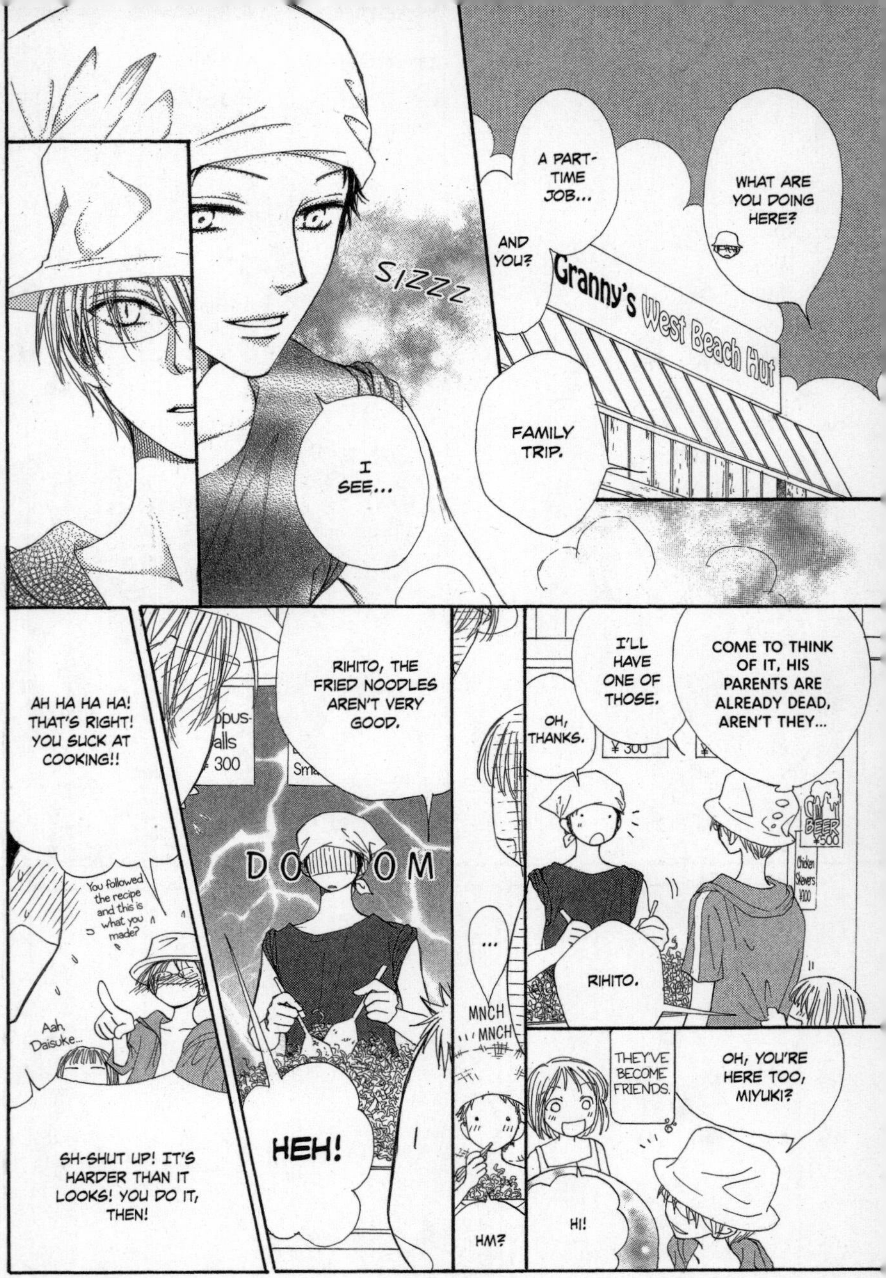
WHAT ARE YOU DOING HERE?
A PART-TIME JOB...
AND YOU?
Granny's West Beach Hut
FAMILY TRIP.
SIZZZ
I SEE...
COME TO THINK OF IT, HIS PARENTS ARE ALREADY DEAD, AREN'T THEY...
I'LL HAVE ONE OF THOSE.
OH, THANKS.
¥300
BEER ¥500
Chicken Skewers ¥100
RIHITO.
OH, YOU'RE HERE TOO, MIYUKI?
THEY'VE BECOME FRIENDS.
HI!
HM?
...
MNCH MNCH
RIHITO, THE FRIED NOODLES AREN'T VERY GOOD.
DO OM
HEH!
AH HA HA HA! THAT'S RIGHT! YOU SUCK AT COOKING!!
You followed the recipe and this is what you made?
Aah, Daisuke...
SH-SHUT UP! IT'S HARDER THAN IT LOOKS! YOU DO IT, THEN!

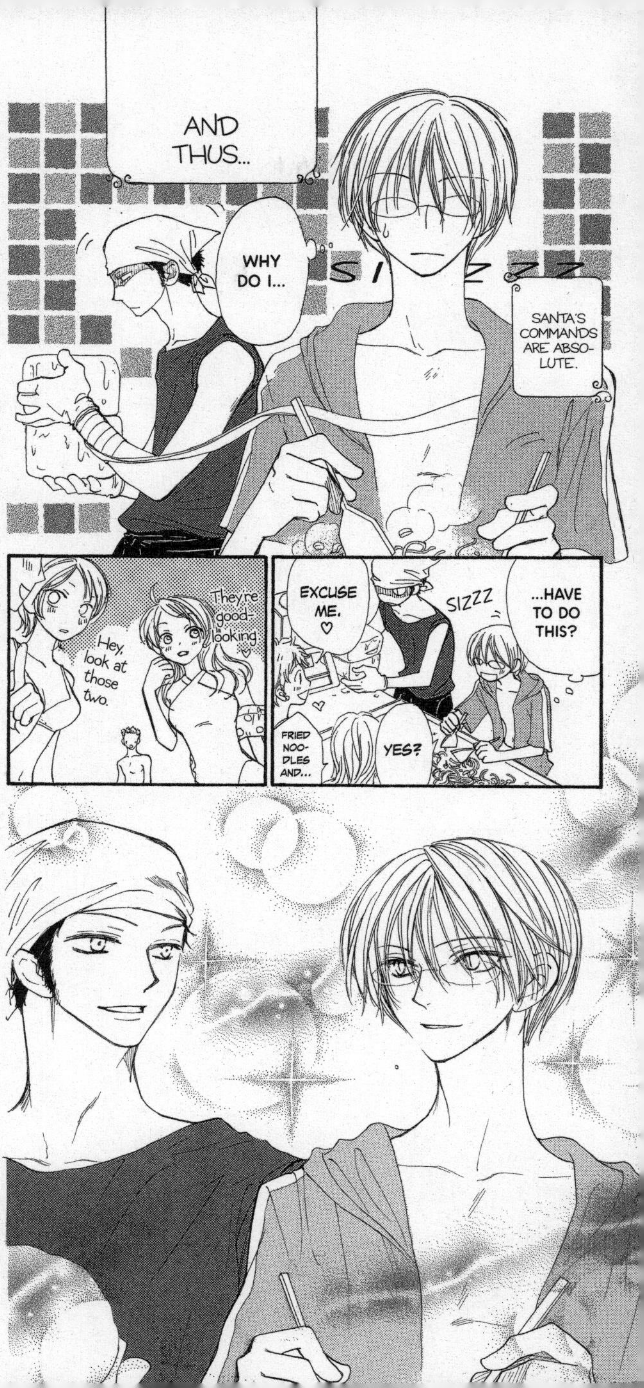
AND THUS...
SANTA'S COMMANDS ARE ABSO-LUTE.
WHY DO I...
...HAVE TO DO THIS?
SIZZZ
EXCUSE ME. ♡
YES?
FRIED NOO-DLES AND...
They're good-looking.
Hey, look at those two.

1/4 Sakura Mail

Part 7

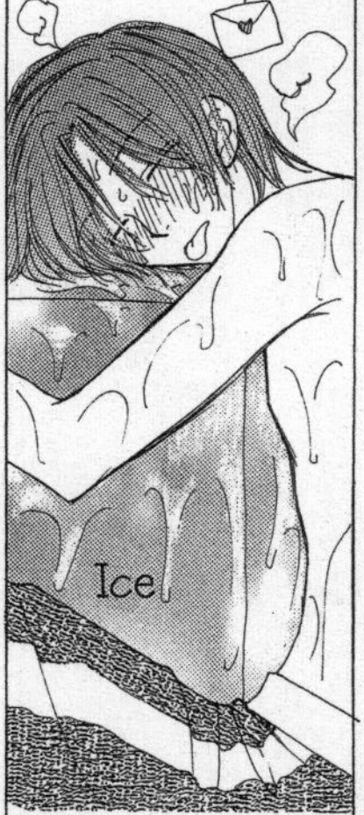
Ice

Another summer story yet again. And if it's about summer, it must have the sea!! So I had them come to swim in the sea again. It's fun to draw naked bodies!! Sooo much fun!! This chapter is filled with muscles. Tateyama is muscular, so I had a very enjoyable time drawing him.

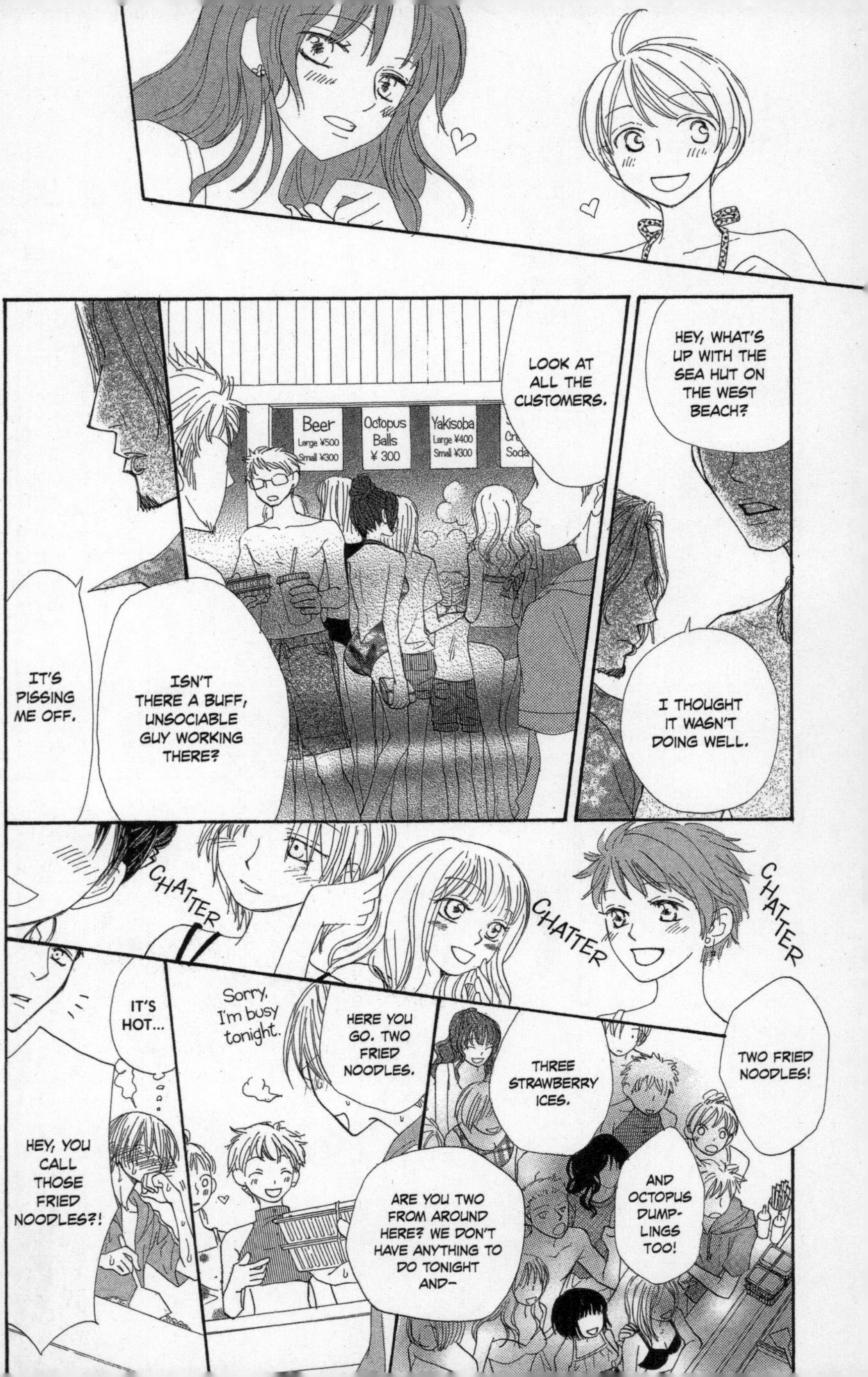
HEY, WHAT'S UP WITH THE SEA HUT ON THE WEST BEACH?
I THOUGHT IT WASN'T DOING WELL.
LOOK AT ALL THE CUSTOMERS.
Beer Large ¥500 Small ¥300
Octopus Balls ¥ 300
Yakisoba Large ¥400 Small ¥300
ISN'T THERE A BUFF, UNSOCIABLE GUY WORKING THERE?
IT'S PISSING ME OFF.
CHATTER
CHATTER
CHATTER
TWO FRIED NOODLES!
THREE STRAWBERRY ICES.
AND OCTOPUS DUMP-LINGS TOO!
ARE YOU TWO FROM AROUND HERE? WE DON'T HAVE ANYTHING TO DO TONIGHT AND-
HERE YOU GO. TWO FRIED NOODLES.
Sorry, I'm busy tonight.
IT'S HOT...
HEY, YOU CALL THOSE FRIED NOODLES?!

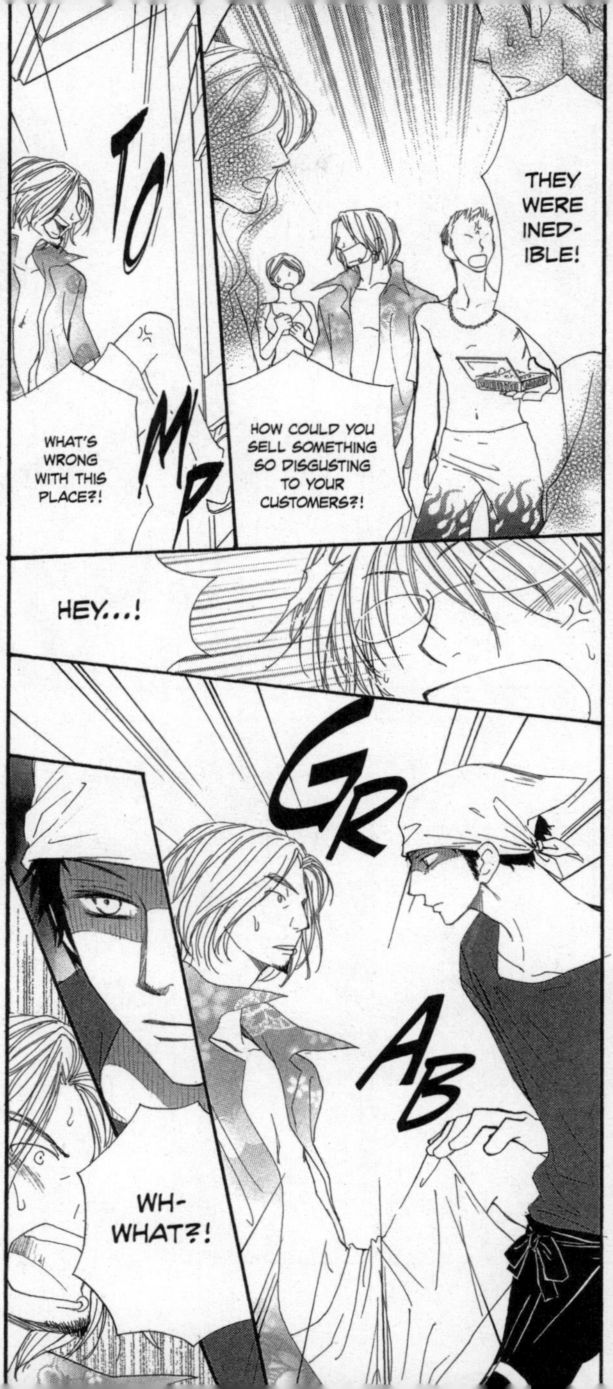
THEY WERE INED-IBLE!
HOW COULD YOU SELL SOMETHING SO DISGUSTING TO YOUR CUSTOMERS?!
TOMP
WHAT'S WRONG WITH THIS PLACE?!
HEY...!
GRAB
WH-WHAT?!

1/4 Sakura Mail

Part 8

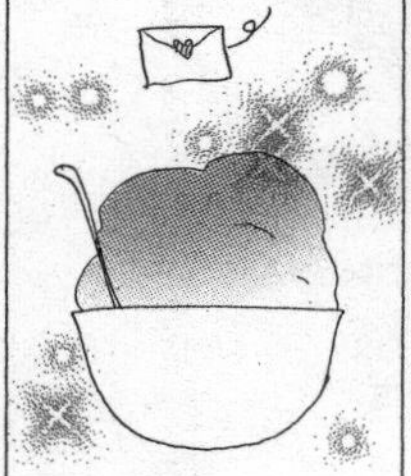

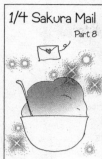

Tateyama is working part-time at the beach hut in this chapter. His boss at the construction site is related to the owners of the beach hut, and he asked Tateyama to help out there during the summer. His little sister Miyuki is really enjoying the vacation at the beach. Miyuki doesn't really care about her brother and Rihito not getting along, and she has grown very fond of Rihito. Daisuke often calls Rihito unintentionally, and Rihito has become Miyuki's favorite because he will always play with her.

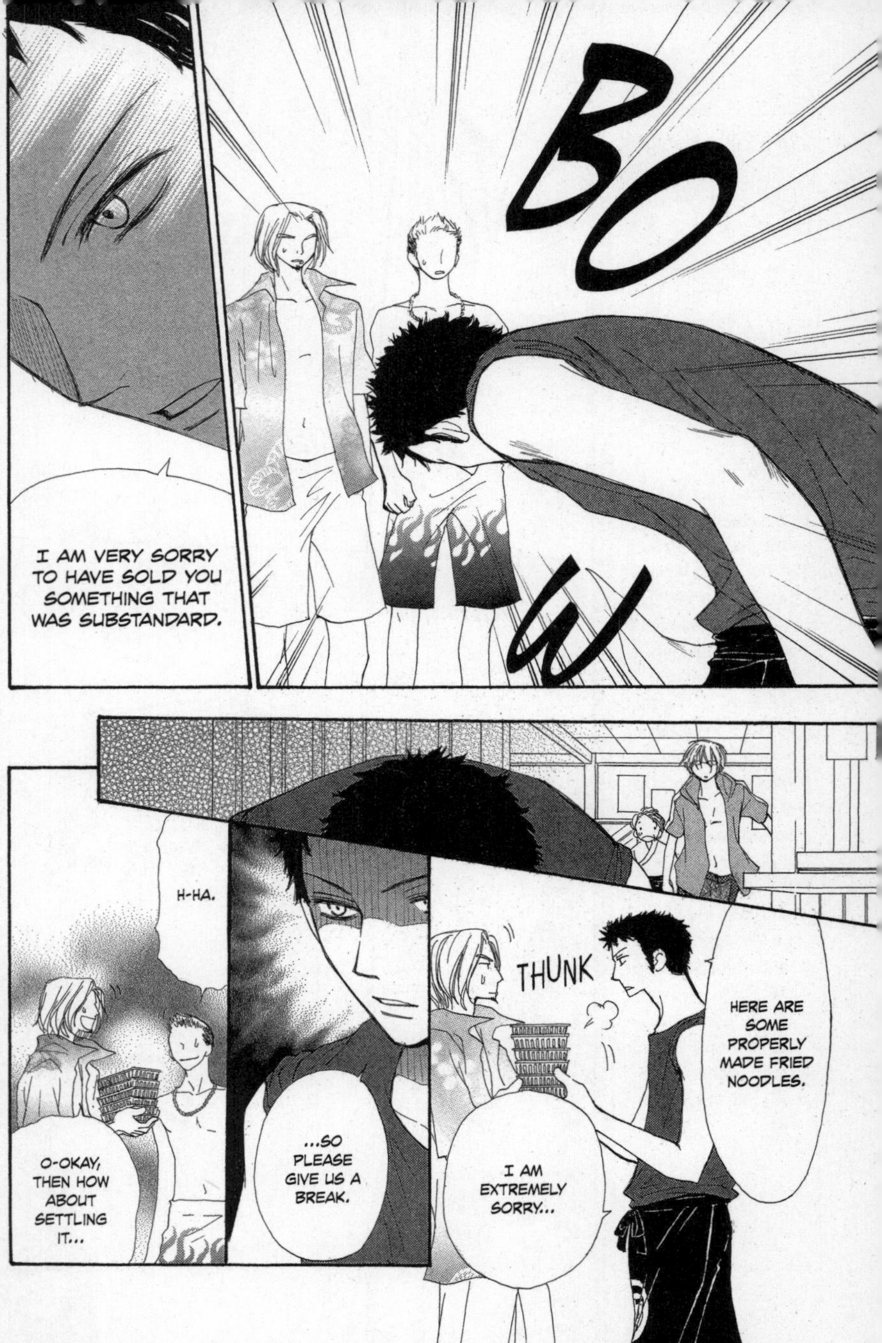
BOW
I AM VERY SORRY TO HAVE SOLD YOU SOMETHING THAT WAS SUBSTANDARD.
HERE ARE SOME PROPERLY MADE FRIED NOODLES.
THUNK
I AM EXTREMELY SORRY...
...SO PLEASE GIVE US A BREAK.
H-HA.
O-OKAY, THEN HOW ABOUT SETTLING IT...

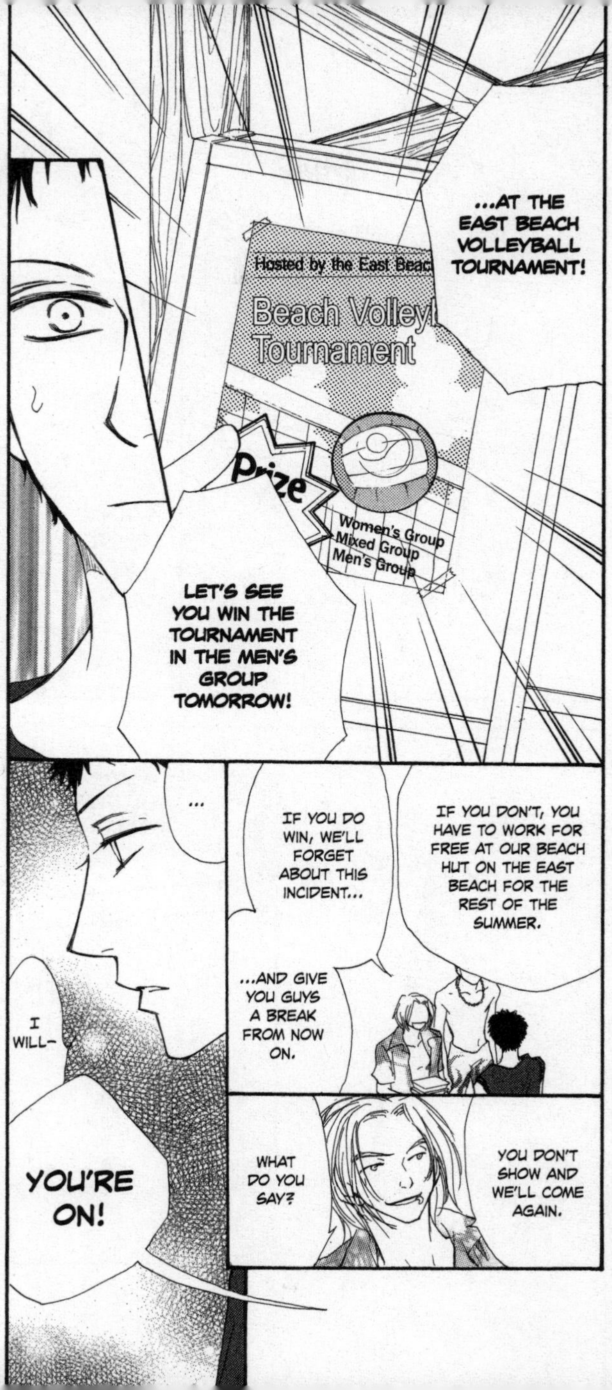
...AT THE EAST BEACH VOLLEYBALL TOURNAMENT!
Hosted by the East Beac
Beach Volley
Tournament
Prize
Women's Group
Mixed Group
Men's Group
LET'S SEE YOU WIN THE TOURNAMENT IN THE MEN'S GROUP TOMORROW!
IF YOU DON'T, YOU HAVE TO WORK FOR FREE AT OUR BEACH HUT ON THE EAST BEACH FOR THE REST OF THE SUMMER.
IF YOU DO WIN, WE'LL FORGET ABOUT THIS INCIDENT...
...AND GIVE YOU GUYS A BREAK FROM NOW ON.
YOU DON'T SHOW AND WE'LL COME AGAIN.
WHAT DO YOU SAY?
...
I WILL-
YOU'RE ON!

1/4 Sakura Mail

Part 9

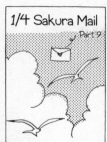

Since Rihito and Daisuke both have younger siblings, I have a habit of calling them "oni-chan." I tell my assistants, "paste the #30 screentone on oni-chan," which confuses them because they don't know which oni-chan I'm talking about. The boys haven't called each other by name in the story either... This is a summer story, so I had them call each other by their roles. But I would like to have them call each other by name sooner or later.

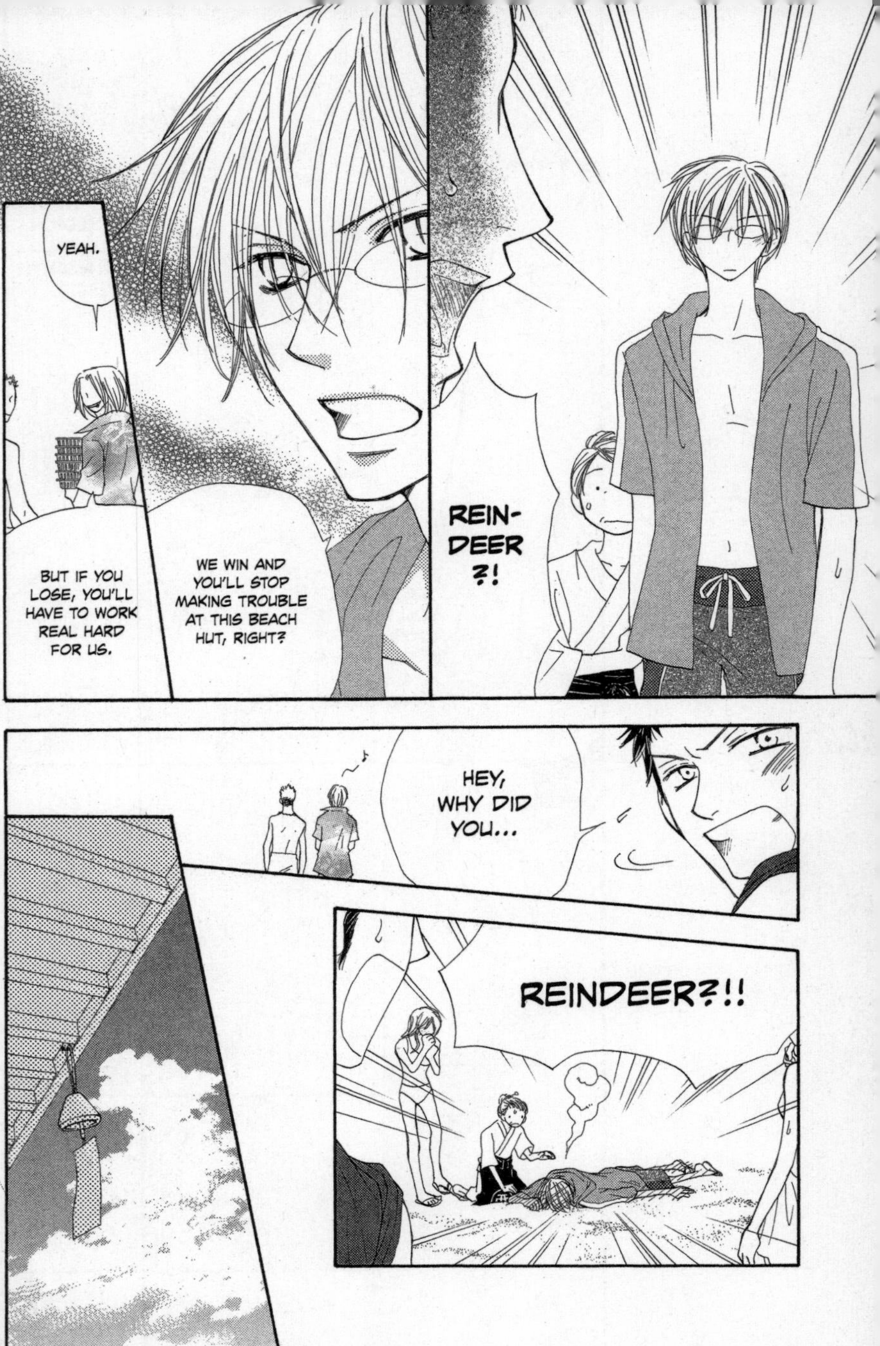
REIN-
DEER
?!
WE WIN AND YOU'LL STOP MAKING TROUBLE AT THIS BEACH HUT, RIGHT?
YEAH.
BUT IF YOU LOSE, YOU'LL HAVE TO WORK REAL HARD FOR US.
HEY, WHY DID YOU...
REINDEER?!!

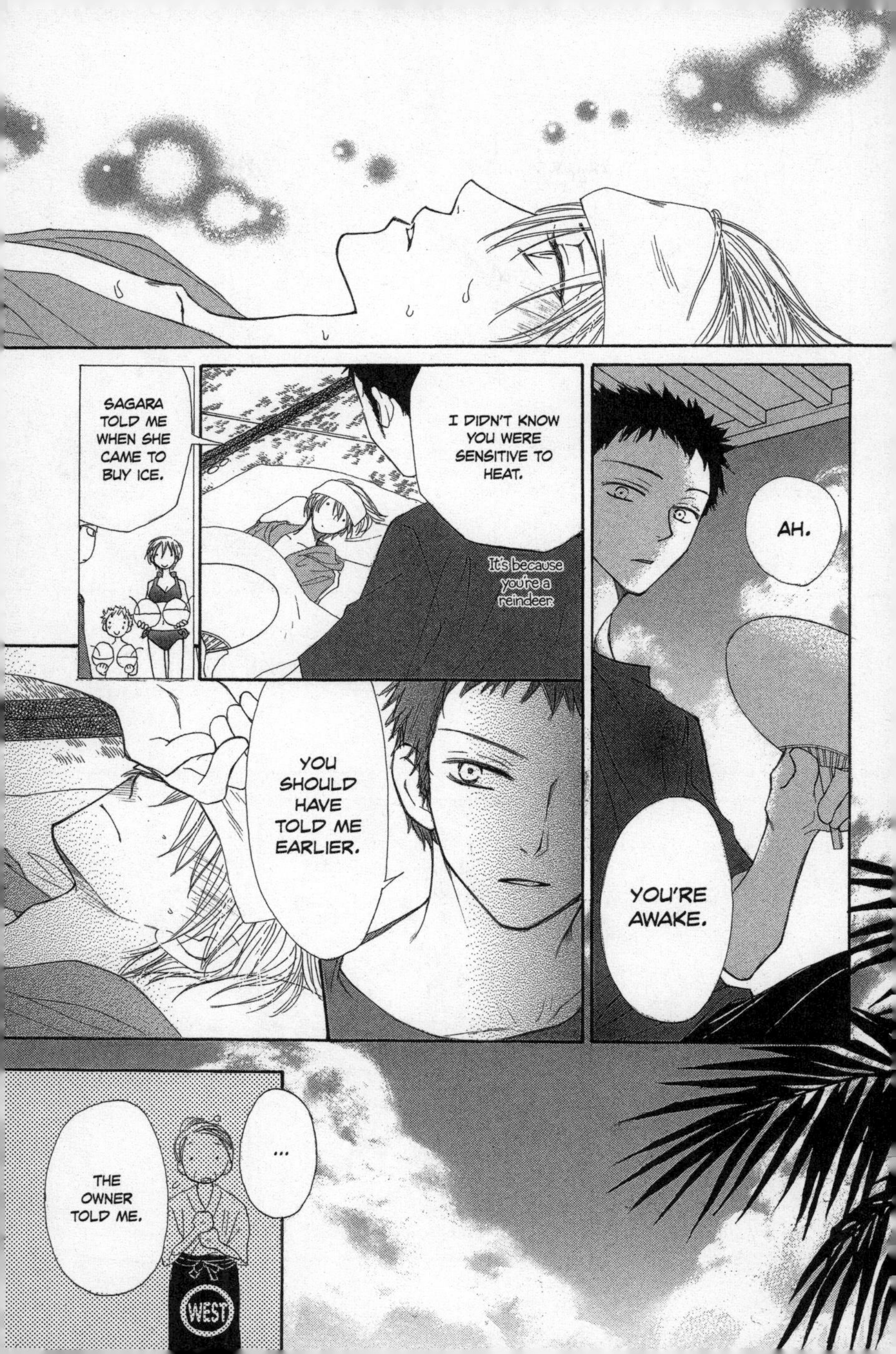
AH.
YOU'RE AWAKE.
I DIDN'T KNOW YOU WERE SENSITIVE TO HEAT.
It's because you're a reindeer.
SAGARA TOLD ME WHEN SHE CAME TO BUY ICE.
YOU SHOULD HAVE TOLD ME EARLIER.
...
THE OWNER TOLD ME.
WEST

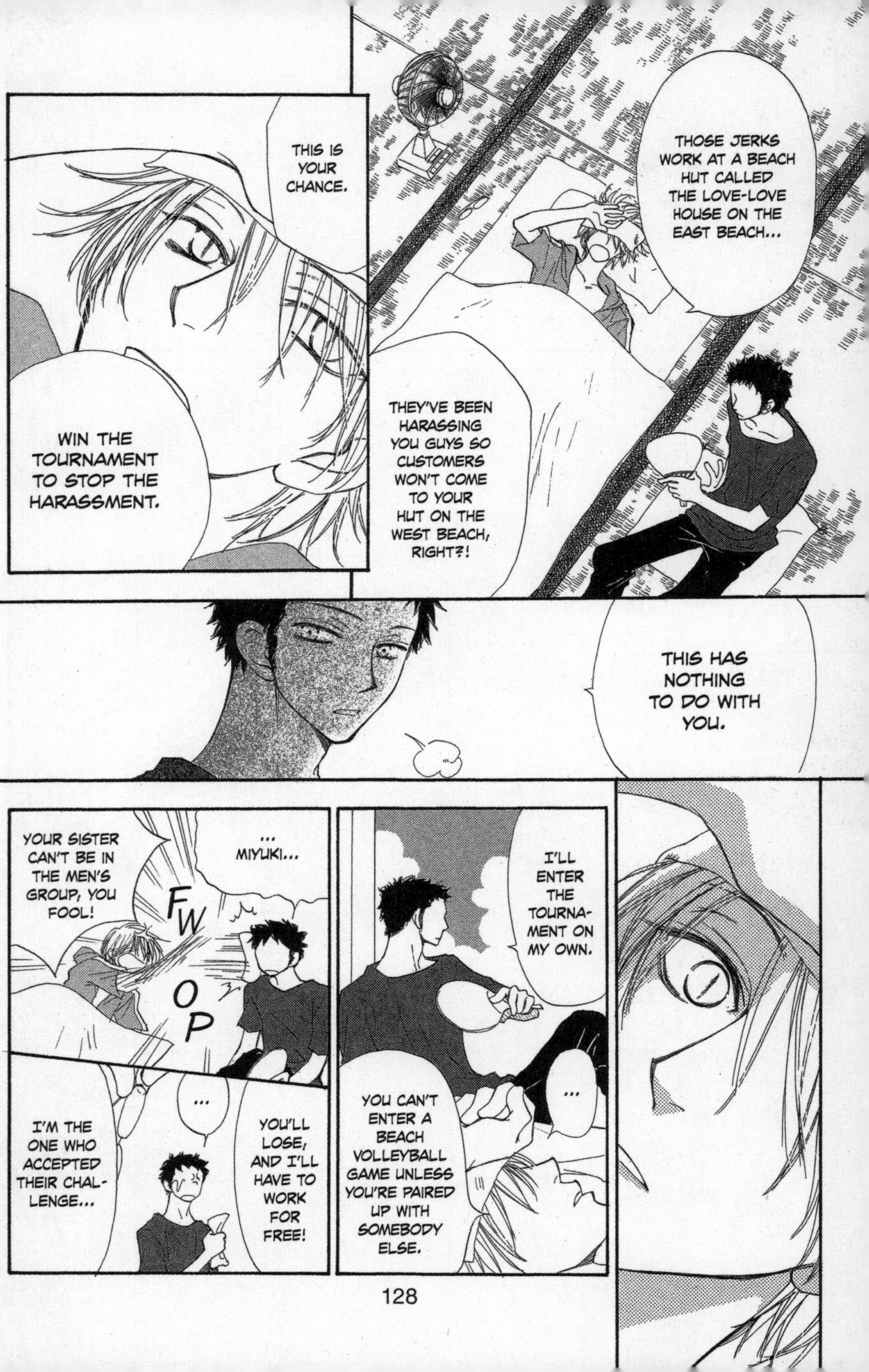
THOSE JERKS WORK AT A BEACH HUT CALLED THE LOVE-LOVE HOUSE ON THE EAST BEACH...
THEY'VE BEEN HARASSING YOU GUYS SO CUSTOMERS WON'T COME TO YOUR HUT ON THE WEST BEACH, RIGHT?!
THIS IS YOUR CHANCE.
WIN THE TOURNAMENT TO STOP THE HARASSMENT.
THIS HAS NOTHING TO DO WITH YOU.
I'LL ENTER THE TOURNAMENT ON MY OWN.
... MIYUKI...
YOUR SISTER CAN'T BE IN THE MEN'S GROUP, YOU FOOL!
FWOP
...
YOU CAN'T ENTER A BEACH VOLLEYBALL GAME UNLESS YOU'RE PAIRED UP WITH SOMEBODY ELSE.
YOU'LL LOSE, AND I'LL HAVE TO WORK FOR FREE!
...
I'M THE ONE WHO ACCEPTED THEIR CHALLENGE...

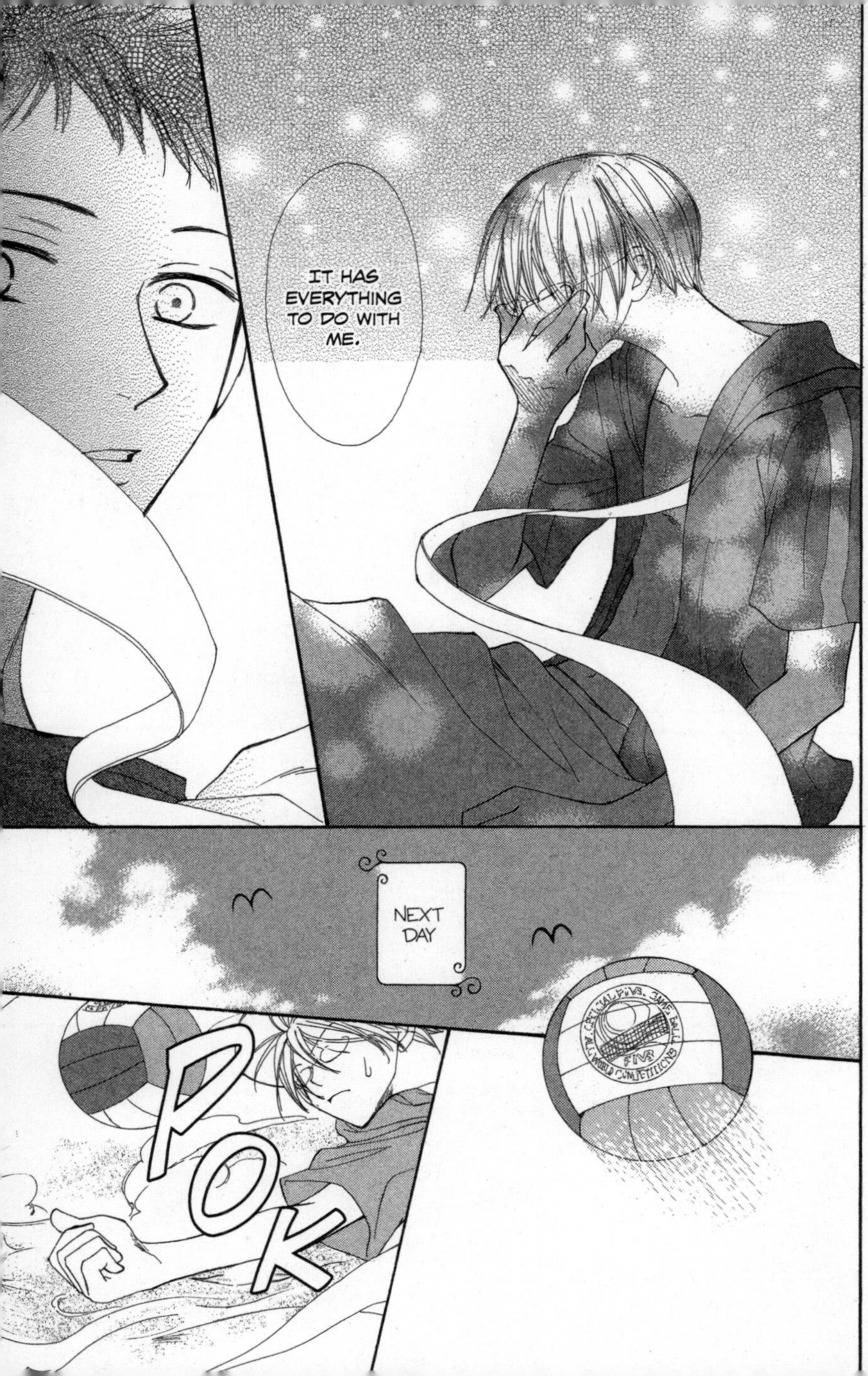
IT HAS EVERYTHING TO DO WITH ME.
NEXT DAY
POK

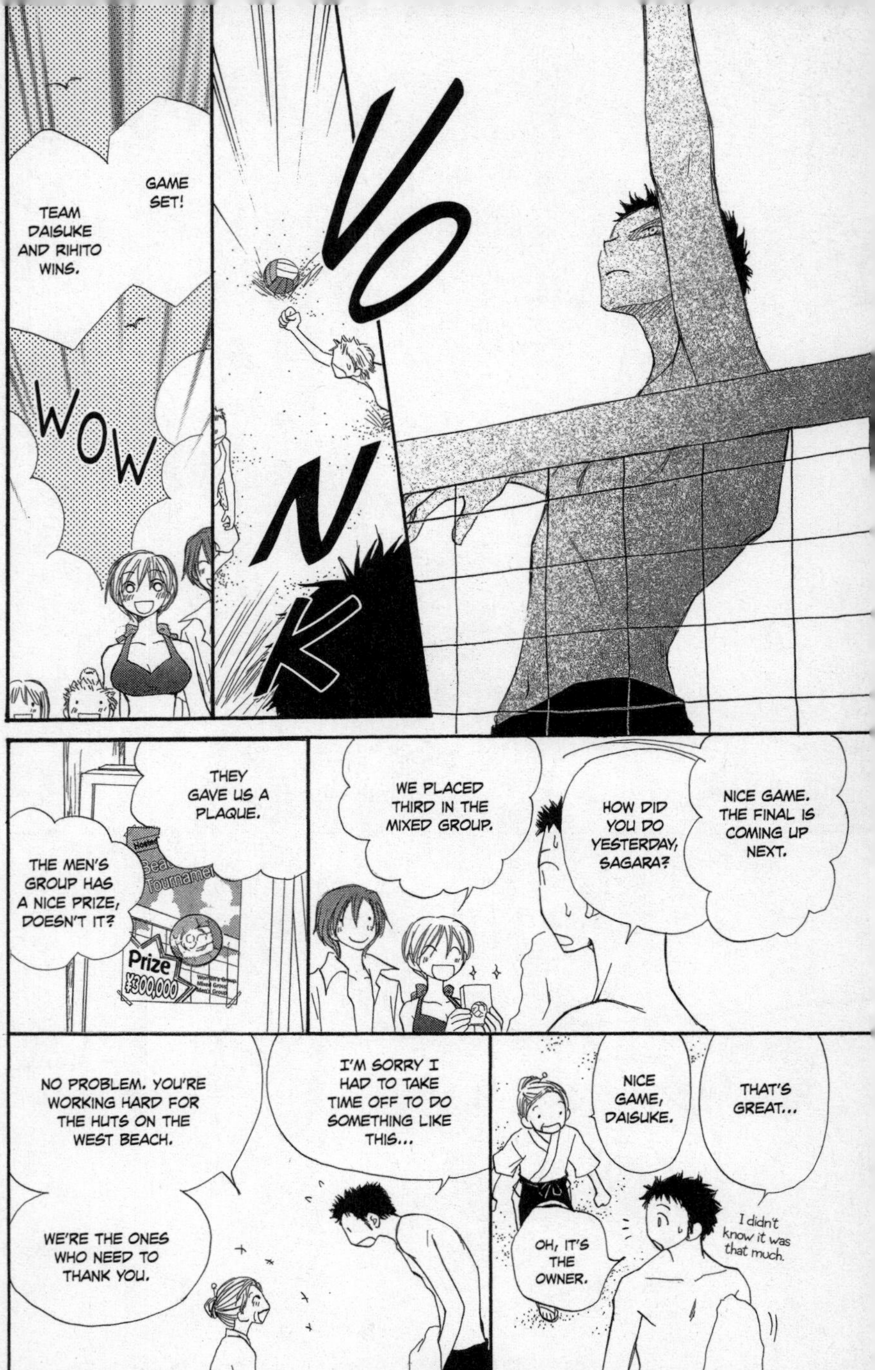
VONK
GAME SET!
TEAM DAISUKE AND RIHITO WINS.
WOW
NICE GAME. THE FINAL IS COMING UP NEXT.
HOW DID YOU DO YESTERDAY, SAGARA?
WE PLACED THIRD IN THE MIXED GROUP.
THEY GAVE US A PLAQUE.
THE MEN'S GROUP HAS A NICE PRIZE, DOESN'T IT?
Prize
¥300,000
THAT'S GREAT...
NICE GAME, DAISUKE.
I didn't know it was that much.
OH, IT'S THE OWNER.
I'M SORRY I HAD TO TAKE TIME OFF TO DO SOMETHING LIKE THIS...
NO PROBLEM. YOU'RE WORKING HARD FOR THE HUTS ON THE WEST BEACH.
WE'RE THE ONES WHO NEED TO THANK YOU.

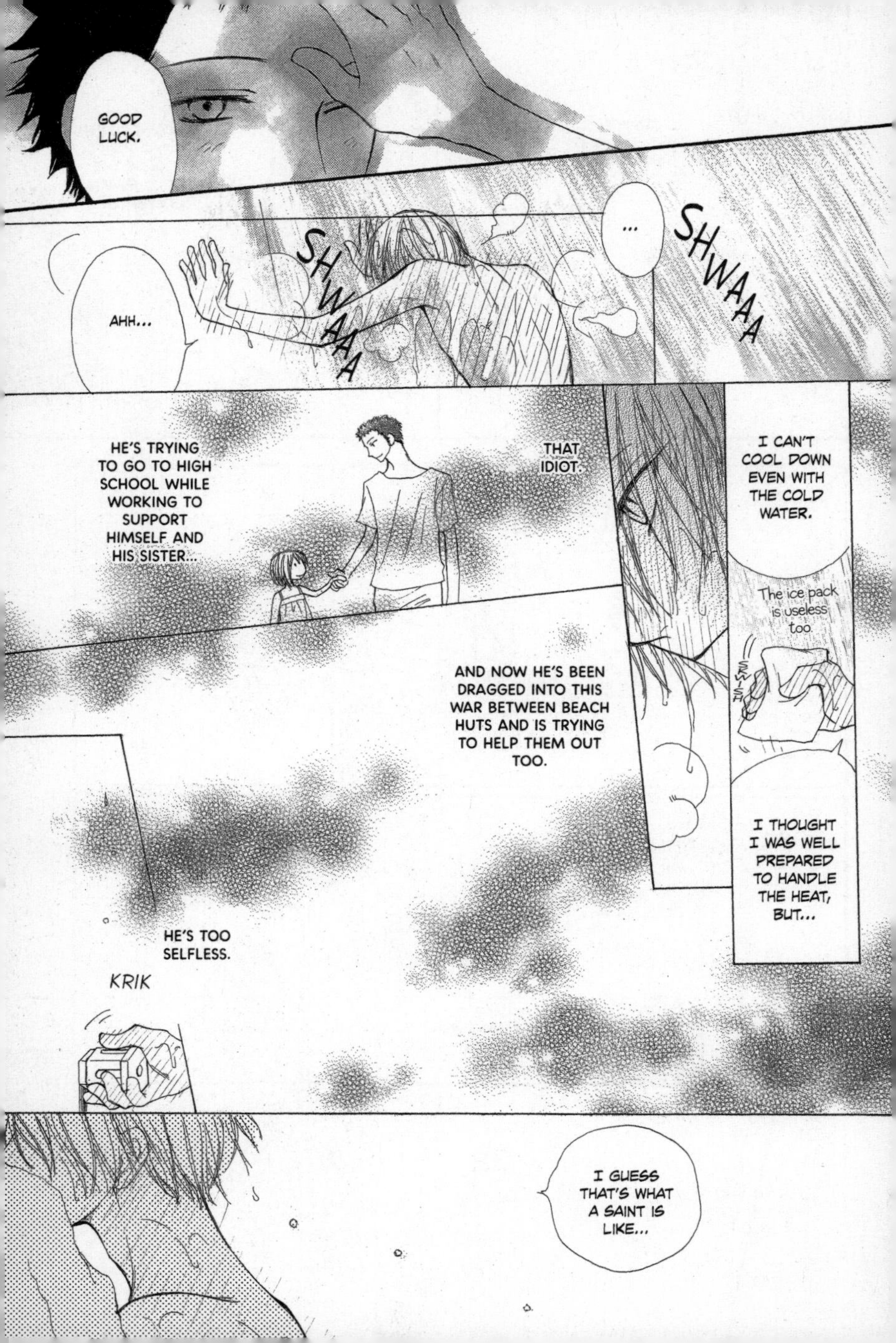
GOOD LUCK.
SHWAAA
...
SHWAAA
AHH...
I CAN'T COOL DOWN EVEN WITH THE COLD WATER.
The ice pack is useless too.
SWISH
I THOUGHT I WAS WELL PREPARED TO HANDLE THE HEAT, BUT...
THAT IDIOT.
HE'S TRYING TO GO TO HIGH SCHOOL WHILE WORKING TO SUPPORT HIMSELF AND HIS SISTER...
AND NOW HE'S BEEN DRAGGED INTO THIS WAR BETWEEN BEACH HUTS AND IS TRYING TO HELP THEM OUT TOO.
HE'S TOO SELFLESS.
KRIK
I GUESS THAT'S WHAT A SAINT IS LIKE...

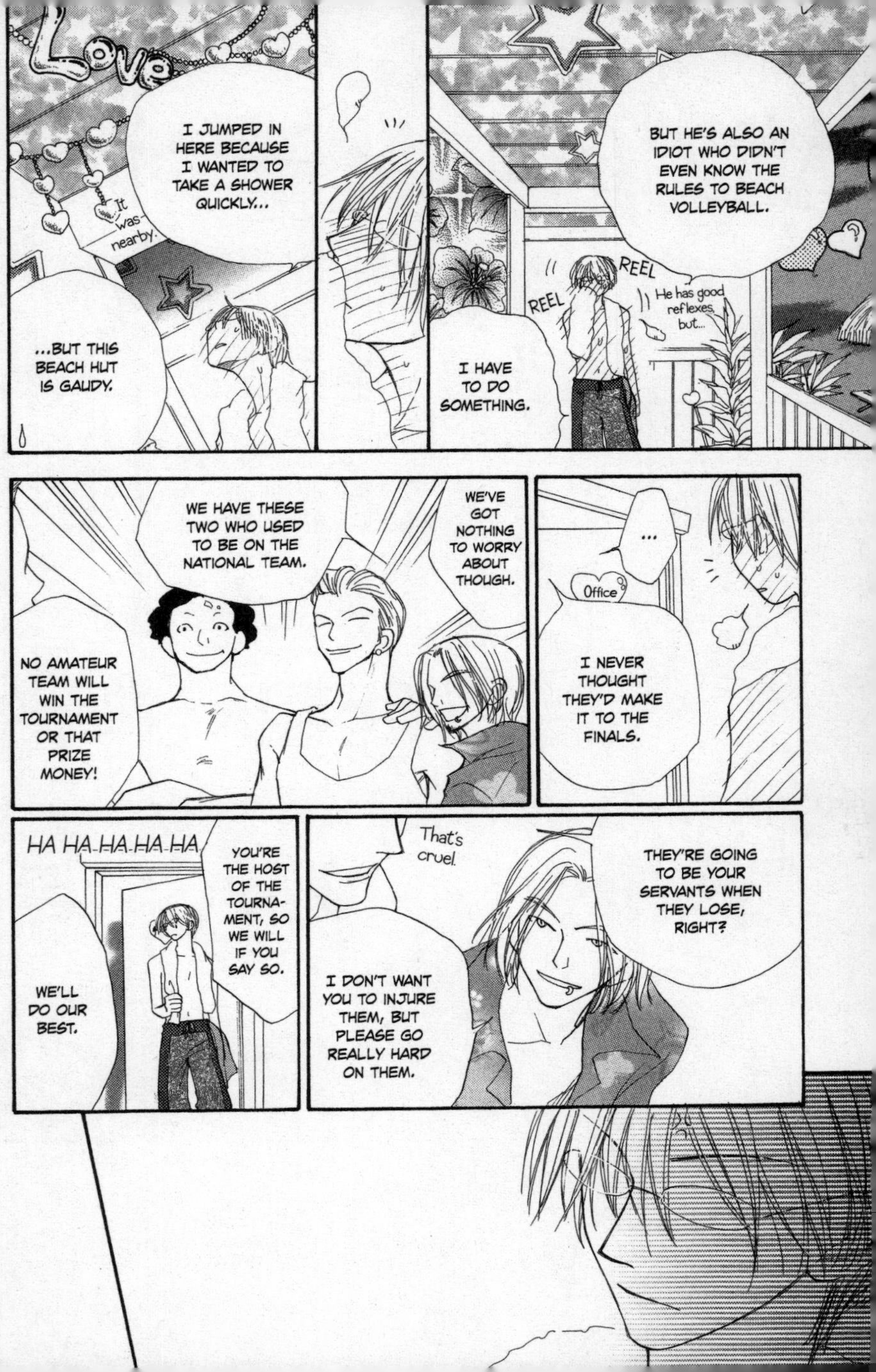
BUT HE'S ALSO AN IDIOT WHO DIDN'T EVEN KNOW THE RULES TO BEACH VOLLEYBALL.
REEL
REEL
He has good reflexes, but...
I HAVE TO DO SOMETHING.
Love
I JUMPED IN HERE BECAUSE I WANTED TO TAKE A SHOWER QUICKLY...
It was nearby.
...BUT THIS BEACH HUT IS GAUDY.
...
Office
I NEVER THOUGHT THEY'D MAKE IT TO THE FINALS.
WE'VE GOT NOTHING TO WORRY ABOUT THOUGH.
WE HAVE THESE TWO WHO USED TO BE ON THE NATIONAL TEAM.
NO AMATEUR TEAM WILL WIN THE TOURNAMENT OR THAT PRIZE MONEY!
THEY'RE GOING TO BE YOUR SERVANTS WHEN THEY LOSE, RIGHT?
That's cruel.
I DON'T WANT YOU TO INJURE THEM, BUT PLEASE GO REALLY HARD ON THEM.
YOU'RE THE HOST OF THE TOURNAMENT, SO WE WILL IF YOU SAY SO.
HA HA-HA-HA-HA
WE'LL DO OUR BEST.

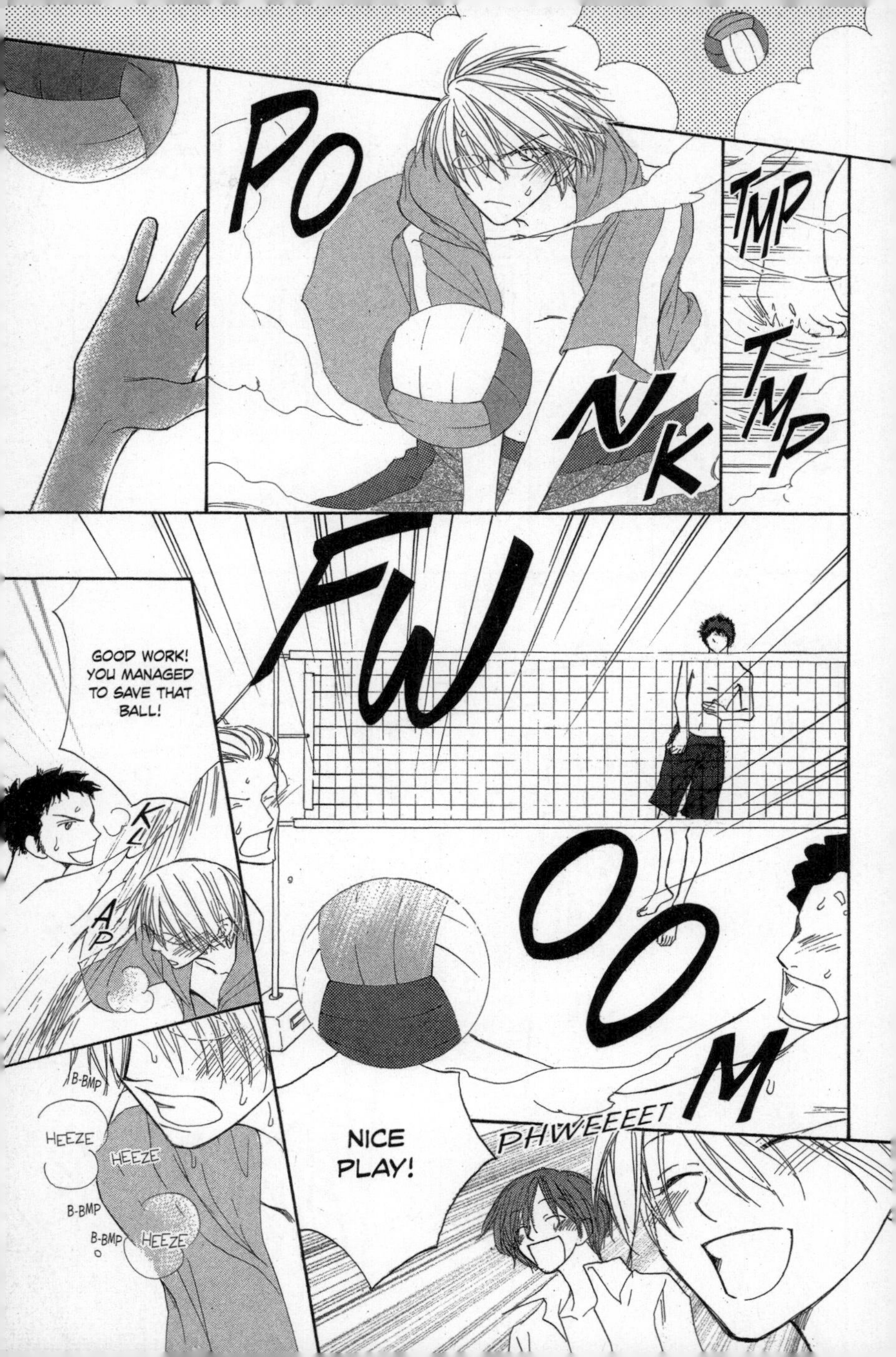
TMP
TMP
PONK
FWOOOM
GOOD WORK! YOU MANAGED TO SAVE THAT BALL!
KLAP
PHWEEEET
NICE PLAY!
B-BMP
HEEZE
HEEZE
B-BMP
B-BMP
HEEZE

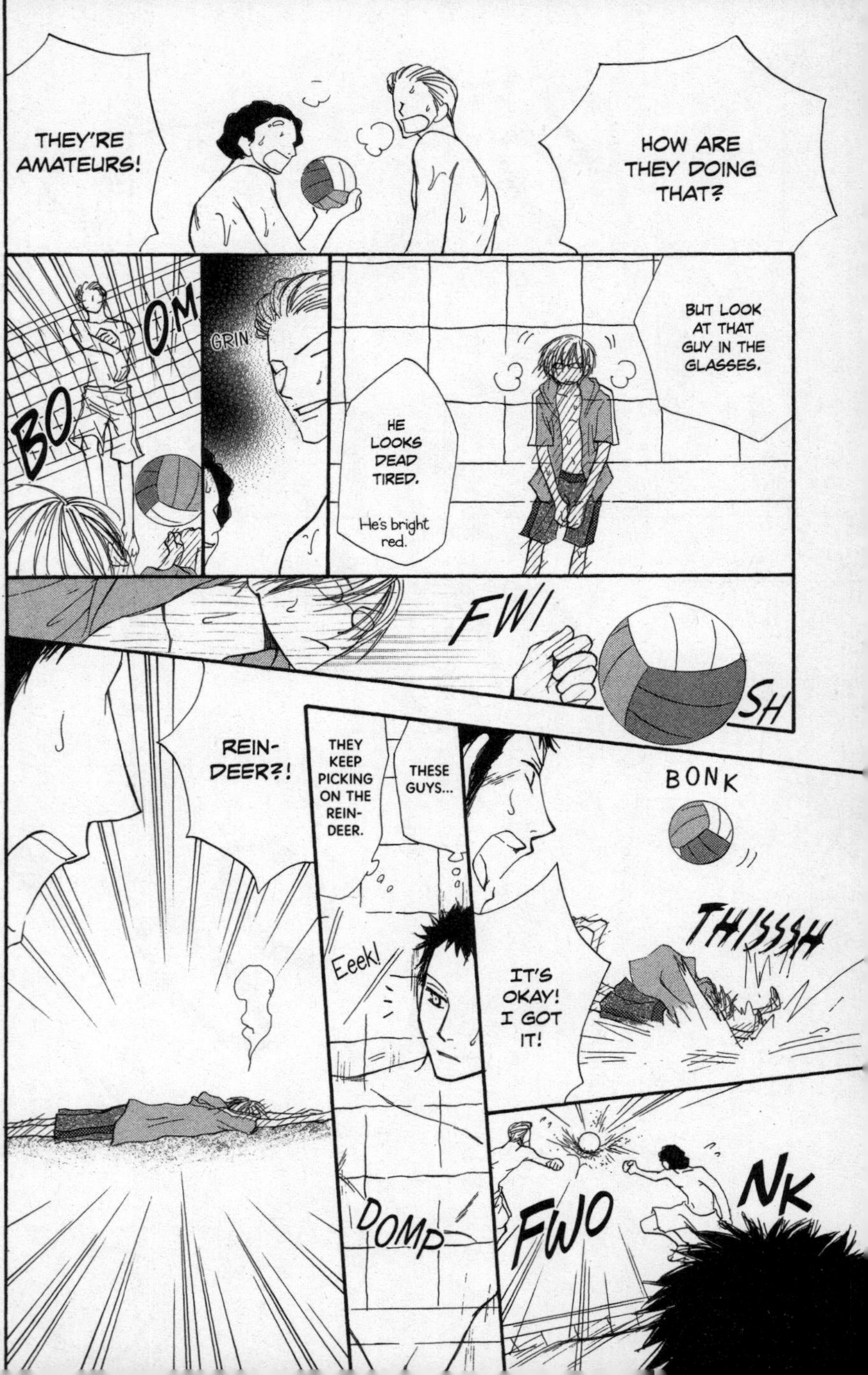
HOW ARE THEY DOING THAT?
THEY'RE AMATEURS!
BUT LOOK AT THAT GUY IN THE GLASSES.
GRIN
HE LOOKS DEAD TIRED.
He's bright red.
BOOM
FWISH
BONK
THISSSH
IT'S OKAY! I GOT IT!
FWONK
THESE GUYS...
THEY KEEP PICKING ON THE REIN-DEER.
Eeek!
DOMP
REIN-DEER?!

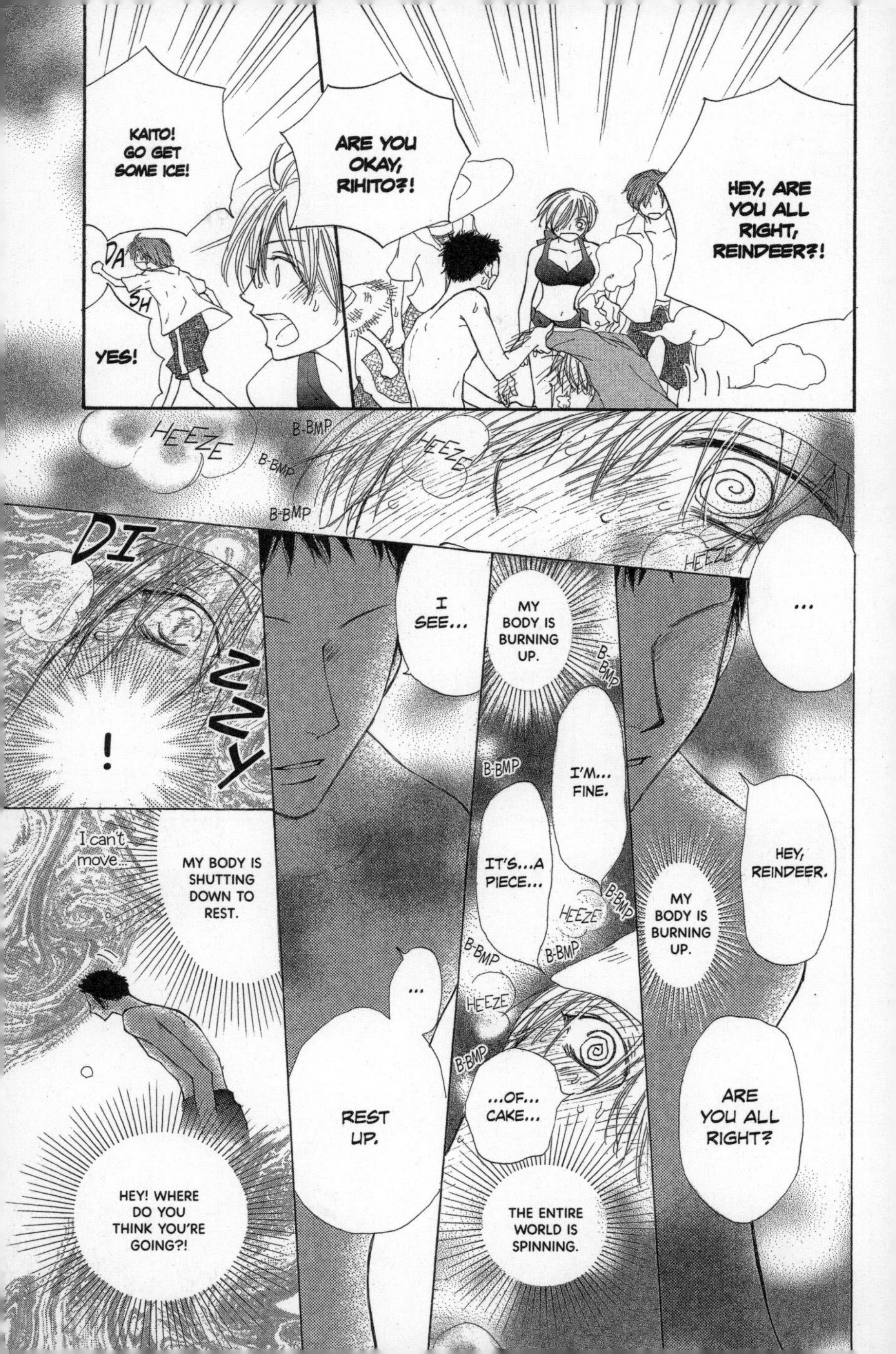
HEY, ARE YOU ALL RIGHT, REINDEER?!
ARE YOU OKAY, RIHITO?!
KAITO! GO GET SOME ICE!
DASH
YES!
HEEZE
B-BMP
B-BMP
B-BMP
HEEZE
HEEZE
...
HEY, REINDEER.
MY BODY IS BURNING UP.
ARE YOU ALL RIGHT?
MY BODY IS BURNING UP.
B-BMP
I'M... FINE.
B-BMP
IT'S...A PIECE...
B-BMP
HEEZE
B-BMP
B-BMP
HEEZE
B-BMP
...OF... CAKE...
THE ENTIRE WORLD IS SPINNING.
I SEE...
...
REST UP.
DIZZY
!
I can't move...
MY BODY IS SHUTTING DOWN TO REST.
HEY! WHERE DO YOU THINK YOU'RE GOING?!

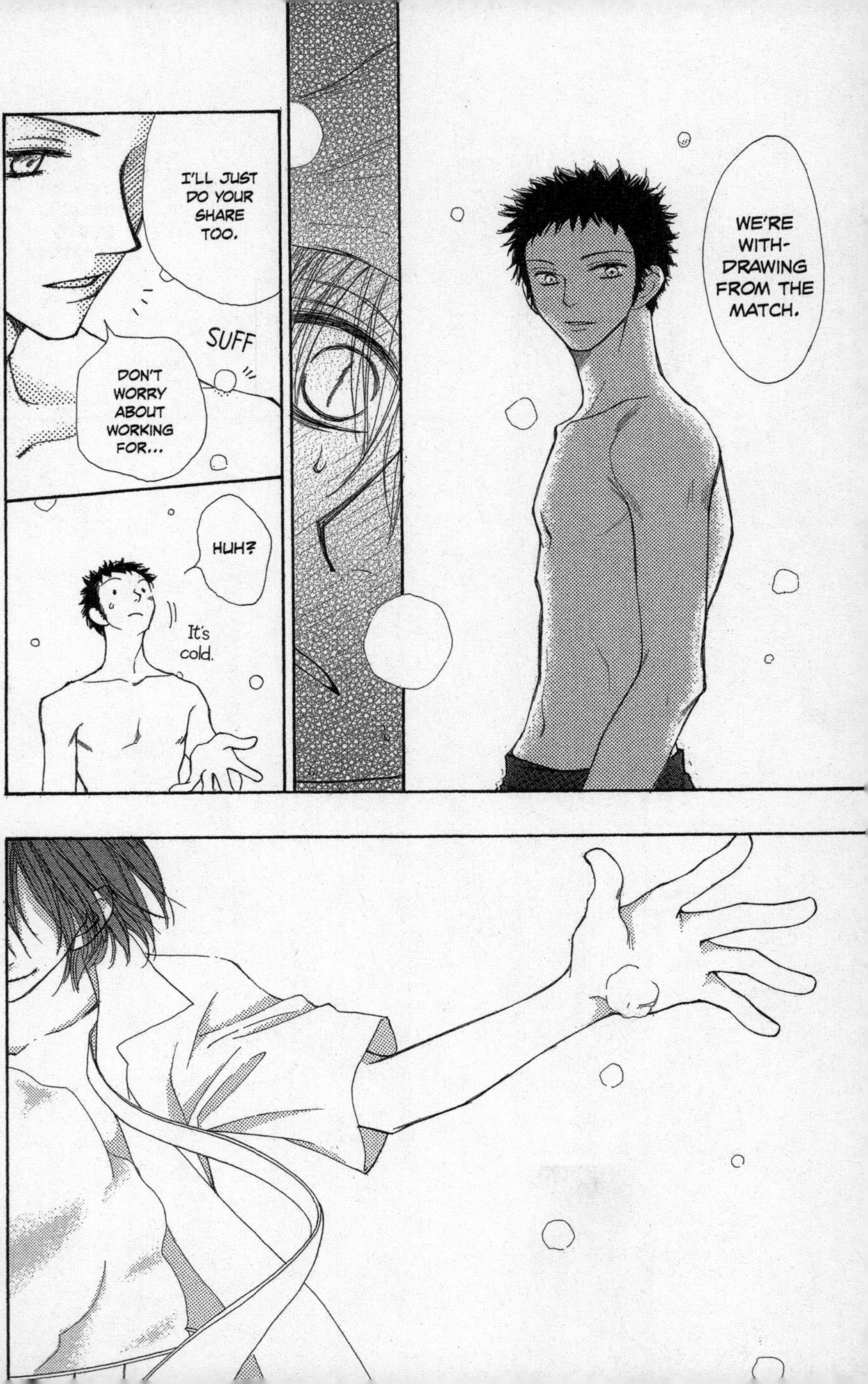
WE'RE WITH-DRAWING FROM THE MATCH.
I'LL JUST DO YOUR SHARE TOO.
SUFF
DON'T WORRY ABOUT WORKING FOR...
HUH?
It's cold.

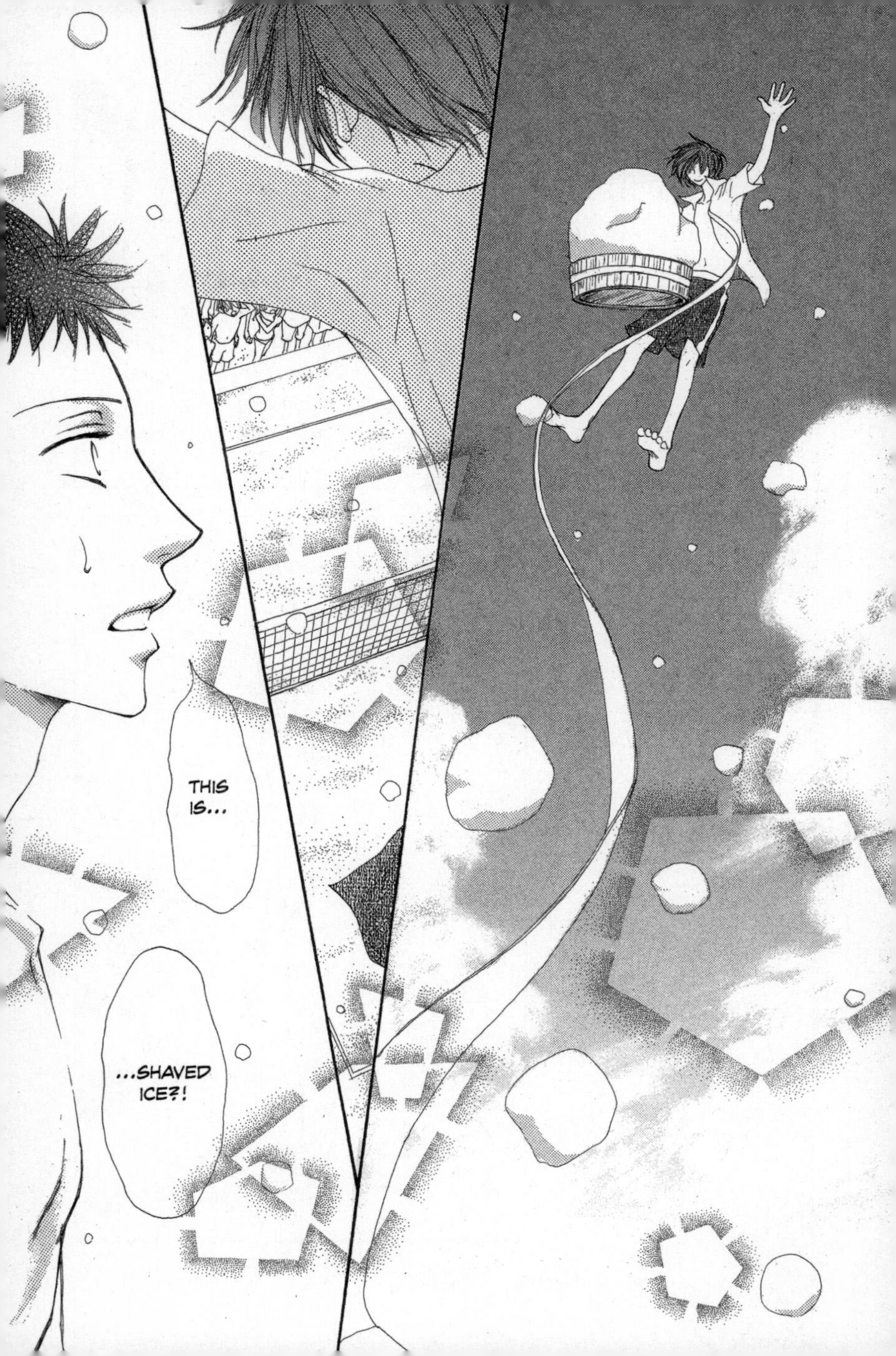
THIS IS...
...SHAVED ICE?!

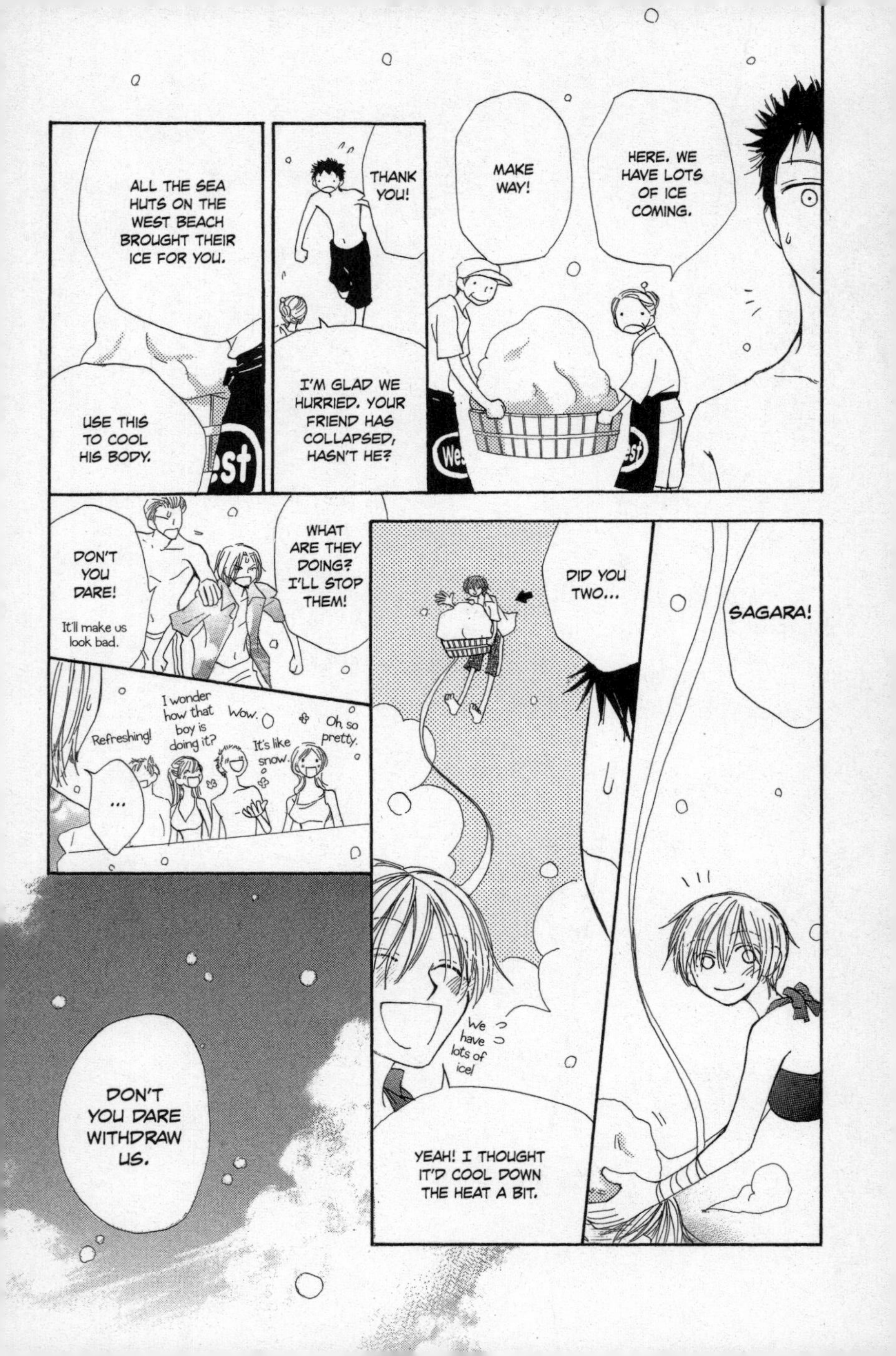
HERE. WE HAVE LOTS OF ICE COMING.
MAKE WAY!
THANK YOU!
I'M GLAD WE HURRIED. YOUR FRIEND HAS COLLAPSED, HASN'T HE?
ALL THE SEA HUTS ON THE WEST BEACH BROUGHT THEIR ICE FOR YOU.
USE THIS TO COOL HIS BODY.
SAGARA!
DID YOU TWO...
We have lots of ice!
YEAH! I THOUGHT IT'D COOL DOWN THE HEAT A BIT.
WHAT ARE THEY DOING? I'LL STOP THEM!
DON'T YOU DARE!
It'll make us look bad.
Oh, so pretty.
It's like snow.
Wow.
I wonder how that boy is doing it?
Refreshing!
...
DON'T YOU DARE WITHDRAW US.

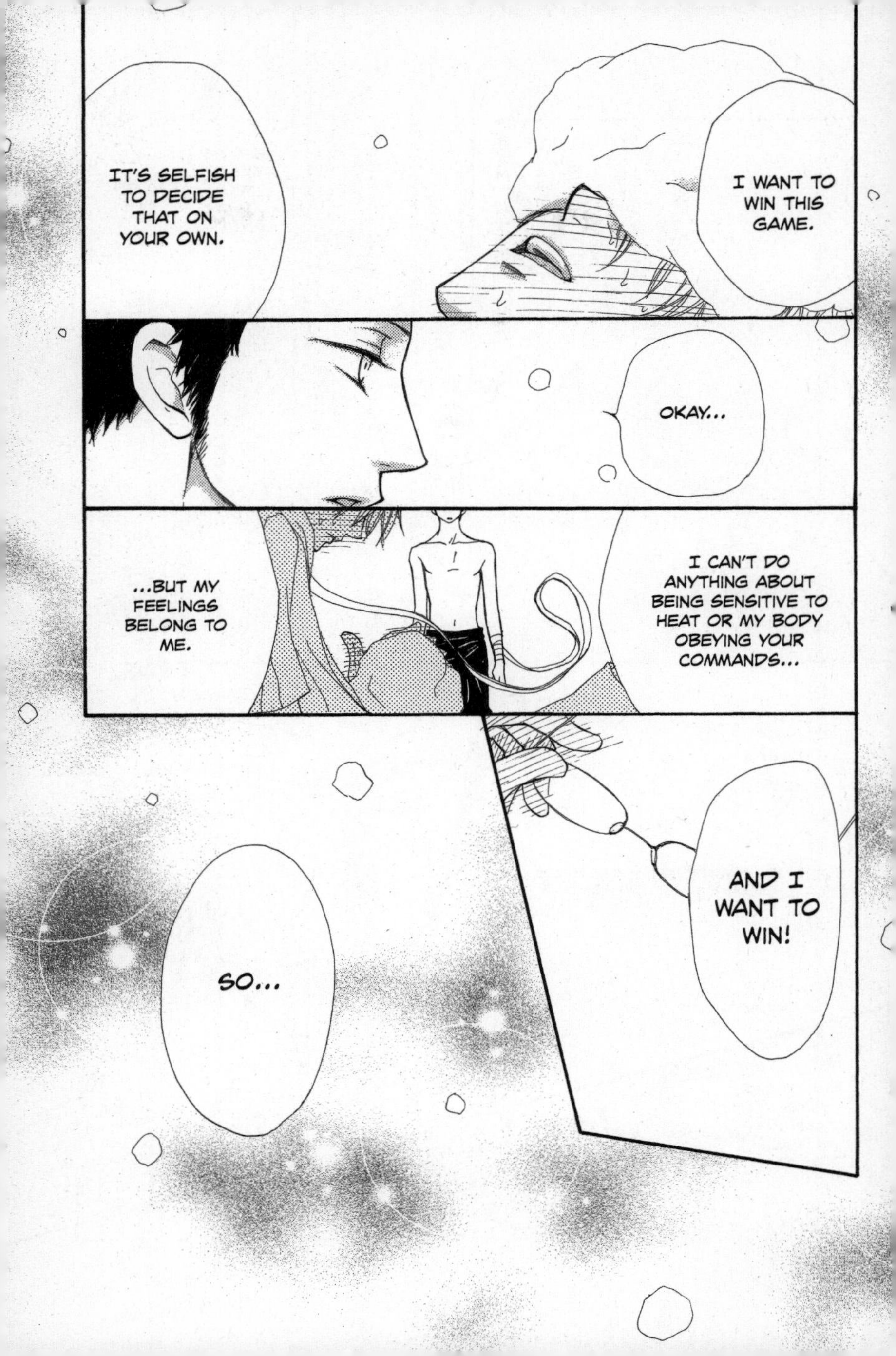
I WANT TO WIN THIS GAME.
IT'S SELFISH TO DECIDE THAT ON YOUR OWN.
OKAY...
I CAN'T DO ANYTHING ABOUT BEING SENSITIVE TO HEAT OR MY BODY OBEYING YOUR COMMANDS...
...BUT MY FEELINGS BELONG TO ME.
AND I WANT TO WIN!
SO...

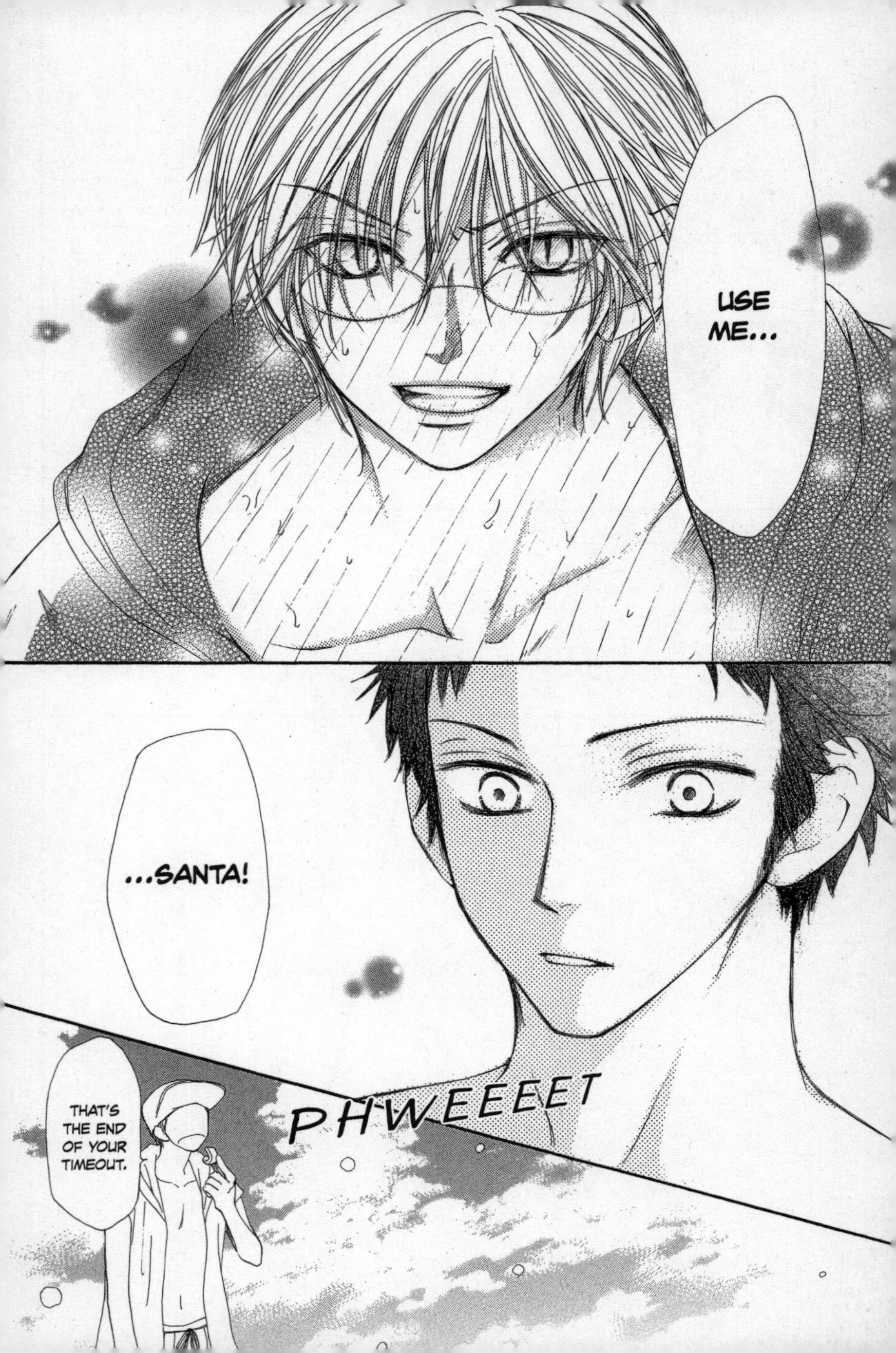
USE ME...
...SANTA!
PHWEEEEET
THAT'S THE END OF YOUR TIMEOUT.

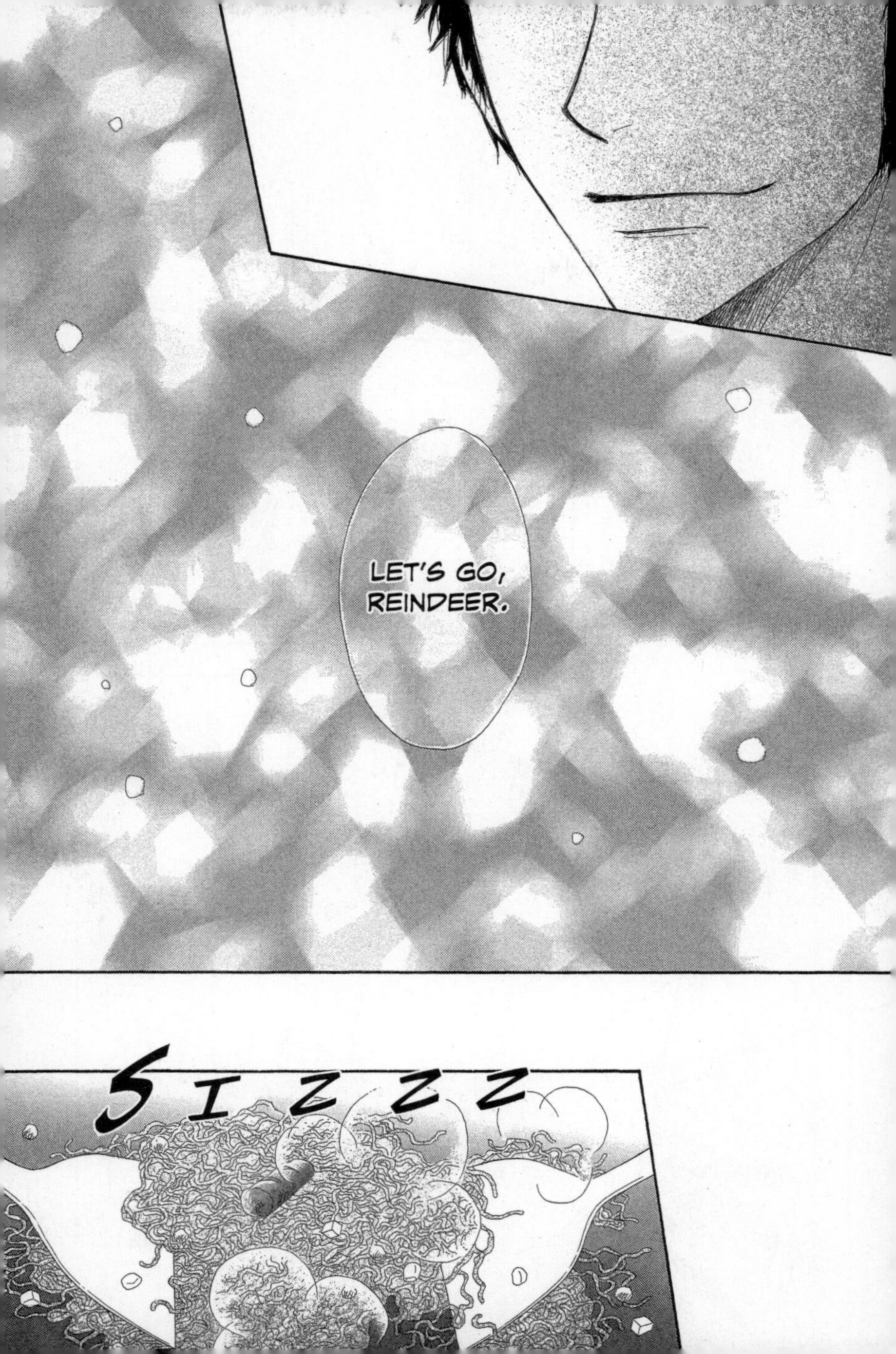
LET'S GO, REINDEER.
SIZZZZ

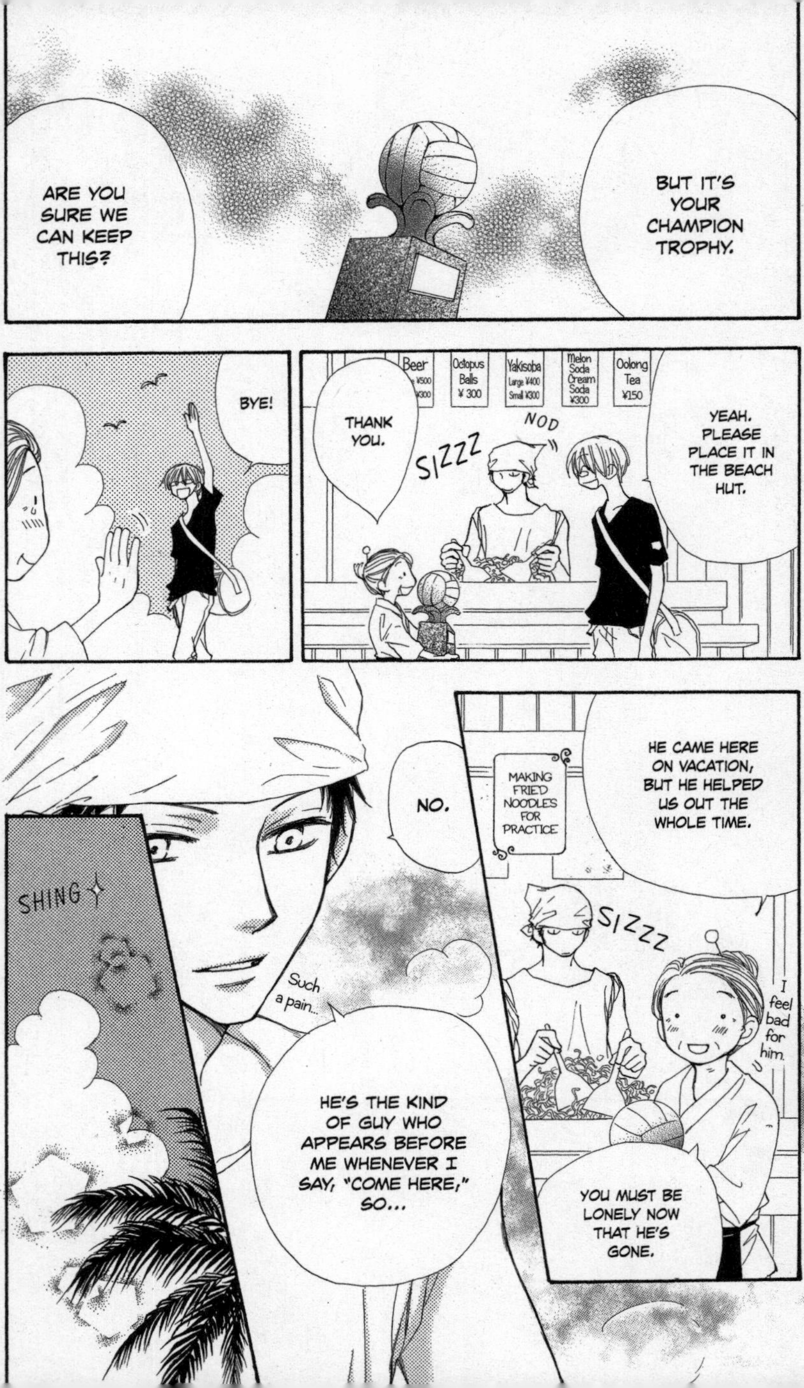
BUT IT'S YOUR CHAMPION TROPHY.
ARE YOU SURE WE CAN KEEP THIS?
YEAH. PLEASE PLACE IT IN THE BEACH HUT.
Oolong Tea ¥150
Melon Soda Cream Soda ¥300
Yakisoba Large ¥400 Small ¥300
Octopus Balls ¥ 300
Beer
NOD
SIZZZ
THANK YOU.
BYE!
HE CAME HERE ON VACATION, BUT HE HELPED US OUT THE WHOLE TIME.
MAKING FRIED NOODLES FOR PRACTICE
SIZZZ
I feel bad for him.
YOU MUST BE LONELY NOW THAT HE'S GONE.
NO.
SHING
Such a pain...
HE'S THE KIND OF GUY WHO APPEARS BEFORE ME WHENEVER I SAY, "COME HERE," SO...

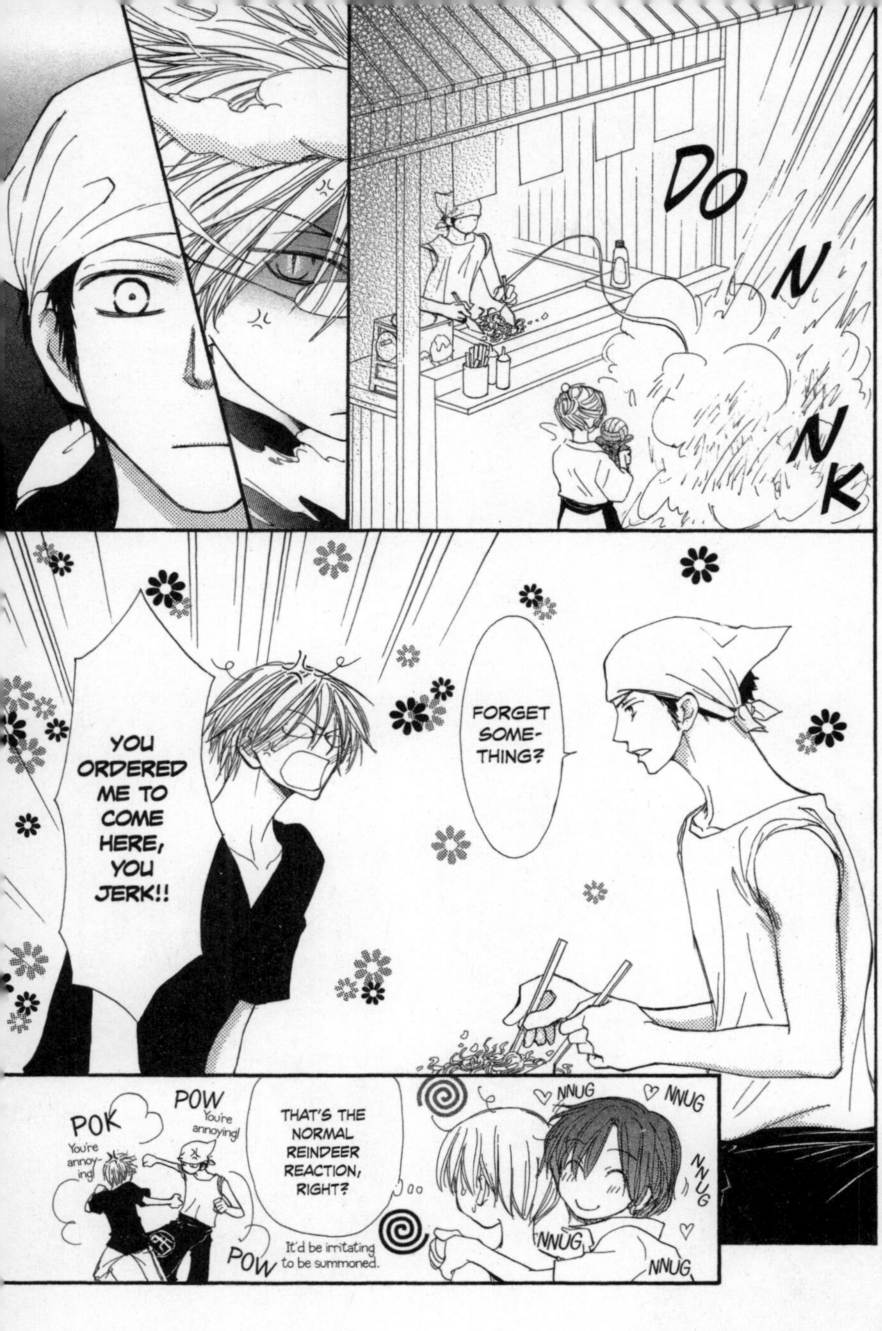
DONNK
FORGET SOMETHING?
YOU ORDERED ME TO COME HERE, YOU JERK!!
NNUG NNUG NNUG NNUG NNUG
THAT'S THE NORMAL REINDEER REACTION, RIGHT?
It'd be irritating to be summoned.
POW
You're annoying!
POK
You're annoying!
POW

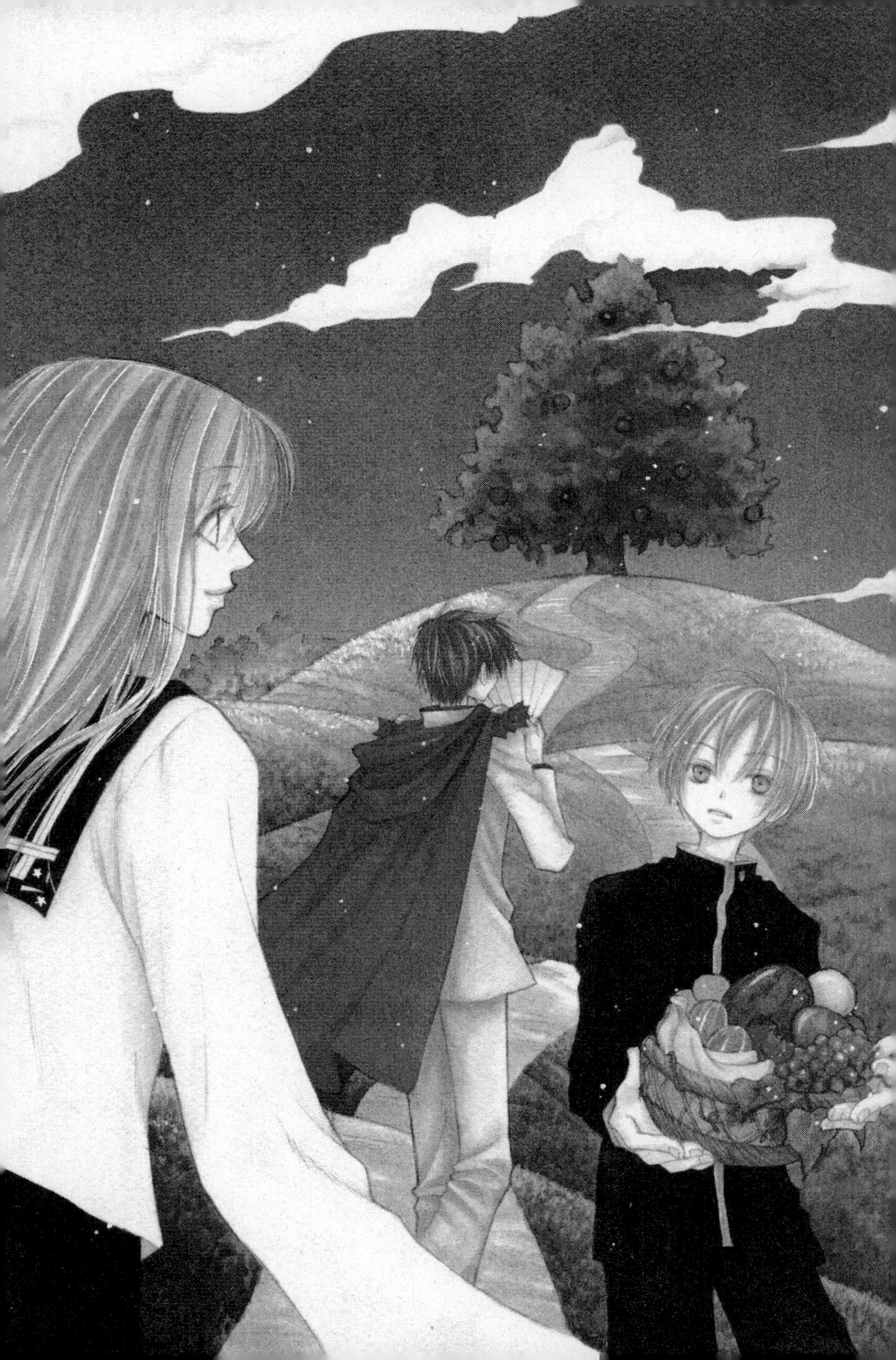

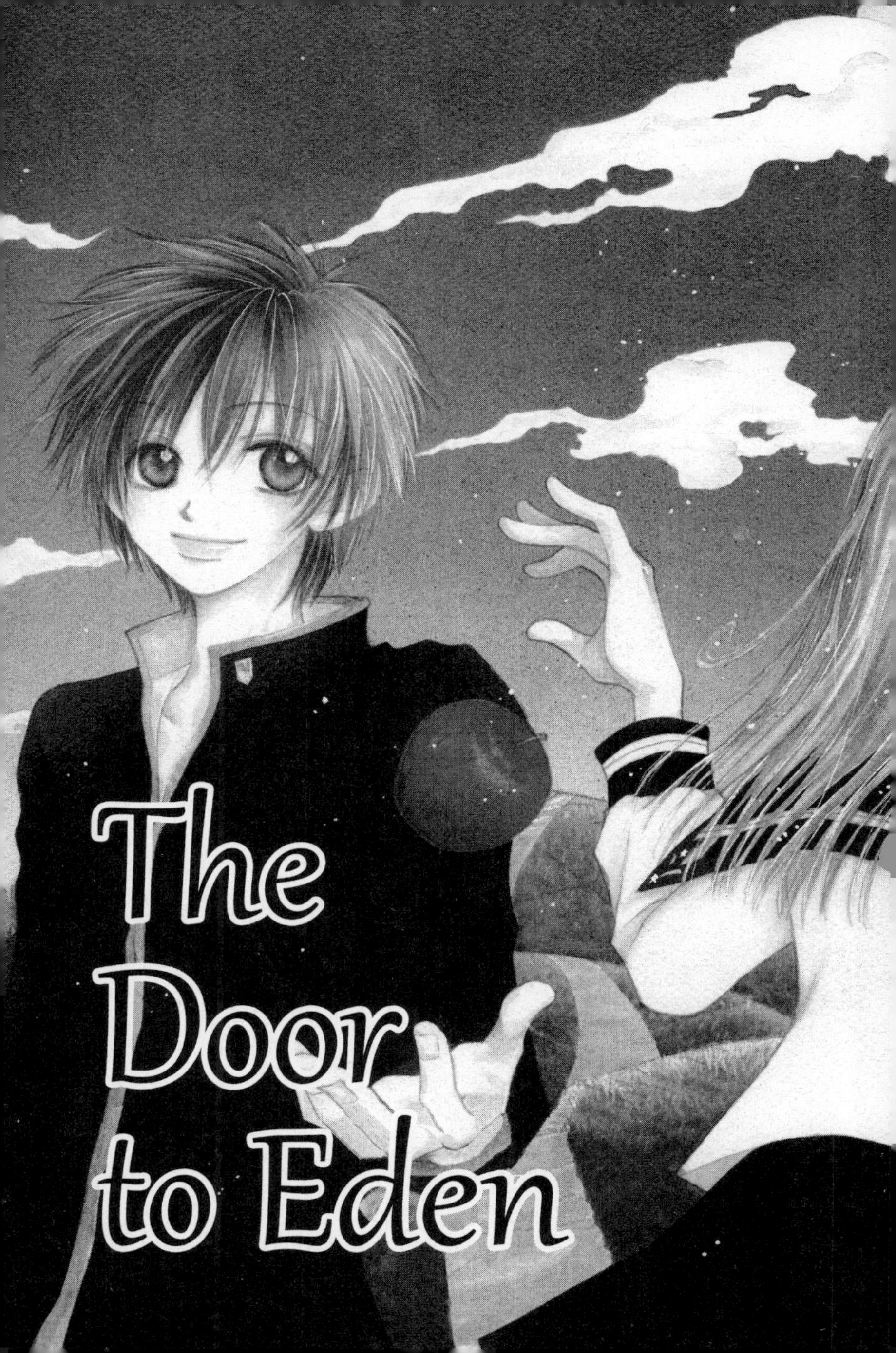
The Door to Eden

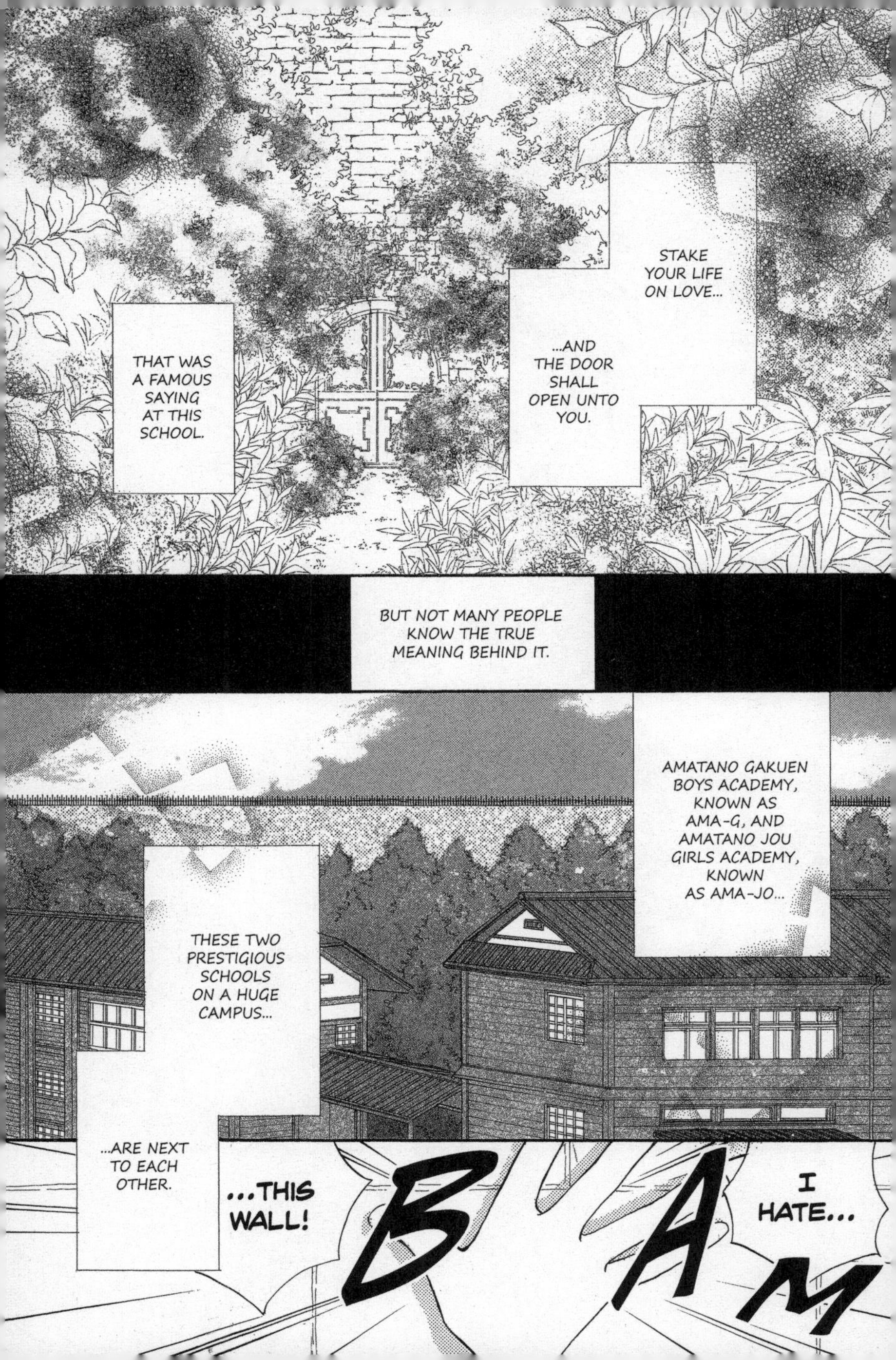
STAKE YOUR LIFE ON LOVE...
...AND THE DOOR SHALL OPEN UNTO YOU.
THAT WAS A FAMOUS SAYING AT THIS SCHOOL.
BUT NOT MANY PEOPLE KNOW THE TRUE MEANING BEHIND IT.
AMATANO GAKUEN BOYS ACADEMY, KNOWN AS AMA-G, AND AMATANO JOU GIRLS ACADEMY, KNOWN AS AMA-JO...
THESE TWO PRESTIGIOUS SCHOOLS ON A HUGE CAMPUS...
...ARE NEXT TO EACH OTHER.
I HATE...
BAM
...THIS WALL!

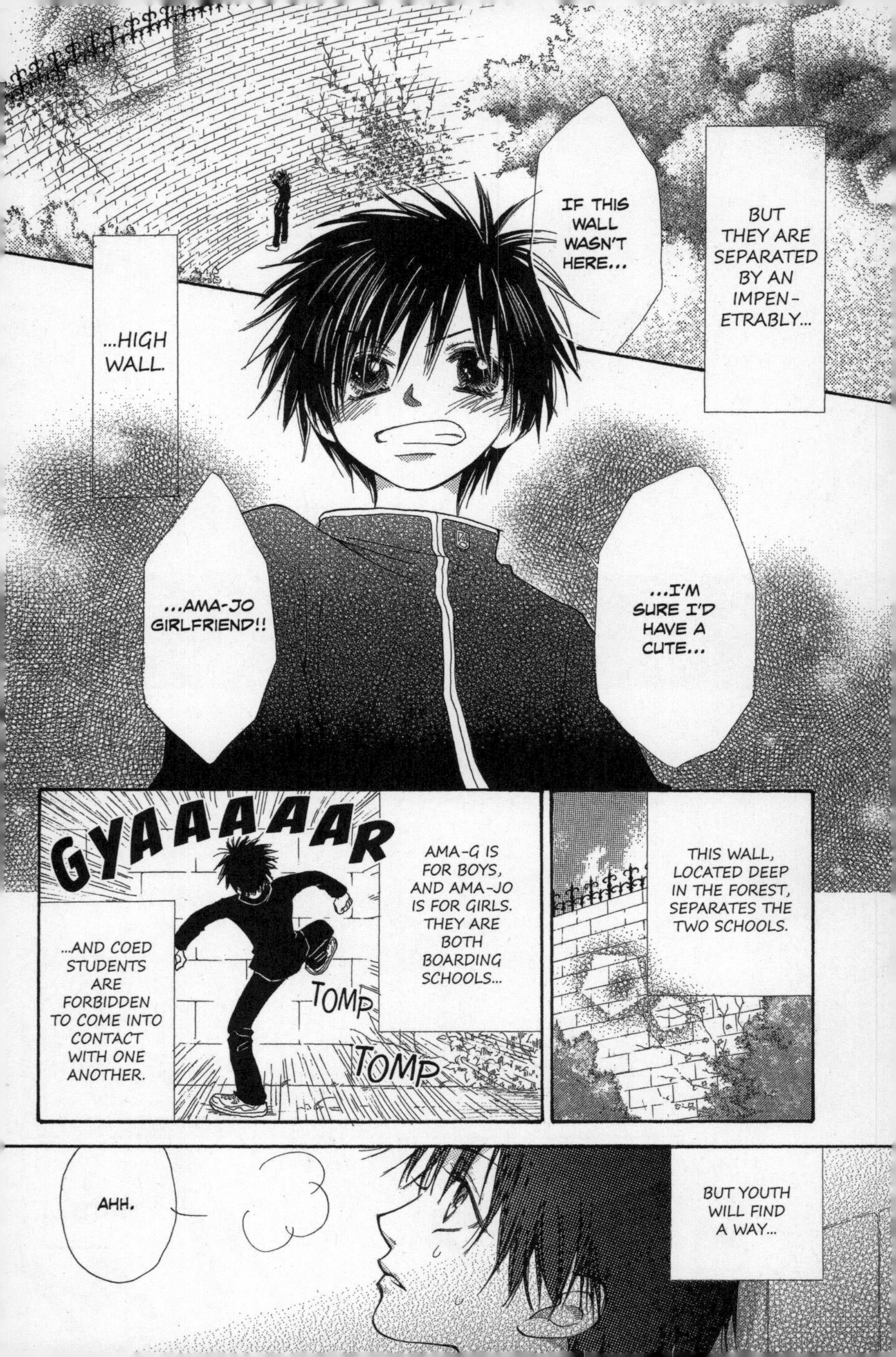
BUT THEY ARE SEPARATED BY AN IMPEN-ETRABLY...
...HIGH WALL.
IF THIS WALL WASN'T HERE...
...I'M SURE I'D HAVE A CUTE...
...AMA-JO GIRLFRIEND!!
THIS WALL, LOCATED DEEP IN THE FOREST, SEPARATES THE TWO SCHOOLS.
AMA-G IS FOR BOYS, AND AMA-JO IS FOR GIRLS. THEY ARE BOTH BOARDING SCHOOLS...
GYAAAAAAR
...AND COED STUDENTS ARE FORBIDDEN TO COME INTO CONTACT WITH ONE ANOTHER.
TOMP
TOMP
BUT YOUTH WILL FIND A WAY...
AHH.

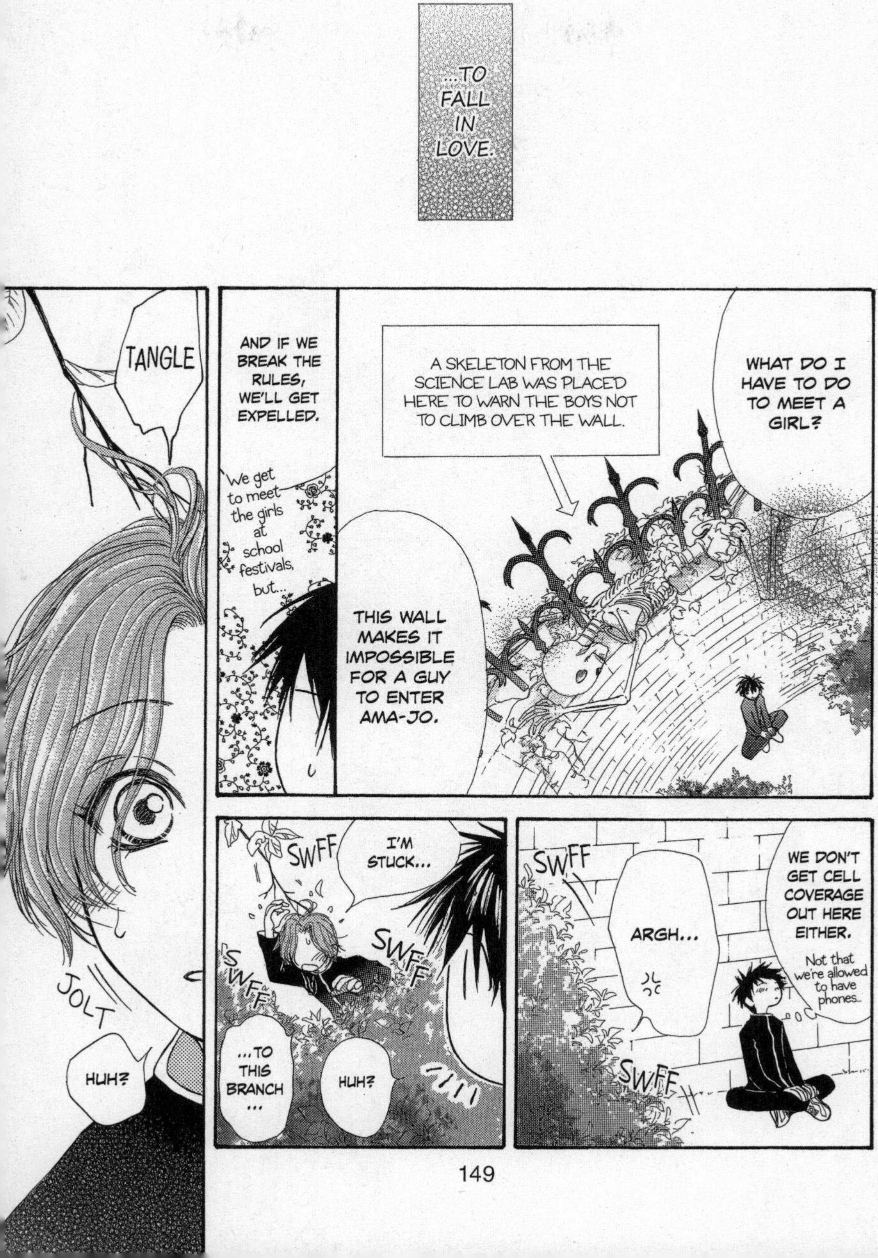
...TO FALL IN LOVE.
WHAT DO I HAVE TO DO TO MEET A GIRL?
A SKELETON FROM THE SCIENCE LAB WAS PLACED HERE TO WARN THE BOYS NOT TO CLIMB OVER THE WALL.
THIS WALL MAKES IT IMPOSSIBLE FOR A GUY TO ENTER AMA-JO.
AND IF WE BREAK THE RULES, WE'LL GET EXPELLED.
We get to meet the girls at school festivals, but...
WE DON'T GET CELL COVERAGE OUT HERE EITHER.
Not that we're allowed to have phones...
SWFF
ARGH...
SWFF
SWFF
I'M STUCK...
SWFF
SWFF
...TO THIS BRANCH...
HUH?
TANGLE
JOLT
HUH?

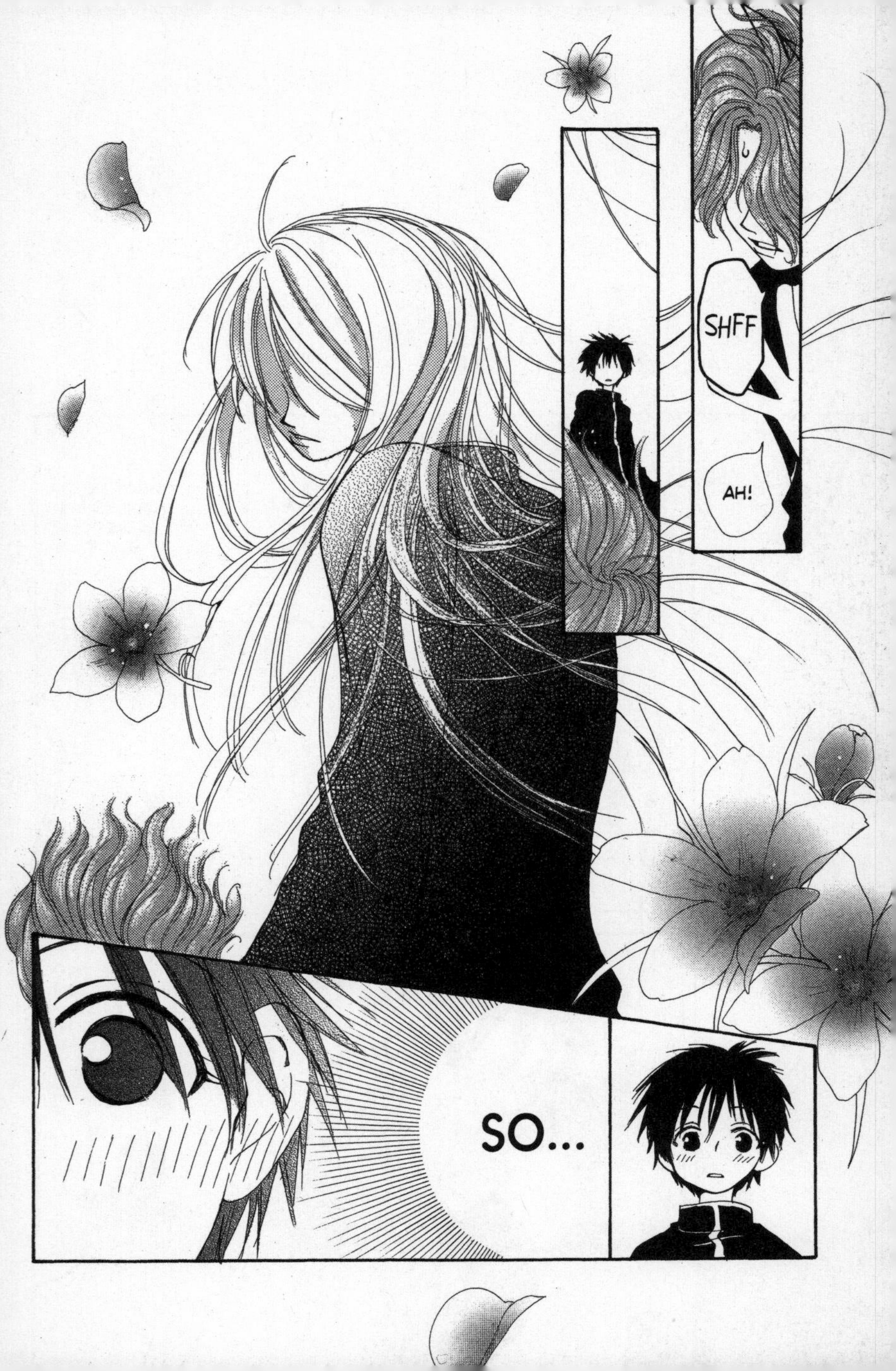
SHFF
AH!
SO...

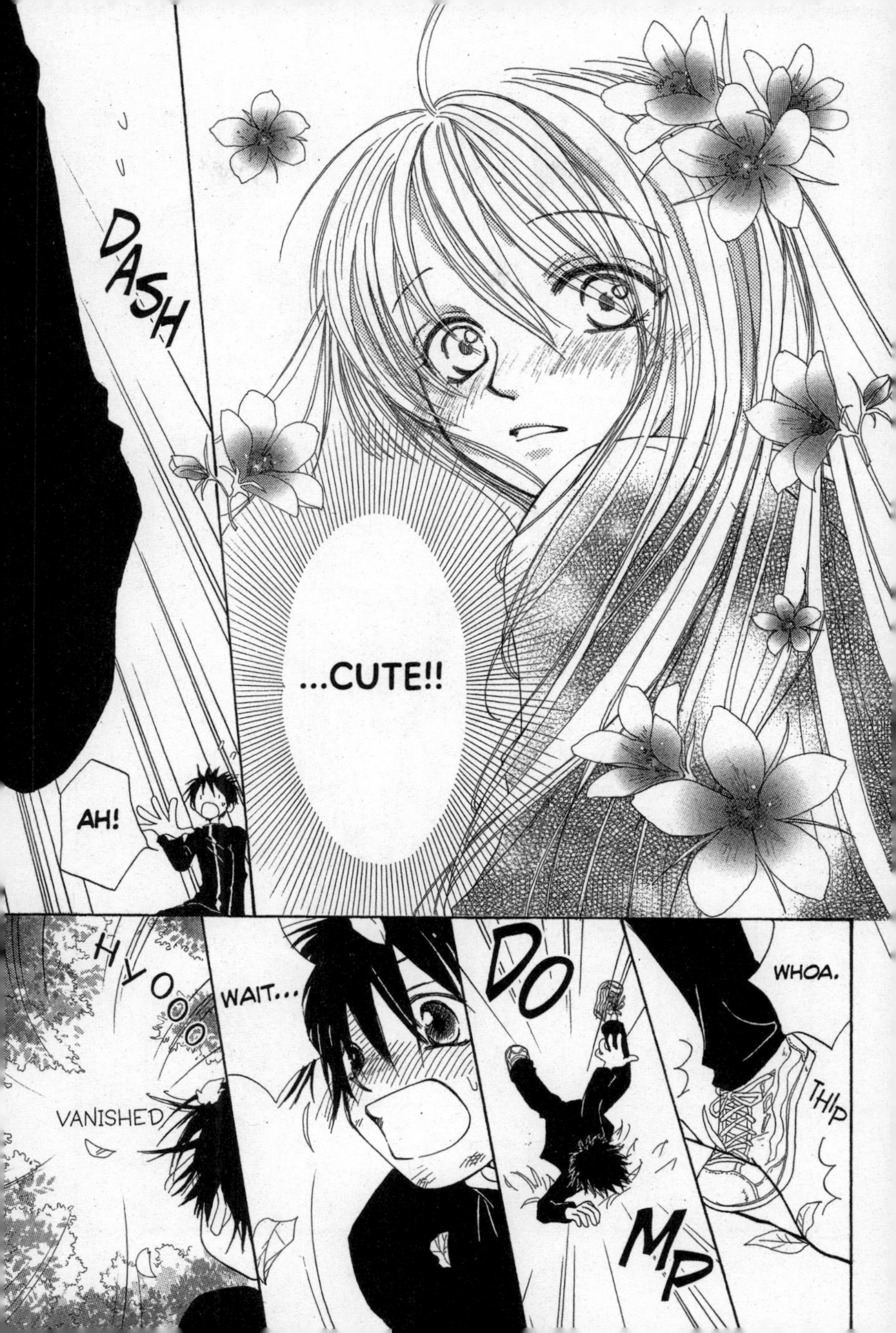
...CUTE!!
DASH
AH!
WHOA.
THIP
DO
MP
WAIT...
HYOOO
VANISHED

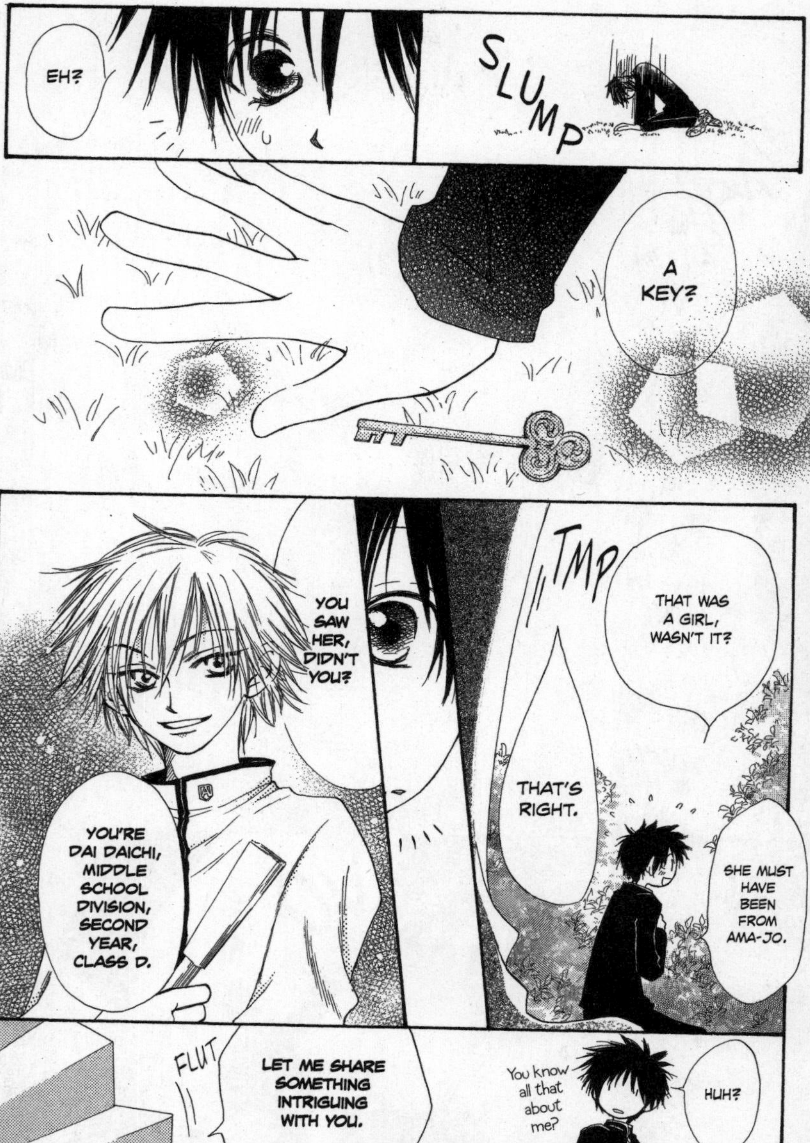
SLUMP
EH?
A KEY?
TMP
THAT WAS A GIRL, WASN'T IT?
THAT'S RIGHT.
SHE MUST HAVE BEEN FROM AMA-JO.
YOU SAW HER, DIDN'T YOU?
YOU'RE DAI DAICHI, MIDDLE SCHOOL DIVISION, SECOND YEAR, CLASS D.
HUH?
You know all that about me?
FLUT
LET ME SHARE SOMETHING INTRIGUING WITH YOU.

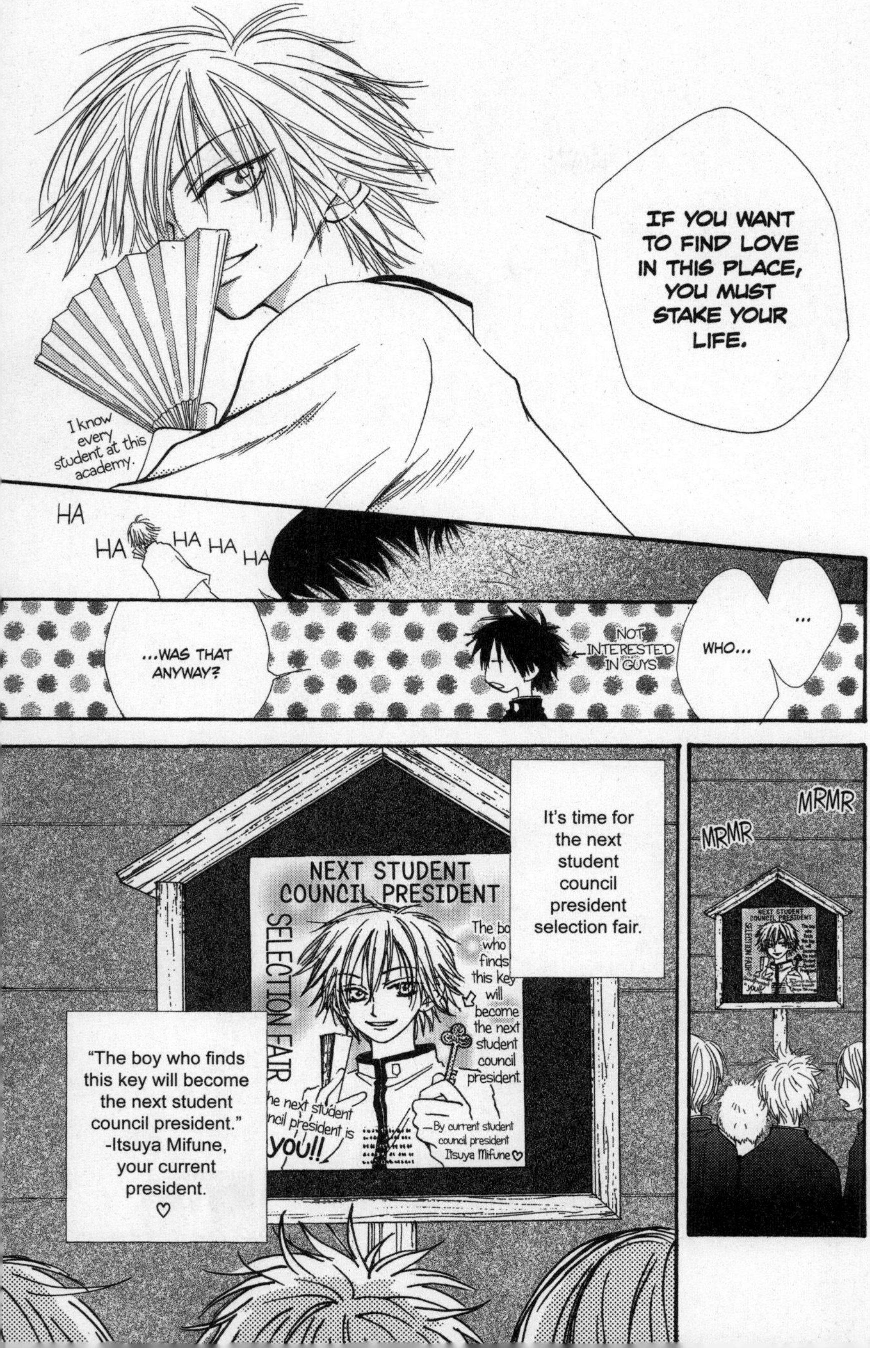
IF YOU WANT TO FIND LOVE IN THIS PLACE, YOU MUST STAKE YOUR LIFE.
I know every student at this academy.
HA
HA HA HA HA
...
WHO...
NOT INTERESTED IN GUYS
...WAS THAT ANYWAY?
MRMR
MRMR
It's time for the next student council president selection fair.
NEXT STUDENT COUNCIL PRESIDENT
SELECTION FAIR
The boy who finds this key will become the next student council president.
By current student council president Itsuya Mifune ♡
"The boy who finds this key will become the next student council president." -Itsuya Mifune, your current president. ♡

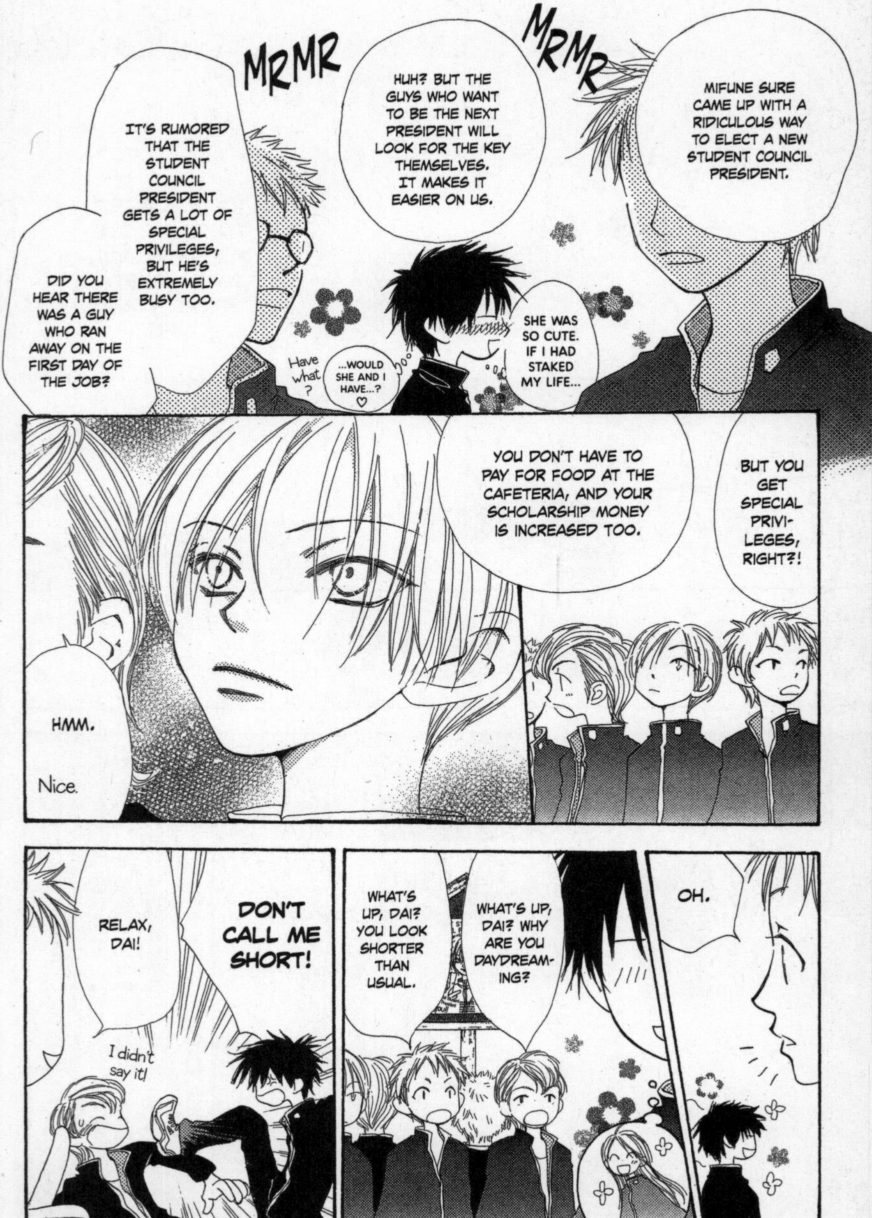
MRMR
MIFUNE SURE CAME UP WITH A RIDICULOUS WAY TO ELECT A NEW STUDENT COUNCIL PRESIDENT.
HUH? BUT THE GUYS WHO WANT TO BE THE NEXT PRESIDENT WILL LOOK FOR THE KEY THEMSELVES. IT MAKES IT EASIER ON US.
MRMR
IT'S RUMORED THAT THE STUDENT COUNCIL PRESIDENT GETS A LOT OF SPECIAL PRIVILEGES, BUT HE'S EXTREMELY BUSY TOO.
DID YOU HEAR THERE WAS A GUY WHO RAN AWAY ON THE FIRST DAY OF THE JOB?
SHE WAS SO CUTE. IF I HAD STAKED MY LIFE...
...WOULD SHE AND I HAVE...? ♡
Have what?
BUT YOU GET SPECIAL PRIVI-LEGES, RIGHT?!
YOU DON'T HAVE TO PAY FOR FOOD AT THE CAFETERIA, AND YOUR SCHOLARSHIP MONEY IS INCREASED TOO.
HMM.
Nice.
OH.
WHAT'S UP, DAI? WHY ARE YOU DAYDREAM-ING?
WHAT'S UP, DAI? YOU LOOK SHORTER THAN USUAL.
DON'T CALL ME SHORT!
RELAX, DAI!
I didn't say it!

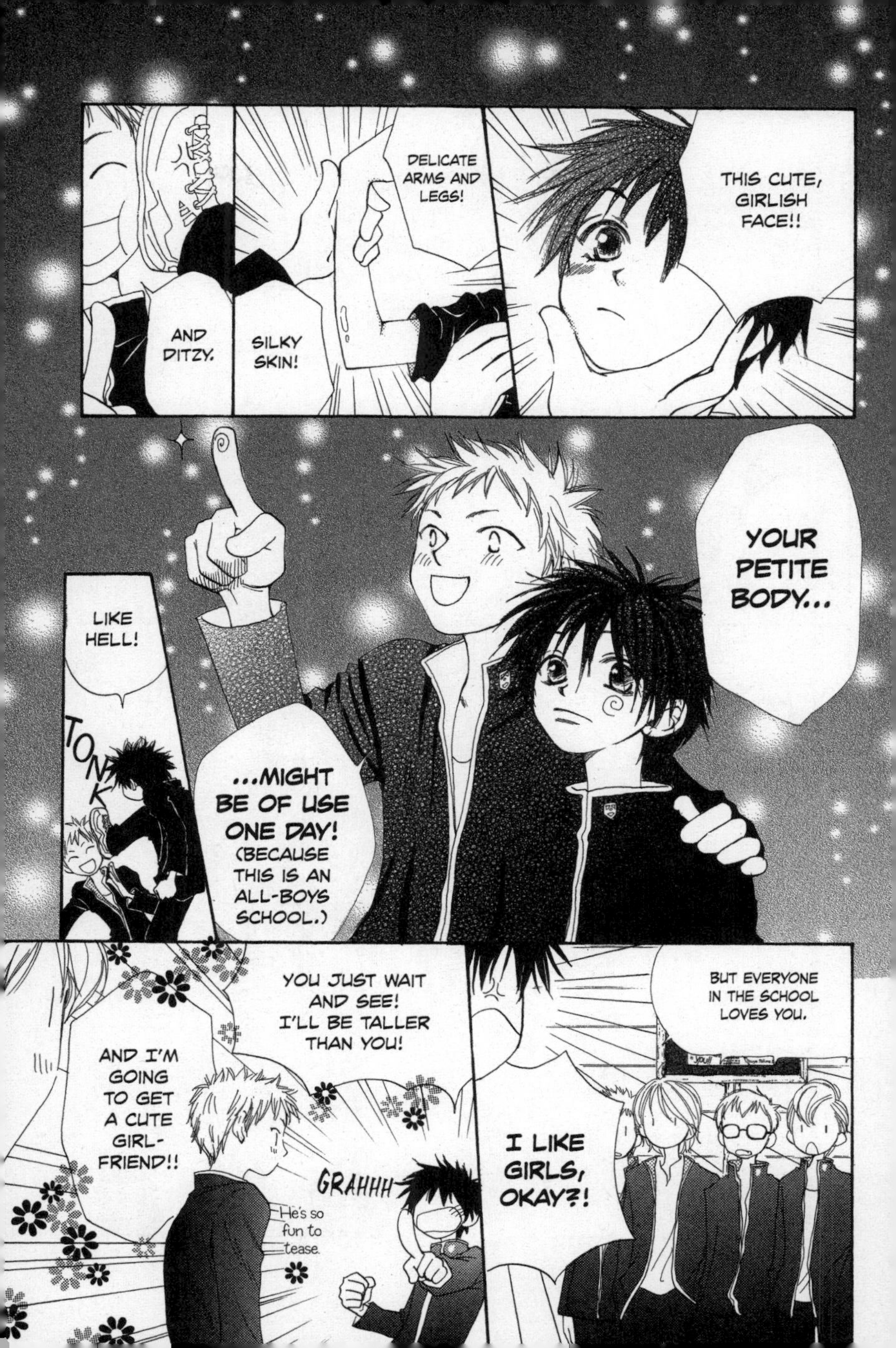
THIS CUTE, GIRLISH FACE!!
DELICATE ARMS AND LEGS!
SILKY SKIN!
AND DITZY.
YOUR PETITE BODY...
...MIGHT BE OF USE ONE DAY! (BECAUSE THIS IS AN ALL-BOYS SCHOOL.)
LIKE HELL!
TONK
BUT EVERYONE IN THE SCHOOL LOVES YOU.
I LIKE GIRLS, OKAY?!
YOU JUST WAIT AND SEE! I'LL BE TALLER THAN YOU!
AND I'M GOING TO GET A CUTE GIRL-FRIEND!!
GRAHHH
He's so fun to tease.

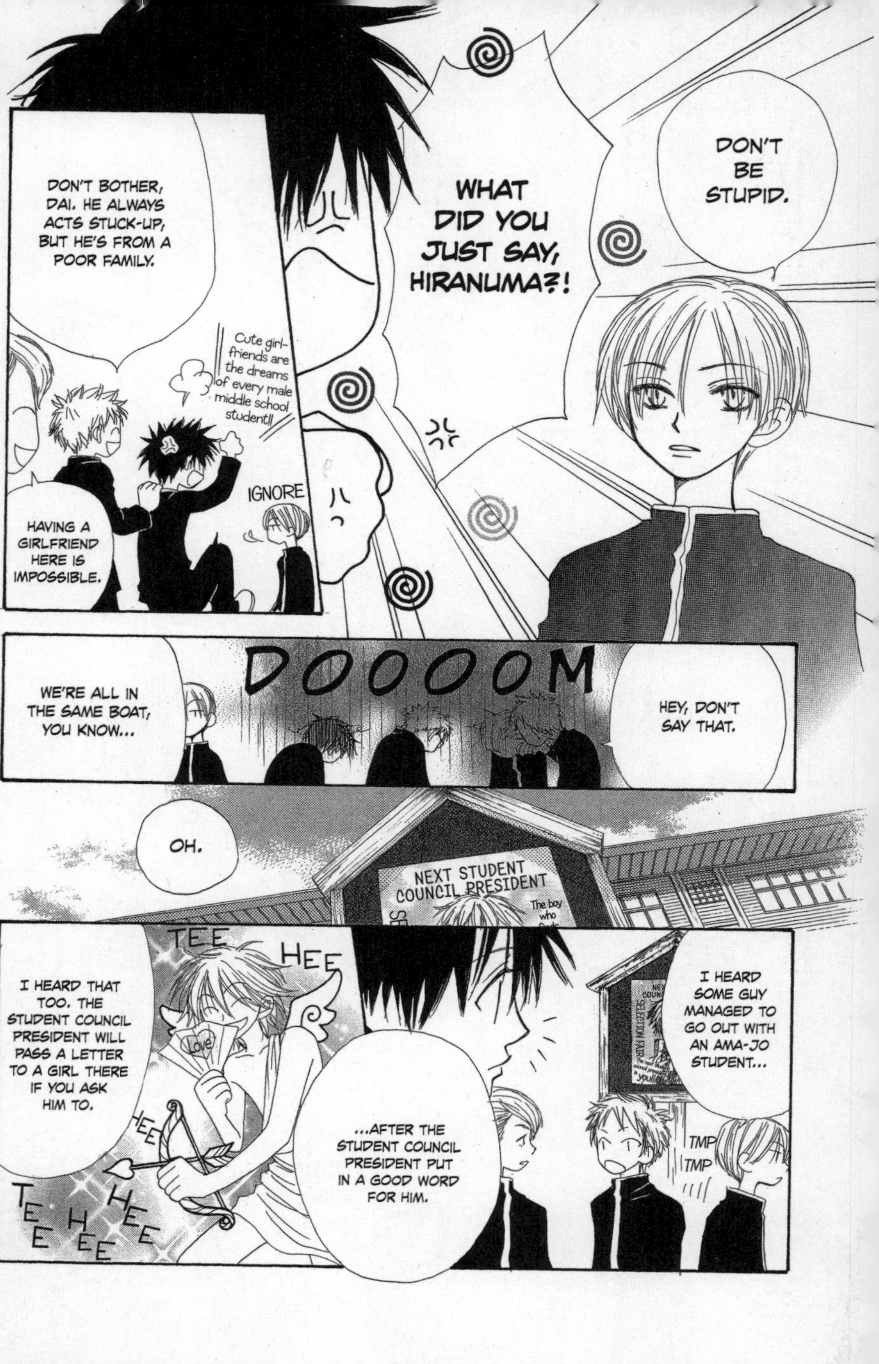
DON'T BE STUPID.
WHAT DID YOU JUST SAY, HIRANUMA?!
DON'T BOTHER, DAI. HE ALWAYS ACTS STUCK-UP, BUT HE'S FROM A POOR FAMILY.
Cute girlfriends are the dreams of every male middle school student!!
IGNORE
HAVING A GIRLFRIEND HERE IS IMPOSSIBLE.
HEY, DON'T SAY THAT.
DOOOOOM
WE'RE ALL IN THE SAME BOAT, YOU KNOW...
OH.
NEXT STUDENT COUNCIL PRESIDENT
I HEARD SOME GUY MANAGED TO GO OUT WITH AN AMA-JO STUDENT...
...AFTER THE STUDENT COUNCIL PRESIDENT PUT IN A GOOD WORD FOR HIM.
TMP TMP
TEE HEE
I HEARD THAT TOO. THE STUDENT COUNCIL PRESIDENT WILL PASS A LETTER TO A GIRL THERE IF YOU ASK HIM TO.
Love
HEE
TEE HEE HEE HEE

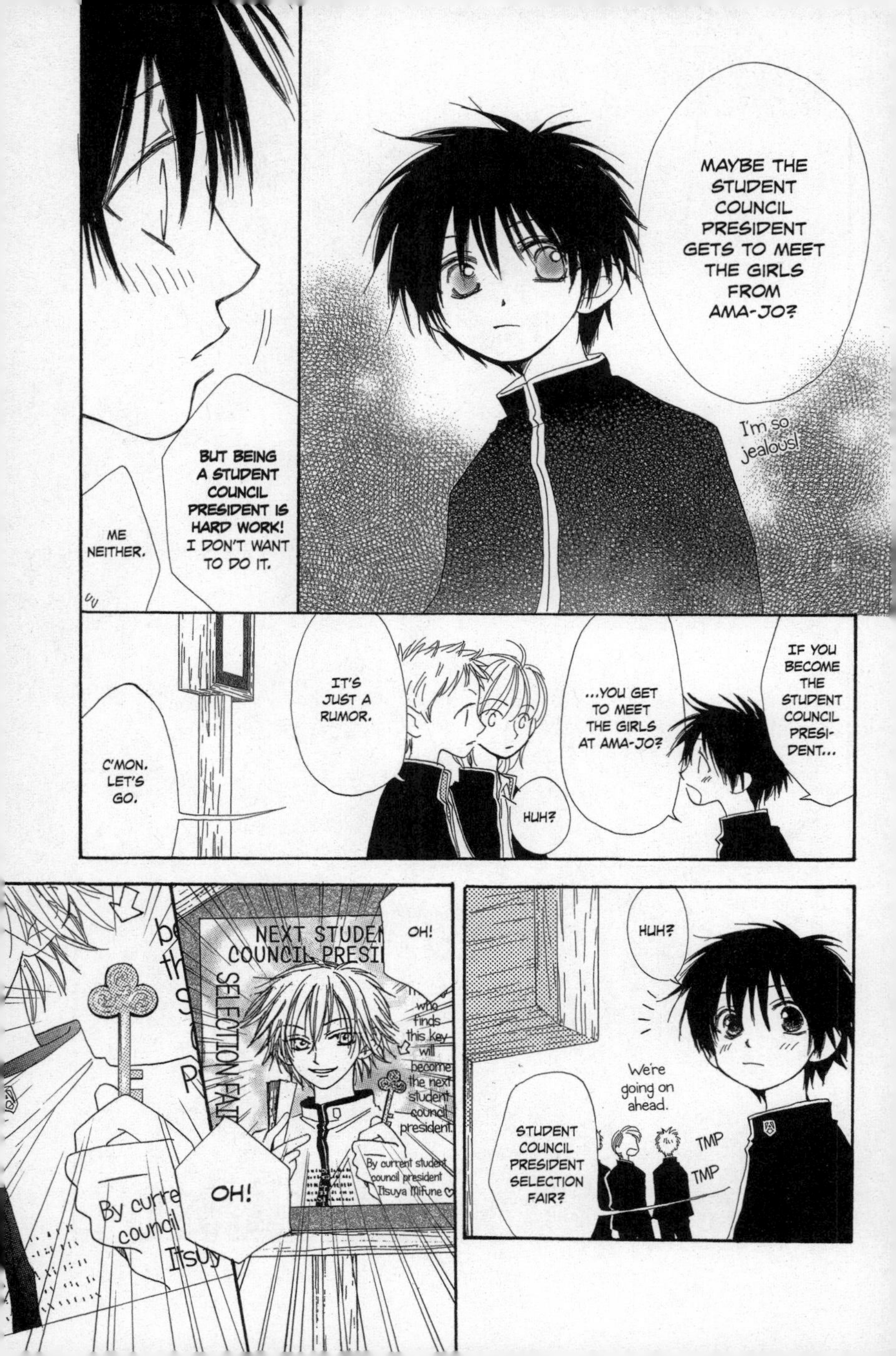
MAYBE THE STUDENT COUNCIL PRESIDENT GETS TO MEET THE GIRLS FROM AMA-JO?
I'm so jealous!
BUT BEING A STUDENT COUNCIL PRESIDENT IS HARD WORK! I DON'T WANT TO DO IT.
ME NEITHER.
IF YOU BECOME THE STUDENT COUNCIL PRESI-DENT...
...YOU GET TO MEET THE GIRLS AT AMA-JO?
HUH?
IT'S JUST A RUMOR.
C'MON. LET'S GO.
HUH?
We're going on ahead.
TMP
TMP
STUDENT COUNCIL PRESIDENT SELECTION FAIR?
OH!
who finds this key will become the next student council president.
By current student council president Itsuya Mifune ♡
OH!

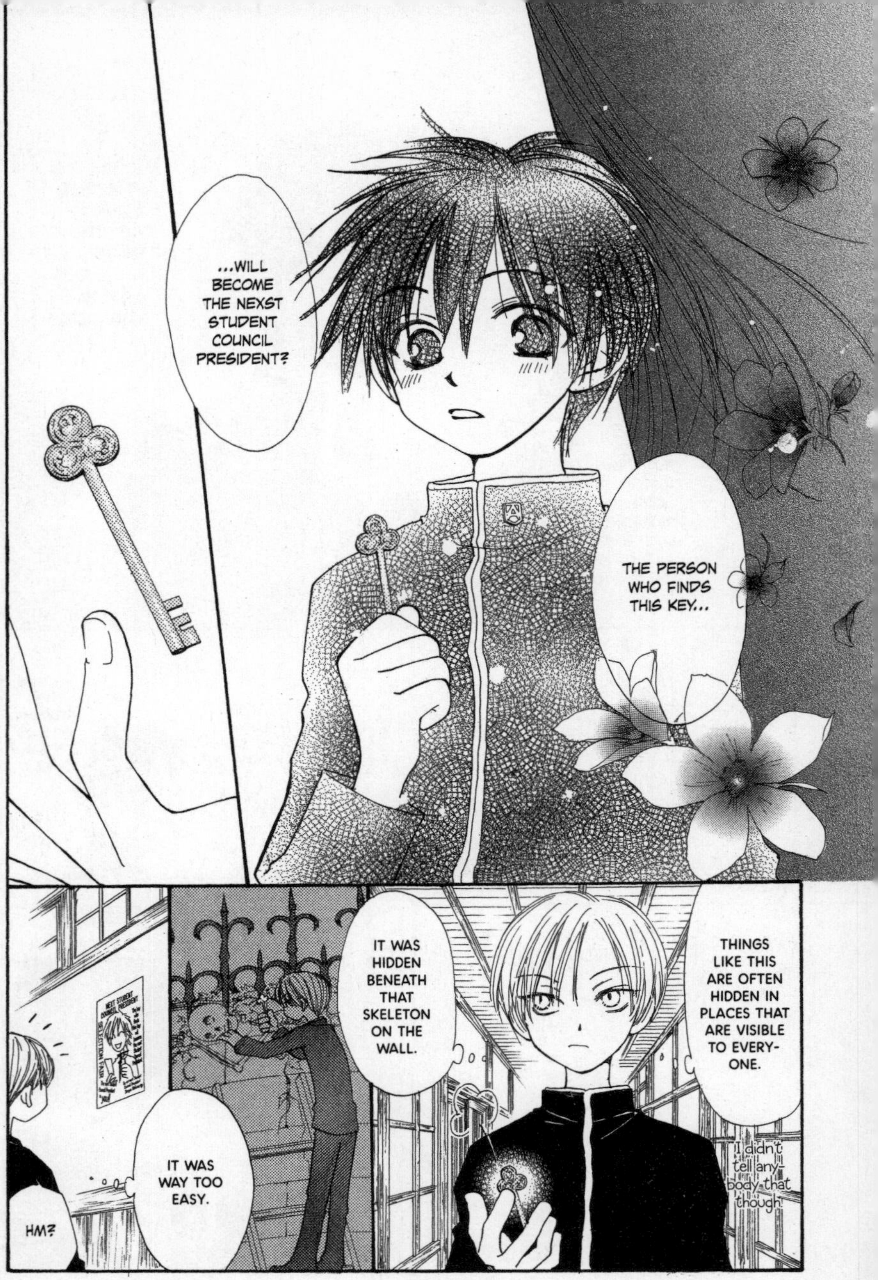
THE PERSON WHO FINDS THIS KEY...
...WILL BECOME THE NEXST STUDENT COUNCIL PRESIDENT?
THINGS LIKE THIS ARE OFTEN HIDDEN IN PLACES THAT ARE VISIBLE TO EVERY-ONE.
I didn't tell any-body that though.
IT WAS HIDDEN BENEATH THAT SKELETON ON THE WALL.
IT WAS WAY TOO EASY.
HM?

1/4 Sakura Mail

Part 10

This is a oneshot I created for the sole reason of wanting to write a story about gender role reversal. But...³ I remember it being an extremely difficult oneshot to create. ♁ I moaned and groaned with my editor and many others. ♁ I reread it after we decided to include it in this manga volume, but after seeing it again, it seems a lot like what I am trying to do in *Penguin Revolution*, my current series...

(continues)

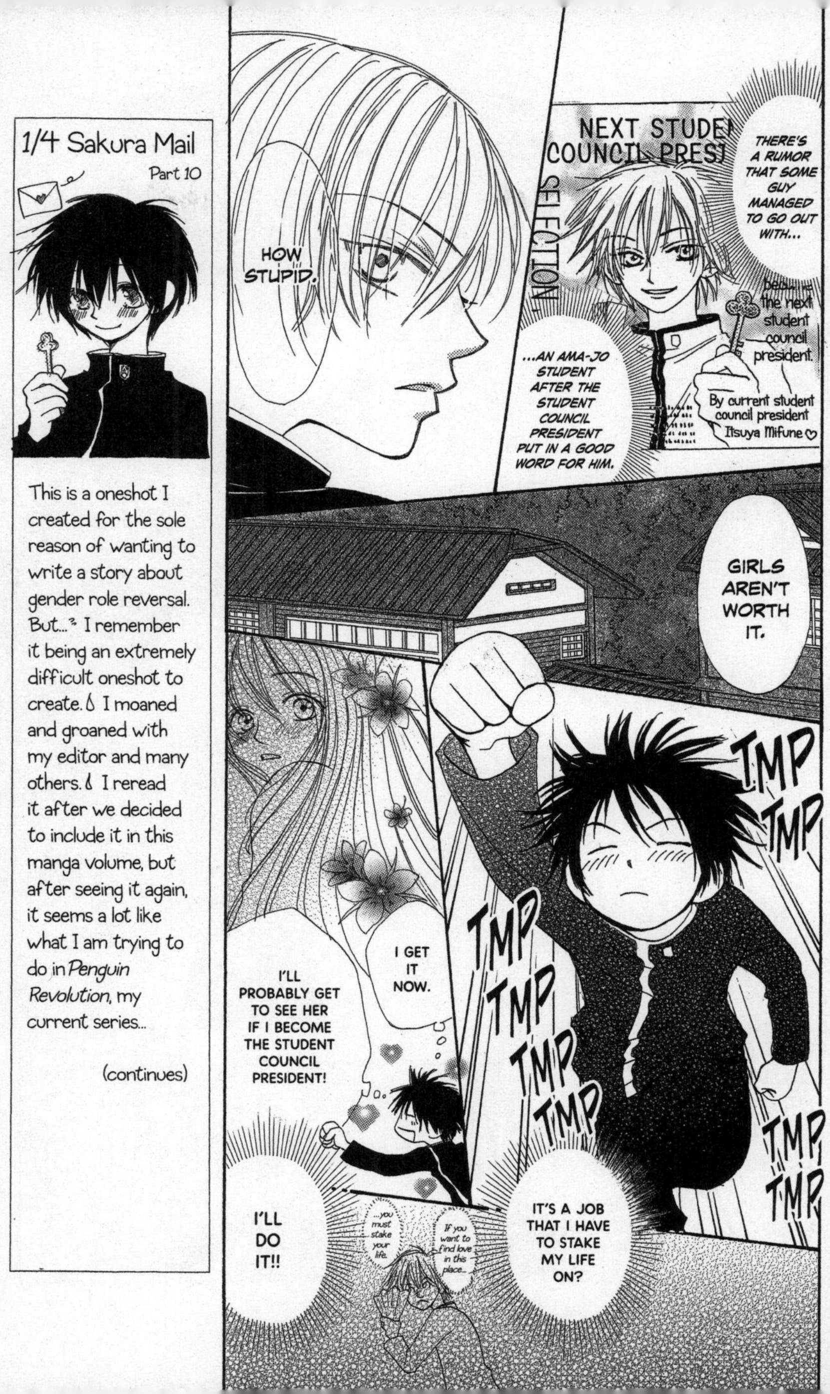
THERE'S A RUMOR THAT SOME GUY MANAGED TO GO OUT WITH...
the next student council president.
By current student council president Itsuya Mifune ♡
...AN AMA-JO STUDENT AFTER THE STUDENT COUNCIL PRESIDENT PUT IN A GOOD WORD FOR HIM.
HOW STUPID.
GIRLS AREN'T WORTH IT.
TMP TMP
TMP TMP TMP TMP
TMP TMP
I GET IT NOW.
I'LL PROBABLY GET TO SEE HER IF I BECOME THE STUDENT COUNCIL PRESIDENT!
IT'S A JOB THAT I HAVE TO STAKE MY LIFE ON?
If you want to find love in this place...
...you must stake your life.
I'LL DO IT!!

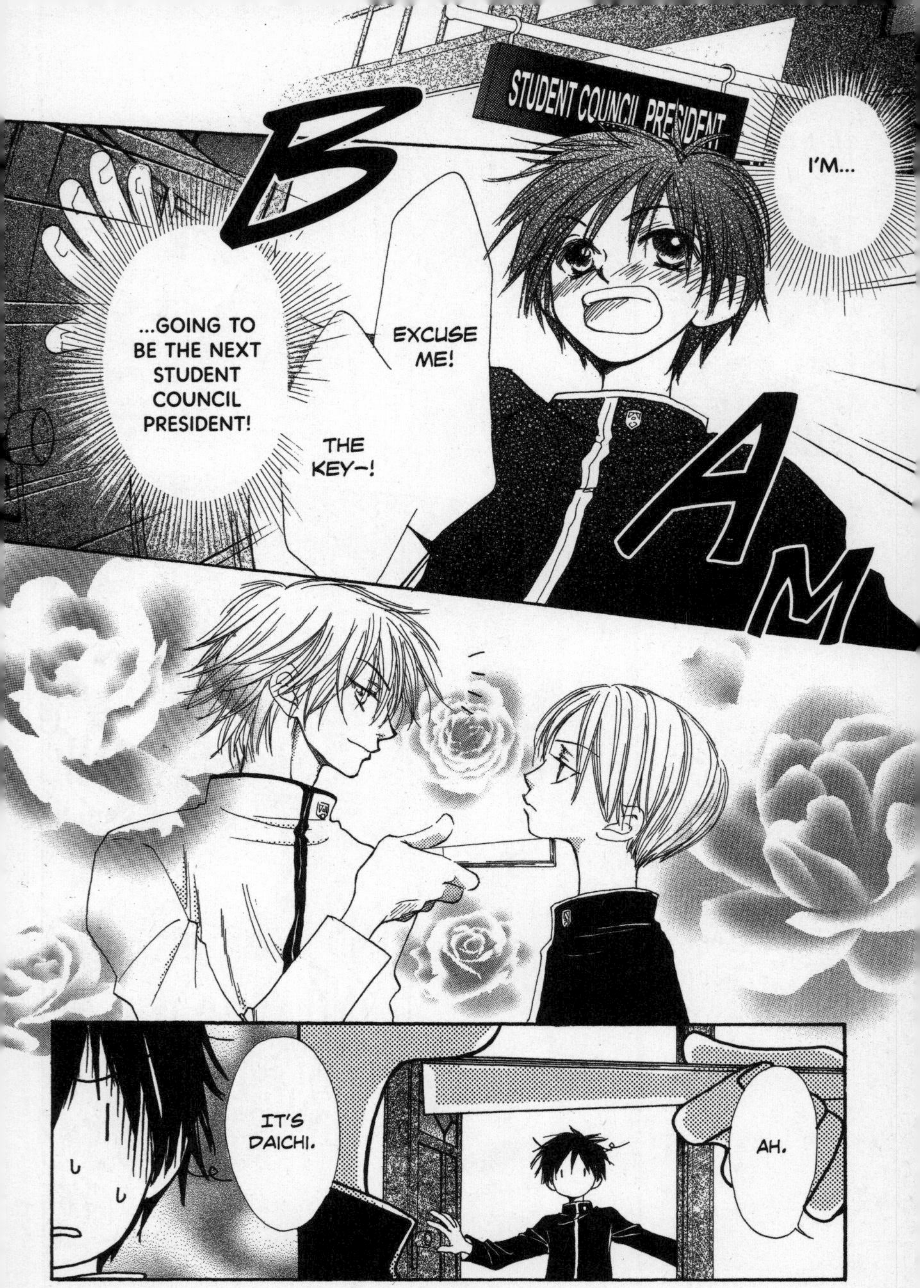
STUDENT COUNCIL PRESIDENT
I'M...
BAM
...GOING TO BE THE NEXT STUDENT COUNCIL PRESIDENT!
EXCUSE ME!
THE KEY–!
AH.
IT'S DAICHI.

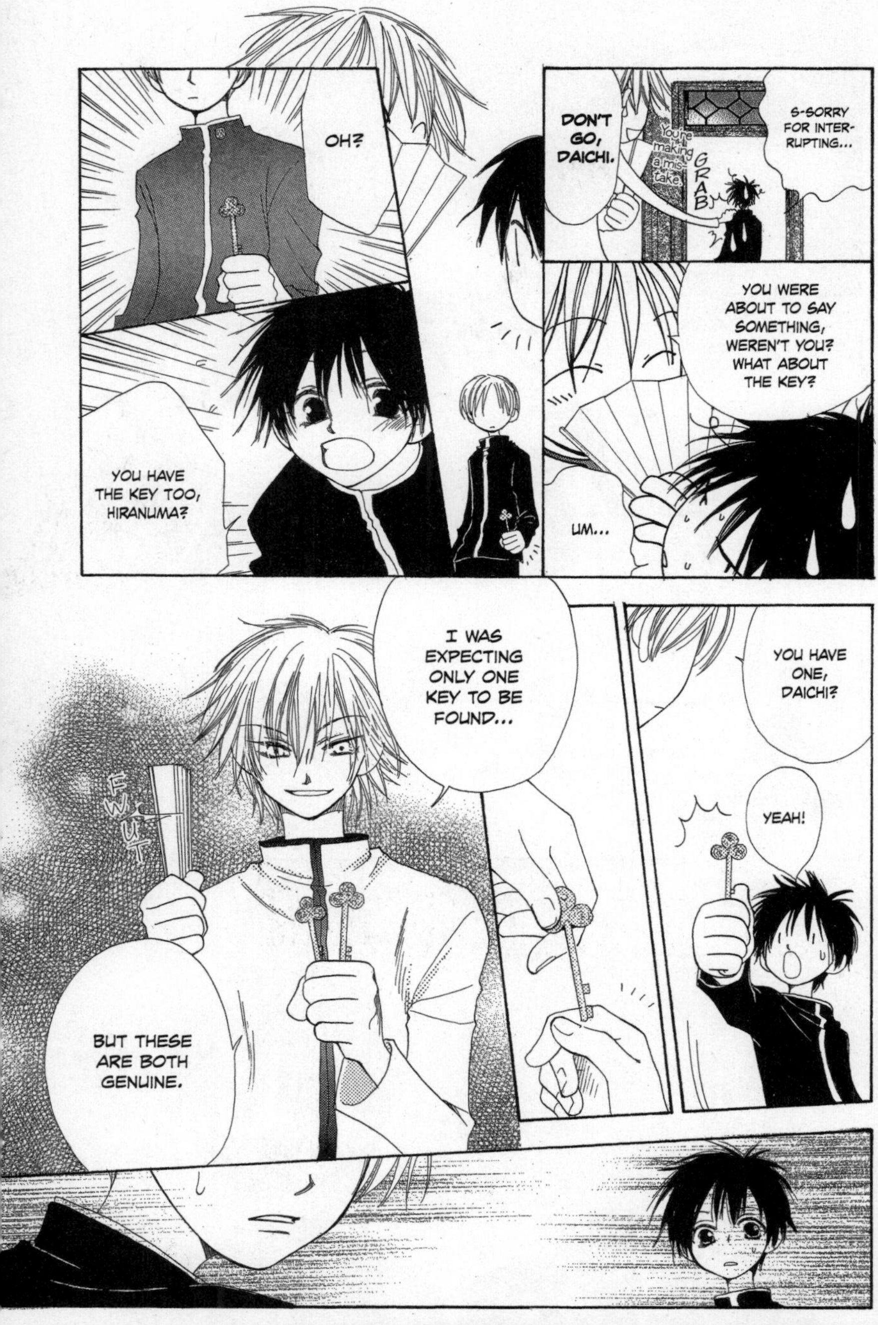
S-SORRY FOR INTER-RUPTING...
DON'T GO, DAICHI.
You're making a mis-take.
GRAB
YOU WERE ABOUT TO SAY SOMETHING, WEREN'T YOU? WHAT ABOUT THE KEY?
UM...
OH?
YOU HAVE THE KEY TOO, HIRANUMA?
YOU HAVE ONE, DAICHI?
YEAH!
I WAS EXPECTING ONLY ONE KEY TO BE FOUND...
FWUT
BUT THESE ARE BOTH GENUINE.

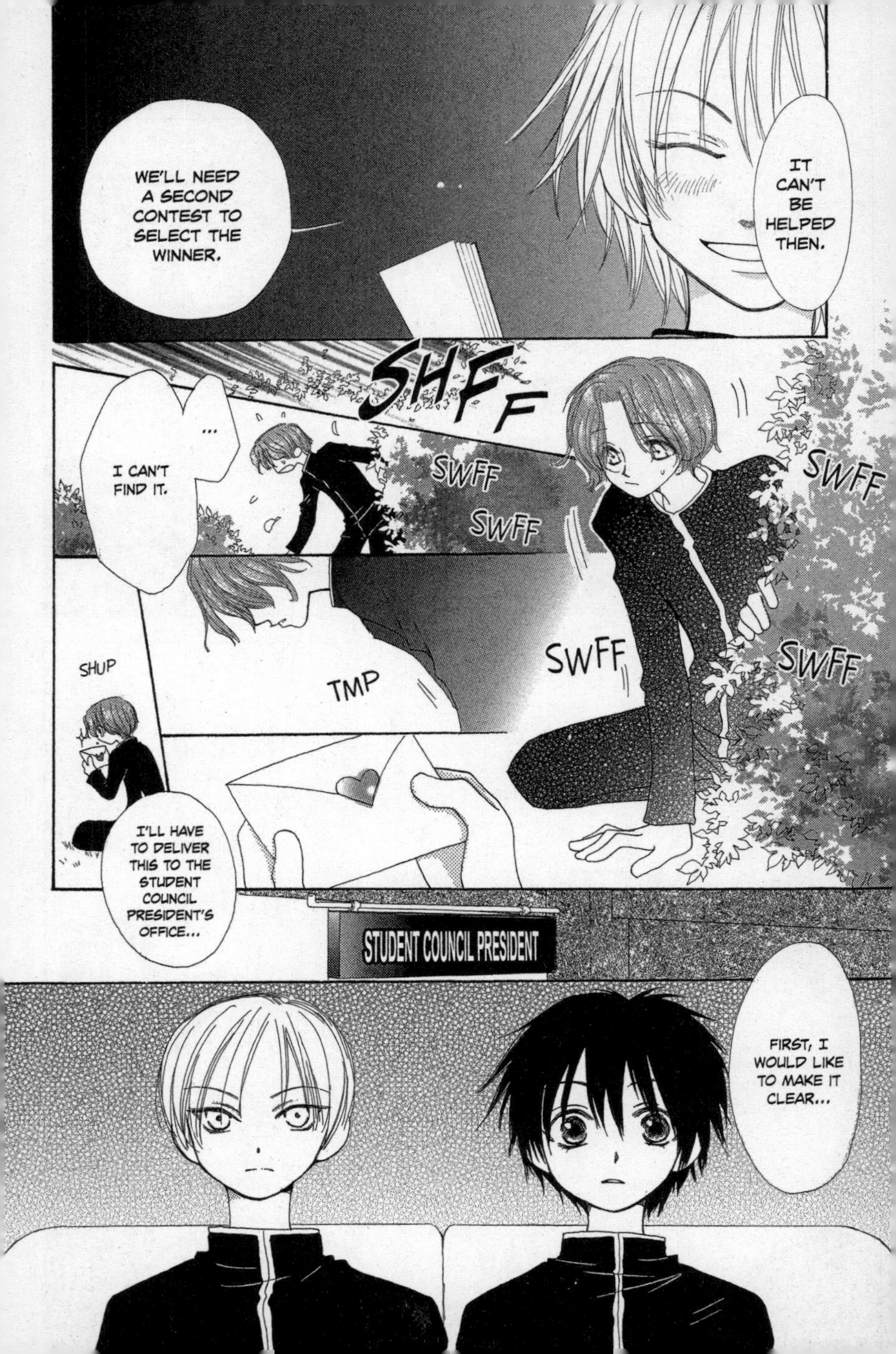

IT CAN'T BE HELPED THEN.
WE'LL NEED A SECOND CONTEST TO SELECT THE WINNER.
SHFF
SWFF
SWFF
SWFF
... I CAN'T FIND IT.
SWFF
SWFF
TMP
SHUP
I'LL HAVE TO DELIVER THIS TO THE STUDENT COUNCIL PRESIDENT'S OFFICE...
STUDENT COUNCIL PRESIDENT
FIRST, I WOULD LIKE TO MAKE IT CLEAR...

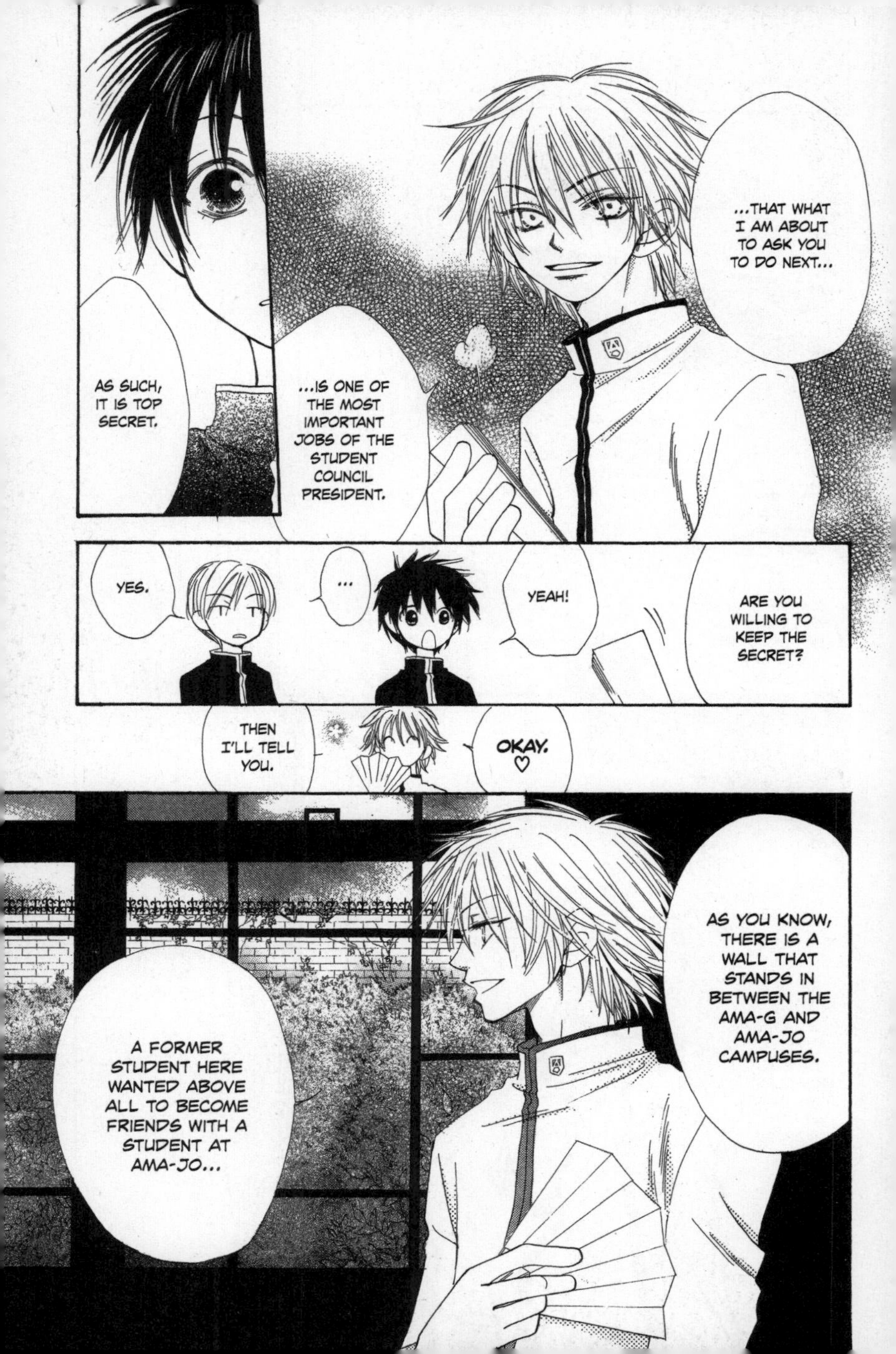
...THAT WHAT I AM ABOUT TO ASK YOU TO DO NEXT...
...IS ONE OF THE MOST IMPORTANT JOBS OF THE STUDENT COUNCIL PRESIDENT.
AS SUCH, IT IS TOP SECRET.
ARE YOU WILLING TO KEEP THE SECRET?
YEAH!
...
YES.
OKAY. ♡
THEN I'LL TELL YOU.
AS YOU KNOW, THERE IS A WALL THAT STANDS IN BETWEEN THE AMA-G AND AMA-JO CAMPUSES.
A FORMER STUDENT HERE WANTED ABOVE ALL TO BECOME FRIENDS WITH A STUDENT AT AMA-JO...

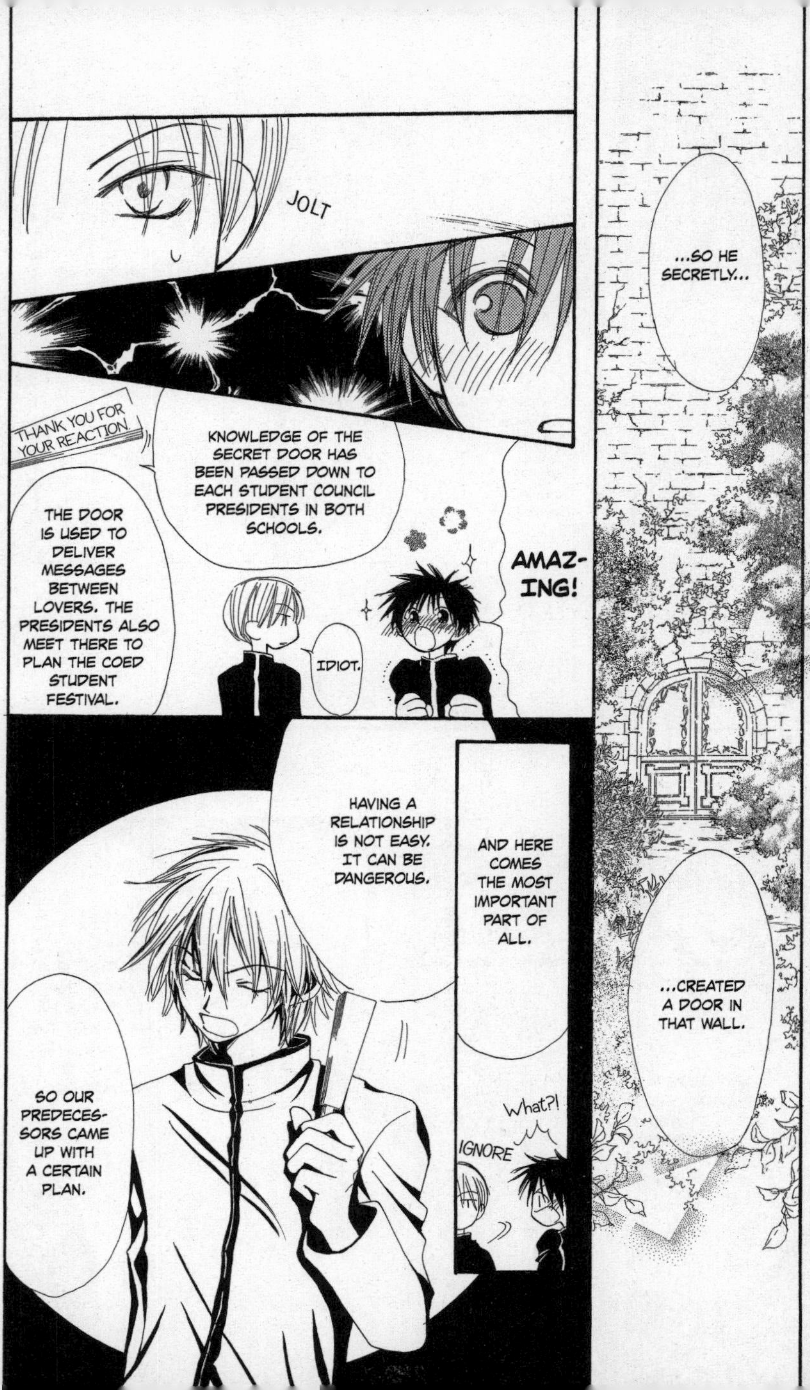
...SO HE SECRETLY...
...CREATED A DOOR IN THAT WALL.
JOLT
AMAZ-ING!
KNOWLEDGE OF THE SECRET DOOR HAS BEEN PASSED DOWN TO EACH STUDENT COUNCIL PRESIDENTS IN BOTH SCHOOLS.
THANK YOU FOR YOUR REACTION.
IDIOT.
THE DOOR IS USED TO DELIVER MESSAGES BETWEEN LOVERS. THE PRESIDENTS ALSO MEET THERE TO PLAN THE COED STUDENT FESTIVAL.
AND HERE COMES THE MOST IMPORTANT PART OF ALL.
What?!
IGNORE
HAVING A RELATIONSHIP IS NOT EASY. IT CAN BE DANGEROUS.
SO OUR PREDECES-SORS CAME UP WITH A CERTAIN PLAN.

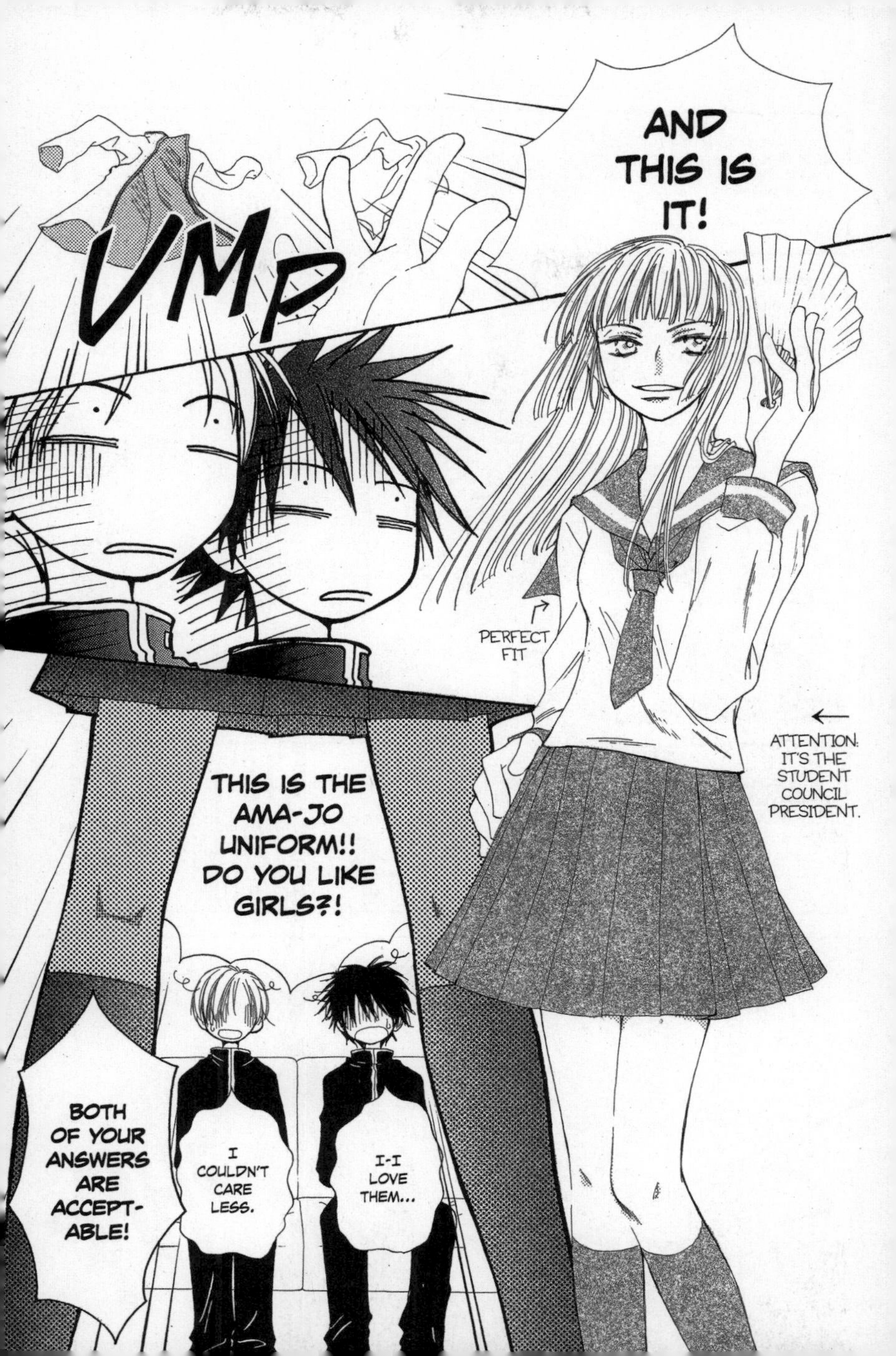

AND THIS IS IT!
VMP
ATTENTION: IT'S THE STUDENT COUNCIL PRESIDENT.
PERFECT FIT
THIS IS THE AMA-JO UNIFORM!! DO YOU LIKE GIRLS?!
I-I LOVE THEM...
I COULDN'T CARE LESS.
BOTH OF YOUR ANSWERS ARE ACCEPT-ABLE!

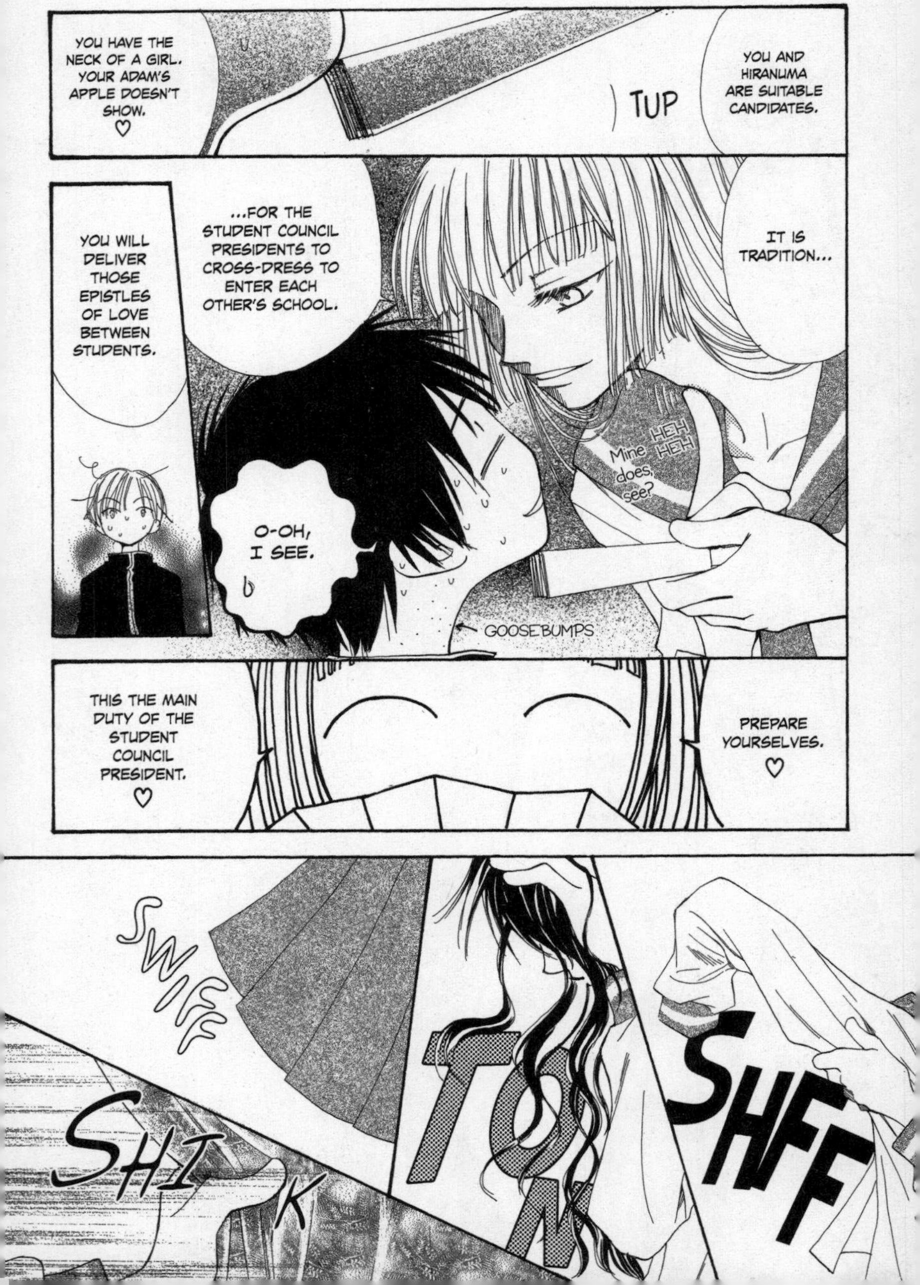
YOU AND HIRANUMA ARE SUITABLE CANDIDATES.
TUP
YOU HAVE THE NECK OF A GIRL. YOUR ADAM'S APPLE DOESN'T SHOW. ♡
IT IS TRADITION...
...FOR THE STUDENT COUNCIL PRESIDENTS TO CROSS-DRESS TO ENTER EACH OTHER'S SCHOOL.
YOU WILL DELIVER THOSE EPISTLES OF LOVE BETWEEN STUDENTS.
HEH HEH
Mine does, see?
O-OH, I SEE.
GOOSEBUMPS
PREPARE YOURSELVES. ♡
THIS THE MAIN DUTY OF THE STUDENT COUNCIL PRESIDENT. ♡
SHFF
TON
SWIFF
SHIK

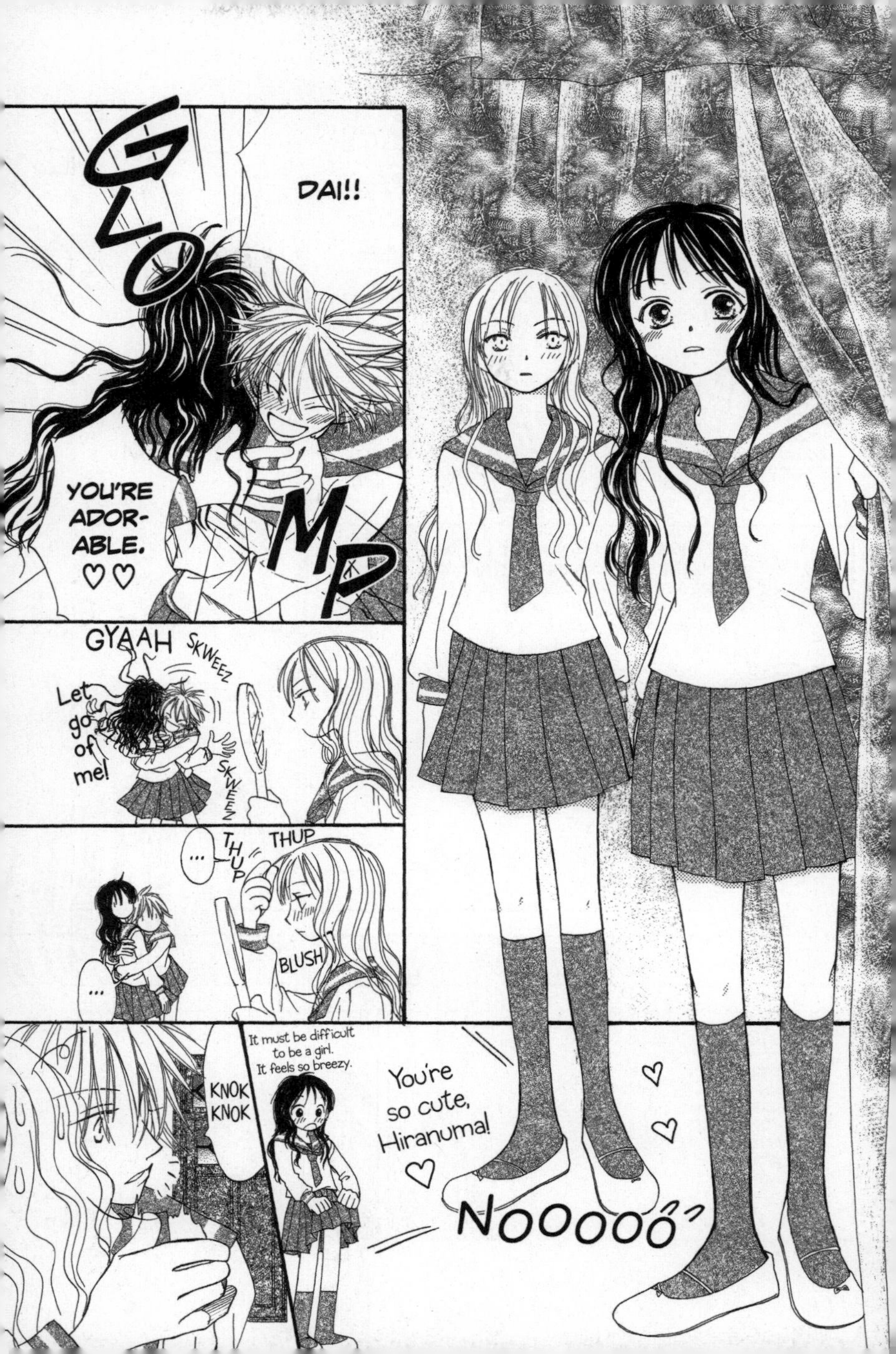

You're so cute, Hiranuma! ♡
NOOOOO
DAI!!
GLOMP
YOU'RE ADORABLE. ♡♡
SKWEEZ
GYAAH
Let go of me!
SKWEEZ
THUP THUP
...
BLUSH
...
It must be difficult to be a girl. It feels so breezy.
KNOK KNOK

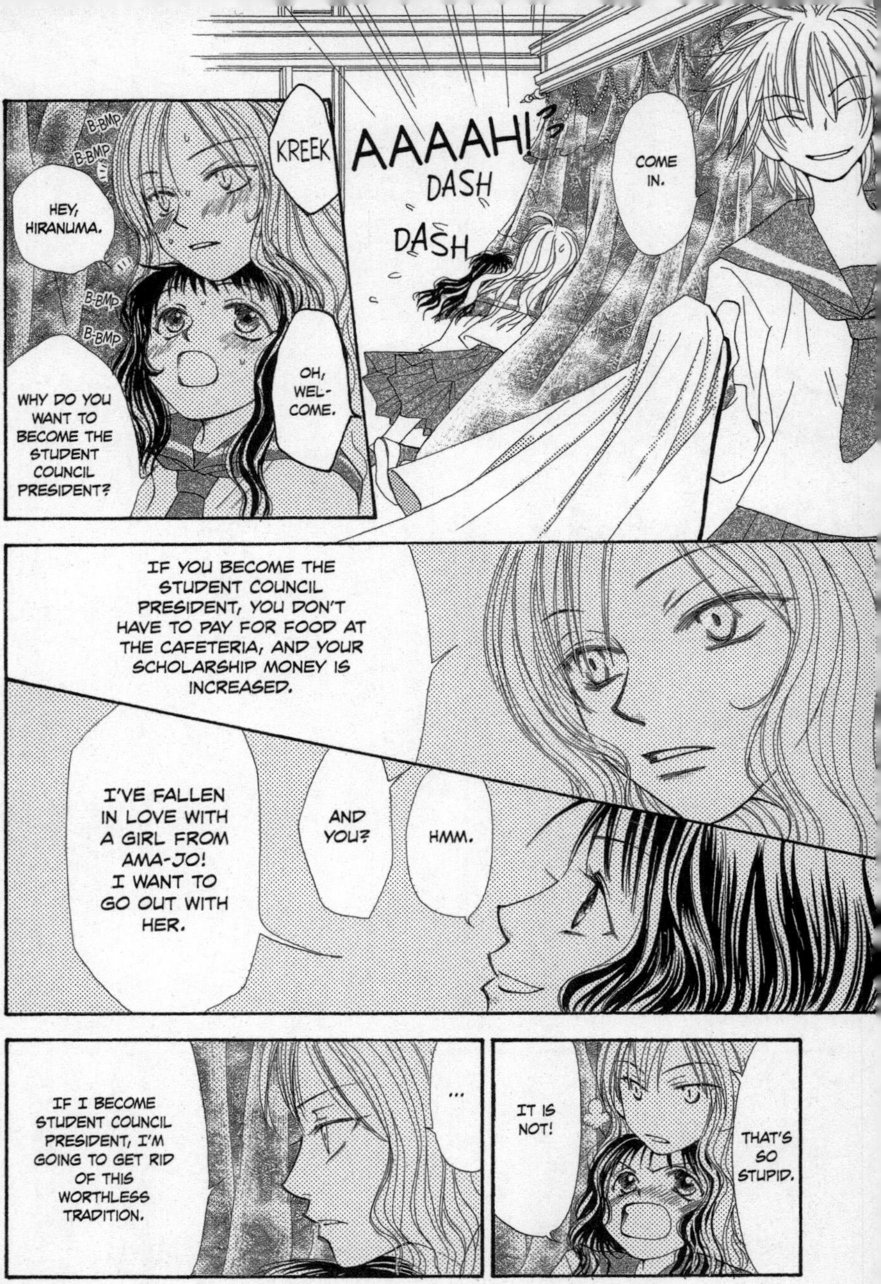
COME IN.
AAAAH!
DASH
DASH
KREEK
B-BMP
B-BMP
HEY, HIRANUMA.
B-BMP
B-BMP
OH, WEL-COME.
WHY DO YOU WANT TO BECOME THE STUDENT COUNCIL PRESIDENT?
IF YOU BECOME THE STUDENT COUNCIL PRESIDENT, YOU DON'T HAVE TO PAY FOR FOOD AT THE CAFETERIA, AND YOUR SCHOLARSHIP MONEY IS INCREASED.
HMM.
AND YOU?
I'VE FALLEN IN LOVE WITH A GIRL FROM AMA-JO! I WANT TO GO OUT WITH HER.
THAT'S SO STUPID.
IT IS NOT!
...
IF I BECOME STUDENT COUNCIL PRESIDENT, I'M GOING TO GET RID OF THIS WORTHLESS TRADITION.

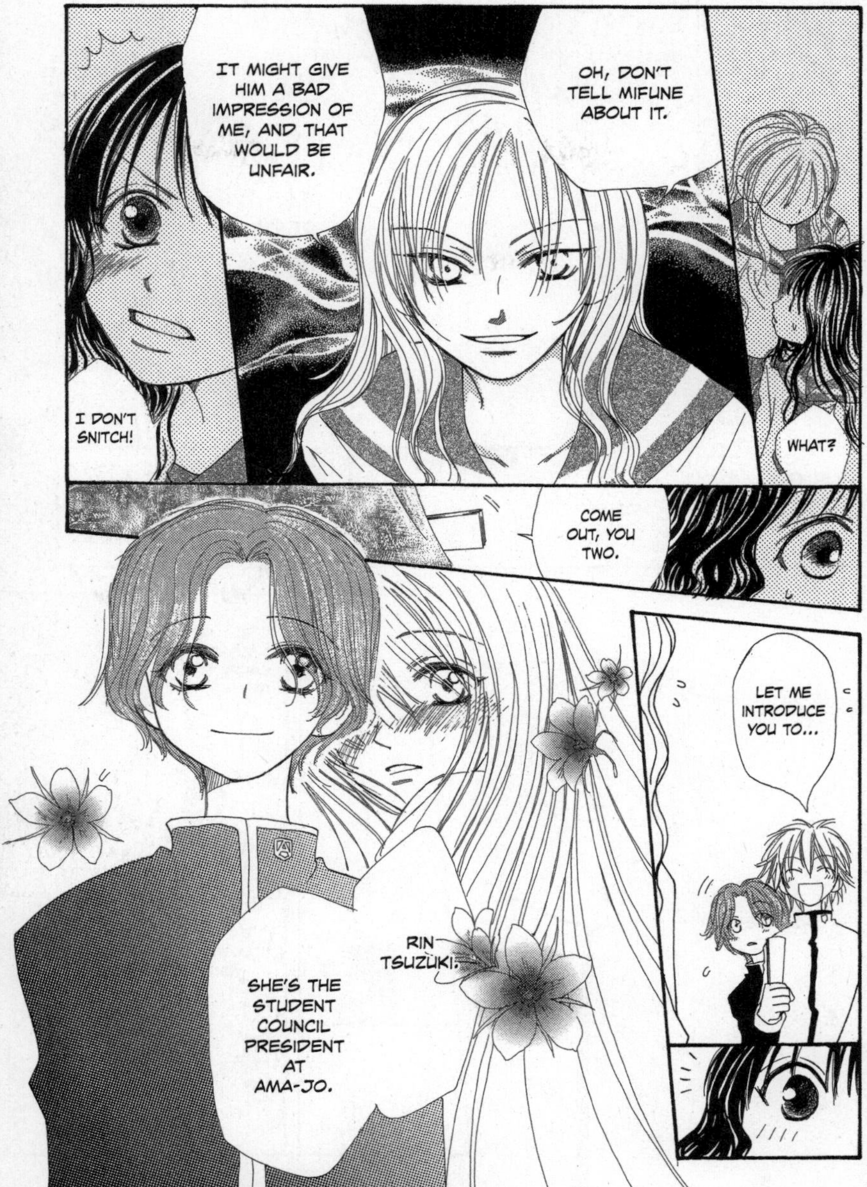
WHAT?
OH, DON'T TELL MIFUNE ABOUT IT.
IT MIGHT GIVE HIM A BAD IMPRESSION OF ME, AND THAT WOULD BE UNFAIR.
I DON'T SNITCH!
COME OUT, YOU TWO.
LET ME INTRODUCE YOU TO...
RIN TSUZUKI.
SHE'S THE STUDENT COUNCIL PRESIDENT AT AMA-JO.

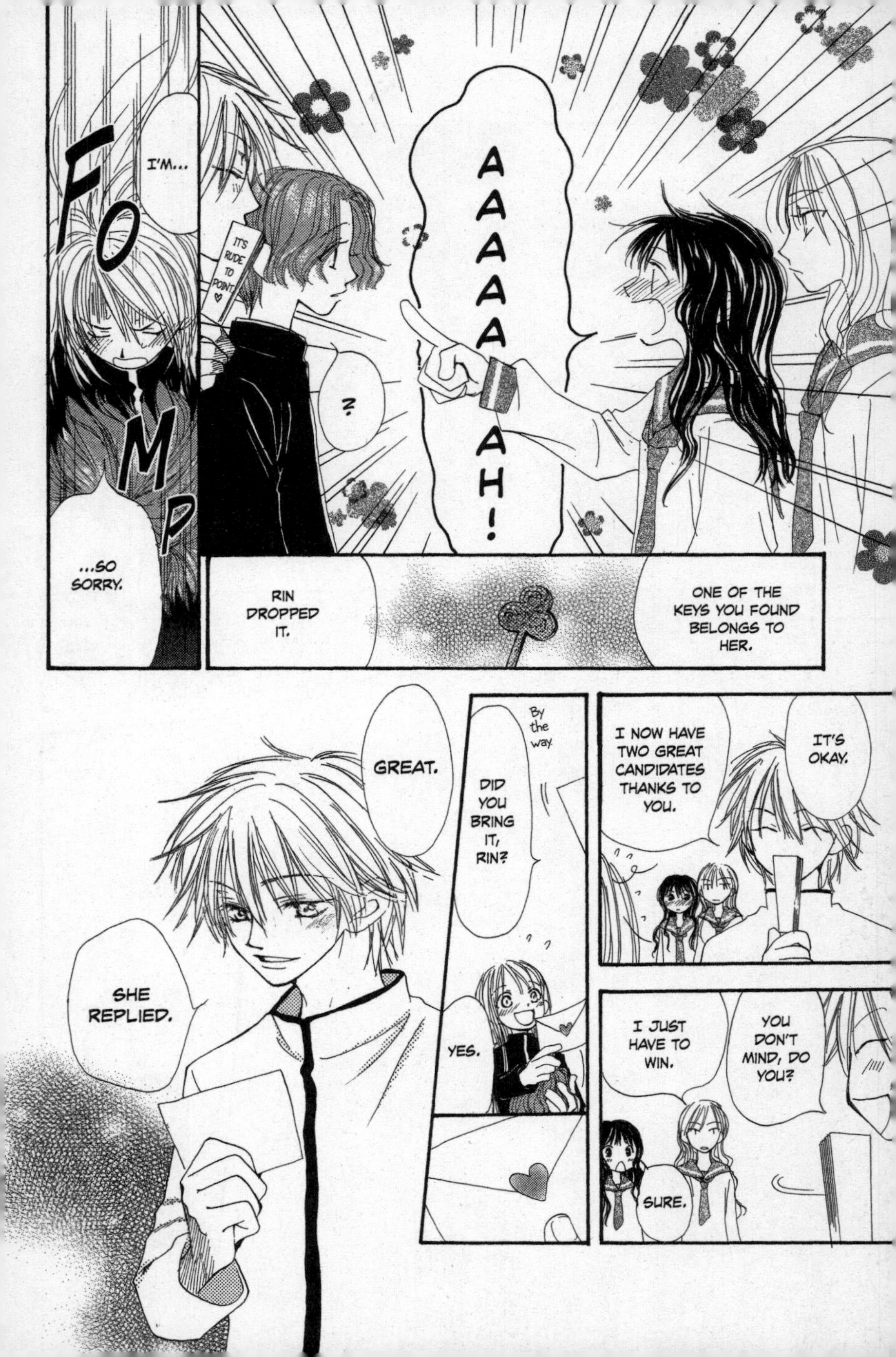
AAAAAH!
?
IT'S RUDE TO POINT ♡
ONE OF THE KEYS YOU FOUND BELONGS TO HER.
RIN DROPPED IT.
FOMP
I'M...
...SO SORRY.
IT'S OKAY.
I NOW HAVE TWO GREAT CANDIDATES THANKS TO YOU.
YOU DON'T MIND, DO YOU?
I JUST HAVE TO WIN.
SURE.
By the way.
DID YOU BRING IT, RIN?
YES.
GREAT.
SHE REPLIED.

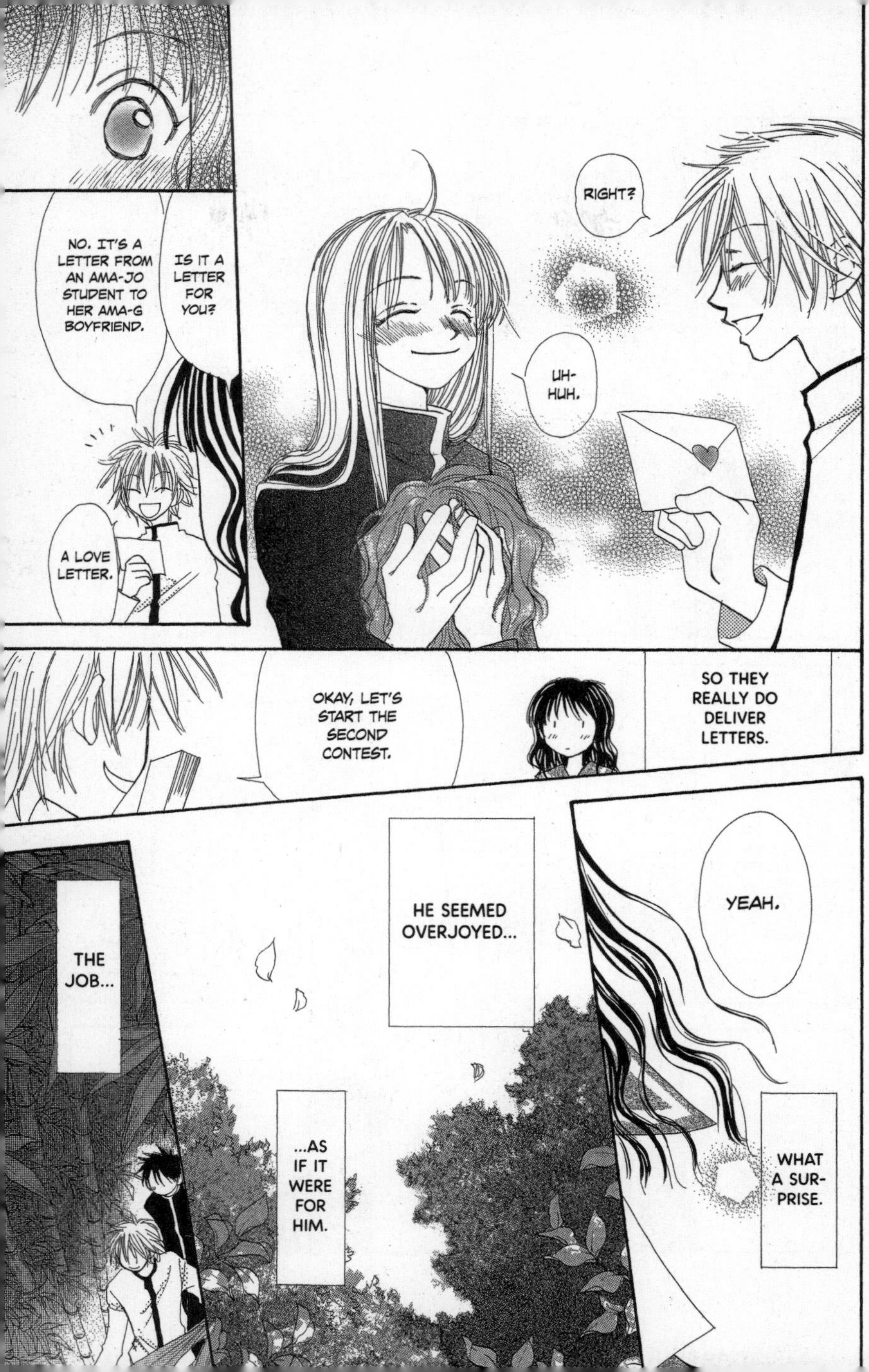
RIGHT?
UH-HUH.
IS IT A LETTER FOR YOU?
NO. IT'S A LETTER FROM AN AMA-JO STUDENT TO HER AMA-G BOYFRIEND.
A LOVE LETTER.
SO THEY REALLY DO DELIVER LETTERS.
OKAY, LET'S START THE SECOND CONTEST.
YEAH.
WHAT A SURPRISE.
HE SEEMED OVERJOYED...
...AS IF IT WERE FOR HIM.
THE JOB...

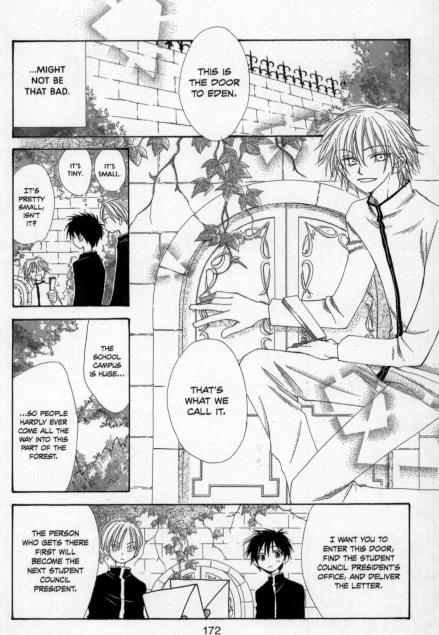

...MIGHT NOT BE THAT BAD.
THIS IS THE DOOR TO EDEN.
THAT'S WHAT WE CALL IT.
IT'S SMALL.
IT'S TINY.
IT'S PRETTY SMALL, ISN'T IT?
THE SCHOOL CAMPUS IS HUGE...
...SO PEOPLE HARDLY EVER COME ALL THE WAY INTO THIS PART OF THE FOREST.
I WANT YOU TO ENTER THIS DOOR, FIND THE STUDENT COUNCIL PRESIDENT'S OFFICE, AND DELIVER THE LETTER.
THE PERSON WHO GETS THERE FIRST WILL BECOME THE NEXT STUDENT COUNCIL PRESIDENT.

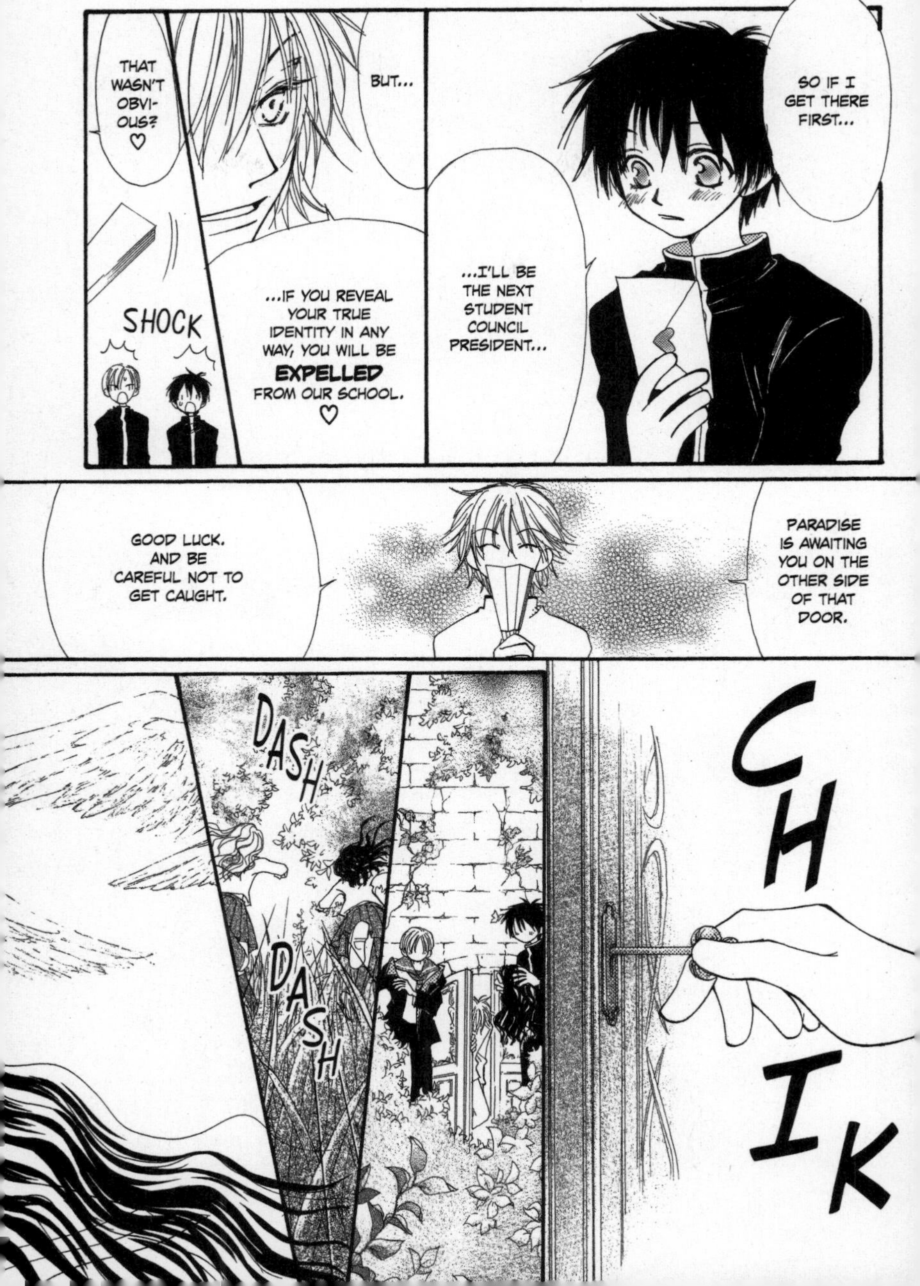
SO IF I GET THERE FIRST...
...I'LL BE THE NEXT STUDENT COUNCIL PRESIDENT...
BUT...
...IF YOU REVEAL YOUR TRUE IDENTITY IN ANY WAY, YOU WILL BE **EXPELLED** FROM OUR SCHOOL. ♡
THAT WASN'T OBVI-OUS? ♡
SHOCK
PARADISE IS AWAITING YOU ON THE OTHER SIDE OF THAT DOOR.
GOOD LUCK. AND BE CAREFUL NOT TO GET CAUGHT.
CHIK
DASH
DASH

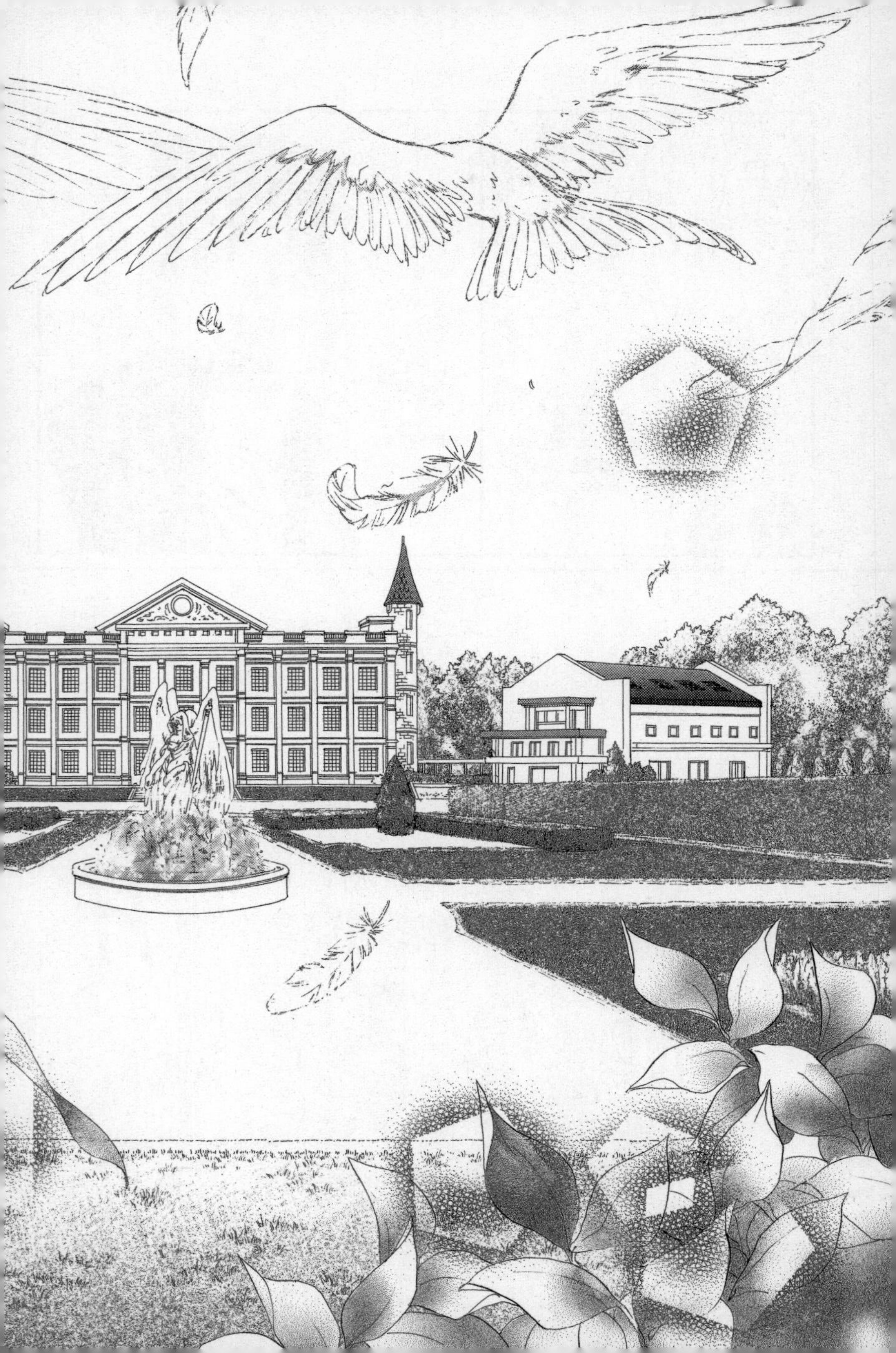

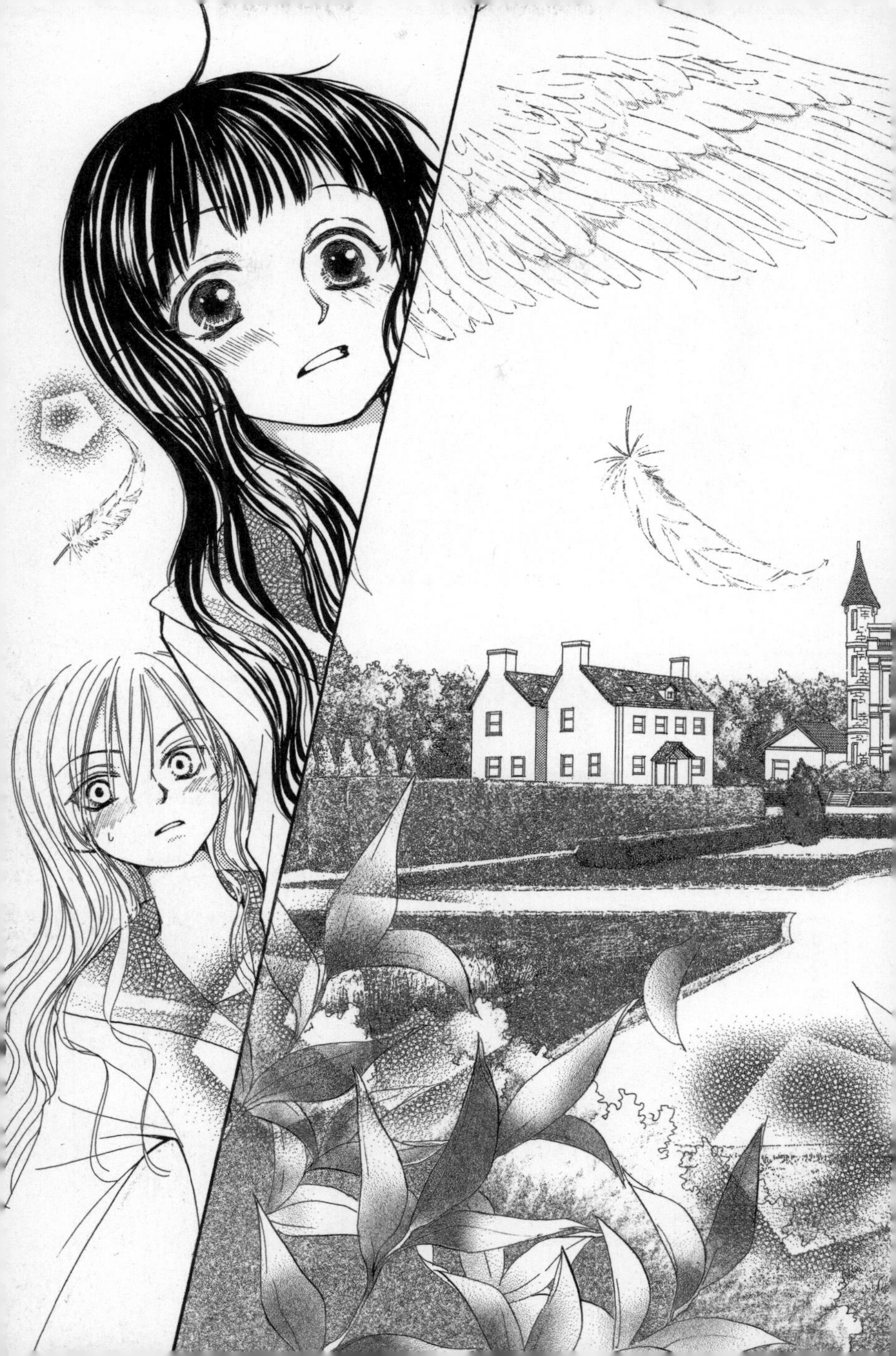

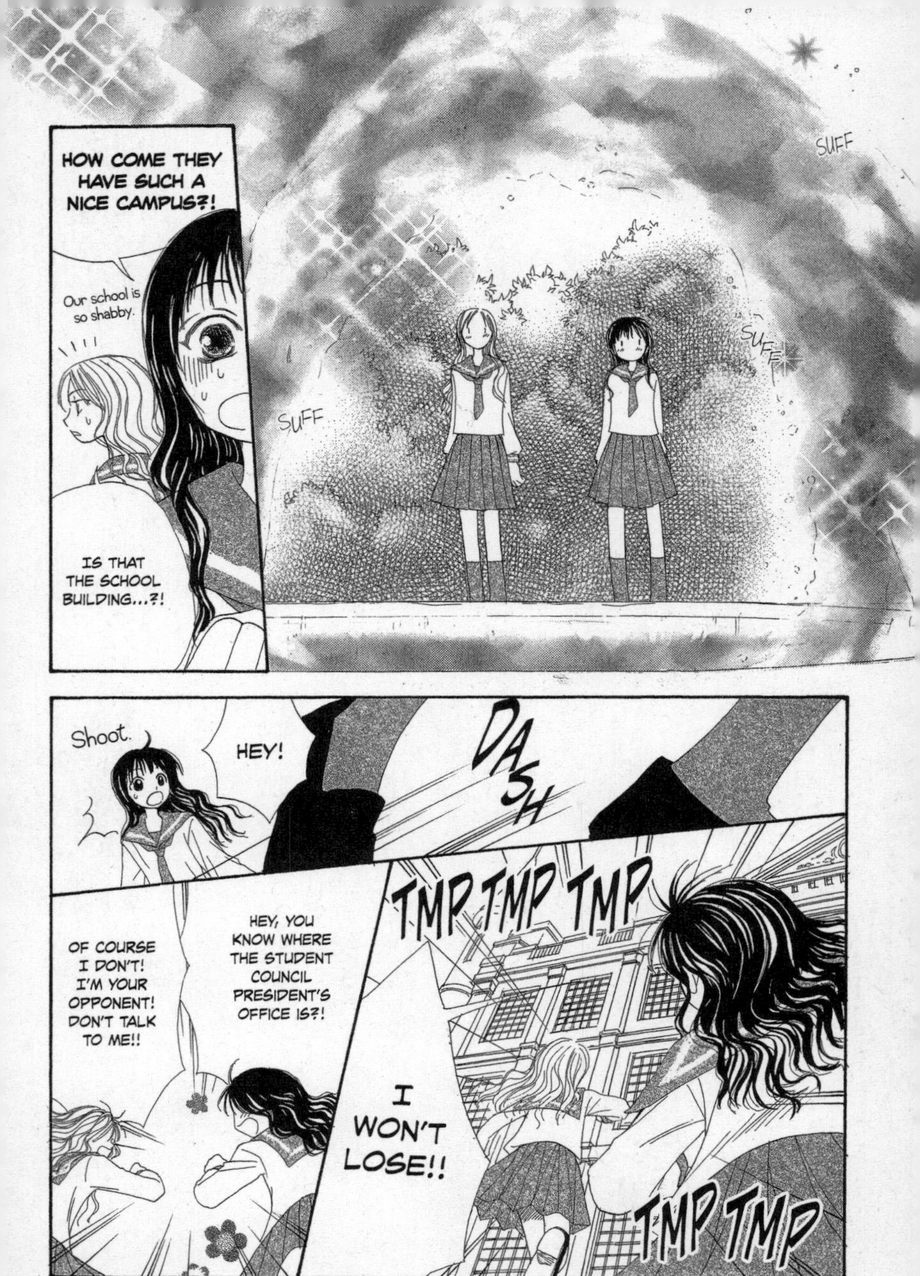
SUFF
SUFF
SUFF
HOW COME THEY HAVE SUCH A NICE CAMPUS?!
Our school is so shabby.
IS THAT THE SCHOOL BUILDING...?!
DASH
HEY!
Shoot.
TMP TMP TMP
I WON'T LOSE!!
TMP TMP
HEY, YOU KNOW WHERE THE STUDENT COUNCIL PRESIDENT'S OFFICE IS?!
OF COURSE I DON'T! I'M YOUR OPPONENT! DON'T TALK TO ME!!

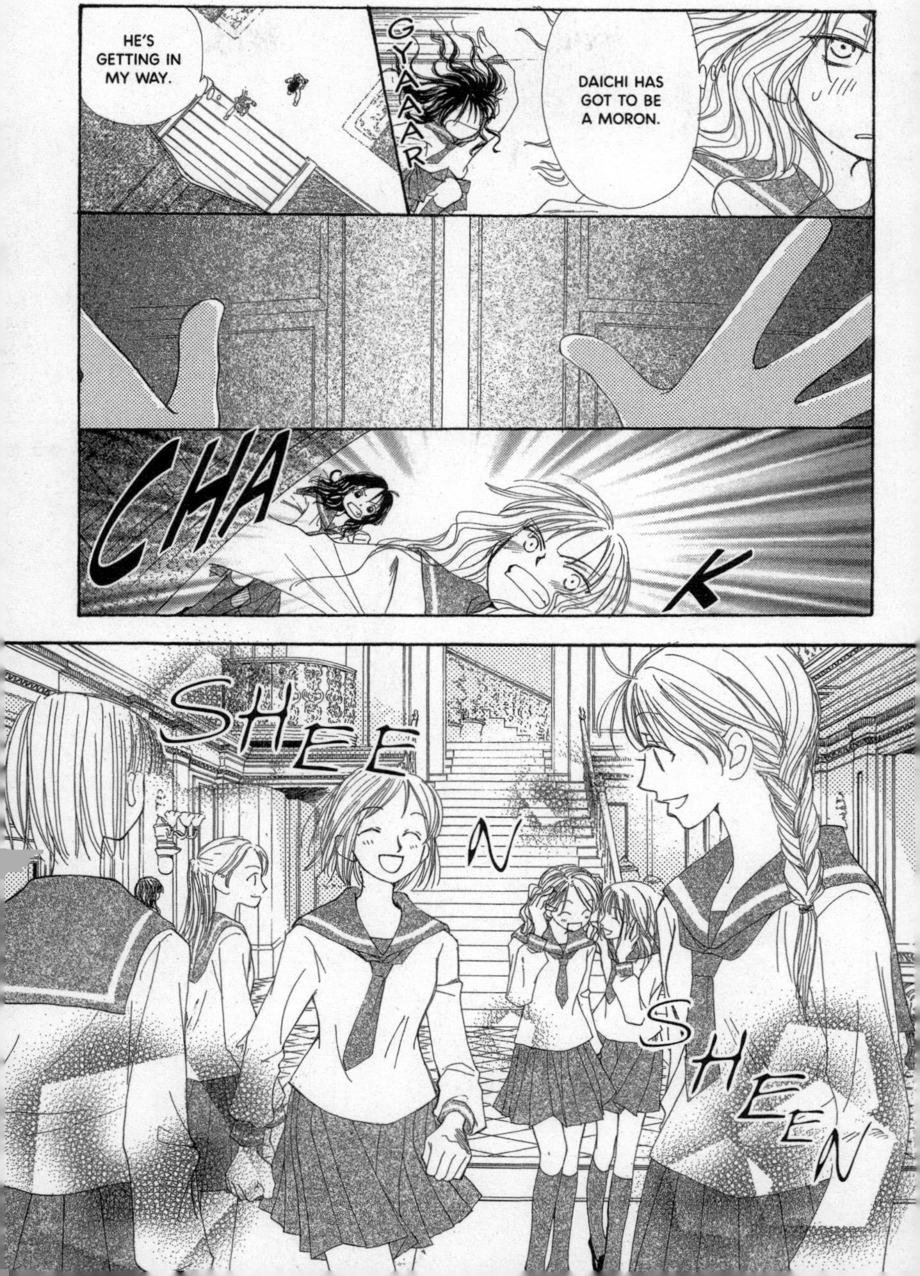
DAICHI HAS GOT TO BE A MORON.
GYAAAR
HE'S GETTING IN MY WAY.
CHA K
SHEEN
SHEEN

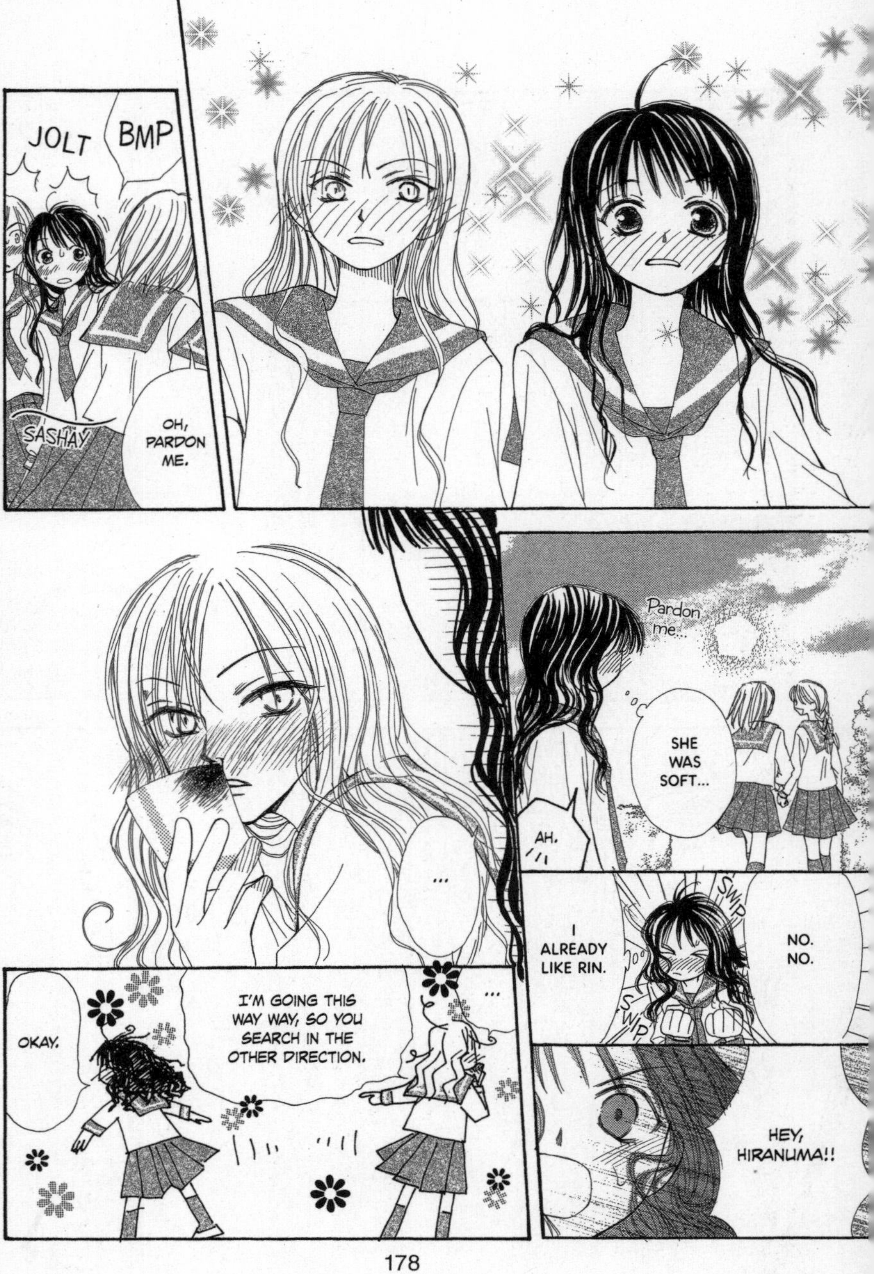
JOLT
BMP
SASHAY
OH, PARDON ME.
Pardon me...
SHE WAS SOFT...
AH.
NO. NO.
I ALREADY LIKE RIN.
HEY, HIRANUMA!!
...
...
I'M GOING THIS WAY WAY, SO YOU SEARCH IN THE OTHER DIRECTION.
OKAY.

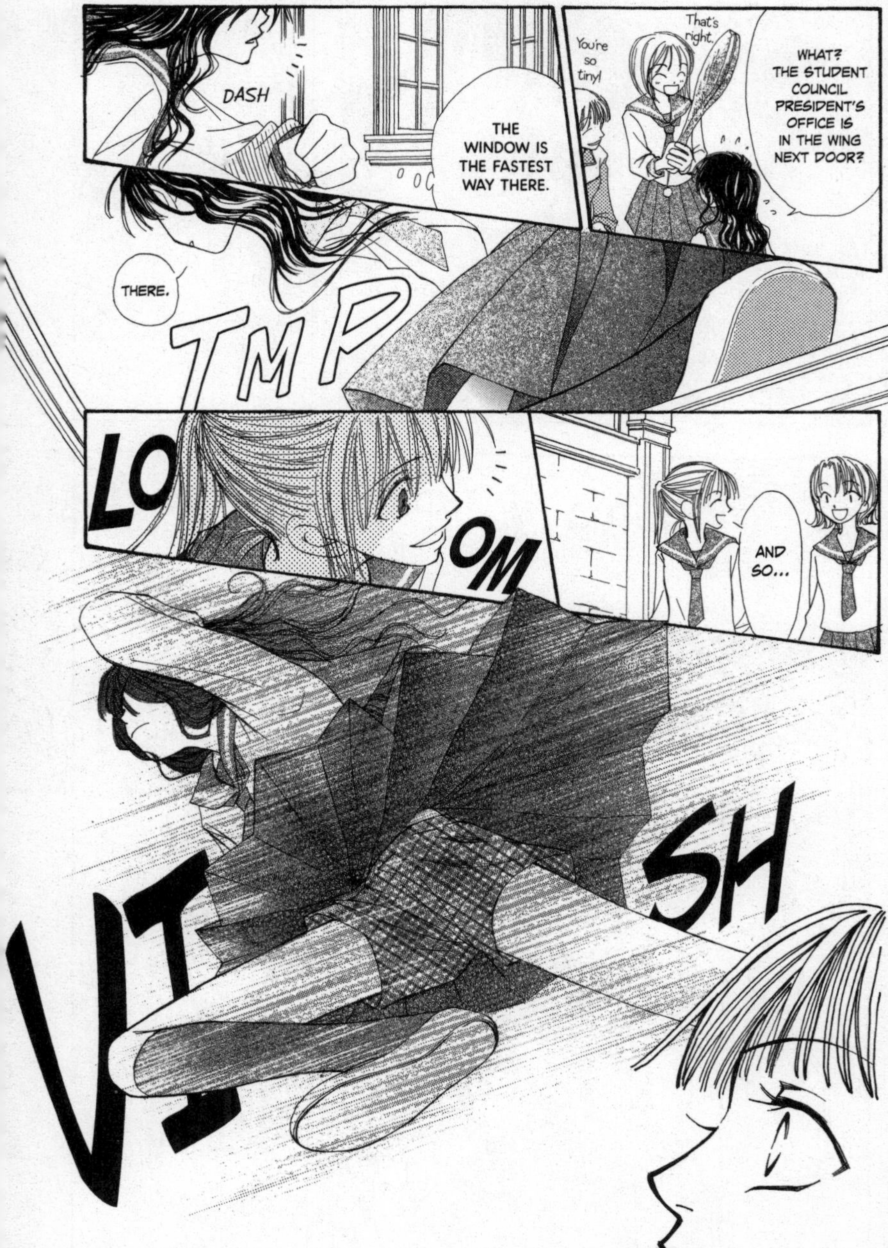
WHAT? THE STUDENT COUNCIL PRESIDENT'S OFFICE IS IN THE WING NEXT DOOR?
That's right.
You're so tiny!
THE WINDOW IS THE FASTEST WAY THERE.
DASH
THERE.
TMP
AND SO...
LO
OM
SH
VI

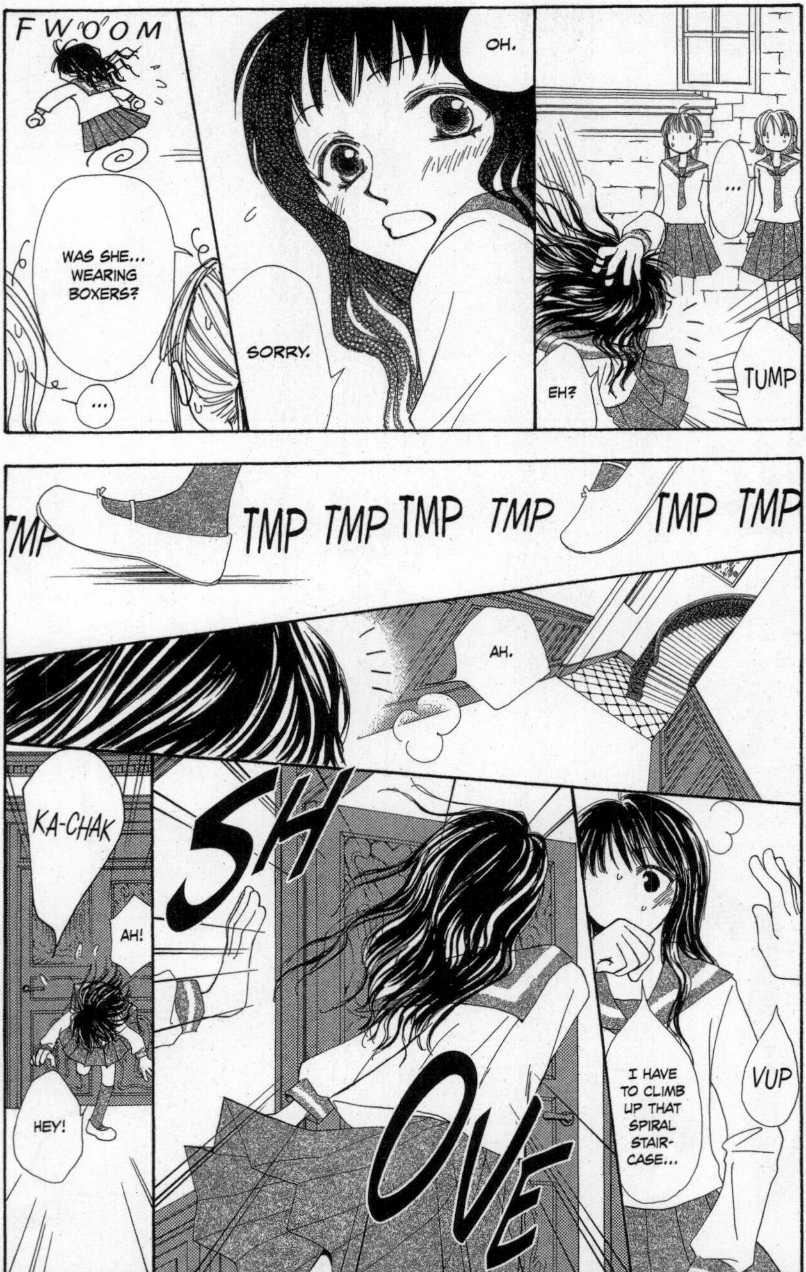
...
TUMP
EH?
OH.
SORRY.
FWOOM
WAS SHE... WEARING BOXERS?
...
TMP TMP TMP TMP TMP TMP TMP
AH.
VUP
I HAVE TO CLIMB UP THAT SPIRAL STAIR-CASE...
SHOVE
KA-CHAK
AH!
HEY!

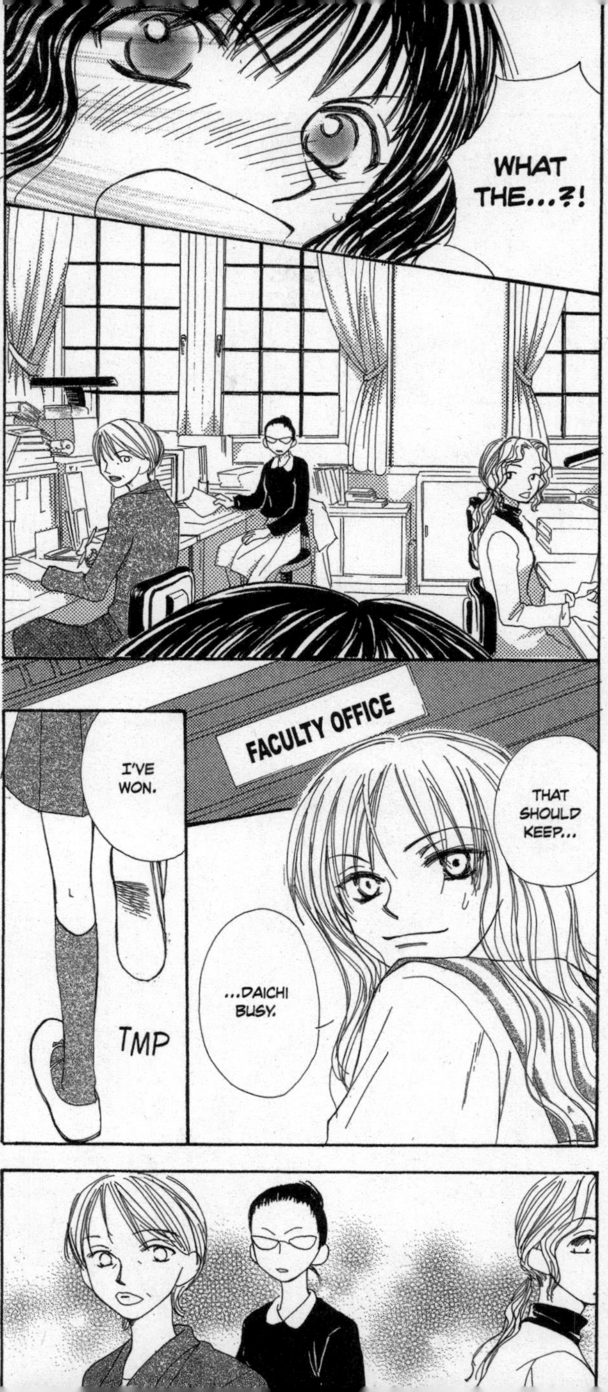
WHAT THE...?!
FACULTY OFFICE
THAT SHOULD KEEP...
...DAICHI BUSY.
I'VE WON.
TMP

1/4 Sakura Mail

Part 11

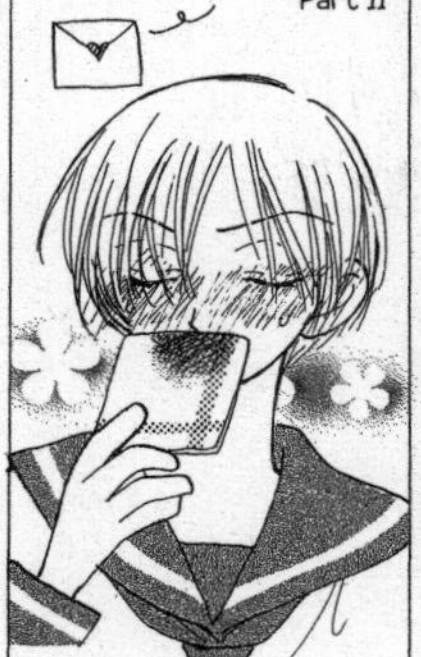

(Did you want to draw a cross-dressing manga that badly, Tsukuba?! Yeah! I did! PHOOF!) It has turned out to be a very embarrassing piece. This oneshot was placed in a manga magazine that was doing a "Cool Men" feature. So I tried my best to make Daichi a nice guy, but I'm not too sure about it... He's probably one of the most foolish main characters I've ever drawn. ♡ Well then, I don't have much space left, so I bid you all farewell.

Sakura Tsukuba

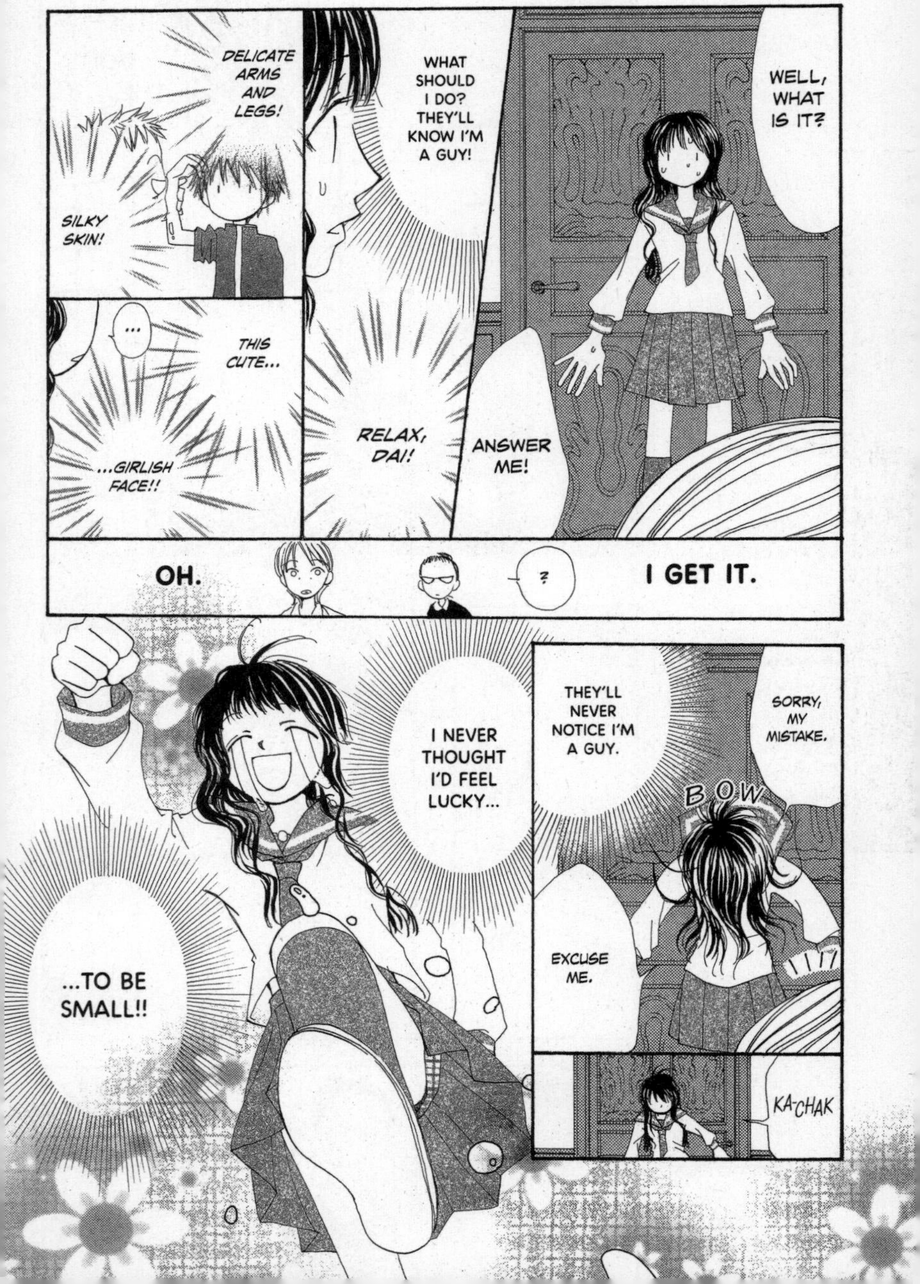
WELL, WHAT IS IT?
ANSWER ME!
WHAT SHOULD I DO? THEY'LL KNOW I'M A GUY!
RELAX, DAI!
DELICATE ARMS AND LEGS!
SILKY SKIN!
...
THIS CUTE...
...GIRLISH FACE!!
OH.
?
I GET IT.
SORRY, MY MISTAKE.
THEY'LL NEVER NOTICE I'M A GUY.
BOW
EXCUSE ME.
KA-CHAK
I NEVER THOUGHT I'D FEEL LUCKY...
...TO BE SMALL!!

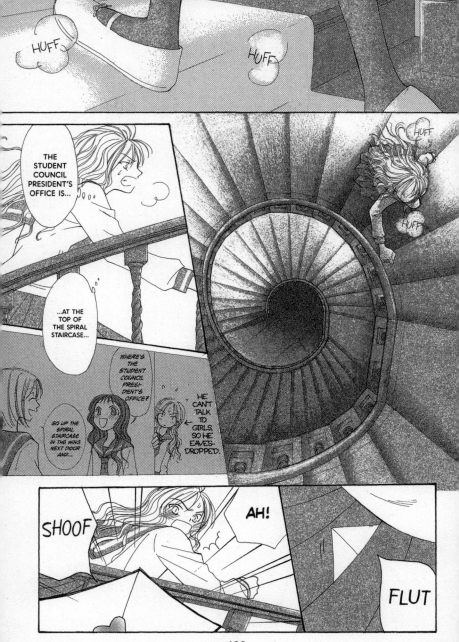

HUFF

HUFF

HUFF

THE STUDENT COUNCIL PRESIDENT'S OFFICE IS...

HUFF

...AT THE TOP OF THE SPIRAL STAIRCASE...

WHERE'S THE STUDENT COUNCIL PRESIDENT'S OFFICE?

GO UP THE SPIRAL STAIRCASE IN THE WING NEXT DOOR AND...

HE CAN'T TALK TO GIRLS SO HE EAVESDROPPED.

SHOOF

AH!

FLUT

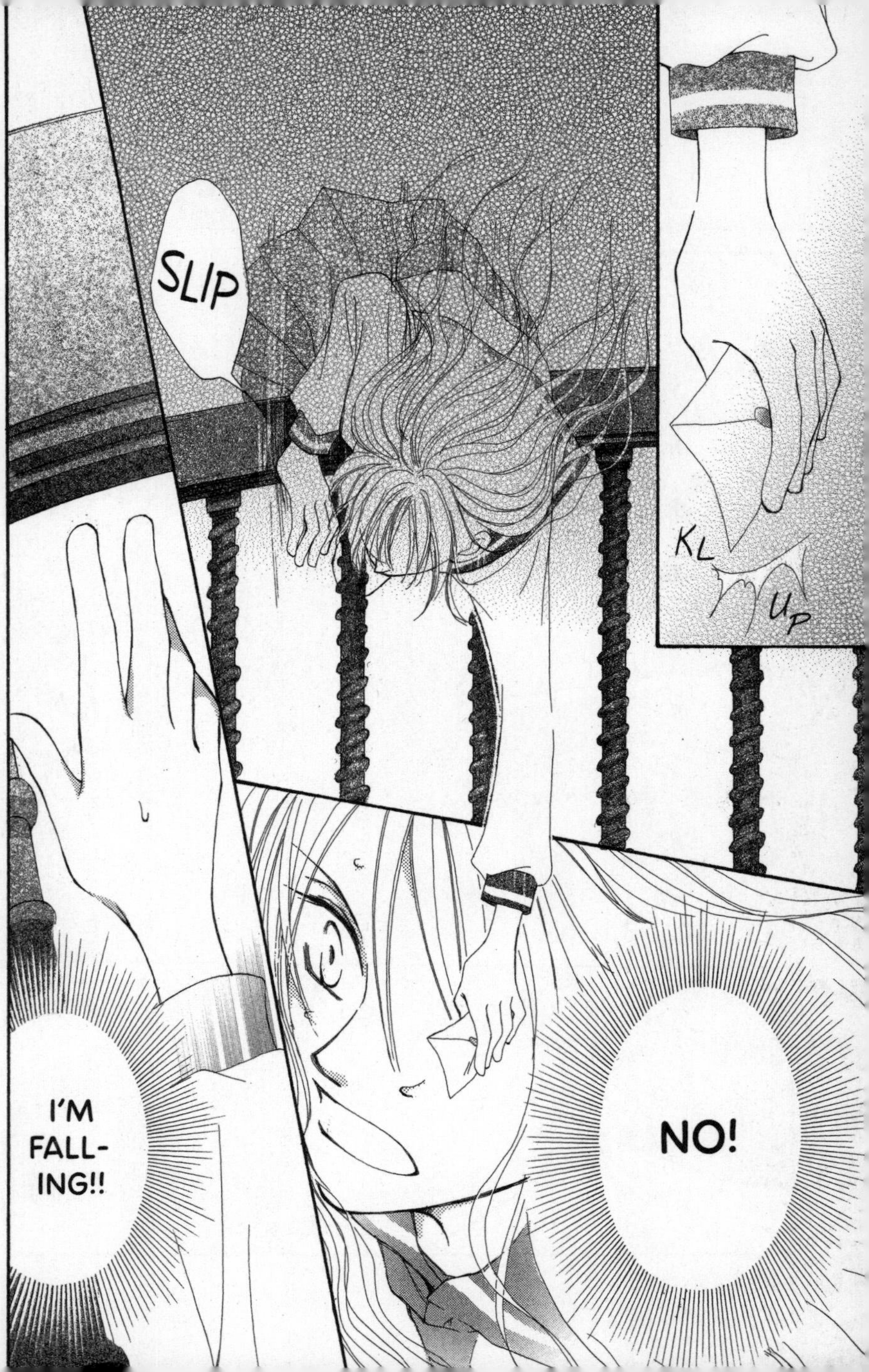
KL
UP
SLIP
NO!
I'M FALLING!!

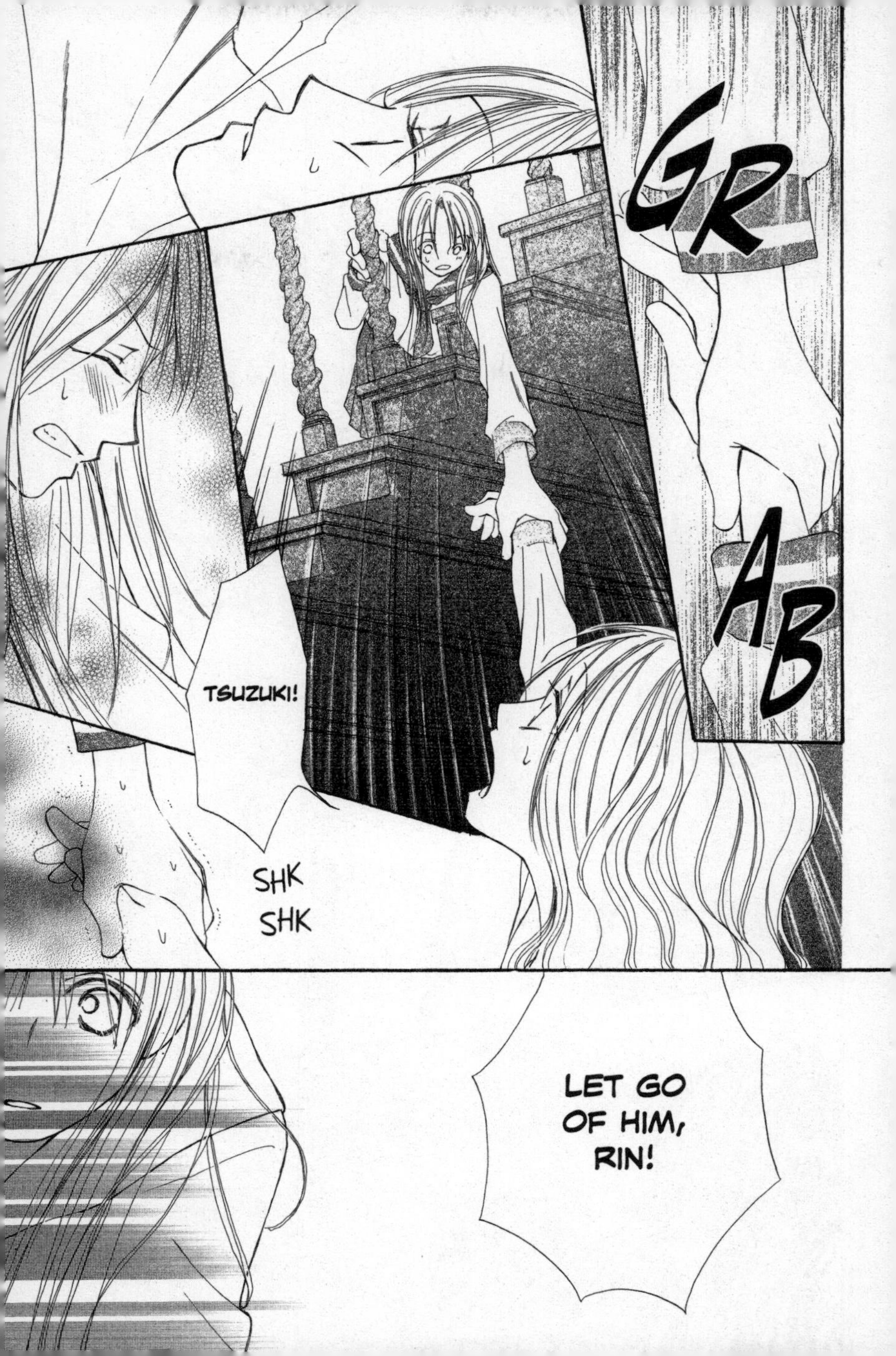
GRAB
TSUZUKI!
SHK SHK
LET GO OF HIM, RIN!

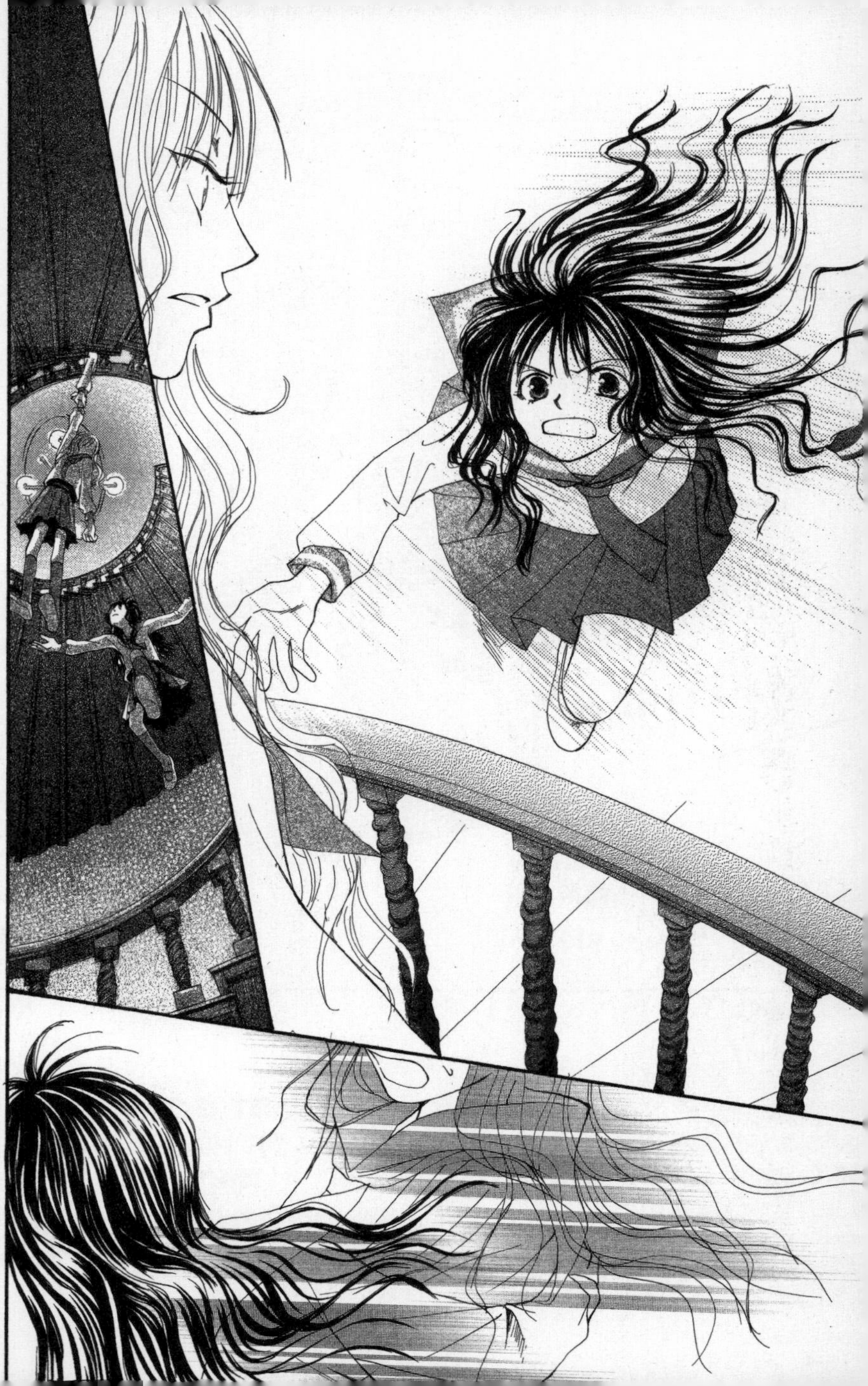

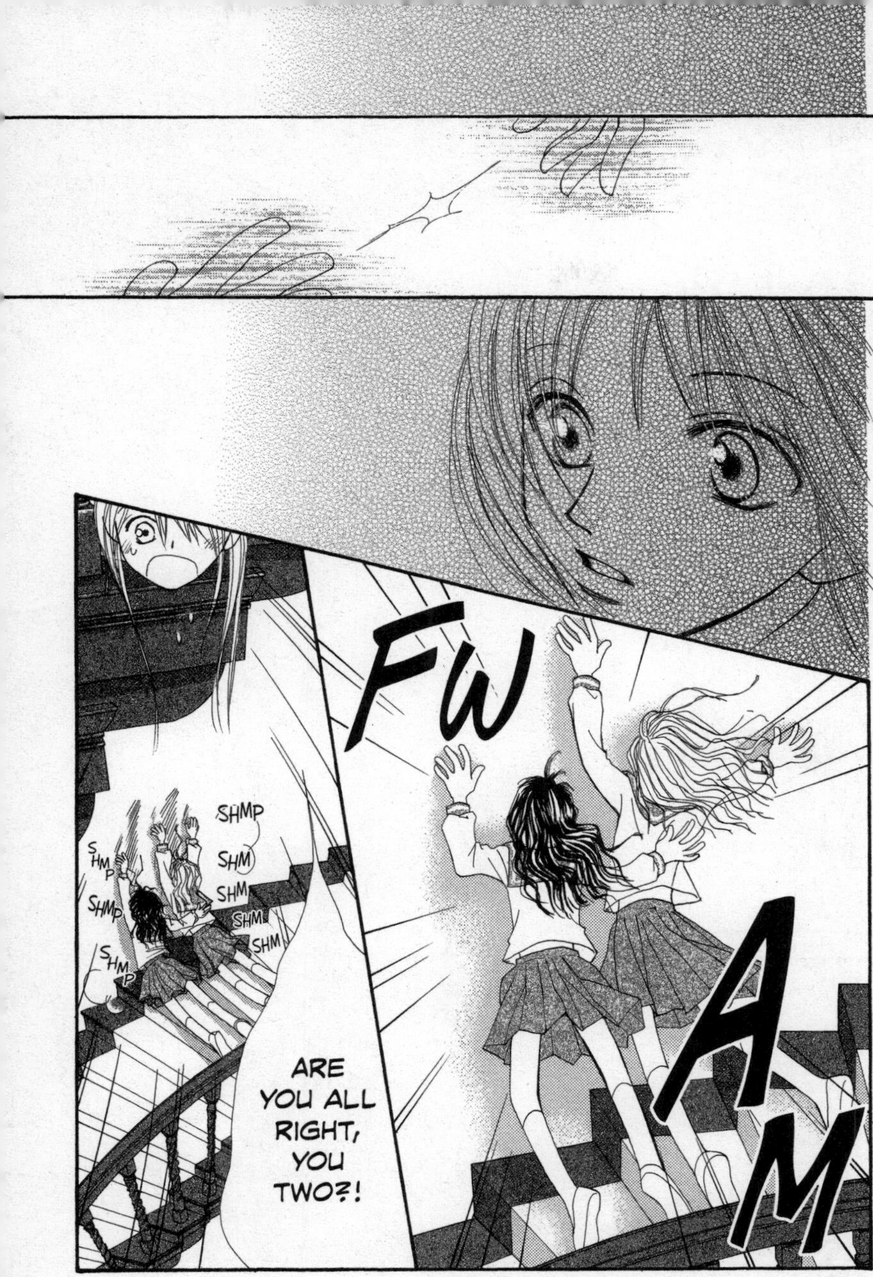
FWAM
SHMP
SHM
SHM
SHMP
SHMP
SHM
SHMP
SHMP
ARE YOU ALL RIGHT, YOU TWO?!

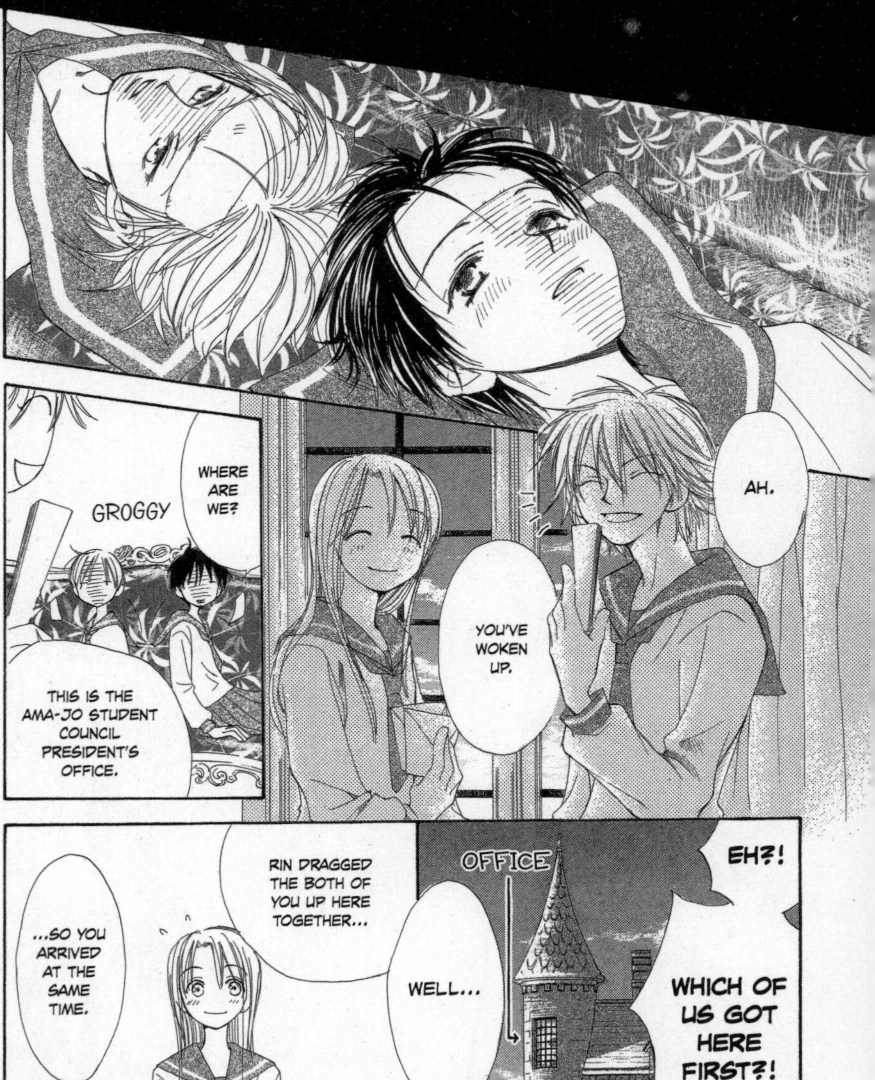
AH.
YOU'VE WOKEN UP.
WHERE ARE WE?
GROGGY
THIS IS THE AMA-JO STUDENT COUNCIL PRESIDENT'S OFFICE.
EH?!
WHICH OF US GOT HERE FIRST?!
OFFICE
WELL...
RIN DRAGGED THE BOTH OF YOU UP HERE TOGETHER...
...SO YOU ARRIVED AT THE SAME TIME.

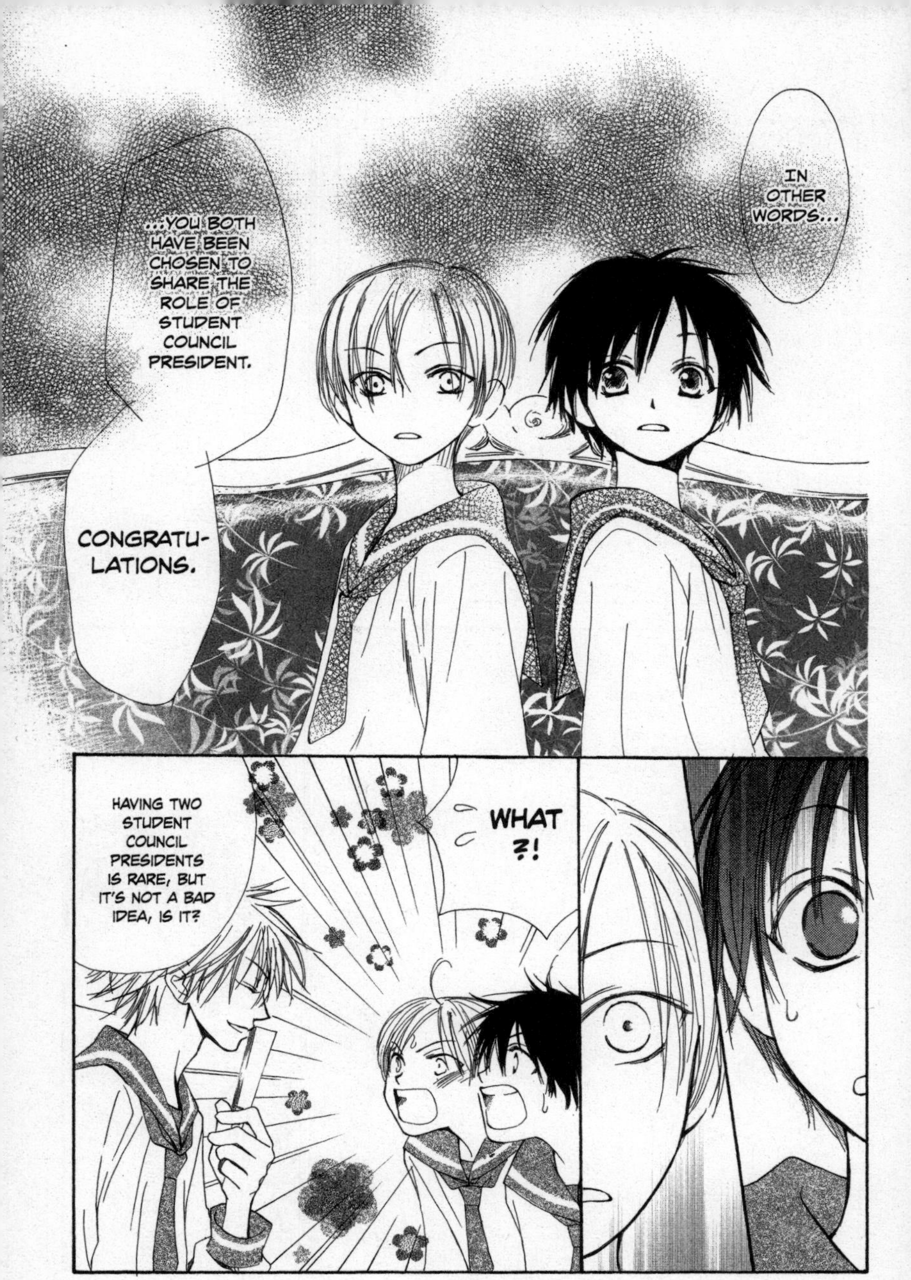
IN OTHER WORDS...
...YOU BOTH HAVE BEEN CHOSEN TO SHARE THE ROLE OF STUDENT COUNCIL PRESIDENT.
CONGRATU-LATIONS.
WHAT ?!
HAVING TWO STUDENT COUNCIL PRESIDENTS IS RARE, BUT IT'S NOT A BAD IDEA, IS IT?

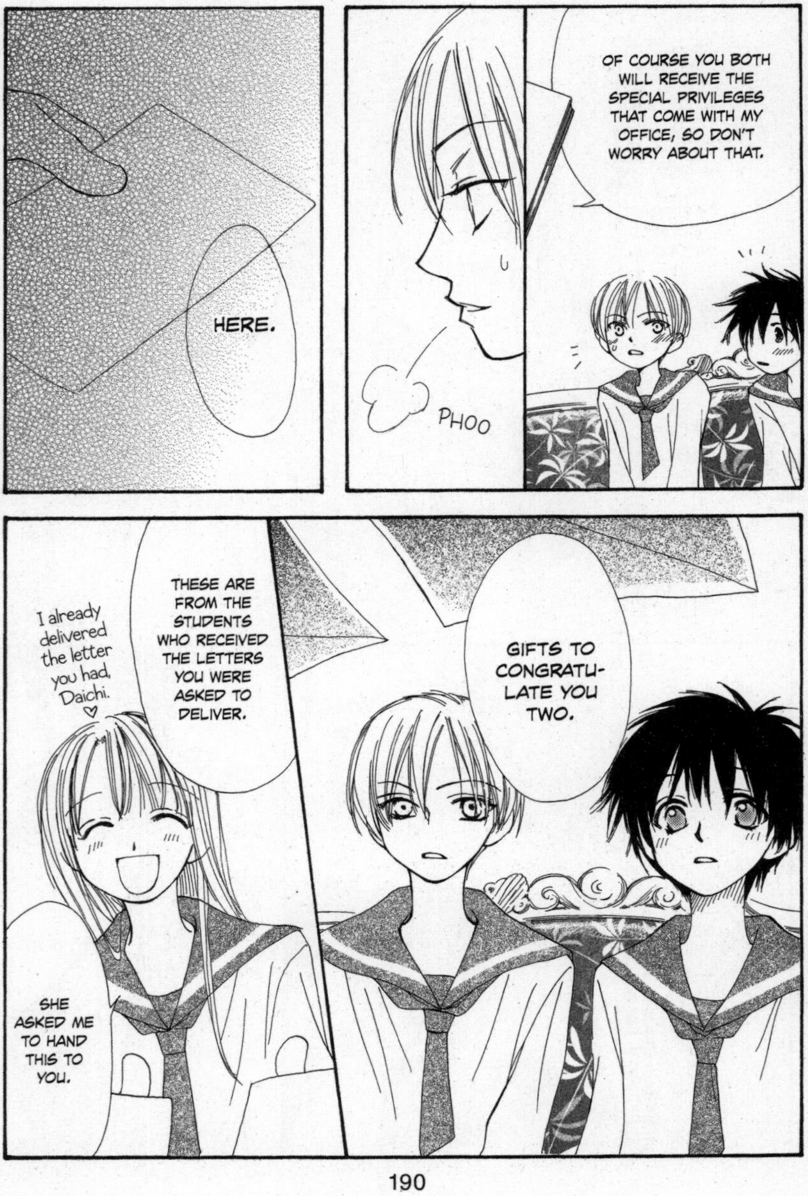
OF COURSE YOU BOTH WILL RECEIVE THE SPECIAL PRIVILEGES THAT COME WITH MY OFFICE, SO DON'T WORRY ABOUT THAT.
PHOO
HERE.
GIFTS TO CONGRATU-LATE YOU TWO.
THESE ARE FROM THE STUDENTS WHO RECEIVED THE LETTERS YOU WERE ASKED TO DELIVER.
I already delivered the letter you had, Daichi. ♡
SHE ASKED ME TO HAND THIS TO YOU.

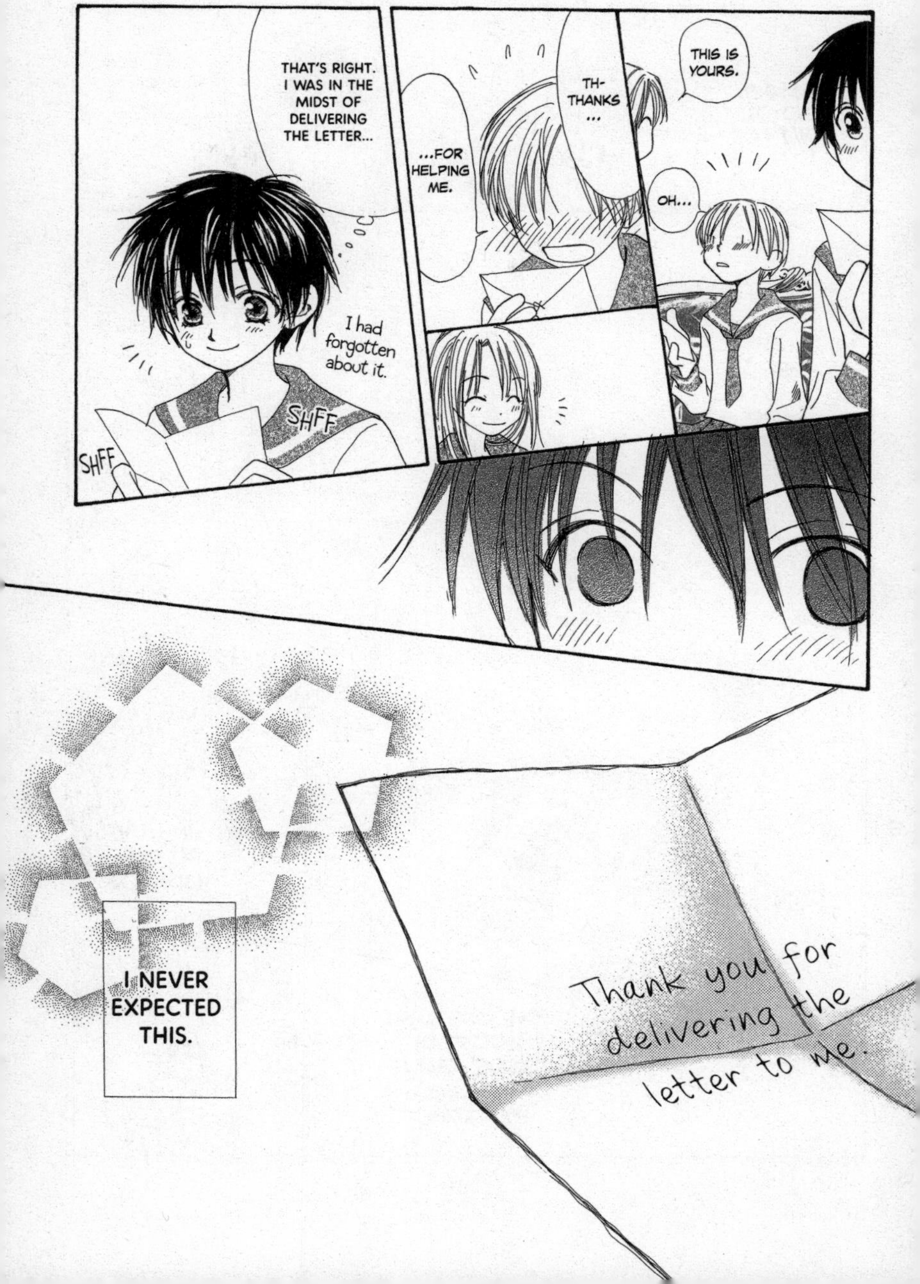
THIS IS YOURS.
OH...
TH-THANKS...
...FOR HELPING ME.
THAT'S RIGHT. I WAS IN THE MIDST OF DELIVERING THE LETTER...
I had forgotten about it.
SHFF
SHFF
Thank you for delivering the letter to me.
I NEVER EXPECTED THIS.

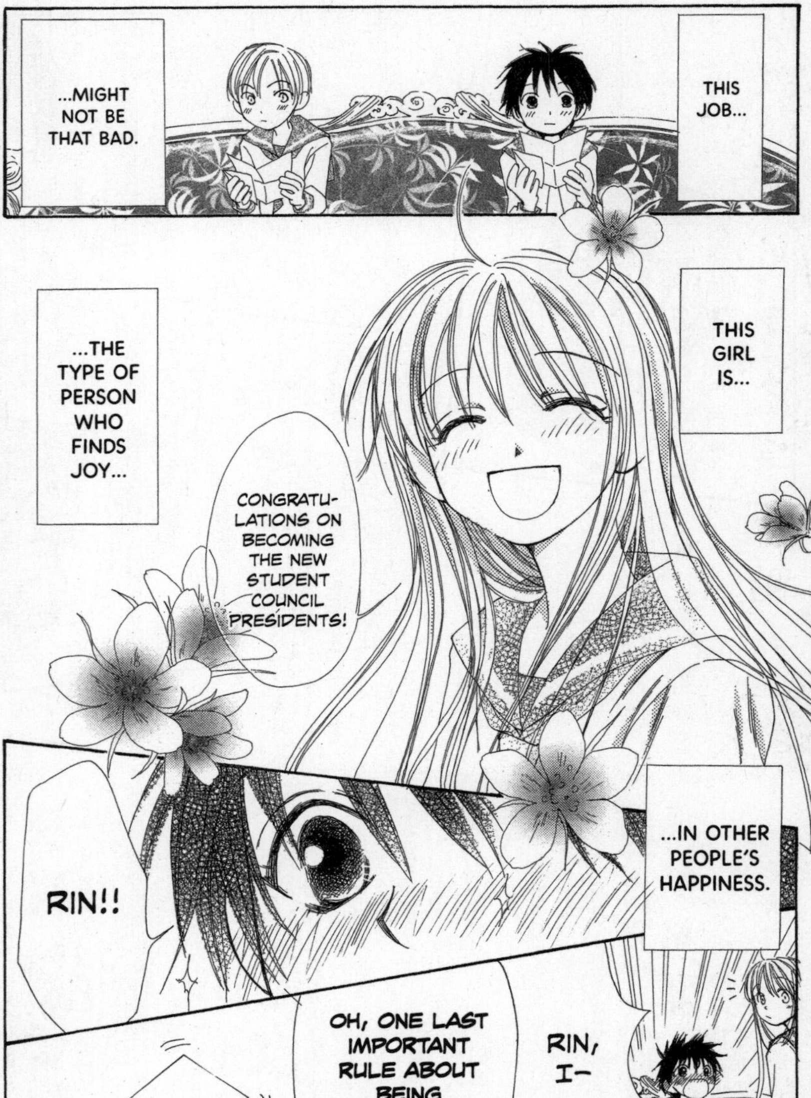

THIS JOB...
...MIGHT NOT BE THAT BAD.
THIS GIRL IS...
...THE TYPE OF PERSON WHO FINDS JOY...
CONGRATULATIONS ON BECOMING THE NEW STUDENT COUNCIL PRESIDENTS!
...IN OTHER PEOPLE'S HAPPINESS.
RIN!!
RIN, I—
OH, ONE LAST IMPORTANT RULE ABOUT BEING PRESIDENT!

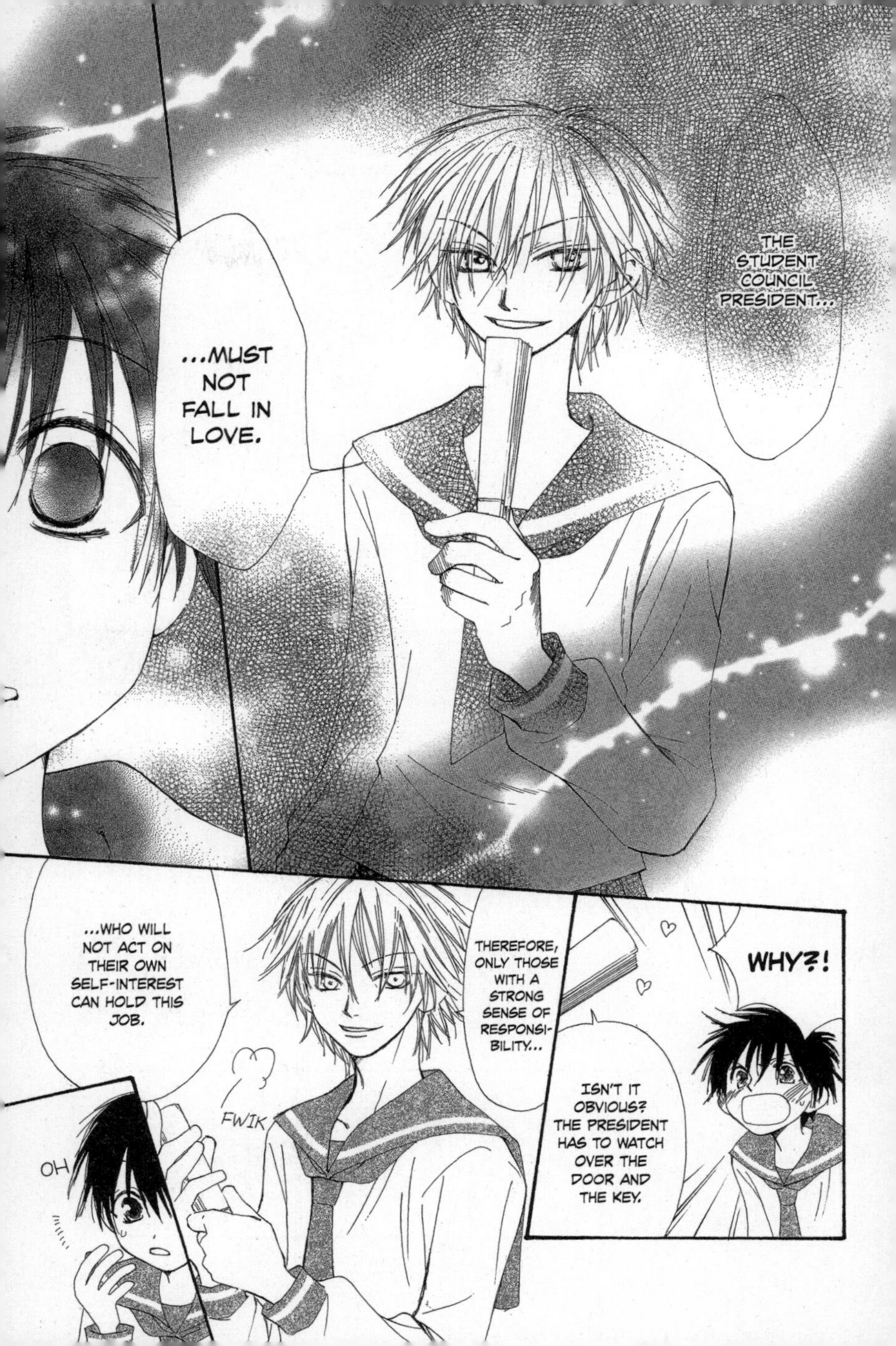
THE STUDENT COUNCIL PRESIDENT...
...MUST NOT FALL IN LOVE.
WHY?!
ISN'T IT OBVIOUS? THE PRESIDENT HAS TO WATCH OVER THE DOOR AND THE KEY.
THEREFORE, ONLY THOSE WITH A STRONG SENSE OF RESPONSI-BILITY...
...WHO WILL NOT ACT ON THEIR OWN SELF-INTEREST CAN HOLD THIS JOB.
FWIK
OH

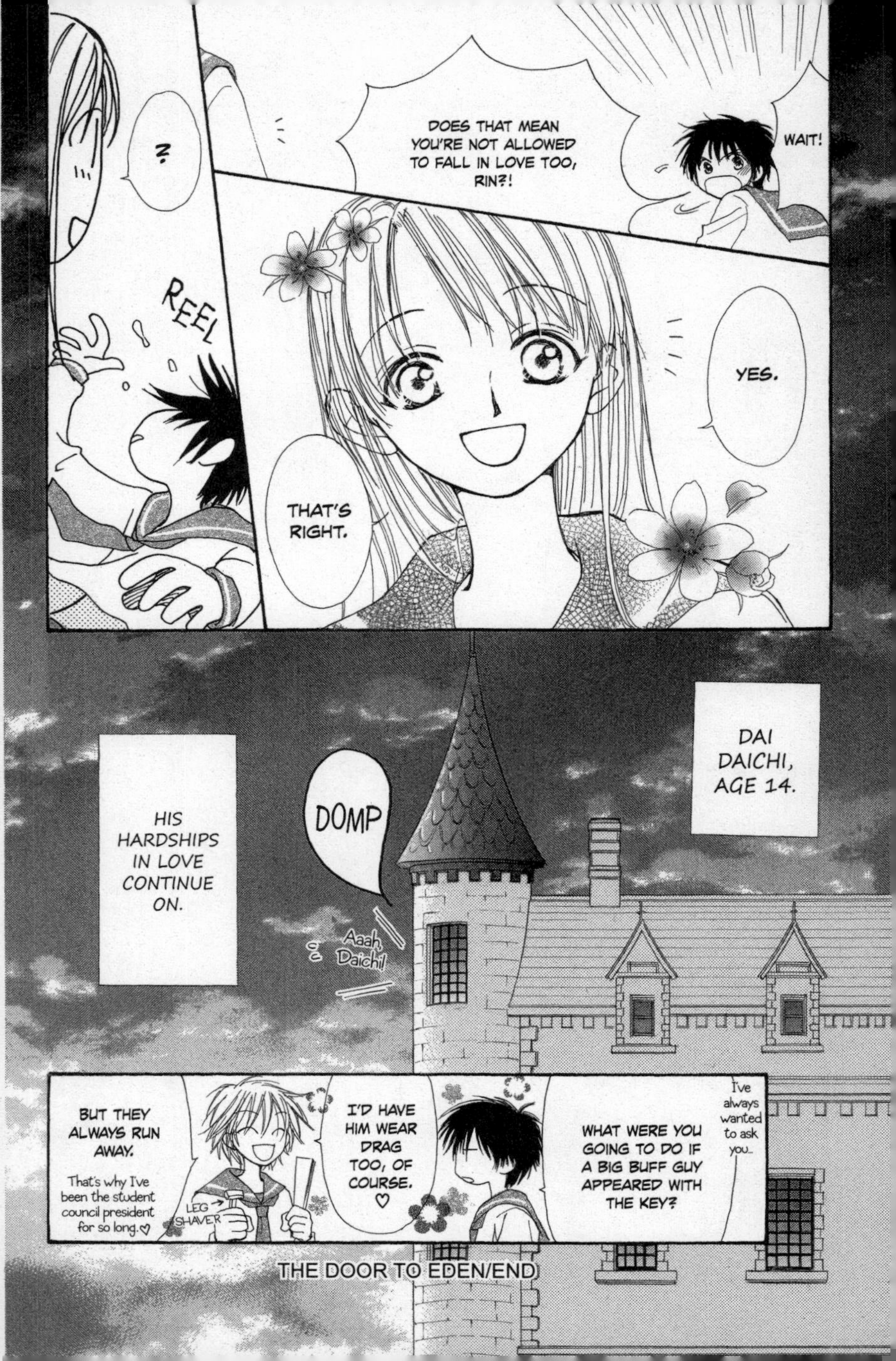
WAIT!
DOES THAT MEAN YOU'RE NOT ALLOWED TO FALL IN LOVE TOO, RIN?!
YES.
THAT'S RIGHT.
?
REEL
DAI DAICHI, AGE 14.
DOMP
HIS HARDSHIPS IN LOVE CONTINUE ON.
Aaah, Daichi!
I've always wanted to ask you...
WHAT WERE YOU GOING TO DO IF A BIG BUFF GUY APPEARED WITH THE KEY?
I'D HAVE HIM WEAR DRAG TOO, OF COURSE. ♡
BUT THEY ALWAYS RUN AWAY.
That's why I've been the student council president for so long.♡
LEG SHAVER

THE DOOR TO EDEN/END

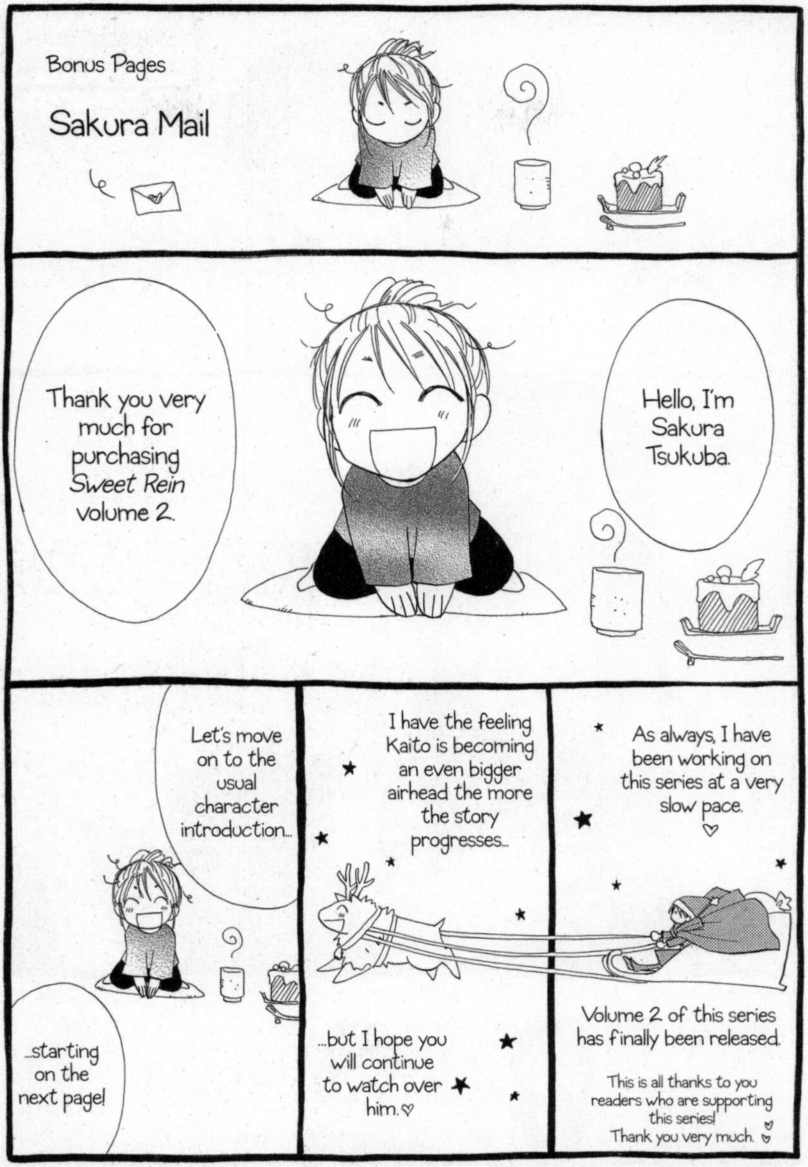

Bonus Pages
Sakura Mail
Hello, I'm Sakura Tsukuba.
Thank you very much for purchasing *Sweet Rein* volume 2.
As always, I have been working on this series at a very slow pace.
Volume 2 of this series has finally been released.
This is all thanks to you readers who are supporting this series! Thank you very much.
I have the feeling Kaito is becoming an even bigger airhead the more the story progresses...
...but I hope you will continue to watch over him.
Let's move on to the usual character introduction...
...starting on the next page!

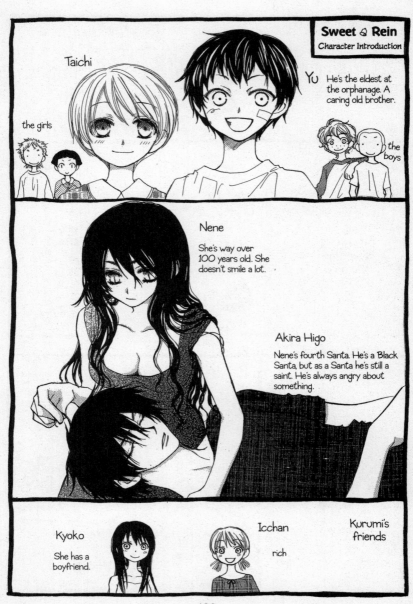

Sweet Rein
Character Introduction
Yu
He's the eldest at the orphanage. A caring old brother.
the boys
Taichi
the girls
Nene
She's way over 100 years old. She doesn't smile a lot.
Akira Higo
Nene's fourth Santa. He's a Black Santa, but as a Santa he's still a saint. He's always angry about something.
Kurumi's friends
Icchan
rich
Kyoko
She has a boyfriend.

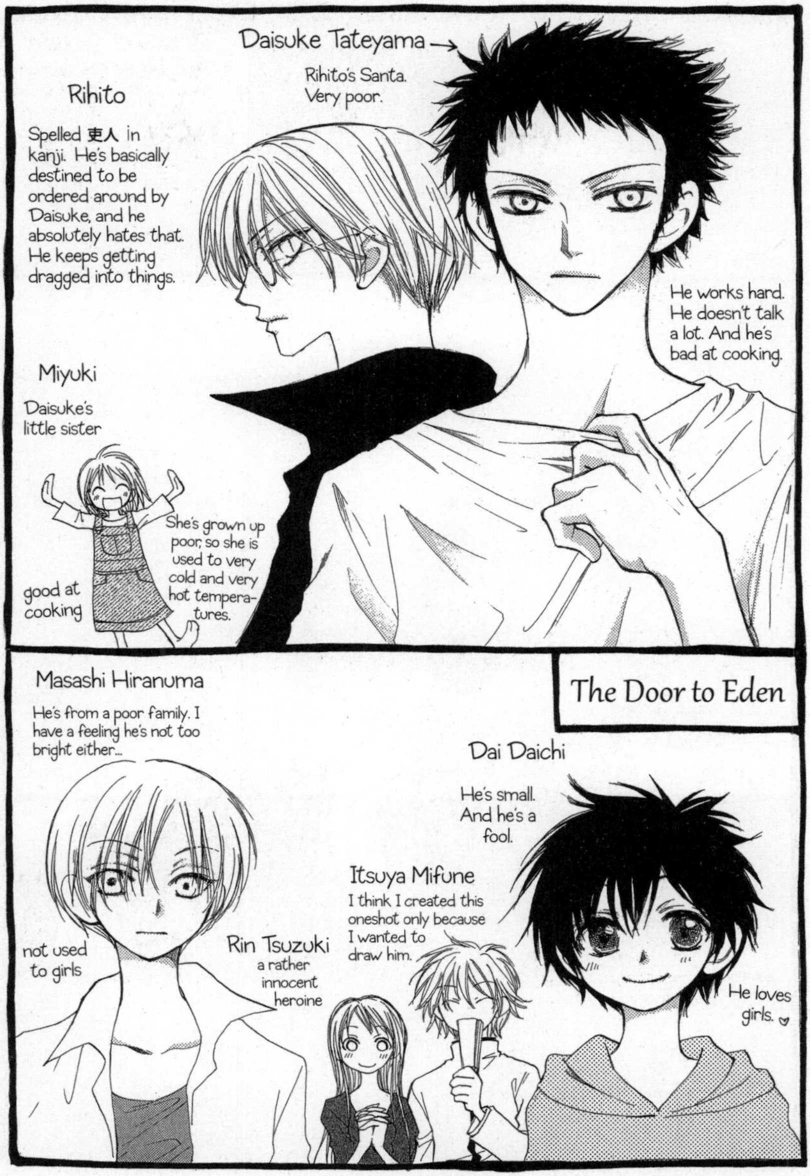

Daisuke Tateyama
Rihito's Santa. Very poor.
He works hard. He doesn't talk a lot. And he's bad at cooking.
Rihito
Spelled 吏人 in kanji. He's basically destined to be ordered around by Daisuke, and he absolutely hates that. He keeps getting dragged into things.
Miyuki
Daisuke's little sister
She's grown up poor, so she is used to very cold and very hot temperatures.
good at cooking
The Door to Eden
Dai Daichi
He's small. And he's a fool.
He loves girls.
Masashi Hiranuma
He's from a poor family. I have a feeling he's not too bright either...
Itsuya Mifune
I think I created this oneshot only because I wanted to draw him.
Rin Tsuzuki
a rather innocent heroine
not used to girls

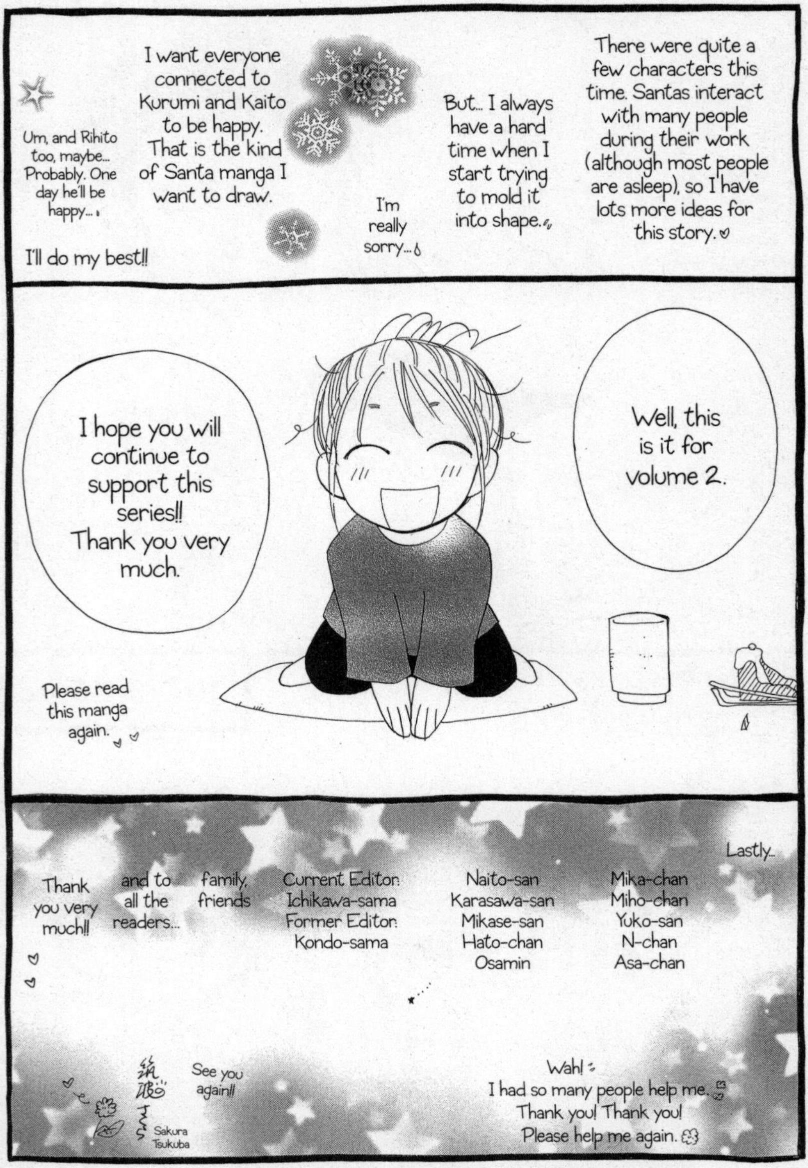
There were quite a few characters this time. Santas interact with many people during their work (although most people are asleep), so I have lots more ideas for this story.
But... I always have a hard time when I start trying to mold it into shape.
I'm really sorry...
I want everyone connected to Kurumi and Kaito to be happy. That is the kind of Santa manga I want to draw.
Um, and Rihito too, maybe... Probably. One day he'll be happy...
I'll do my best!!
Well, this is it for volume 2.
I hope you will continue to support this series!! Thank you very much.
Please read this manga again.
Lastly...
Mika-chan Miho-chan Yuko-san N-chan Asa-chan
Naito-san Karasawa-san Mikase-san Hato-chan Osamin
Current Editor: Ichikawa-sama Former Editor: Kondo-sama
family, friends
and to all the readers...
Thank you very much!!
Wah! I had so many people help me. Thank you! Thank you! Please help me again.
See you again!!
Sakura Tsukuba

Sakura Tsukuba is from Saitama
Prefecture. In 1994 she debuted with
Hikari Nodokeki Haru no Hi ni, a title
which won the LaLa Manga Grand
Prix Kasaku Award. Her other works
include *Land of the Blindfolded*
(recipient of the Hakusensha Athena
Shinjin Taisho award) and *Penguin
Revolution*.

Sweet Rein

Volume 2
Shojo Beat Edition

Story and Art by
Sakura Tsukuba

Translation/Tetsuichiro Miyaki
Adaptation/Nancy Thistlethwaite
Touch-up Art & Lettering/Inori Fukuda Trant
Design/Izumi Evers
Editor/Nancy Thistlethwaite

YOROSHIKU • MASTER by Sakura Tsukuba
© Sakura Tsukuba 2007
All rights reserved.
First published in Japan in 2007 by HAKUSENSHA, Inc., Tokyo.
English language translation rights arranged
with HAKUSENSHA, Inc., Tokyo.

The stories, characters and incidents mentioned
in this publication are entirely fictional.

Printed in the U.S.A.

Published by VIZ Media, LLC
P.O. Box 77010
San Francisco, CA 94107

10 9 8 7 6 5 4 3 2 1
First printing, April 2014

www.viz.com

www.shojobeat.com

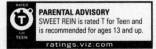

What happens when the hottest boy in school
...is a girl?!?

Find out in these **3-in-1** collections of the hit shojo series!

Hana-Kimi

Story & Art by **HISAYA NAKAJO**

Mizuki Ashiya has such a crush on a track star named Izumi Sano that she moves from the U.S. to Japan to enroll in the all-male high school he goes to! Pretending to be a boy, Mizuki becomes Sano's roommate...

...but how can she keep such a big secret when she's so close to the guy she wants?

IN STORES NOW!

3-in-1 Vol. 1 ISBN: 978-1-4215-4224-9
3-in-1 Vol. 2 ISBN: 978-1-4215-4225-6
3-in-1 Vol. 3 ISBN: 978-1-4215-4229-4

Only **$14.99 US / $16.99 CAN** each!

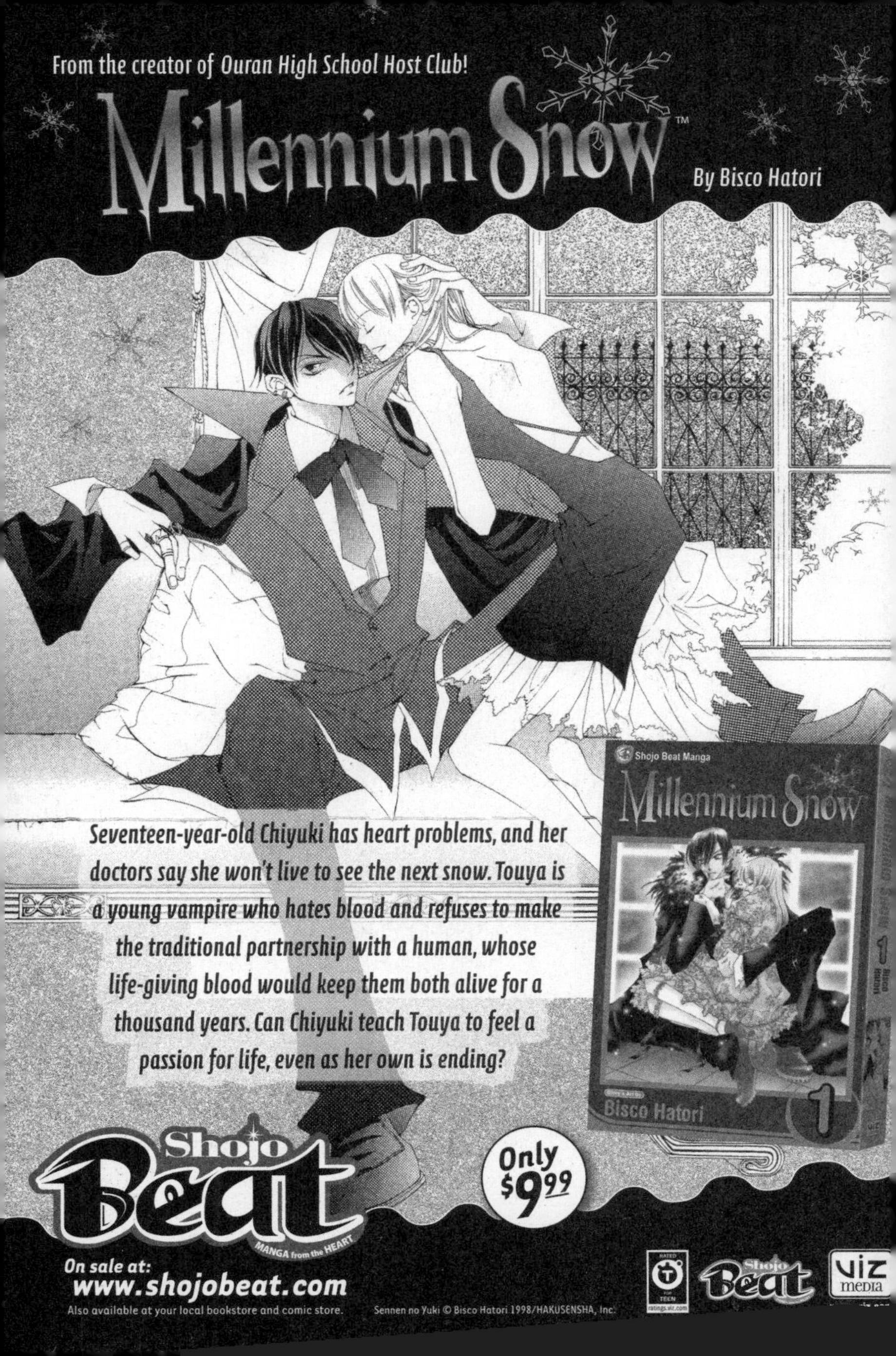
From the creator of Ouran High School Host Club!
Millennium Snow™
By Bisco Hatori
Shojo Beat Manga
Millennium Snow
1
Bisco Hatori
Seventeen-year-old Chiyuki has heart problems, and her doctors say she won't live to see the next snow. Touya is a young vampire who hates blood and refuses to make the traditional partnership with a human, whose life-giving blood would keep them both alive for a thousand years. Can Chiyuki teach Touya to feel a passion for life, even as her own is ending?
Shojo Beat
MANGA from the HEART
Only $9.99
On sale at:
www.shojobeat.com
Also available at your local bookstore and comic store.
Sennen no Yuki © Bisco Hatori 1998/HAKUSENSHA, Inc.
Shojo Beat
VIZ media

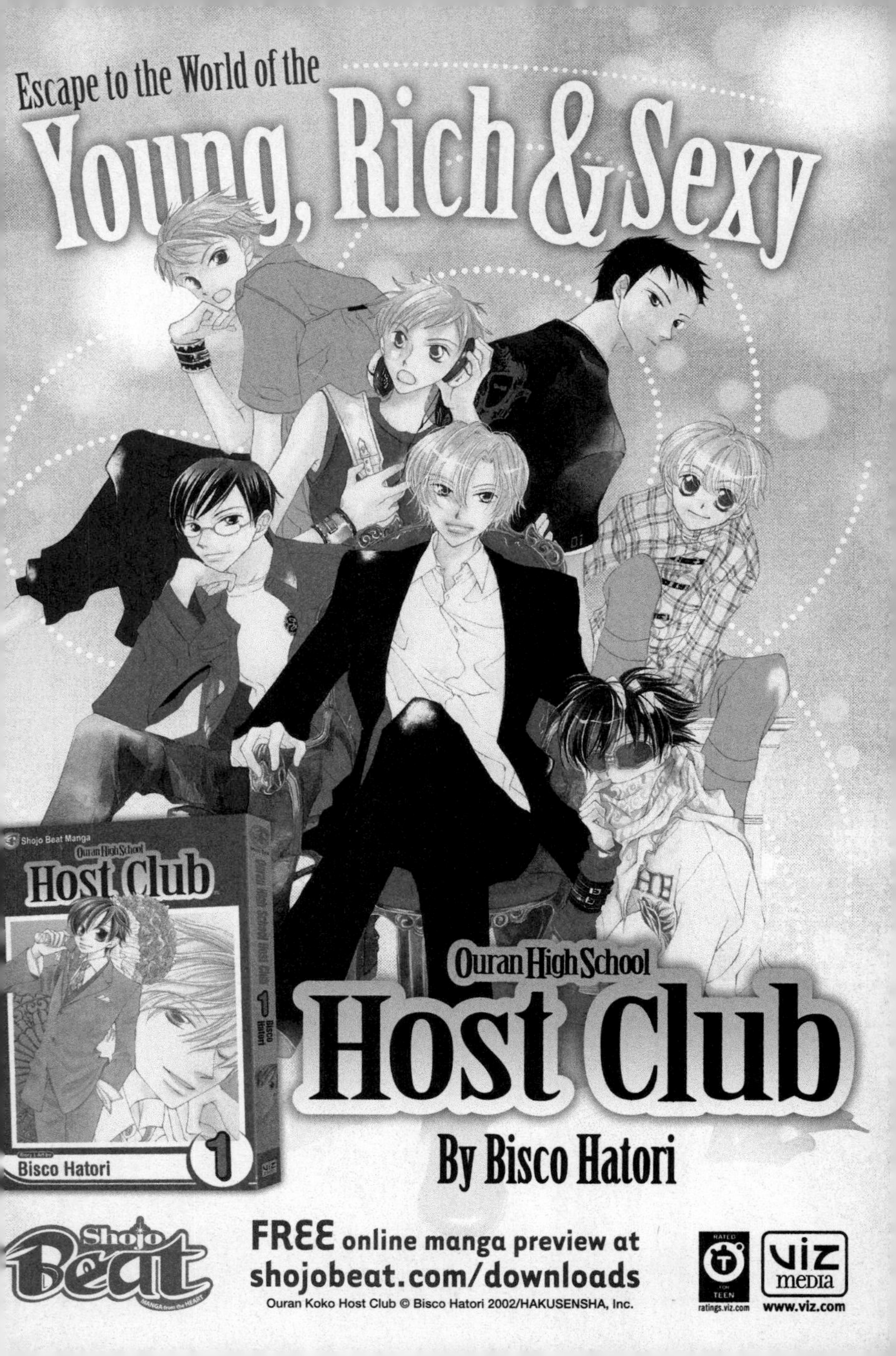
Escape to the World of the
Young, Rich & Sexy
Shojo Beat Manga
Ouran High School
Host Club
Bisco Hatori
1
Ouran High School
Host Club
By Bisco Hatori
Shojo Beat
MANGA from the HEART
FREE online manga preview at
shojobeat.com/downloads
Ouran Koko Host Club © Bisco Hatori 2002/HAKUSENSHA, Inc.
RATED T TEEN
ratings.viz.com
VIZ media
www.viz.com

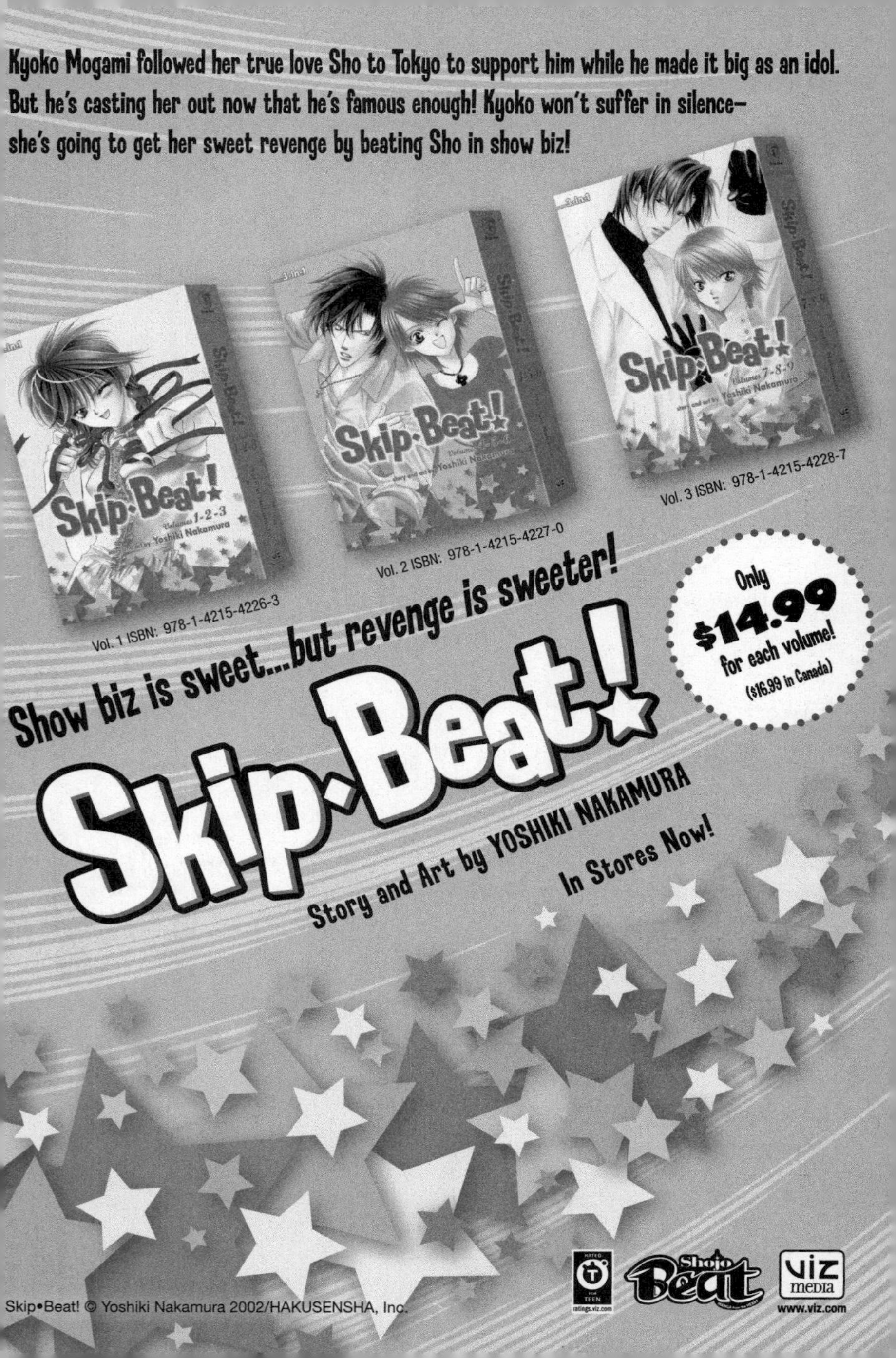

You may be reading the wrong way!

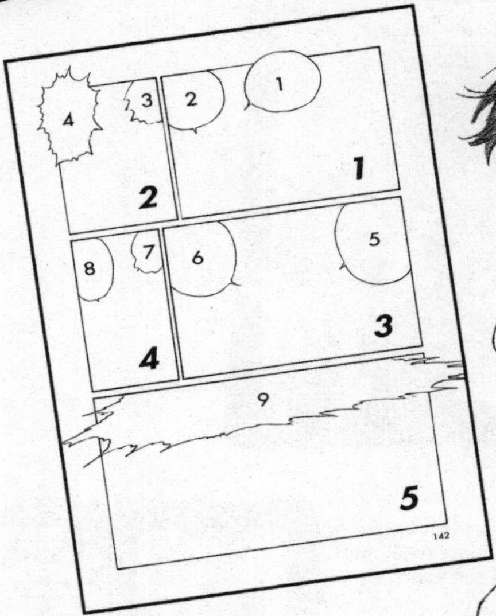

1
2
3
4
5
6
7
8
9
1
2
3
4
5
142

This book reads right to left to maintain the original presentation and art of the Japanese edition. The diagram above shows how to follow the panels. Turn to the other side of the book to begin.

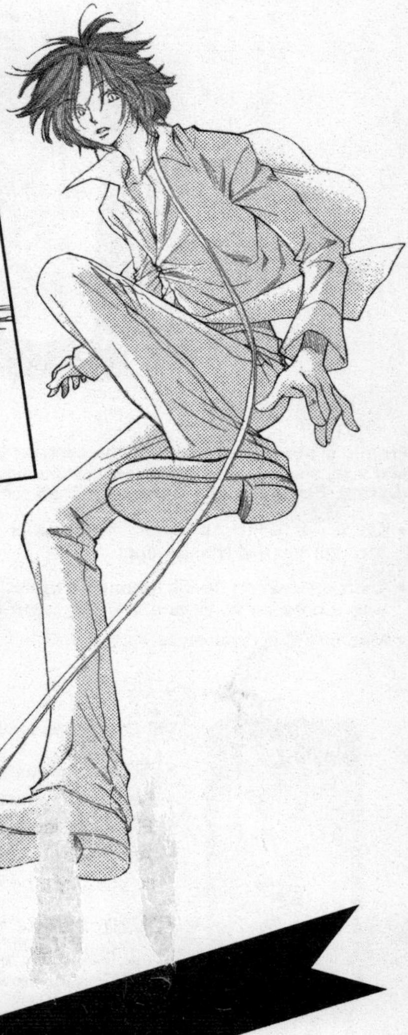